Working with Computers

Working with Computers

ROBERT H. BLISSMER

ROLAND H. ALDEN

HOUGHTON MIFFLIN COMPANY   Boston

Dallas   Geneva, Illinois   Palo Alto   Princeton, New Jersey

Contents

Preface xiv

End-User Agreement xix

P A R T I

Concepts

1 Introducing Personal Computers 4

Preview 4

An Overview of Computers 5
    What You Can Do With a Personal Computer 6
    Acquiring Computer Skills 8

What Is a Computer System? 8

What Is Hardware? 9
    Input Devices 11
    The Processor 11
    Memory 12
    Mass Storage 14
    Output Devices 16

What Is Software? 18

Types of Computer Systems 20

Computers and Communications 22
    Small-Scale Systems 22
    The Single-User System 22
    The Multiuser System 24
    Distributed Processing Systems 26

Computer Systems in Business 26
  Transaction-Oriented Systems 26
  Workgroup Systems 27
  Management Information Systems (MIS) 28

Using a Computer System 30
  Using the Operating System 31
  Using the Keyboard 32

Installing Works 34
  Handling Disks 34
  Loading DOS 35
  Formatting Your Blank Disks 36
  Copying Works 37
  Copying the Graphics Display File 39
  Copying Example Files 39
  Ending the Session 40

Review 41

2   Getting Started with Microsoft Works 43

Preview 43

A Quick Tour of Works 44
  Word Processor 44
  Spreadsheet 44
  Database 45
  Communications 45

Interacting with a Personal Computer 46
  The User Interface 47
  The Display Screen 48
  The Keyboard 49

Getting Started 55
  The NEW Dialog 57
  Word Processing Exercise 58
  Editing with the Word Processor 61
  Saving 62
  Printing 63

Review 66

3   Computers and Problem Solving 69

Preview 69

Problem Solving 70
  What Is a Problem? 70
  What Is a Solution? 70

Computers as Problem-Solving Tools 71
  What Computers Do Best 71
  What People Do Best 73

The Problem-Solving Process 74
  Get to Know the Problem 75
  Define the Problem 76
  Identify Alternative Solutions 77

       Choose the Best Alternative 77

       Implement the Solution 78

       Evaluate the Results 78

    Variations on Problem Solving 79

       Decision Making 79

       Top-Down Design 80

       The Design Process 81

       Writing 82

    The Spreadsheet Tool 85

       A Spreadsheet Example 85

       What-If Budget Analysis 87

       Printing the Spreadsheet 91

  Review 92

PART II

Applications

4 *Introducing Word Processing 96*

Preview 96

Word Processing and Problem Solving 97

Some Word Processing Basics 98

    What Is a Document? 98

    How to Create a New Document 100

    What You Will See 100

Experimenting with Word Processing 101

    Selection 102

    Copy 104

    Move 105

    Editing Shortcuts 106

    Scrolling 107

    Editing and the Display 108

    Paragraphs 110

Writing a Sample Letter 111

    Editing: Correcting Mistakes 112

    Revising: Adding New Text 112

    Saving the Document 113

    Printing the Document 114

    The Layout Dialog 114

Review 117

5 *Working with Word Processing 119*

Preview 119

Writing the First Draft 120
   Revising the First Draft 121
   Search and Replace 121

Writing Additional Drafts 124
   Format Menu 124
   Page Breaks 125
   Tabs 127
   Headers and Footers 129
   Switching Between Documents 131

Additional Formatting 132

Advanced Word Processing Features 133
   Writing Enhancements 134
   Printing Enhancements 135
   Display Enhancements 135

Desktop Publishing 136

Review 140

6 *Introducing Spreadsheets 141*

Preview 141

Spreadsheets and Problem Solving 142

The Electronic Spreadsheet 144
   What You Will See 144
   Moving Around in the Spreadsheet 145
   Entering Information into the Spreadsheet 146
   Editing the Spreadsheet 147

A Sample Spreadsheet Problem 149
   Designing the Layout 150
   Building a Spreadsheet Model 152
   Entering Text 152
   Entering Formulas 153
   Entering Numbers 154
   Changing Formats 154
   Adding to the Spreadsheet 156
   Recalculating the Spreadsheet 156
   Saving and Printing the Spreadsheet 157
   Additional Printing Features 158
   Additional Format Features 160

Review 162

7 *Working with Spreadsheets 163*

Preview 163

Putting the Spreadsheet to Work 163
   Building a Sales Analysis Model 164
   What-If Analysis 169

Spreadsheets and Integration 171
   Writing a Memo 171
   Building a Sales Forecast Model 171

      What if You Change the Forecast? 175
      What the Spreadsheet Can't Do 176
   Additional Spreadsheet Features 177
      Templates 177
      Very Large Spreadsheets 177
      Linking Multiple Spreadsheets 178
      Macros 178
   Review 179

8   *Introducing Databases 181*
   Preview 181
   Database Programs and Problem Solving 182
   A Sample Database Application 183
   Designing a Database 184
      Starting the Database Program 186
      The Form Design Screen 186
      Tips on Database Design 188
   Entering and Editing Data 189
      Entering Data 189
      Editing Data 191
      Removing Data 191
   Querying for and Sorting Data 191
      Querying the Database 192
      Complex Searches 194
      Sorting Records 195
      Printing Data 196
   Review 197

9   *Working with Databases 199*
   Preview 199
   The Application Development Process 200
      Getting to Know the Application 200
      Specifying the Requirements 200
      Identifying the Constraints 202
      Implementing the Database Program 203
      Evaluating the Results 204
   Generating the Registration Form 206
   Generating Reports 207
      Sorting and Grouping the Records 208
      Defining the Report 209
      Viewing and Printing the Report 212
   Additional Database Features 212
      Relational Databases 212
      Database Size 213
      Wildcard Searches 214
      Data Security 214
      Data Integrity 214
   Review 217

x

10 *Working with Charts 219*
Preview 219
Visualizing Numbers 220
Inside a Chart 221
Chart Styles 223
Building a Chart 226
Charting from the Database 234
Printing Graphs 237
Review 239

PART III

Connections

11 *Introducing Communications 242*
Preview 242
Communications Basics 243
Computer Networks 243
    Electronic Mail 245
    Information Utilities 246
    Local-Area Networks 248
Communication Hardware and Software 248
    Terminals 248
    Modems 248
    Communication Software 251
A Sample Works Communications File 251
    Making the Connection 254
    Advanced Features 254
Communications Industry Issues 254
Review 257

12 *Computers at Work 259*
Preview 259
Computers in the Office 260
    Five Primary Functions 261
    Human Factors: Ergonomics 264
Information Systems 267
    Computerization of Basic Business Transactions 267
    Management Information Systems 269
    Decision Support Systems 273
Computers in Industry 273
    Manufacturing and Robotics 273
    Finance, Banking, and Retailing 278

Computers in the Professions 281
    Health Care 282
    Law 284
    Journalism 285
Review 287

13 Computers and Society's Institutions 289

Preview 289
Computers in Government 290
    The Federal Government 290
    Local Government 294
    Law Enforcement 295
Computers in Education 297
    Computer-Assisted Instruction 298
    Drawbacks to CAI 300
Computers and the Arts 301
    Motion Pictures 301
    Art 302
    Literature 303
    Music 304
Computers in Science 305
    Simulation 306
    Supercomputers 306
    Space Exploration 307
Review 309

14 Computers and Ethics 313

Preview 313
Privacy 314
    The Computer as a Threat to Privacy 314
    Safeguarding Privacy 316
Computer Crime 318
    Computer-Abetted Crime 318
    Hackers and Computer Trespassing 320
    Safeguarding Security 322
Emerging Issues in Information Ethics 324
    Information Malpractice 326
    Intellectual Property Rights 326
    The Value of Information 327
    The Value of Human Capital 327
    Equal Access to Information 327
Review 329

15 Buying a Personal Computer 331

Preview 331
Know Your Applications 332
    Get to Know the Problem 332
    What Do You Want the Computer to Do? 333

Information Sources 334
  Computer Users 334
  Computer Magazines 334
  Books 335
  Computer Shows 335
  User Groups 335
  Computer Stores 336
  Documentation 337
  Courses 337
How to Buy an MS-DOS-Based Computer 338
  IBM Products 339
  Model Considerations 340
  Disk Storage Considerations 341
  Display Considerations 341
  Printer Considerations 342
  Communication Considerations 342
  A Note on IBM Compatibility 342
  A Note on Operating Systems 343
How to Buy an Apple Macintosh 343
  Memory Considerations 344
  Disk Storage Considerations 344
  Printer Considerations 344
How to Buy a Home Computer 345
  The Apple II Family 345
How to Buy a Portable Computer 346
Choose the Best Alternative 347
How to Make Your Purchase 348
Review 351

Appendixes

A   Using MS-DOS and Works 353
The Keyboard and MS-DOS 353
All About Files 354
MS-DOS Commands 355

B   Special Mouse Shortcuts 358
The Works Mouse 358
The Mouse and Menus 359
The Mouse and Dialog Boxes 359
The Mouse and Scroll Bars 359
The Mouse and Selecting 361
The Mouse and the Keyboard 361

C   Spreadsheet and Database Functions 362

D   Menus and Commands   370

Summary of Commands by Application and Menu   371
Main Menu Bar Commands   371
Word Processor Commands   372
Spreadsheet Commands   375
Chart Screen Commands   379
Database Commands   381
Form and List Screen Commands   383
Query Screen Commands   386
Communications Commands   389

Glossary   391

Art Credits   401

Index   404

Preface

In business, government, and education, computers and computer software are tools which people use daily to learn, work, communicate, and create. To compete successfully in such a climate it's important that every student learn and master the general problem-solving skills necessary to effectively use computers and application software.

The Challenge

However useful computers might be, learning how to use them — and how not to use them — can be difficult. The student's challenge is threefold: first, to learn the basic concepts and principles common to all computer technology; second, to learn the skills required to effectively use a computer; and third, to understand the connections between computers and the various environments in which they are used — school, the workplace, and society.

The Solution

Working with Computers answers the challenge. The text is designed for a one-term first course in computers; no prior computer experience is presumed or needed. *Working with Computers*

- is a hands-on, practical introduction to computers.
- teaches students fundamental problem-solving skills.
- engages students in problem-solving that involves word processing, spreadsheets, databases, reporting, graphing, and communications.
- explains how computers are used in various occupational and professional fields.

■ points out problems that can arise when computers are misused.

■ demonstrates how computers can be productive and creative tools.

After studying *Working with Computers* and using the accompanying Microsoft Works integrated software, students will

■ know how to use computers to solve a wide variety of problems.

■ gain insight into the expanding capabilities of computers.

■ understand the interconnected technological, social, and economic issues that surround the use of computers.

■ have the computer skills needed to enter the job market with confidence.

Organization

Part I, *Concepts*, covers computer fundamentals and discusses the needs that personal computers fill. Chapter 1 orients students to computers in general and to personal computers in specific. Chapter 2 introduces software — both application and operating system — and prepares students to use the Works software. Chapter 3 continues the orientation. It explains the problem-solving process and points out several specific examples of when computers are useful and when they are not.

Part II, *Applications*, covers in detail how to use application software. Students learn the concepts and principles of four of the five application programs step-by-step and apply the software to problems. Each chapter introduces a major application area — word processing (chapters 4 and 5), spreadsheets (chapters 6 and 7), databases (chapters 8 and 9), and charts (chapter 10). As the chapters progress, new aspects of the total software package unfold: the concept of integration (passing data between applications); the fundamentals of file management; how to develop applications; and advanced software features.

Part III, *Connections*, recognizes the need to present computers in a broader context. It is a comprehensive summary of the issues that will concern every computer user in the next decade. Chapter 11 introduces the important topic of computer-to-computer communications. Chapter 12 explores computers at work in offices, banks, factories, and the professions. Chapter 13 examines the use of computers in government, education, the arts, and the sciences. Chapter 14 covers the ethical issues involved in using computers. Finally, Chapter 15 provides a systematic approach to acquiring software and hardware. It builds on the problem-solving method used throughout the text and applies it to a problem students might face — that of buying their own personal computer systems.

Appendixes provide technical information about Works, DOS, and using a mouse, as well as explanations of all the Works commands and spreadsheet and database functions.

Microsoft Works

Microsoft Works is an integrated word processor, spreadsheet, charting, database, and communications program. It is a first-rate example of the software tools that are available for personal computers today. Works represents an answer to what is most needed in today's introductory and computer literacy course — easy to use, comprehensive, reliable, and productive software.

Works will run on almost any MS-DOS-based personal computer; it requires only 384K of memory and two floppy disk drives. The textbook edition of Works is as functional as the retail version, with the following exceptions:

- The word processor supports a maximum of 10 single-spaced pages (approximately 25,000 characters).
- The spreadsheet is 32 columns by 256 rows.
- The database supports a maximum of 256 records, up to 32 fields per record, and up to 79 characters per field.
- The charting program does not include additional fonts.
- The spelling checker, computer-based help and tutorials, and macro system are omitted.

The retail version includes support for numerous printers, additional fonts, and higher data capacities. The files produced by the textbook edition are fully compatible with the retail version.

By working with the Works software students will

- learn more about what computers can and cannot do.
- solve relevant problems with the help of a computer.
- learn to use application software.
- apply the principles they learn to other application software such as Lotus 1-2-3, dBase, and WordPerfect.

These objectives will serve students well, whether they become casual everyday or extremely knowledgeable computer users. Hands-on experience with Works is of immediate value. Works can be used for a variety of coursework and assignments, in both this and other classes. Works helps students prepare for a computerized world and is a valuable contribution toward an introductory course that is innovative, exciting, practical, and relevant.

Learn by Doing

Working with Computers begins with a gentle introduction to the most popular application, word processing. Over the course of 15 chapters, students learn to use several applications to solve a variety of practical problems. Along the way they are exposed to topical issues surrounding computers and the roles they play. With a straightforward yet uncompromising approach, *Working with Computers*

- covers the background and orientation material required for an introductory computer course.
- reinforces the material by providing examples, problems, and exercises that require students to use the Works software.

No attempt is made to teach every command and detailed feature of the Works software. Instead, Works is used to demonstrate fundamental concepts common to all applications software, in the context of application exercises students are motivated to complete. The emphasis is on learning by doing.

Teaching Tools

As a textbook, *Working with Computers* contains a number of learning aids, including

- comprehensive hands-on exercises with clear, concise step-by-step instructions that will not intimidate the novice software user.
- software exercises that help build confidence by presenting students with challenging problems.
- discussion questions, often featuring contemporary, controversial topics of interest to the whole class.
- project-oriented exercises to encourage learning from sources outside the classroom and lab.
- an instructor's manual and test bank that includes chapter overviews and teaching hints, suggested projects, answers to discussion questions, tips for using the software exercises, and true/false, multiple choice, and matching questions and answers.

Acknowledgments

We are grateful to Microsoft Corporation for permitting us to include the Works software with this book.

We would also like to gratefully thank those professors who reviewed early drafts of the manuscript and made numerous helpful comments:

Ronald Anderson	University of Minnesota
Harvey R. Blessing	Essex Community College
William Burkhardt	Carl Sandburg College
Lawrence Campo	Macomb Community College
James A. Davis	Oregon Institute of Technology
Larry Dold	San Joaquin Delta College
E. Edward Eill	Delaware County Community College
David F. Harris	College of the Redwoods
Seth Hock	Columbus State Community College
Laurence J. Krieg	Washtenaw Community College
David John Marotta	Lane Community College
William M. Moldrup	Merced College
Wesley Nance	Cerritos College
Alex W. Nichols	Cleveland State Community College
Dr. Ronald D. Peterson	Weber State College
Leonard Presby	William Paterson State College of NJ
Ellie Rosen	Santa Monica College
Sharon Szabo	Schoolcraft College
Robert Taylor	Berkshire Community College
Louis A. Wolff	Moorpark College

Robert H. Blissmer
Roland H. Alden

End-User License Agreement

MICROSOFT SOFTWARE LICENSE

<u>READ THIS FIRST</u>. Your use of the Microsoft software (the "SOFTWARE") is governed by the legal agreement below.

BY OPENING THE SEALED DISKETTE PACKAGE YOU ARE AGREEING TO BE BOUND BY THE TERMS AND CONDITIONS BELOW. IF YOU DO NOT AGREE WITH SUCH TERMS AND CONDITIONS, YOU SHOULD RETURN THE UNOPENED DISKETTE PACKAGE TOGETHER WITH THE BOOK TO THE PLACE WHERE YOU OBTAINED THEM FOR A REFUND.

1. <u>GRANT OF LICENSE</u>. Microsoft grants to you the right to use one copy of the enclosed SOFTWARE on a single terminal connected to a single computer (i.e. with a single CPU). You must not network the SOFTWARE or otherwise use it on more than one computer or computer terminal at the same time.

2. <u>COPYRIGHT</u>. The SOFTWARE is owned by Microsoft or its suppliers and is protected by United States copyright laws and international treaty provisions. Therefore, you must treat the SOFTWARE like any other copyrighted material (e.g. a book or musical recording) *except* that you may either (a) make one copy (b) transfer the SOFTWARE to a single hard disk provided you keep the original solely for backup or archival purposes. You may not copy the written materials.

3. <u>OTHER RESTRICTIONS</u>. You may not rent or lease the SOFTWARE, but you may transfer the SOFTWARE and written materials on a permanent basis provided you retain no copies and the recipient agrees to the terms of this Agreement. You may not reverse engineer, decompile or disassemble the SOFTWARE.

4. <u>DUAL MEDIA SOFTWARE</u>. If the SOFTWARE package contains both $3\,^1/_2$" and $5\,^1/_4$" disks, then you may use only the disks appropriate for your single-user computer. You may not use the other disks on another computer or loan, rent, lease, or transfer them to another user except as part of the permanent transfer (as provided above) of all SOFTWARE and written materials.

DISCLAIMER OR WARRANTY AND LIMITED WARRANTY

THE SOFTWARE AND ACCOMPANYING WRITTEN MATERIALS (INCLUDING IN-STRUCTIONS FOR USE) ARE PROVIDED "AS IS" WITHOUT WARRANTY OF ANY KIND. FURTHER, MICROSOFT DOES NOT WARRANT, GUARANTEE, OR MAKE ANY REPRESENTATIONS REGARDING THE USE, OR THE RESULTS OF THE USE, OF THE SOFTWARE OR WRITTEN MATERIALS IN TERMS OF CORRECTNESS, ACCURACY, RELIABILITY, CURRENTNESS, OR OTHERWISE. THE ENTIRE RISK AS TO THE RESULTS AND PERFORMANCE OF THE SOFTWARE IS ASSUMED BY YOU. IF THE SOFTWARE OR WRITTEN MATERIALS ARE DEFECTIVE YOU, AND NOT MICROSOFT OR ITS DEALERS, DISTRIBUTORS, AGENTS, OR EMPLOYEES, ASSUME THE ENTIRE COST OF ALL NECESSARY SERVICING, REPAIR OR CORRECTION.

Microsoft warrants to the original LICENSEE that (a) the disk(s) on which the SOFTWARE is recorded is free from defects in materials and workmanship under normal use and service for a period of ninety (90) days from the date of delivery as evidenced by a copy of the receipt. Further, Microsoft hereby limits the duration of any implied warranty(ies) on the disk to the respective periods stated above. Some states do not allow limitations on duration of an implied warranty, so the above limitation may not apply to you.

Microsoft's entire liability and your exclusive remedy as to the disk(s) shall be at Microsoft's option, either (a) return of the purchase price or (b) replacement of the disk that does not meet Microsoft's Limited Warranty and which is returned to Microsoft with a copy of the receipt. If failure of the disk has resulted from accident, abuse, or misapplication, Microsoft shall have no responsibility to replace the disk or refund the purchase price. Any replacement disk will be warranted for the remainder of the original warranty period or thirty (30) days, whichever is longer.

NO OTHER WARRANTIES. MICROSOFT DISCLAIMS ALL OTHER WARRANTIES, EITHER EXPRESS OR IMPLIED, INCLUDING BUT NOT LIMITED TO IMPLIED WAR-RANTIES OF MERCHANTABILITY AND FITNESS FOR A PARTICULAR PURPOSE, WITH RESPECT TO THE SOFTWARE, THE ACCOMPANYING HARDWARE. THIS LIMITED WARRANTY GIVES YOU SPECIFIC LEGAL RIGHTS. YOU MAY HAVE OTHERS, WHICH VARY FROM STATE TO STATE.

NO LIABILITY FOR CONSEQUENTIAL DAMAGES. IN NO EVENT SHALL MICROSOFT OR ITS SUPPLIERS BE LIABLE FOR ANY DAMAGES WHATSOEVER (INCLUDING WITHOUT LIMITATION DAMAGES FOR LOSS OF BUSINESS PROFITS, BUSINESS INTERRUPTION, LOSS OF BUSINESS INFORMATION, OR OTHER PECUNIARY LOSS) ARISING OUT OF THE USE OR INABILITY TO USE THIS MICROSOFT PRODUCT EVEN IF MICROSOFT HAS BEEN ADVISED OF THE POSSIBILITY OF SUCH DAMAGES. BECAUSE SOME STATES DO NOT ALLOW THE EXCLUSION OR LIMITATION OF LIABILITY FOR CONSEQUENTIAL OR INCIDENTAL DAMAGES, THE ABOVE LIMITATION MAY NOT APPLY TO YOU.

Working with Computers

PART I

Concepts

We think you should learn about computers. Why? You're probably going to spend the next couple of years in college, then move on to your first or a new job. You're going to spend a good portion of your time gathering information, writing, calculating, solving problems, and communicating. If you think of computers and their programs as tools for accomplishing all these tasks, you can imagine how useful they might be.

Learning about computers requires hands-on experience. But there is no need for the mechanics of using computers and programs to overwhelm the bigger picture. Before you begin using computers, you need an overview.

Part I prepares you for hands-on skills by teaching you some basic computer concepts. Chapter 1 introduces personal computers. You'll learn about the computer as a system of interrelated components, hardware and software concepts, an overview of the uses for computers, and an introduction to the MS-DOS operating system. Chapter 2 prepares you to work with application software. In it, we discuss the role of the user interface and some techniques that computers use to communicate with people. Then we introduce you to the Works software, beginning with the word processor.

Problems can't be solved with a computer until they have been well thought out. Chapter 3 provides you with some general-purpose tools for problem solving, an organized method for solving problems, and some approaches for solving specific problems. Then we introduce you to the Works spreadsheet program.

Personal computers are indeed powerful problem-solving tools. And, thanks to dramatic improvements in performance, coupled with equally dramatic declines in cost, these tools are now within the grasp of everyone. In fact, the personal computer may prove to be one of the most important tools of our time.

- After you complete Chapter 1, you will have learned to use MS-DOS to prepare two diskettes: one for your copy of the Works software and one for your personal files.
- After you complete Chapter 2, you will have used the word processor to edit and print a document.
- After you complete Chapter 3, you will have used the spreadsheet program to juggle your income, rent, and car expenses into a balanced budget that meets a savings goal.

1

Introducing Personal Computers

Preview   Today the personal computer is a tool that almost anyone can use. Using a personal computer is a matter of (1) knowing what can be done with a personal computer, (2) understanding the basic concepts and terminology of computers, and (3) acquiring the hands-on skills needed to operate a personal computer.

This chapter will give you the necessary background to begin using a personal computer. You'll take a brief tour of computer systems. You'll learn what a computer system is and what hardware is. You'll learn to recognize the hardware components of a computer system. You'll begin to understand what software is, and you'll become acquainted with the different types of computer systems. Finally, you'll learn what an operating system is and does.

Along the way, you'll encounter some concepts basic to all computer systems, as well as some computer terminology. With this background, you'll be ready for hands-on experience with a personal computer.

In this chapter, you'll learn:

- Some uses for computers
- The concept of the computer as a system of interrelated components
- The hardware components of a computer
- Types of software for computers
- The three categories of computer systems
- Trends in single-user, multi-user, and networked computer systems
- Business uses of computers
- The functions of application software
- The role of operating-system software
- How to use your operating system

An Overview of Computers

Today it is possible to have at your fingertips more computing power than was available to any computer scientist only 30 years ago. How can this be? There are two explanations. First, computers have evolved at a dizzying speed over the last 30 years. Remarkable technological advances have made computers steadily smaller, less expensive, and easier to use. The result is the **personal computer** — a computer small enough to fit on a desktop, affordable enough to be owned by one person, yet powerful enough to perform many different tasks. The computer you will use in this class is a personal computer. It is a highly capable assistant, and it greatly simplifies the task of learning basic computer skills.

Meanwhile, an equally remarkable evolution has occurred in **software** — the programs or instructions that control the operation of a computer. Computers are such flexible tools because their functions are determined by software. Changing the software in a computer transforms it into a completely different tool. Thus, the same computer can assist you whether you are writing a term paper, alphabetizing a list of names, or preparing a budget.

The first computer users were a handful of scientists and technicians who painstakingly wrote their own software and regarded the computer as a highly specialized tool. However, most of today's computer users rely on a very active commercial software industry to provide the programs that make their computers useful. You will be using an example of such software — the textbook edition of the Microsoft Works program that accompanies this text — to put these concepts into practice.

What You Can Do With a Personal Computer

What can you accomplish with the computing power of a personal computer? Because you can change its function by changing the software, the personal computer is a **general-purpose tool**. It can help you write, calculate, analyze, organize, draw, and communicate. The following scenario may help you to envision how you might use a personal computer.

Chris Wilson is attending freshman orientation at Altair Community College. This morning's meeting will explain how freshmen are going to use the personal

A WORD ABOUT
The Personal Computer Revolution

Since the middle of the 1970s, the personal computer revolution has been widely proclaimed. Intrigued by the prospect of having one at home or business, people have bought personal computers in record numbers. Since the first personal computer was offered in kit form in 1975, over 100 million have been sold.

At first, people bought personal computers, not so much to make practical use of them, but to see for themselves what a computer could do. They played games, wrote programs, and experimented with application software. Schools put them to use, first for drill and practice, then for teaching programming, and now for teaching application skills. Businesspeople put them to use in accounting, word processing, record keeping, and inventory control.

Later, people began to discover the limitations of computers. While the computers kept on selling, some of the computer revolution's promises remained unfulfilled. They could be ornery machines, unnecessarily complicated and hard to use. Often, using them meant learning a new language filled with technical jargon. Sometimes they couldn't perform as advertised, and people were frustrated by the shortcomings or nonexistence of software to do the things they wanted to do. But there are grounds for optimism. Personal computers are improving and have become powerful agents of change in society.

As a result of naturally occurring evolution, personal computers will become more and more capable, through advances in hardware technology — an order of magnitude more capable than the personal computers being sold today.

As the personal computer matures, today's most sophisticated applications will seem like child's play compared to those available a decade from now. Tomorrow's personal computers will be powerful enough to let people do things they have yet to imagine.

computers they are required to buy. This is the third year that Altair has required all incoming students to own a personal computer. By a special arrangement with a computer manufacturer, Altair offers personal computers to its students at about half the retail price. Altair has also built a state-of-the-art campus communications network, to which students can link their personal computers.

At the meeting, each student is given a "software toolkit," a set of computer programs to use for research, homework, and term papers. One of the programs in the toolkit is a word processor, which students are to use to write papers for all their classes. Chris's English composition instructor is going to assign the class one written paper per week. She will also expect the papers to be revised and handed back in, since the word processor makes the mechanics of revision almost effortless.

Chris's economics classes will be using another program in the toolkit, called a spreadsheet program. In studying the effects of inflation, the class will use the spreadsheet program to project future inflation rates and analyze the impacts of alternative rates.

Another program in the toolkit, the database program, will help Chris to index and retrieve lists of references for research papers. The toolkit also includes a drawing program for use in art classes, and a music synthesizer for music classes. At Altair, every personal computer also comes equipped with a set of communication tools, including a communications program. Students can use these tools to tap into the library's computerized card catalog and indexes. They can also use them to communicate with each other and with their professors by sending and receiving "electronic mail" over the communications network.

Altair is confident that its students will be able to do more and better work because the personal computer and software toolkit will free them from the tedious aspects of schoolwork to concentrate more fully on learning.

This scenario is very close to being realized. It is so close to reality, in fact, that all of the software tools we have described, except for the drawing program and music synthesizer, are available with this book. Your personal toolkit is a program called the textbook edition of Microsoft Works. It combines a word processor, a spreadsheet with charting, a database with reporting, and communications. You are going to use Works in this class to learn how to use a personal computer. And after you are finished with the class, you can continue to use Works for other personal or school projects.

Acquiring Computer Skills

The most important step in learning what a computer can do for you is to begin to use one. There really is no substitute for hands-on experience. When you sit down at a personal computer and begin to use it, you'll find that learning by doing can be fun. You'll gain the practical skills you need to benefit most fully from using a computer. And you'll begin to get a feeling for the personal computer's potential and functions.

If you are unfamiliar with personal computers, you will first need to understand some of the basic features of all computer systems. You really don't need a lot of technical knowledge to use a computer. But you do need to understand the answers to a few basic questions: What is a computer system? What is hardware? What is software? How does a computer work? How do you use one? Armed with common sense and the answers to these questions, you will be ready to begin to use a personal computer.

What Is a Computer System?

A **system** is a set of parts, each with a specific purpose, which work together to accomplish a desired goal. A **computer system** consists of the computer itself, often called *hardware*; the programs that control the computer, called *software*; the problem-solving procedures for accomplishing a given task with a computer; and the people who use the computer system to do productive work.

All of the work that a computer system performs is **information processing** of one kind or another. Information processing differs from other work in that the value of its product — information — is determined by its relevance to the problem being solved. Information processing does not have to be done by computer. Typing is information processing; so is adding a list of numbers with paper and pencil.

Thinking is also information processing. It makes sense to use a computer for information processing when the information produced with its aid is more timely, more convenient, more accurate, or more effective than could be produced by other means.

When all the parts of a computer system are working together effectively, the result is information that is highly valuable in a particular problem-solving context. Let's examine in more detail each of the parts that make a computer system work.

What Is Hardware?

Hardware — the electronic and mechanical components of the computer — is the tangible part of a computer system. It consists of a collection of parts or subsystems, each of which performs unique functions. Take a look at Figure 1.1, which identifies the parts of a computer. Broadly speaking, the physical parts of a computer system are: **input devices**, which convert data into a form that the computer can use; a **processor**, which performs the actual information processing and supervises and controls the operation of the entire system; a **memory**, which stores information used by the processor; **mass storage devices**, which store information before and after processing; and **output devices**, which convert the results of

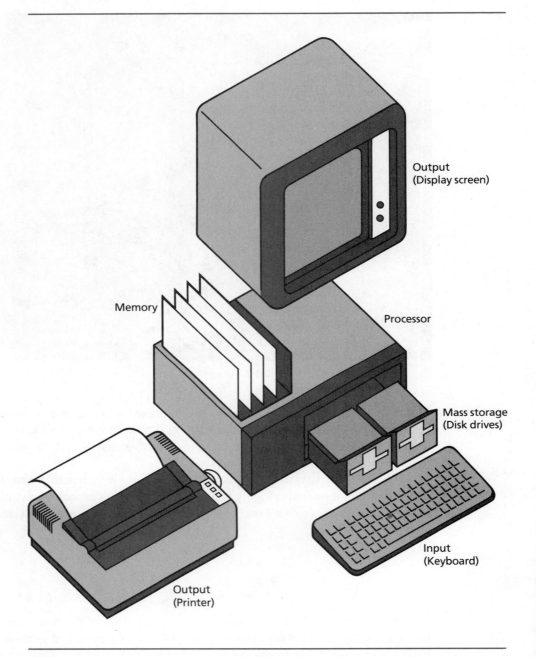

Figure 1.1
Parts of a computer.

processing into information that people can use. Let's look at these hardware parts in more detail, to see how each performs its functions.

Figure 1.2
As the user rolls the mouse next to the computer, the movement of a ball on the underside of the mouse translates into cursor movement on the screen. Buttons on the mouse allow the user to select what the cursor is pointing to.

Input Devices

Input devices have a twofold purpose. First, they accept the commands from the user that tell the computer system what to do. Second, they accept data that have been assembled for processing. **Data** are raw facts that are used to create information. An input device converts data and commands into a form the computer can use.

The most widely used input device for a personal computer is a **keyboard** — a device resembling a typewriter keyboard, which converts finger pressure on the keys into electronic codes the computer can recognize. You will use a keyboard to input data and commands to the personal computer you use in this class. Some personal computers augment the keyboard with a pointing device called a *mouse*, shown in Figure 1.2. The mouse can also be used to input commands, and in Appendix B, Special Mouse Shortcuts, we will describe how you can use a mouse with Works.

The Processor

The processor is the part of the computer that controls its operation and does the actual processing. It is the "brain" of the computer system. Though the comparison between a brain and a processor should not be overstretched, it remains a useful analogy for describing what the processor does. Data and programs enter the computer via an input device and are temporarily stored in the computer's memory to await their turn for processing.

The processor operates cyclically. It begins with the first instruction in a program, carries out the task specified by the instruction, and goes on to the next instruction. The processor repeats this step-by-step operation until processing is complete. In doing so, it controls all the other functions performed by the system. The processor performs the tasks of information processing and control by means of simple arithmetic and logical operations, such as comparing two numbers and making a decision based on the comparison. All of this happens at incredible speed. The length of time it takes a processor to execute an instruction is measured in millionths of a second.

Today processing and control take place in a miniature package called a **microprocessor** — a tiny silicon chip that contains all the circuitry necessary to carry out the instructions it receives. Advances in technology have transformed yesterday's bulky, refrigerator-sized components into microscopic versions etched on quarter-inch flakes of silicon. And each new generation of chips manages to cram in more components. As Figure 1.3 shows, the components on today's chips measure in at only two microns. (A micron equals 39 millionths of an inch.)

Memory

Memory is a storage area inside the computer. The processor needs a place to store data and programs while it executes individual instructions one at a time. In a personal computer, memory consists of a collection of silicon chips. These memory chips are of two types: random-access memory (RAM) and read-only memory (ROM).

Random-access memory, or **RAM**, is the processor's temporary working area. It remains empty until the processor needs to use it, that is, until data and programs are sent to it from an input device. It is also temporary memory, because it is **volatile**. In other words, it loses its contents when the power is turned off. RAM is often called *read/write memory*, meaning that the processor can both read its contents and write new instructions or data into it.

Read-only memory, or **ROM**, is a permanent memory, containing data and instructions loaded into it at the time the computer was built. Its name signifies that its contents cannot be changed; the processor can read from ROM but cannot write new information into it. In contrast to RAM, ROM is **nonvolatile.** It does not lose its contents when the power is shut off.

Why does a computer system need two different kinds of memories? Remember that a computer is a general-purpose tool; you can give it many different sets of instructions. Each time you give it a new program, the program is stored in RAM. Thus it is RAM that gives the computer much of its flexibility. Meanwhile, however, certain tasks are being repeated over and over again, always in the same way. One example is starting up the computer, often called **booting.** A set of instructions known as a **bootstrap program** is permanently stored in ROM. When the

The Everyday, Everywhere Machine

Not so long ago, the term *computer* conjured up images of cavernous, climate-controlled rooms lined with banks of refrigerator-sized machines that fed on a steady diet of paper tape and punch cards. The only people with access to these buzzing, whirring, electronic wizards were scientists, whose knowledge of the devices was regarded with a kind of suspicious awe. Today when we think of computers, we envision the compact units found on desktops in offices, schools, and homes. Computers seem to be everywhere. They receive credit for many of the conveniences we enjoy and blame for many inconveniences. As you will discover in this essay, computers are, indeed, everywhere—including a few places that may surprise you.

1. Many checkout counters use laser scanning systems to read the Universal Product Code (UPC) on merchandise. The scanner senses the widths of the stripes in the UPC and converts the data into signals the computer can understand. These systems not only speed up checkouts but also help stores keep an accurate inventory.

Computers in Disguise

2,3. The ubiquitous automatic teller machine (ATM) is a computer people commonly come into contact with. From bank lobbies to ski lodges, ATMs allow around-the-clock deposits, withdrawals, statement updates, and numerous other basic banking activities.

4. Even our leisure hours benefit from the service of computers. A computer on board this pleasure fishing vessel is used to measure water depth and help locate fish.

5. Computerized stadium scoreboards provide the most visible evidence of the computer's involvement in professional sports. Behind the scenes, everything—from highly sophisticated sports training facilities to speed guns that clock the speed of major league fastballs—depends on computer technology.

6. Often we interact with a computer without even knowing that we are, such as when we fill our car with gasoline. The digital readout on modern gas pumps is a sure sign that a computer is at work behind the scenes.

7. At home or abroad, we rarely are beyond the reach of computers. Here a waitress in a Tokyo restaurant uses CATNET, a nationwide credit verification system introduced by IBM in Japan.

8. Computers are found in household appliances such as microwave ovens and stereos. On this refrigerator, for example, an electronic food care warning system monitors the temperature of the refrigerator and freezer and warns the user if the door is ajar or the unit needs service.

In the Home

9. Computers first entered many households in the form of video games, and entertainment is a popular use of home computers.

10. Small size, relatively low prices, and the availability of a wide range of software have made the personal computer an essential tool in the home office, especially for self-employed individuals.

11. Many programs for young children are games with an educational theme. Most children warm up quickly to computers and are eager to experiment with them. Unlike adults, children are unlikely to be intimidated by the machines.

At the Office

Computers, both visible and not-so-visible, are changing the way nearly all work is done.

13. In this office, the traditional telephone has given way to an Integrated Voice/Data Terminal (IVDT). The IVDT features a speaker phone, a 200-entry phone list, a built-in calculator, and it can be connected to a larger computer.

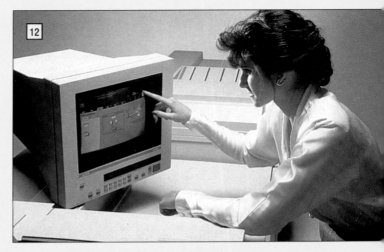

12. This computerized office copier features touch screen controls and allows the user to set up one job while another is being performed.

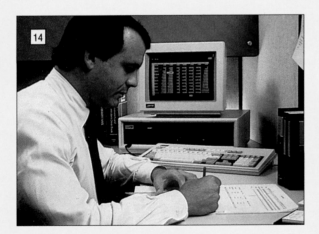

14. Specialized office tasks, as well as basic office equipment, have benefited tremendously from computers. Spreadsheet programs, for example, are "electronic worksheets" that can be used to create financial projections and analyze alternative business plans.

15. Desktop publishing is one of the fastest growing office uses of computers.

Institutions

Many of our society's most basic institutions like schools and law enforcement agencies rely increasingly on computers.

16. Computers are slowly becoming a part of classroom learning for students of all ages. Education experts generally agree that we are still a long way from realizing the computer's full potential as a teaching tool.

17. Working with computers, students can master new concepts at their own speed. Figuring out the best way to use a computer for problem solving can be a thought-provoking activity in itself.

18. Personal computers can be an invaluable aid in preparing reports, essays, and assignments.

19. At the National Institute for Deaf Children, in Paris, a child learns to speak more clearly with the aid of an IBM Personal Computer. Responding to a speech pattern displayed on the monitor, the child adjusts his pitch until he makes the correct sound.

Window 1

20. This compact neonatal monitoring device gives precise measurements of an infant's heart and lung functions.

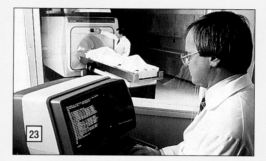

23. Computerized axial tomography (CAT) scanners create detailed, high-resolution three-dimensional images. These images enable doctors to make precise diagnoses without surgery.

21,22. Law enforcement and health care workers need quick answers from large databases. Usually these requirements are met by connecting desktop terminals to a central host computer. The connection can be made with a dedicated wire running directly between the two, with a permanently leased telephone line, or with dial-up telephone service.

Portables

25. Portable computers can provide instant price quotes for complicated sales. Once an order for a sale has been taken, the portable computer can transmit the order over a telephone line to the corporation's host computer, and receive immediate confirmation.

26. Portable computers that require AC electrical power and that weigh about 20 pounds or more are often called *transportable computers.* They can be used both at work and at home.

24. Computers no larger than a briefcase can run on batteries in any location. Despite their small size, they can have memory capacities rivaling much larger computers.

27. Most transportable computers fold into a suitcase-sized unit. This computer includes a full-size detachable keyboard, a 9-inch display, a disk drive, two expansion slots that allow optional circuit boards to be plugged into the computer, a built-in printer, and 800 kilobytes of memory.

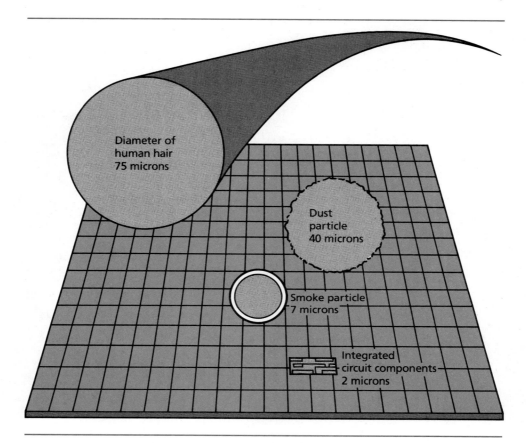

Figure 1.3

Chip sizes. In an area the size of the diameter of a human hair, a chip can contain a grid of hundreds of circuits, each made of lines 2 microns wide.

computer is turned on, the bootstrap program is activated and takes care of loading other programs into memory.

Computer memories are rated in terms of their capacity to store information. The smallest unit of information in a computer system is called a **bit** (short for *bi*nary dig*it*). A bit is represented inside the computer by a tiny electronic component, which can be either on or off. Thus, one bit can express either of two alternatives: on or off, 0 or 1, yes or no, and the like. Two bits can represent four alternatives, and so on. Figure 1.4 illustrates how a computer represents information with electronic currents.

But while the processor deals with bits, people communicate by means of characters (letters, numbers, punctuation marks, and other symbols). Eight bits (which can represent 256 alternatives) are more than enough to represent all the commonly used and understood characters. A group of eight bits, treated as a unit and used to represent one character, is called a **byte**. In other words, a byte is a unit of storage that can hold one character of information.

Random-access memory. IBM's 1-million-bit dynamic random-access memory (DRAM) chip, used in some IBM computers.

Computer memories are measured in terms of the number of bytes of information they can hold. Table 1.1 shows some commonly used abbreviations for memory capacity. Typical memory sizes for personal computers are 512K, 640K, and 1024K. K stands for kilo, which means 1,000. Because computers count in powers of two — not powers of ten, as people do — 1K is actually 1,024 bytes, and 512K is actually 524,288 bytes. But for simplicity's sake, people speak of K as 1,000. The same technological advances that have made microprocessors small and inexpensive are also driving down the size and cost of memory. Thus, it is no longer unusual to find personal computers with memories of 2 million or more bytes.

Mass Storage

Because RAM is temporary memory (it loses its contents when the power of the computer system is shut off), special devices are needed to store data and programs outside the computer before and after processing. The most common mass storage medium is called a disk.

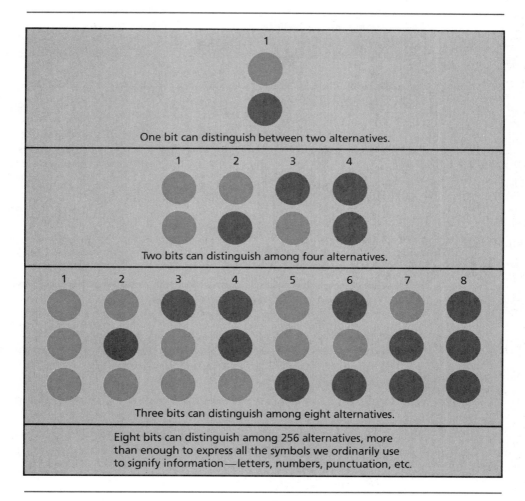

One bit can distinguish between two alternatives.

Two bits can distinguish among four alternatives.

Three bits can distinguish among eight alternatives.

Eight bits can distinguish among 256 alternatives, more than enough to express all the symbols we ordinarily use to signify information—letters, numbers, punctuation, etc.

Figure 1.4
Representing information with electronic currents.

A **disk** is a circular platter coated with a magnetic material. It stores information in the form of tiny magnetic spots on its surface. A disk is like a miniature electronic filing cabinet, in that it organizes information by grouping it into **files** — sets of logically related information. The Works disks contain several data files for storing information and several program files containing the programs that process that information.

A **disk drive** is a device that can read the information on the disk and write new information on it. It does so by mounting the disk on a spindle and spinning it around, much as a record player plays a record. But whereas a phonograph record stores its contents in a single spiral groove, a disk is sectioned off into multiple concentric tracks, each of which is divided into multiple sectors. The disk

TABLE 1.1
Commonly used abbreviations for memory size

Abbreviation	Number of bytes	Uses
K (kilobyte) or thousand	1024	Common memory sizes for personal computers (512K to 2048K)
MB (megabyte) or million	1,048,576	Memory size for mini-computers and mainframes (4MB to 64MB)
GB (gigabyte) or billion	1,073,741,824	Mass storage systems for very large computers (1GB to 16GB)
TB (terabyte) or trillion	1,094,511,627,776	Experimental mass storage systems such as laser disks (up to 1TB)

drive moves different sectors into contact with the read/write head. When you insert a disk and activate the drive, the computer copies information either from the disk into memory or from memory to the disk.

There are two broad categories of disks: *floppy disks*, also called *diskettes*, which are flexible, and *hard disks*, which are rigid. Figure 1.5 is a diagram of a 5¼-inch floppy disk. Common floppy disks are either 5¼ inches or 3½ inches in diameter. The 3½-inch disks are enclosed in a rigid plastic container, which makes them less susceptible to damage. Disks, like memory, are rated according to their capacity. Each 5¼-inch Works disk has a capacity of 360K bytes. This is large enough to store several program and data files.

Hard disks have a speed and capacity advantage over floppy disks. A typical hard disk for a personal computer might store 20 million bytes — 20 megabytes — of information. Hard disks combine large storage capacities with fast access to information, but they cost far more than an equivalent number of floppy disks. As a personal computer user's needs grow, he or she often accumulates a large number of data and program files. A single hard disk can store many different programs, along with larger files. The hard disk's capacity and speed offer the user a more convenient way to organize, manage, and access a larger number of files.

Output Devices

Output devices convert the results of processing into a form that people can use. A **display screen**, often called a *monitor*, is the most common output device. Most use the same cathode-ray tube (CRT) technology as a television screen, slightly modified for computer use. The display screen is how the computer communicates with you, the user. It provides you with immediate feedback by displaying the

A WORD ABOUT
Mass Storage and the Optical Disk

New storage technologies are reducing the costs of disk storage. For most personal computer systems, magnetic disks will continue to dominate, and the introduction of new recording techniques will provide improved performance at lower cost. In ten years, diskettes with capacities in the tens of megabytes and hard disks with capacities in the hundreds of megabytes to gigabytes (hundreds of millions to billions) will be commonplace. Even so, magnetic disks face stiff competition from their optical cousins.

Optical disks are widely used for video and audio recording and are beginning to play an important role in computer data storage. For example, a version of the compact disk (CD) is now available for computers. It's called the compact disk read-only memory or CD ROM. A single disk will store 540 megabytes. This is equivalent to 1,500 floppy disks, 270,000 pages of text, 5,000 images, or 16 hours of sound.

Products like Microsoft Bookshelf take advantage of this large capacity to store multi-

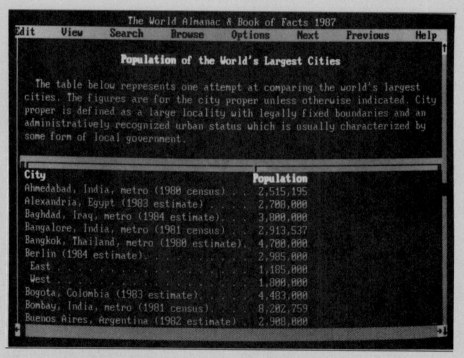

The *1987 World Almanac* and *Book of Facts* on Microsoft Bookshelf makes the PC a valuable research tool by providing easy access to more than one million timely facts.

volume reference works. On one compact disk, Bookshelf stores ten of the most useful reference tools for writing, including a dictionary, *The Chicago Manual of Style*, *Bartlett's Familiar Quotations*, an almanac, a thesaurus, a spelling checker, business information sources, and the *U.S. ZIP Code Directory*. Users can access Bookshelf from within a word processor while editing a document; look up information in seconds without leaving the keyboard; and copy information into the document. Other products contain everything from the Bible to Shakespeare's works to complete encyclopedias, all on a single disk.

Optical disks on which people can record are already replacing microfilm storage and retrieval systems. Their use is quite versatile, since they can store data, voices or music, still images, and even television programs.

However, optical disk technology has two crucial limitations. First, it's not yet easy to erase information from optical disks. Once their huge capacity is filled, obsolete data can't be erased to make room for new data. Also, reading data on optical disks can be somewhat slower than on magnetic disks. In spite of these limitations, though, optical disks can be very useful; new and creative uses for them are being found every day.

characters you type on the keyboard or showing you the results of your instructions to the computer. Display screens can be monochrome (one color) or full color.

A **printer** is an output device that provides permanent paper output. When you turn off a computer, the image on the monitor disappears. Paper output means you can retain your output or, in this class, hand it in to your instructor.

What Is Software?

Software, you will recall, is the collective name for the programs that control the hardware. Hardware is the tangible part of a computer system; software is the intangible part. It is software that determines what tasks the computer system performs.

At first, software may not strike you as a particularly ingenious or unique idea. After all, when you put a new tape into your stereo, you can dramatically change the music that it produces. However, you are merely changing the music, not the function of the stereo. The stereo will never do anything other than play music. But putting a new program into a computer can completely transform the function of the computer. New software gives the computer new capabilities.

Computer hardware is more like a musical instrument than a simple playback device. This is because the combination of hardware and software, like the combination of instruments and music, is a medium of expression. In this class, you will use the Works software to write, calculate, analyze, organize, and express solutions to problems.

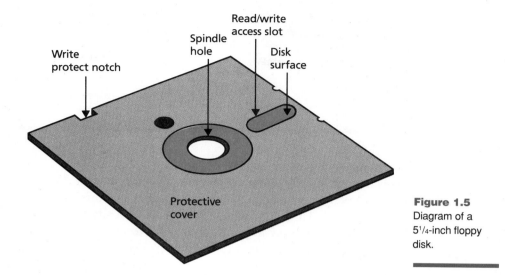

Write
protect notch

Spindle
hole

Read/write
access slot

Disk
surface

Protective
cover

Figure 1.5
Diagram of a
5¼-inch floppy
disk.

Though software is intangible, it does have a physical form. A **software package** consists of one or more floppy disks on which the programs reside. It is accompanied by a set of books or manuals called **documentation**. The documentation usually includes a *user's guide*, a *technical reference manual*, and a *quick reference card* that summarizes the functions of the program and how to use them. Along with the program itself, there may be another disk containing a **tutorial** — an interactive program that helps you learn how to use the software.

There are four kinds of packaged software: (1) general-purpose application software, (2) special-purpose application software, (3) programming languages, and (4) operating-system software (Table 1.2).

The first category, **general-purpose application software**, is software designed to handle a wide variety of tasks that call for the same general capabilities. For example, word processing is a general-purpose application; you can use a word processor to write a term paper, a business letter, a love letter, or a poem. Today there are six categories of general-purpose software: word processing packages, spreadsheets, databases, communications packages, graphics packages, and integrated programs like Works that combine several of these applications into a single, multifunction program.

Special-purpose application software is tailored to the specific needs of particular kinds of businesses or professions. For example, a lawyer who is contemplating buying a word processor might prefer a program specifically designed to prepare legal documents and contracts. A doctor might find a medical billing, accounting, and patient-tracking system more useful than a general-purpose database. A scientist is likely to want a special-purpose statistical-analysis package instead of a general-purpose spreadsheet.

The third category, **programming languages**, consists of programs that are used to write other programs. A programming language is a set of precise rules for

TABLE 1.2
Four categories of software

General-purpose application
Special-purpose application
Programming language
Operating system

formulating statements so that a computer can be programmed to understand them. You may be familiar with the names of some programming languages, such as BASIC or Pascal. Thanks to the development of ready-to-use software, you no longer need to know how to program in order to use a computer. Computer systems are designed to serve two types of users. Most users now use existing programs; the small minority of users known as programmers spend their time writing and developing new programs. We will assume that you are in the first category.

The fourth category is **operating-system software** — the programs that control the operation and manage the resources of a computer system. In personal computers that use disk drives, the operating system is usually called a **disk operating system** or, more casually, **DOS** (rhymes with "boss"). Most personal computers, such as IBM, Tandy, Compaq, and Hewlett-Packard, use MS-DOS (Microsoft disk operating system), which, for simplicity's sake, we will call DOS.

Types of Computer Systems

To help you place personal computers in perspective, we are now going to examine computer systems of all sizes. Computer systems range in size from a personal computer system used by one person to massive systems of interconnected computers that support thousands of people. Today the personal computer plays a prominent role in computer systems of all magnitudes. The trend is toward smaller, faster, and cheaper ones that deliver more computer power per dollar.

Computer systems are categorized on the basis of memory capacity and computational power. Memory size is measured in bytes. The kilobyte (K) is the equivalent of 2^{10}, or approximately 1,000, bytes. Because all three categories of computers can have very large memories, we will compare their memory capacities in megabytes (MB), the equivalent of 2^{20}, or approximately 1 million, bytes.

Processing power is measured in **MIPS**, which stands for *million instructions per second*. Keep in mind, when you read these numbers, that the value of any computer system is determined by what serves its users best and most economically, not necessarily by its power or speed.

As we have already discussed, personal computers, also called **microcomputers,** are desktop-sized, microprocessor-based computer systems. Used in a wide variety

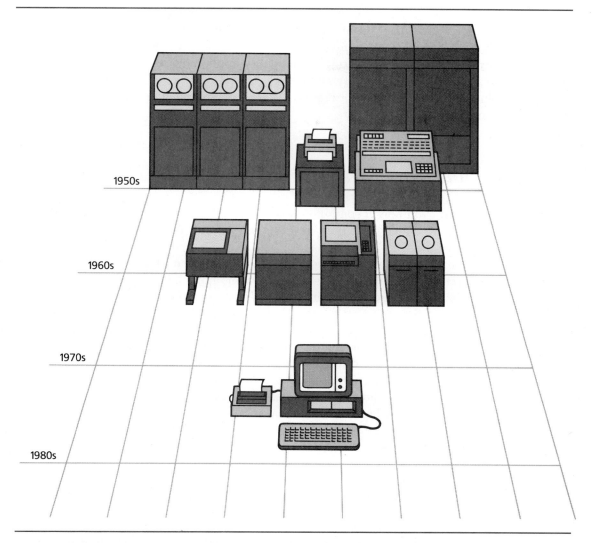

1950s

1960s

1970s

1980s

Today's desktop-sized computers are faster and more powerful than the room-sized computers of the 1950's.

of business, professional, academic, and personal undertakings, personal computers possess up to 16 megabytes of memory and operate at speeds up to 2 MIPS.

At the other end of the spectrum are **mainframes** — room-sized, high-performance computers, capable of running complex programs that would be impractical or impossible on smaller computer systems. They are used by large corporations, government agencies, and universities to process large volumes of information and to perform high-speed processing. A mainframe computer may possess up to 256 megabytes of memory and operate at speeds of up to 40 MIPS — 40 million instructions per second. They are also expensive and require an air-conditioned environment and trained staffs of operators.

In the middle are **minicomputers** — medium-sized, medium-capacity computer systems whose performance rivals that of small mainframes. They are typically used as divisional or departmental computers in business and as the primary computer system in scientific or laboratory applications. A minicomputer has up to 32 megabytes of memory and operates at speeds of up to 4 MIPS. Because of its simpler design, it does not require a special environment or a large staff, as does a mainframe.

Computers and Communications

The rapid evolution of computer systems has intermixed computers and communications so closely that they have become, for all practical purposes, a single integrated industry.

There are two aspects to computer communications. First, the components of a computer system (the processor, memory, and input and output devices) need to communicate with one another. Second, computers need to communicate with other computers. A group of interrelated computers capable of exchanging information is called a **network**.

The channels for transmitting information between computers are direct wiring (if the components of a computer system are close together), telephone lines, cable systems, and satellite systems. Today most communications traffic is carried on ordinary voice telephone lines. This is made possible by a hardware component called a **modem**, which enables two computers to exchange data over standard telephone lines. Figure 1.6 shows two personal computers linked by their modems and the phone lines. **Communications software** performs the "behind-the-scenes" operations necessary for hardware devices to communicate with one another.

Small-Scale Systems

In the last five years, personal computers and minicomputers have become powerful enough to perform many of the information-processing tasks that once were reserved for mainframe computers. Users of computer systems, in turn, are attracted to the prices of smaller systems and their ease of use.

The structure of computer systems is also changing. In the past, mainframe computers were connected to **terminals** — devices without independent computing capability, used only to enter and receive information. Today it is considered more effective to distribute processing among several computers, which may be widely dispersed geographically. Now let's look at several kinds of computer systems, to see what role personal computers are playing in them.

The Single-User System

In business, personal computers have interpersonal functions as well. Personal computers can handle much of the communication that businesspeople need to

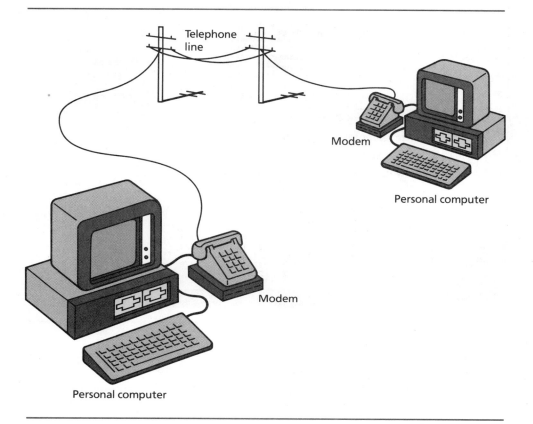

Figure 1.6
Two personal computers linked via modem and phone line.

exchange with their associates and customers. By equipping a personal computer with a modem and communications software, for example, one can send and receive **electronic mail**. To send electronic mail, you type a message using word processing software, and then transmit it — via communications software, a modem, and the telephone lines — to the recipient's electronic mailbox, a storage location in the system's central computer. The recipient accesses his or her mailbox, reads the mail, and sends a reply to your electronic mailbox. Sender and receiver need not be interacting at the same time to use electronic mail.

Personal computers can also access electronic libraries, which deliver stock quotes, business news, reference material, and miscellaneous services, such as airline schedules, hotel reservations, and shopping services. Electronic libraries are stored in a mainframe or minicomputer's disk-filing system, and you can subscribe to one just as you would subscribe to a newspaper or a magazine. Figure 1.7 shows a screen displaying daily stock prices, accessed through an electronic information utility.

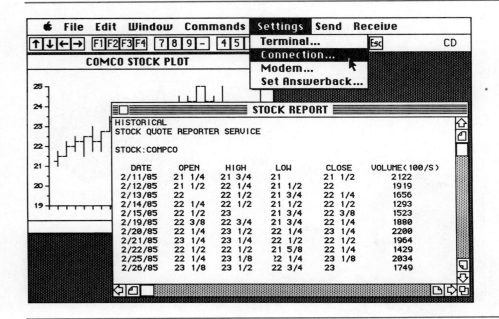

Figure 1.7
Communications software lets you share information with other personal computers, mainframes, and subscription services by sending and receiving data quickly and easily.

The Multiuser System

Multiuser systems allow several users to share a computer's processor, memory, disk storage, and software simultaneously. The key to multiuser systems is their ability to share data and program files. For example, computerized accounting systems typically use five general-purpose software packages: accounts receivable, accounts payable, inventory, payroll, and general ledger. If these programs are integrated — that is, if they have the ability to exchange data with each other — the information contained in the organization's accounting system can be shared by storing the data and program files on a hard disk and by sharing the files among several personal computers. Multiuser systems come in three types: (1) shared-logic systems, (2) multiprocessor systems, and (3) local area networks. Figure 1.8 shows a multiuser system.

Shared-logic systems connect several terminals to a single microcomputer or minicomputer processor. Shared-logic systems work best when all users are performing the same application. For example, in a small law firm with a shared-logic word processing system, the legal secretaries share a common set of document files. Each secretary uses a terminal connected to the central processor and disk storage device. Since the users are all sharing a common processor, adding more users makes the system perform less efficiently for each user. And if the processor fails, the entire system goes down with it.

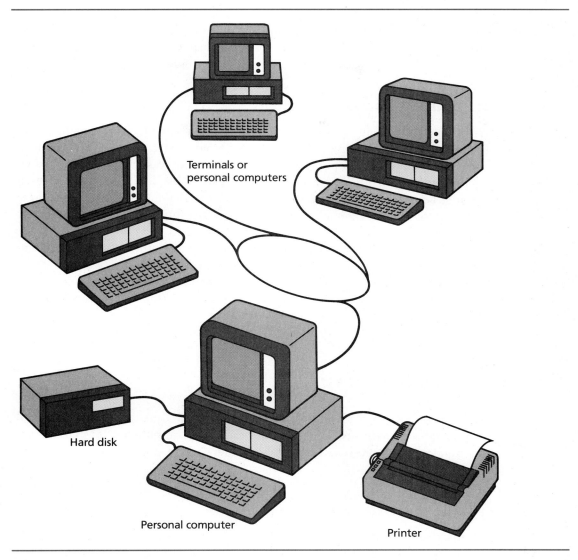

Terminals or
personal computers

Hard disk

Personal computer

Printer

Figure 1.8
A multiuser system.

Multiprocessor systems connect each terminal to its own processor but place the processors in a central location and assign one processor to control the network and the shared disk. In this configuration, the failure of a single processor does not disable the whole system. However, since the processors share a single central location, they can all be incapacitated by a power failure or other disruption.

Local area networks link freestanding personal computers for purposes of sharing such resources as a mass storage device or a high-speed printer. Each user can use his or her personal computer without affecting the performance of the overall system and also use the network to communicate with other users. The rate at which information is transmitted from one computer to another is determined by the type of communication channel used (usually ordinary wires or cable systems).

Distributed Processing Systems

Distributed processing systems are computer systems in which information processing is distributed among physically separate computer systems. For example, each of a nationwide corporation's regional sales offices might have its own minicomputer system. Each sales office is responsible for processing its own customer accounts and sends only a summary of sales information to corporate headquarters. Figure 1.9 shows how a typical distributed processing system is organized.

By distributing information processing and storage among several different locations, large organizations achieve higher performance, faster response times, and a degree of flexibility that is not possible when all data processing is centralized on a single large computer. Another advantage of distributed systems is greater reliability, since the failure of a local system affects only that system.

Computer Systems in Business

The trend in computer systems of all sizes is toward a greater number of small computers, each dedicated to a particular individual, application, or department. This trend is largely responsible for the proliferation of computers in businesses, large and small.

Transaction-Oriented Systems

In **transaction-oriented systems**, processing is activated by a distinct input called a **transaction**. An airline reservation system, for example, processes individual requests for flight schedules, reservations, and seat assignments from thousands of terminals throughout the world.

The credit approval systems of major credit card companies link a central computer to terminals in thousands of retail outlets. At the point of purchase, the clerk inserts the customer's credit card into a magnetic reader. The device reads the number from the card and initiates a phone call to the central computer, where the card number is checked against the customer's credit limit.

These systems are called **on-line systems** because the input is transmitted directly from the point of origin to a central location, where it is processed. Figure 1.10 shows how a typical on-line system is organized. The time it takes an on-line system to process a transaction is called its *response time*. On-line systems are characterized by their rapid response times. Users of an airline reservation or

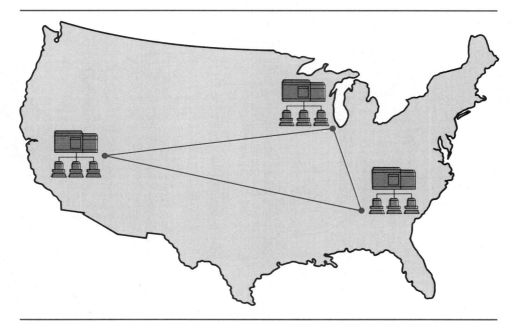

Figure 1.9
A distributed processing system.

credit approval system can't wait more than a couple of minutes to complete their transactions.

Other transaction-oriented systems include banking systems with automated teller machines, stock market quotation systems, and hotel reservation and billing systems.

Workgroup Systems

Workgroup systems apply computer and communication technologies to the enhancement of office functions and procedures. All of the most fundamental office functions — writing, revising, filing, copying, and communicating — have been computerized. Workgroup systems also include videoconferencing systems and voice and electronic mail systems. More specialized applications include image processing, typesetting, production text processing, engineering design, graphic design, conference scheduling, and electronic filing.

The typical Workgroup system is designed to serve the needs of a small (5 to 25) group of people who spend most of their time communicating with each other and far less time communicating with people in other locations.

There are similar sized computer systems that perform similar functions in settings other than offices. Groups of engineers often use networks of specially designed personal computers to design and test new products. Factory automation

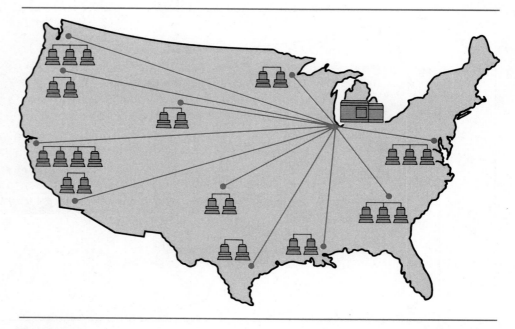

Figure 1.10

A transaction-oriented on-line system connects computers distributed over a wide geographic area to a central computer system that provides access to valuable data.

systems supervise and regulate the manufacturing process. Systems that link information processing with industrial robots actually handle parts and materials, production, assembly, inspection, and packaging.

Management Information Systems (MIS)

Management information systems (MIS) are computer systems that gather information about an organization and make it available on time, and in a useful form, to those managing the organization. MIS typically take advantage of computers of all sizes to help make information more accurate and useful, as well as available when and where it is needed. The vast quantity of information that large corporations and government agencies need to operate, and the speed with which that information is created and used, have made computer-based management information systems critical to such operations.

A university management information system, for example, might support administrative functions, such as student grading, class scheduling, accounting, library operations, faculty research, and teaching. A staff of professionals manages and operates the computer system and provides user services, such as entering data, running programs, and interpreting output. In the last five years, however, minicomputers and personal computers have begun to supplant this centralized approach.

Management information systems are often organized hierarchically. At the top of the hierarchy are one or more mainframes that serve as a repository for organizational information. This information is stored in databases — the collections of data on which organizations base their activities and decisions. A **database** is a collection of various types of information, organized according to a logical structure that eliminates redundancies in the information. If a database consists of more than one file, software establishes the relationships among the files.

A large organization might have large-scale databases for its financial data, personnel data, and inventory data. These databases become so large that mainframe processing speeds and capabilities are needed to structure, maintain, update, and retrieve the data.

Lower on the hierarchy are the minicomputer and personal computer subsystems found at the departmental and divisional level. In a hierarchical system, minicomputers often serve as **front-end processors**. That is, they collect information from local sources, perform a limited amount of processing on it, and send it on to the mainframe. At the lowest level, personal computers serve as workstations for individuals. The workstation is a multifunction device. At times it operates as a terminal under the control of the mainframe or minicomputer; at other times, it is under the direct control of the user.

Multinational corporations often set up very large **wide-area networks** to link their management information systems and databases even on different continents. A typical multinational, such as an oil company or computer hardware manufacturer, might have a central MIS facility with several mainframes, regional offices with mainframes or minicomputers, and thousands of personal computers on the desks of administrative and clerical workers.

How does such a system serve the diverse needs of a large organization? Personal computers used as standalone systems automate decision-making procedures. Personal computers located in the same facility can be connected by a local area network for purposes of sharing information. Users who need to access information from the central corporate mainframe databases can use their personal computers as terminals. And any two computers in the worldwide network can communicate through the wide-area communication network.

Another example of a large-scale management information system is a large retail chain with thousands of stores distributed throughout the United States. This system combines a wide-area communications network with distributed processing. At each store, sales transactions are recorded by the point-of-purchase terminals that are replacing traditional cash registers. Since it would be impractical for every terminal to be connected to the mainframe computers at the retailer's headquarters, transactions are stored and forwarded daily to regional centers. There they are processed and forwarded to the retailer's mainframe database system.

Organizations of every size and kind are acquiring computer systems. Meanwhile, these systems are evolving in response to advances in hardware and software. As a result, our society is heading into an era in which most of the workforce will be creating, processing, and communicating information. We will discuss these aspects of computers in more detail in Part III, "Connections".

Using a Computer System

Using a computer system involves giving it commands or procedures to carry out. The goal of a computer user is to get the computer to do some useful work. With this in mind, it may be helpful to view a computer system as a hierarchy of resources, with the user at the highest level, the application software at the next highest level, the operating system at the middle level, and the hardware at the lowest level of the hierarchy.

At the highest level, the user has an **application** in mind. He or she wants to apply the computer to a particular problem, such as writing a term paper, analyzing a set of numbers, or organizing a list of names. The rest of the computer system is simply a means to this end.

In general, application software performs the high-level work, while the operating system performs the low-level work. By low-level work, we really mean routine work — work that is common to almost all applications. Take, for example, storing information in files. Whether you write with a word processor, analyze problems with a spreadsheet program, or organize lists of information with a database program, you will need to put your information in files.

As we noted earlier, a blank disk is analogous to a filing cabinet without drawers, indexes, dividers, or folders. It is simply "raw" storage space. To be useful as storage, it has to be labeled, indexed, and organized so that users can access the information that is stored there.

This level of organizing and managing the storage space on a disk is accomplished by the operating system. Figure 1.11 illustrates how a disk is organized. The operating system sections the disk into concentric circles called **tracks.** Each track is then divided into **sectors.** The operating system also creates a directory, to keep account of which tracks and sectors are in use by which files. As Figure 1.11 illustrates, the operating system consults the directory for the address of the appropriate sector and then moves it into contact with the read/write head. A directory is necessary because files are typically in a constant state of change. New files are created, and old files are deleted. Information is added to and deleted from existing files. Unless the disk space is managed efficiently, the information stored on it could become as chaotic as that in a disorganized filing cabinet.

Guided by the user, the operating system keeps the disk's filing system in order. It can be instructed to name or rename a file, copy files from one disk to another, read information from a file, or write information to a file. The operating system can also inform the user of how much space is left on a disk and how big the files are.

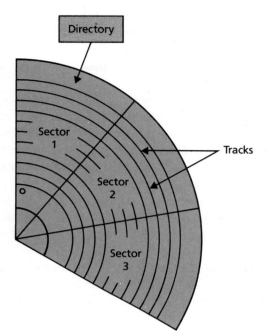

Figure 1.11
How a disk is organized. The operating system divides the disk into tracks and then divides the tracks into sectors. It also creates a directory that lists the location of files on the disk.

The application software is not concerned with such details. An application program simply "asks" the operating system to do such tasks. The net effect of this hierarchical organization is to insulate the user from all of the "housekeeping" details except those that are necessary to accomplish the tasks at hand. Of course, the user could be responsible for all these details, but that would defeat the goal of using a computer. Hierarchical organization makes it far easier for a user to get the computer to do useful work.

Why doesn't the application program take care of these tasks directly instead of using the operating system? First, tasks like storing and retrieving data from a disk are routine operations. It makes sense to develop these programs once and then just to let different application programs use them over and over again. Second, and just as important, it would not be feasible for two or more application programs to share a resource, such as a disk, without a "third party" — the operating system — to ensure that they do not interfere with each other.

In addition to managing the disks, the operating system also handles other standard procedures such as displaying characters on the screen, accepting input from the keyboard, and sending information to the printer.

Using the Operating System

It might sound as if the user never comes into direct contact with the operating system. In fact, the user does interact with it through a special program that provides an operating system user interface. You often interact with the operating system to run application programs and to communicate with the disk drives and the printer. When the operating system is copied into memory, it takes control of the computer. To run an application program, you then specify its name to the operating system.

The more you use a computer system, the more you will tend to accumulate files and disks. As your "library" of files and disks grows, you will want to learn how to use the file-managing operations of the operating system. These include such commands as: look at a directory, check a disk, copy, save, erase, and rename a file or a disk. These commands are useful for rearranging information on your disks and for making room for new files.

You are about to begin using a personal computer by applying the concepts you have just learned to a few simple operating-system tasks. You will learn how to format your disks, load and run programs, examine your disks, and make copies of disks and files.

The operating system you use will be the MS-DOS operating system from Microsoft, the same company that developed the Works software. MS-DOS is usually supplied by the manufacturer of a particular computer, and it comes with different names and in different variations and versions. IBM, for example, calls it PC-DOS, but in this book we will always call it DOS. In addition, DOS has been revised several times to (1) add more capability, (2) take advantage of newer personal-computer hardware, and (3) fix bugs or mistakes. The original version of DOS was numbered 1.00.

The Works software requires that the version of DOS be number 2.0 or greater. For instance, Version 2.1 or 3.0 will work, but Version 1.1 will not. When you turn on the computer and load DOS, information about the specific version of DOS, including the version number, is displayed on the screen.

Depending on the version of DOS you are using, what you see on your computer screen may differ slightly from the illustrations in this chapter. Don't worry; if your version is 2.0 or greater, the commands you enter and the results you get will be correct.

Using the Keyboard

With DOS, you use the keyboard to enter the commands that tell the computer what to do. The display screen will give you feedback as you instruct the computer. Typing skill is not necessary at this stage, since these commands are simple and short. But take the time to familiarize yourself with the layout of the keyboard; in Chapter 2 we will look at the entire keyboard in more detail. Figure 1.12 shows two typical keyboard layouts. Look at it now to locate the [Backspace] key, the [Enter] key, and the [Shift] key.

Occupying the middle of the keyboard are the traditional typewriter keys, used primarily to enter text and numbers. These keys consist of the letters of the alphabet, numbers, a space bar, and punctuation marks. There are also two [Shift]

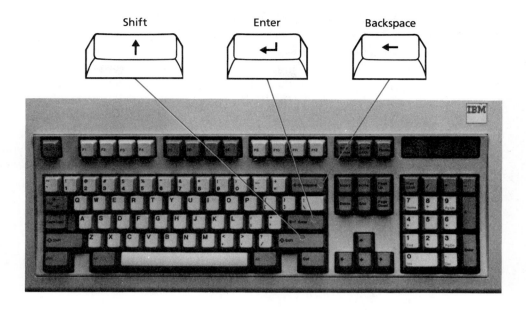

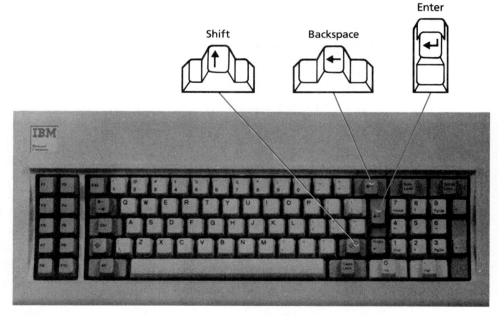

Figure 1.12
Typical keyboard layouts. Top: enhanced keyboard; Bottom: standard keyboard.

keys and a [Caps Lock] key. Letters typed while the [Shift] key is held down appear as capitals. The [Caps Lock] key holds the [Shift] down until it is released.

The [**Backspace**] key is used to erase the character to the left of the cursor when typing letters or numbers. If you hit the wrong key, simply press the [Backspace] key. This moves the cursor one position to the left and simultaneously erases the character. Holding the [Backspace] key down will repeatedly erase characters as the cursor moves to the left.

The [**Enter**] key (sometimes called the *return* key) is used to enter commands, respond to prompts, and begin new paragraphs. For example, if you type an operating system command, such as DIR, the command will not be performed until you press the [Enter] key. The operating system then accepts the command and drops the cursor down one line.

Installing Works

Before you begin, be sure you have the following hardware components:

- An MS-DOS-compatible personal computer, equipped with a keyboard, two floppy disk drives, and a display device
- A DOS disk that includes a level of DOS compatible with your computer
- The Works program disk that accompanies this book
- Two blank floppy disks

If the computer you will be using has only one floppy disk drive or a hard disk drive, your instructor will give you slightly different instructions; ask for these instructions now and use them instead of those that follow. You also need to know what kind of graphics display is used in your computer; ask for this information now.

There are four steps required to install Works: (1) loading the disk operating system (DOS); (2) formatting two blank disks, one for your working copy of the Works program and one for your personal files; (3) copying the original Works program disk to your working copy disk; (4) copying a file that adjusts Works to the graphics display in your computer; and (5) copying the example files used in this book to your personal disk.

Recall that starting up the computer is called *booting*. Use the following procedure to boot the computer. The computer you are using has two floppy disk drives. The left (or top) one is called drive **A**. The right (or bottom) one is called drive **B**.

Handling Disks

Floppy disks are vulnerable to dirt, dust, magnetic fields, mishandling, and human error. Proper handling of disks is essential to prevent damage. Never touch the

Figure 1.13
The correct way to insert a floppy disk into a disk drive. The label faces up and enters the drive last.

exposed surfaces of the disk. Handle the disk only by its protective jacket. When they are not in use, always keep disks in their storage envelopes. Never place a disk on top of the display device or any other source of a strong magnetic field. Never place a disk where you might inadvertently spill a soft drink or a cup of coffee on it. And don't place a disk in a flexible notebook or backpack, where it might easily bend.

Loading DOS

1. Remove the DOS disk from its outer storage envelope, handling it by the label. Remember not to touch the exposed magnetic surface of the disk.

2. Open the door of disk drive A and insert the disk with the label facing up, as shown in Figure 1.13. Insert the exposed end of the disk first. Don't forget to close the disk drive door. If it's left open, the drive will not work.

3. Most DOS-compatible computers have an on/off switch on the right side, near the back of the machine. The display device may have its own on/off switch, or it may go on automatically with the computer. Locate the switch or switches, and turn both devices on. If the computer is already on, locate the [Ctrl] and the [Alt] key on the left-hand side of the keyboard, and the

[Del] key on the right-hand side. Press all three keys simultaneously.

4. After a few seconds' delay, a red light on disk drive A will go on. You'll hear clacking and whirring as the disk begins to spin. The computer is copying the operating system from the disk into memory. When it is finished, it will beep, and the operating system will display a **prompt** — a request for input from the user, which will look like this:

```
Current date is Tue 1-01-1980
Enter new date: _
```

Note: If, instead of the date prompt, a message appears asking you to insert a DOS disk into drive A, you may have inserted the wrong disk. Remove it, insert the DOS disk into drive A, and press the [Enter] key.

5. To the right of the prompt will be a **cursor** — a short, blinking underline. Its purpose is to let you know where the next character you type will appear. If the date appearing on the display is incorrect, type in today's date, using the format *month-day-year*. If you make a mistake typing, you can use the [Backspace] key to erase the mistake. Once you have correctly entered the date (or if it was already correct), press the [Enter] key.

6. The operating system will then prompt you like this:

```
Current time is 0:00:33:55
Enter new time: _
```

Type in the current time (if it is incorrect), using the military format *hours:minutes*, with a colon between the two numbers. (On the 24-hour military clock, 1:30 P.M. equals 13:30 and so on.) Then press the [Enter] key. Next the operating system will display a copyright notice, followed immediately by the DOS prompt *A>* and the blinking underline cursor. The **A>** prompt is the signal that the system is ready to carry out any operating-system commands that you type in on the keyboard.

Congratulations! You have just loaded DOS into the computer's memory. You are now ready to begin using the computer. By the time you finish this section, you'll have completed your first exercise using a personal computer.

Formatting Your Blank Disks

The first step is to format your two blank disks. To do this, you will use the FORMAT program, which is located on the DOS disk. Its purpose is to prepare a disk to accept DOS files. Note that, when you type DOS commands, you can use either capital or lower case letters. Before you begin, the DOS operating-system disk should be in drive A, and the system should be displaying the DOS prompt A>.

1. Insert a blank disk in drive B.

2. Type in the command FORMAT B:/S and press the [Enter] key. Don't forget the space after FORMAT, the colon following the B, and note that you use the forward slash (/) — not the backward slash (\) — before the S.

    You will be prompted to:

    ```
    Insert new diskette for drive B:
      and strike any key when ready
    ```

3. Press any key to begin the formatting operation. (Depending on your version of DOS, you may see the words "Head" and "Cylinder" displayed with numbers.) The screen displays:

    ```
    Formatting...
    ```

    Once the process is complete, the screen will display messages like the following:

    ```
    Formatting...Format complete
      System transferred
    362496 bytes total disk space
    40960 bytes used by system
    321536 bytes available on disk
    Format another (Y/N)?
    ```

4. Press N (depending on your version of DOS, you may need to press [Enter] also) to end the FORMAT program. Remove the newly formatted disk from disk drive B, label it "Works Files," and include today's date and your name. In the future you will use this disk to start the computer with DOS before you use the Works program. This disk will also hold all the files you create with the Works program.

Copying Works

Now you will format a disk to be used to hold a working copy of the Works program disk.

1. Again, insert a blank disk in drive B.

2. Type in the command FORMAT B: and press the [Enter] key.

    This time, the "/S" has been omitted, meaning that the **system files** needed by DOS will not be copied to this disk. You won't be able to use this disk to start the computer with DOS, but there will be more room on the disk for the Works program files.

You will be prompted to:

```
Insert new diskette for drive B:
  and strike any key when ready
```

3. Press any key to begin the formatting operation. The screen displays:

```
Formatting...
```

Once the process is complete, the screen will display messages like:

```
Formatting...Format complete
362496 bytes total disk space
362496 bytes available on disk
Format another (Y/N)?
```

4. Press N (depending on your version of DOS, you may need to press [Enter] also) to end the FORMAT program. Remove the newly formatted disk from disk drive B, label it "Works Program Copy," include today's date and your name.

5. Now put the newly formatted "Works Program Copy" back into disk drive B.

   Locate the original Works program disk that comes with this book. To avoid accidental erasure you may want to **write-protect** this disk by covering a notch on the floppy disk jacket with a piece of special tape, as shown in Figure 1.14. Your instructor can provide you with the tape.

6. Remove the DOS disk from drive A and put the original Works program disk into drive A.

Figure 1.14

Write protection via covering the notch on a floppy disk.

You will now copy all the files from the original Works disk in drive A to your working disk in drive B by using the DOS COPY command. If you ever accidentally erase a file on your working disk, you will be able to replace it by going back to the original disk.

7. Type in the command COPY A:*.* B: and press the [Enter] key.

This command will copy all the files on the disk in drive A to the disk in drive B. As the files are copied, their names appear on the screen. Your screen display will look like:

```
A:WORKS.EXE
A:WORKS.INI
A:COMM.SCD
A:EPSON.GPD
A:HIEPSON.GPD
A:EPSONFX.PRD
A:EGA.GSD
A:HERCULES.GSD
A:CGA.GSD
A:TANDY.GSD
A:MCGA.GSD
A:SURVEY.WPS
A:BUDGET.WKS
A:COUNTRY.WDB
    14 Files(s) copied
```

Copying the Graphics Display File

In order to display graphs, the Works software must be adjusted for the specific graphics display in your computer. Your instructor can tell you which graphics display is installed in your computer. Works can use any of the following displays:

1. Color Graphics Adapter (CGA)
2. Enhanced Graphics Adapter (EGA)
3. Hercules Monochrome Adapter
4. IBM Models 25/30 Multicolored Graphics Array (MCGA)
5. Tandy Model 1000

After you determine which kind of graphics display your computer has, type one of the following commands:

1. If your computer has a CGA graphics display, type in the command COPY B:CGA.GSD B:SCREEN.GSD and press the [Enter] key.

2. If your computer has an EGA graphics display, type in the command COPY B:EGA.GSD B:SCREEN.GSD and press the [Enter] key.

3. If your computer has a Hercules graphics display, type in the command COPY B:HERCULES.GSD B:SCREEN.GSD and press the [Enter] key.

4. If your computer has an MCGA graphics display, type in the command COPY B:MCGA.GSD B:SCREEN.GSD and press the [Enter] key.

5. If your computer has a Tandy graphics display, type in the command COPY B:TANDY.GSD B:SCREEN.GSD and press the [Enter] key.

Copying Example Files

The "Works Program Copy" disk contains some data files used as examples in later chapters of this book. These files belong on the "Works Files" disk, where you will also store all the other files you create with Works. To copy these files, the disk labeled "Works Program Copy" should first be in drive B.

1. Remove the original Works program disk from drive A and put the "Works Files" disk in drive A.

2. Type in the command COPY B:*.W* A: and press the [Enter] key.

   This command will copy all the Works data files on the disk in drive B to the disk in drive A. Your screen display will look like:

```
B:SURVEY.WPS
B:BUDGET.WKS
B:COUNTRY.WDB
   3 Files(s) copied
```

Ending the Session

At the end of your session with the computer, remove any disks you have been using from the drives and place them in their storage envelopes. Check with your instructor or lab supervisor to see whether the computer should be turned off or left on for use by the next class.

In Chapter 2, you will begin to learn how to use the Works program.

Review

Key Terms

Personal computer
Software
General-purpose tool
System
Computer system
Information processing
Hardware
Processor
Memory
Input device
Output device
Mass storage device
Data
Keyboard
Microprocessor
Random-access memory (RAM)
Volatile
Read-only memory (ROM)
Bit
Byte
Disk
File
Disk drive
Display screen
Printer
Software package
Documentation
Tutorial
General-purpose application software

Special-purpose application software
Programming language
Operating-system software
Disk operating system (DOS)
MIPS
Mainframe
Minicomputer
Network
Modem
Communications software
Terminal
Electronic mail
Multiuser system
Shared-logic system
Multiprocessor system
Local area network
Distributed processing system
Transaction-oriented system
Transaction
On-line system
Workgroup system
Management information system (MIS)
Database
Front-end processor
Wide-area network
Application
Prompt
Cursor
Write-protect

Discussion Questions

1. How is it possible for you to have more computing power at your fingertips than was available to any computer scientist 30 years ago?
2. What makes a personal computer a general-purpose tool?
3. Briefly outline the components of a computer system.
4. What is RAM? What is ROM?
5. Why does a computer system have two different kinds of memories?
6. Approximately how many characters of information is 360K bytes?
7. What are the two aspects of computer communications?
8. What is the key to a multiuser system?
9. What are the advantages of distributed processing in comparison to centralized processing?

10. What is an application? Name some examples of applications.

11. Name one technique that an operating system uses to organize the storage space on a disk.

12. What purpose does the hierarchical organization of a computer system's resources serve?

13. Give two reasons why it is desirable for the operating system to handle details of storing and retrieving information on a disk.

14. Why is it useful to write-protect a disk?

Software Exercises

The following exercises will help reinforce what you have already learned about DOS and will acquaint you with some new commands. To begin the exercises, place your "Works Files" disk in drive A and your Works program disk in drive B. Then boot the computer by pressing the [Ctrl], [Alt], and [Del] keys simultaneously.

1. When DOS displays the date prompt, type some random characters, but don't press the [Enter] key. Correct your typing "errors" by pressing the [Backspace] key until all the characters are erased. Then enter the correct date and press the [Enter] key. Do the same exercise at the time prompt.

2. DOS is usually forgiving if you make a mistake while typing in a command. At the A> prompt, type in some numbers, such as 333, then press [Enter]. DOS will display the error message "Bad command or file name". Unfortunately, DOS doesn't tell you what to do, so if you ever do get such an error message, check to be sure your commands and file names are correctly spelled.

3. Recall that each DOS disk uses a directory to keep track of files. To display the directory of the disk in drive A, type DIR A: and press [Enter]. DOS will display the directory of your "Works Files" disk. To display the directory of your Works program disk, type DIR B: and press [Enter]. Note that each directory entry contains the name of the file, its size in bytes, and the date and time it was created or last changed.

4. You will be creating many files throughout this course. There will be times when you will want to check the contents of a file without using Works. The TYPE command gives you a quick way to do this. To display the contents of the file named SURVEY.WPS, type TYPE A:SURVEY.WPS and press [Enter] key. You can use the TYPE command to check the contents of any of your data files. (Don't worry if you see some strange characters when you do!)

2
Getting Started with Microsoft Works

Preview The Microsoft Works software consists of four integrated application programs — a word processor, a spreadsheet program with charting, a database program with reporting, and a communications program.

All of the Works programs use similar commands. Once you have learned to use one of the applications, you can put that learning to use with the other applications.

This chapter will lead you through the Works environment, explaining the concepts and commands of the user interface. In the process, you will gain an understanding of how software and users communicate with each other. Then you will start up the Works software and use the word processor to edit and print a file.

In this chapter, you'll learn:

■ The Works applications
■ The purpose and function of a user interface
■ The use of the display screen and keyboard
■ How to use the Works user interface
■ How to use DOS with Works
■ The Works word processor

A Quick Tour of Works

The Works software consists of four applications: a word processor, a spreadsheet program with charting, a database program with reporting, and a communications program. Each application is designed to help you perform certain tasks.

In addition, Works is an **integrated program**; that is, it allows the applications to work together, so that they can be even more useful. For instance, information from the spreadsheet, database, and communications programs can be moved into the word processor to become part of a report. Information can be extracted from the database and moved into the spreadsheet for analysis and graphing. You can even capture information from other computers, using the communications program, and move that information into the spreadsheet or database.

Word Processor

A **word processor** applies the computer to the work of writing. It is used to create **documents** by entering and editing text. Documents can be either long reports or short memos and can include graphs and numerical information from the spreadsheet application. Documents can also contain special fields that are used to access information from a database; with these fields, the word processor can print out multiple copies of a document corresponding to multiple records in a database. This feature can be used to automate the printing of form letters, for instance.

The word processor allows you to print text in boldface, underlined, italic, strikethrough, superscript, and subscript formats when your computer is equipped with a suitable printer. Figure 2.1 shows samples of text printed in these formats using the word processor.

Spreadsheet

A **spreadsheet** program dedicates the computer to the work of calculating and analyzing numbers. Numbers, formulas, and text can be entered into a spreadsheet. When a number or formula changes, all the other numbers and formulas are instantly updated to reflect the change. In effect, the spreadsheet makes editing numbers easy, in much the same way that a word processor makes editing text easy.

The Works spreadsheet also has a **charting** feature. This software will draw many different kinds of charts, including pie charts, bar graphs, and line graphs. The numbers that drive a chart come from the spreadsheet, and it is easy to change numbers on the spreadsheet and then view the results as a chart. Because charts make complex numerical relationships easier to comprehend, the combination of spreadsheet and charting is particularly useful.

The word processor allows you to print text in **bold face,** <u>underlined</u>, *italic,* ~~strikethrough~~, ^{superscript} and $_{subscript}$ formats when your computer is equipped with a suitable printer.

Figure 2.1
Sample text printouts.

The spreadsheet includes many functions that can be used in formulas. Functions perform complex calculations for you. For instance, the function PMT can be used to compute the monthly payment for a loan, given the interest rate, loan amount, and term. The spreadsheet includes financial and mathematically oriented functions, as well as miscellaneous functions that make spreadsheet calculations easier. All of these functions are detailed in Appendix C, "Spreadsheet and Database Functions."

Database

A **database** harnesses the computer to the work of organizing and retrieving information. The Works database is very similar to the spreadsheet, and once you have learned to use the spreadsheet, the database should be instantly familiar.

The database allows you to create a structure for information, called a **record**. A record is made up of **fields**, which are similar to the units in the spreadsheet called **cells**. The database also allows you to create a form, which is a way of looking at and editing the fields in one record. A form on the screen is similar to a common printed form.

The database also includes a **query facility**, which allows you to limit your view of the information to just those records that match certain constraints; you can then sort these records. The reporting feature allows you to print out information about these records in a very organized format. In addition, you can print form letters using the word processor.

The database shares with the spreadsheet many functions that can be used in formulas to calculate the value of fields. See Appendix C, "Spreadsheet and Database Functions," for the details of these functions.

Communications

The **communications** program allows your personal computer to access other computers, including mainframe computers and computers that are very far away. Through a process called *terminal emulation*, the work area of your screen becomes a window into another computer.

The information that you see, the information that comes from the other computer, can be captured in a file for use by the other Works applications. In some circumstances, you can transfer information you created with Works applications to another computer.

Works communications allows your personal computer to communicate, either by directly connecting it to another computer or by using a modem to call the other computer using a telephone line. Using a modem and the telephone, you can call many publicly available computer systems and gain access to information and services, such as the latest news, airline reservation systems, stock prices, and electronic mail services.

You'll learn to use these specific applications throughout this course, but first we'd like to introduce a few concepts that are applicable to all personal computers. Then we'll let you put them to use with the Works software.

Interacting with a Personal Computer

Learning to operate a personal computer is, in many ways, like learning to drive a car. In learning to drive, you place yourself in an environment — the driver's seat — that equips you with the means to control the operation of a car. You give the car instructions by turning the wheel and stepping on the gas and the brake. The windows, rearview mirrors, and instrument panel give you feedback and enable you to view your progress as you drive. The car/driver interface, in other words, enables the driver to control the car and communicates information to the driver.

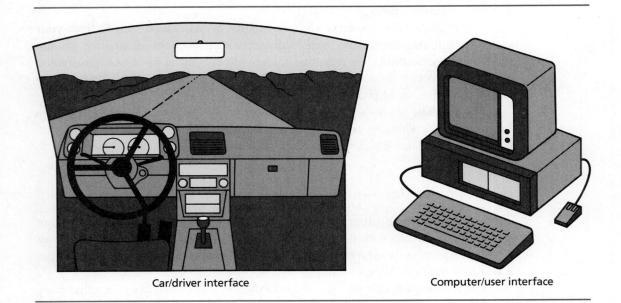

Car/driver interface   Computer/user interface

You do not have to understand how a car works to learn to drive. You do, however, need to be familiar with the car/driver interface. Though it is complex, most learners take it for granted because they are already familiar with cars. By contrast, the computer is a new technology, and few first-time users are already familiar with it.

Computers differ from cars and other industrial products in one important way. As we saw in Chapter 1, the hardware is simply a vehicle for the software, which is very abstract and intangible. The programs and data files that computers process consist of intangible information, stored in magnetic form on disks.

Learning how to use a personal computer is primarily a matter of learning to use software. To enable the user to manipulate the software, the computer system has to provide an environment in which objects, such as files and programs, and actions, such as commands and feedback, are made concrete to the user.

The User Interface

Two-way communication with the software occurs through the **user interface** — software that acts as an intermediary between an application program and the person using it. The user interface permits you to communicate with the computer and to interpret what the computer system communicates to you.

There are several techniques of two-way communication. In Chapter 1, you learned how to give commands to the operating system by typing them in at the keyboard. You also saw the computer's feedback on the display screen. This type of two-way communication works well if you already know the commands or if you have a reference guide that lists the available commands.

As an alternative, most programs display a **menu** of the commands available to the user. Instead of typing in the command, the user can simply select the command he or she wants to use. Many programs will also display a list of files, so that the user can select a file instead of typing in the file name.

Some user interfaces are very ingenious in the way they visually represent the software and the functions of control. Some use graphic images called **icons** to represent the options in a menu. Figure 2.2 shows an example of a menu that uses icons. Some also divide the display screen into **windows**, variable-sized rectangles capable of simultaneously displaying different parts of a file or different application programs.

Some user interfaces augment the keyboard with a pointing device called a *mouse*, which controls the cursor. You point to menu items and options by moving the mouse around on a flat surface next to your computer. The mouse's movements are replicated by the movement of the cursor on the screen. To select the item at which the cursor is pointing, you simply press a button on the mouse. IBM's Personal System/2 and Apple's Macintosh are examples of computers whose user interface is designed around a mouse pointing device. These systems also use icons and other graphic symbols to communicate with the user. You can use a

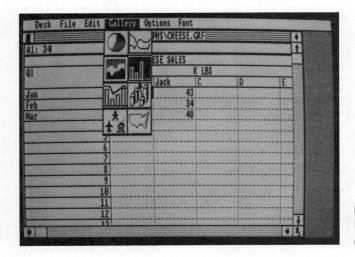

Figure 2.2
Menu with icons.

mouse with the Works software, too; see Appendix B, "Special Mouse Shortcuts," for instructions.

If the user makes a mistake, the user interface should point it out and give instructions to correct it. These and other instructions often take the form of a **dialog**, consisting of one or more questions from the system and the user's responses to them. A dialog resembles a conversation between you and the user interface.

Among the most interesting challenges for designers of user interfaces has been to develop hardware and software for blind, deaf, and physically handicapped users. There are several systems that can translate text into speech and several ingenious devices for translating movements of the head, toe, finger, or eye into computer commands.

Creating user interfaces for the handicapped forces designers to question their assumptions and think about how people would interact with computers if keyboards and display screens were not the standard conventions of computer use. Their research and experimentation are leading to new ways of interacting with computers, which may ultimately benefit all computer users. Figure 2.3 shows a screen reader that enables blind or visually impaired users to hear text displayed on the screen just as a sighted user would see it.

The Display Screen

The display screen is the primary vehicle by which the user interface communicates to you, the user. It provides you with information and feedback. In effect, the display screen becomes a window through which you receive feedback from the software.

Software can use several techniques to make your interaction with it more concrete. After you select a menu item, it is highlighted in **reverse video** to indicate that it has been selected. Figure 2.4 shows a menu with the selected command highlighted in reverse video.

Often there isn't enough room on the display screen to see the entire contents of a file. For example, many documents you write on the word processor will be too long to display all at once on the screen. To view other parts of the document, you will use a technique called **scrolling**, which we will discuss later.

The Keyboard

The other side of two-way communication — the actions you initiate to control the operation of the computer system — uses the keyboard. As you have already seen, a personal computer's keyboard has several more keys than a traditional typewriter keyboard. These additional keys are used to give the computer instructions

Figure 2.3
IBM screen reader.

A WORD ABOUT
The Friendly Frontier

How can computers be made easier to use? One of the often-studied problems in research laboratories is the "person-to-computer interface," or simply the *user interface*. The long-term goal of such research is to make the person-to-computer interface as fluid and fluent as the person-to-person interface. In addition to experiments with language understanding, several interesting experiments are under way which may pave the way to more flexible user interfaces.

Personal computers allow you to point at items on a display, either by moving a mouse or putting your finger on a touch-sensitive screen. Could a computer system respond to your hand movements? At the Massachusetts Institute of Technology (MIT), experiments were conducted in which the user wore a wristwatch-size band to detect arm movements. This enabled the user to move objects on a large display screen by pointing to them. In addition, a speech recognizer allowed the user to specify commands to create objects and to tell the computer to change their shapes and colors. By combining pointing with talking, researchers were able to reduce some of the problems associated with speech recognition.

By the same token, could a computer respond to where you are *looking?* In an experimental eye-tracking system, researchers outfitted users with special eye-tracking glasses and asked them to watch simultaneous video programs projected on a single screen. If the glasses detected that the user was staring at one particular program, the system would enlarge that image. By monitoring which part of the display screen the user was

The gaze-orchestrated dynamic windows experiment at MIT helps researchers study how people focus their visual attention when confronted with complex displays.

looking at, software might be able to better under-stand what the user was interested in, and to respond accordingly. In addition, the system might be able to make an inference as to when to move on or gauge the effectiveness of its displays by checking to see whether users look in the right places. If a user did not look at a relevant spot, for example, the system could reemphasize different parts of its display.[1]

[1]Richard Bolt, "Conversing with Computers," *Technology Review*, February–March 1985, pp. 38–40.

The goal of these and other experiments is to make computers as easy to talk to as another person. In person-to-person communication, of course, people use gestures, speech, eye movements, and body language and adapt their method of communicating based on previous history of interaction with specific people. Will software ever be able to accomplish the same things? Although such software is years away, these experiments give researchers clues to developing software that resolves ambiguities and makes the computer system more responsive.

and commands. The user interface should make important and frequently used commands highly accessible and infrequently used ones accessible only when they are needed. Commands can be activated quickly by pressing one or more special keys on the keyboard. It is harder to memorize the meanings assigned to such keys, but pressing keys can be faster than choosing a command from a menu. Figure 2.5 shows a keyboard from an MS-DOS personal computer.

On either the far left-hand side of the keyboard or in a row above the number keys are ten **function keys** (some computers may have more than ten), labeled F1 through F10. Function keys are often used to enter commands; their specific meaning depends on the software being used.

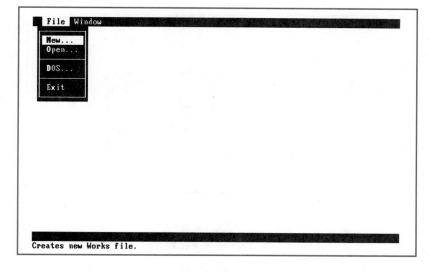

Figure 2.4
Pull-down menu with reverse video highlight.

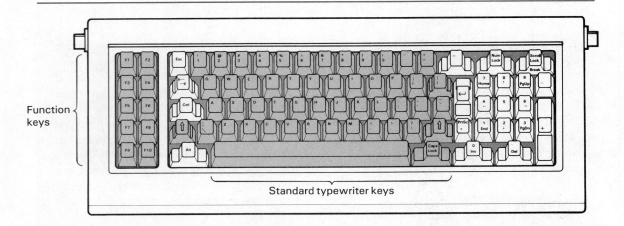

Figure 2.5
Keyboard layout.

Immediately to the left and right of the traditional typewriter keys are other special keys, which are also used to give commands to a program. Most of these keys appear in a slightly different color than the typewriter keys. Take a look at Figure 2.6.

■ The [**Esc**] (escape) key is often used to cancel, or "escape from," an operation in progress. For example, in the Works software, [Esc] cancels a command.

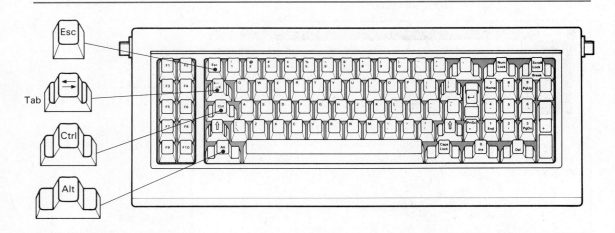

Figure 2.6
Keyboard showing placement of [Esc], [Tab], [Alt], and [Ctrl] keys.

A WORD ABOUT
Display Technology

Computer graphics, the methods and techniques used to draw pictures or show images on display screens, will benefit from new low-cost, high-resolution display technology. By way of analogy, imagine the display screen as a spreadsheet with a very large number of visible rows and columns. Instead of the intersection of row and column being a cell, it is a picture element, sometimes called a *pixel*. The number of rows multiplied by the number of columns is the number of pixels. Your television screen displays 525 rows by 484 columns, or 254,100 pixels. Today's Macintosh SE computer displays 175,104 pixels, and the IBM PS/2 with Video Graphics Array (VGA), 256,000 pixels.

The trend in display technology is more pixels in more colors. Today's color displays are based on CRT (cathode ray tube) technology, the same technology used in a television set. The best of these displays provide over 1 million pixels in thousands of colors. In the future, thin flat-panel displays will provide the same resolution for use in portable computers.

Better displays make possible new applications that combine complex moving images with traditional computer graphics. One vision of the future, being developed at MIT, includes personal computers that replace both the television set and the VCR. Such a computer would receive television broadcasts, and then special software would

The SR-12P by Princeton Graphic Systems (©1986).

edit and reorganize the programs to suit the viewer's needs. For instance, you might prefer a news program that combines coverage from ABC and NBC for international events, includes PBS for political reports, and tunes in the local station for weather and sports. You could view these reports in any order you chose, easily skip some, and save others for future reference.

- The **[Tab]** key, which is inscribed with left and right arrows, is used to move the cursor to a prespecified location left, right, up, or down from its current position. In the Works software, you will frequently use the [Tab] key to move the cursor in dialog boxes.

- In the word processor, the [Tab] key is used much as it would be on a typewriter; the cursor is moved to the next "tab stop," which can be anywhere on a line. In the spreadsheet and database programs, the [Tab] key moves the cursor to cells or fields, respectively.

- The **[Alt]** (alternate) key, like the function keys, is often used in conjunction with other keys as a shorthand method for entering instructions or commands. In the Works software, the [Alt] key activates the menu bar, and pressing the [Alt] key in combination with other keys will display menus and activate commands.

- The **[Ctrl]** (control) key, like the [Alt] key, is used as a shorthand way of entering instructions or commands. It is always used in conjunction with another key; pressing it by itself causes nothing to happen. Different programs use the [Ctrl] key in different ways; the Works word processor uses the [Ctrl] and [Enter] key combination to signal the start of a new page.

- To the right of the [Enter] key is a dual-function set of keys, which acts as (1) **cursor-movement keys** and (2) a numeric keypad. The four keys inscribed with arrows indicate the direction in which the cursor will move when the key is pressed. They can also be used to enter numbers by pressing the [Num Lock] key. The [Num Lock] key is like a toggle switch. Press it once and it activates the numeric keypad function; press it again and it toggles back to the cursor-movement function.

- *Important:* You will be using the cursor-movement keys constantly. If it appears that the cursor is not responding, you may have unintentionally pressed the [Num Lock] key. Try pressing it again to toggle back to the cursor-movement function.

- Below the numeric keypad are the **[Ins]** (insert) key and the **[Del]** (delete) key shown in Figure 2.7. The [Ins] key is sometimes used to toggle between insert and overstrike modes of typing. In the insert mode, new characters will be inserted *between* existing characters; in overstrike, new

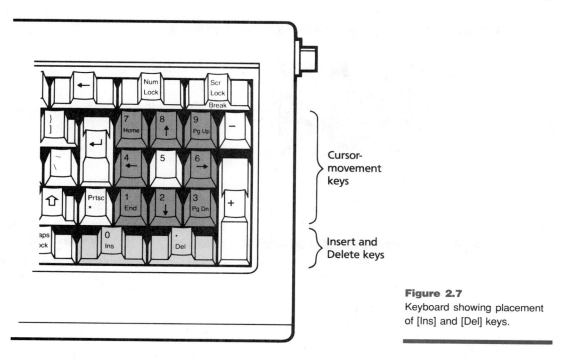

Figure 2.7
Keyboard showing placement
of [Ins] and [Del] keys.

characters replace old characters. The [Ins] key is not used in the Works software. The [Del] key is used to delete characters or other selected text. It functions differently from the [Backspace] key in that it does not move to the left before deleting a character. It deletes the character or characters highlighted by the cursor.

Getting Started

We've introduced a lot of concepts so far, and there's more ground to cover. So, to apply some of these principles, let's use the Works software to help explain them. Here's how to get started. *Note:* This section assumes that you have installed Works onto two floppy disks according to the instructions in Chapter 1.

1. Remove your "Works Files" disk from its storage jacket and insert it into disk drive A. Be sure to close the disk drive door.

2. Remove your "Works Program Copy" disk from its storage jacket, handling it by its label, and insert the disk into disk drive B. Be sure to close the disk drive door.

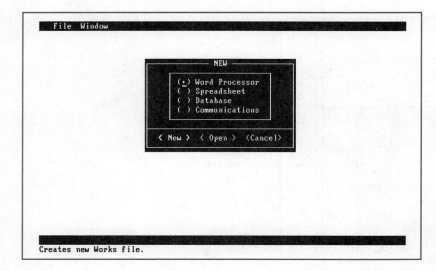

Figure 2.8
The initial Works screen.

3. If the computer is already turned on, see step 4 below. If it is off, turn the computer on. If the display device has a separate power switch, turn it on, too. Now go to step 5.

4. If the computer is on, you can use the system restart procedure. Simultaneously press the [Ctrl] and [Alt] keys with your left hand while pressing the [Del] key with your right hand.

   Important: A system restart completely clears the computer's memory, so any files that have not been previously saved will be lost. Use it with caution.

5. The display screen may prompt you to enter the date and time. (Refer to page 36 if you've forgotten how to do so.) Remember to press the [Enter] key after each. Then the A> prompt will appear. Type B:WORKS and press the [Enter] key.

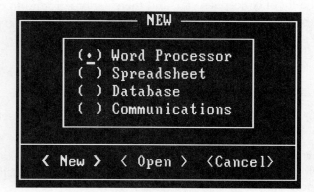

Figure 2.9
NEW dialog box.

Figure 2.10
Alert dialog box.

Now the red light on disk drive B will go on, and the computer will copy the software from the disk into memory. A title and copyright screen will appear briefly, and then you'll have your first look at the Works software: the main menu bar and the NEW dialog box. Figures 2.8 and 2.9 show what you'll see.

You are now ready to begin using the Works software. By the time you finish this chapter, you'll have completed your first assignment using the word processor.

The NEW Dialog

A **dialog box** is a special tool you use to tell the Works software how you want to proceed with a particular command. Dialog boxes usually appear when you choose commands on menus that end with ellipses (...). Commands that don't end with ellipses perform an action immediately; commands that do require you to make choices before Works can carry out the command. These commands display in the middle of the screen a dialog box, which presents those choices to you. When you first start Works, the NEW dialog box is automatically displayed, as in Figure 2.8.

The NEW dialog box is used to start up a new Works application. You must tell Works which application you want to start and whether you want the application to create a new file that will initially be empty or whether you want to open a file that already exists on one of your disk drives.

When you have provided the information and made your choices, you press the [Enter] key to finish performing the command. If you change your mind, you can press the [Esc] key; the dialog box will disappear, and the command will not be performed.

Dialog boxes can also appear even if you have not chosen a command from a menu. These dialogs appear because the software needs to alert you to an unusual situation or ask you a question. They are sometimes called *alert boxes*. Figure 2.10 shows one of these alert boxes.

Word Processing Exercise

Your instructor wants to survey your class to find out something about each student's prior experience with and attitudes toward computers. You are going to use the word processor to fill out the survey form. In the process, you will learn the basic word processing operations of cursor movement, scrolling, and entering text.

You are going to use the word processor to:

1. Select and open the document called "Survey."
2. Answer the survey questions.
3. Save the document on your disk.
4. Print the completed survey to hand in to your instructor.

By the time you have completed this assignment, you will have learned the basic skills of using a word processor. The following instructions will lead you through the process step by step:

---

1. First, use the NEW dialog to start the word processor and open the file called SURVEY.WPS.

   The NEW dialog contains four fields: three buttons labeled <New> <Open> and <Cancel> and an option box containing the words "Word Processor," "Spreadsheet," "Database," and "Communications." A blinking cursor appears in the box under the bullet next to "Word Processor." You can move the blinking cursor from field to field by pressing the [Tab] key. Press the [Tab] key once to move the blinking cursor to the <New> button. Now press the [Tab] key three more times to move the blinking cursor to the <Open> and <Cancel> buttons and back to the bullet next to "Word Processor."

   You use the [Tab] key to move the cursor forward to the next field; you can use the [Shift] and [Tab] keys together to move the cursor backwards to the previous field. Only when the cursor is in a field can you make choices with that field. The first field in the NEW dialog — the box containing the choices "Word Processor," "Spreadsheet," "Database," and "Communications" — is called an **option box**. This option box is used to tell Works which application you want to start. Once the blinking cursor is inside an option box, you can use the up arrow and down arrow keys to move the bullet up and down the list of of options. Try moving the bullet with the arrow keys now.

   Since we want to start the word processor, move the bullet next to the option "Word Processor." Now press the [Tab] key twice to move the blinking cursor under the button labeled <Open>. You want to "press" the <Open> button to tell Works to open an already – existing file. If you wanted to start the word processor with a new blank file, you would choose the <New> button instead. Now "press" the <Open> button by pressing the [Enter] key on the keyboard.

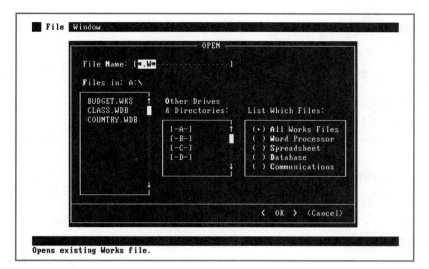

Figure 2.11
OPEN dialog box.

2. The NEW dialog disappears and is replaced by the OPEN dialog box. Figure 2.11 shows the OPEN dialog box. This dialog box is used to browse through the files located on the computer's disk drives and to choose one to open.

   The OPEN dialog contains several fields. The first is labeled "File Name" and is a **text box**. If you know the name of the file you want to open, you can just type it in here. Note that this field does not contain a blinking cursor, but the text within the bracket characters [*.W*...] is highlighted. Such highlighting replaces the blinking cursor when more than one character is about to be edited. You will learn more about editing text later, once the word processor is started.

   Now press the [Tab] key to move the blinking cursor to the box labeled "Files in: A:\." This box is called a **list box**; it is similar to an option box, except that the list of choices is arbitrarily long. Here it is displaying a list of the Works files on the disk in drive A. You should now use the up and down arrow keys to browse through the list and highlight the file name SURVEY.WPS.

   If you can't find SURVEY.WPS in the list, make sure that the option box captioned "List Which Files" is set to option "All Works Files" or "Word Processor." If you still can't find the file, you may be accessing the wrong directory or disk. You can use the "Other Drives & Directories" list box to try to find the file. If you've set up your disks according to the instructions in Chapter 1, the file should be on drive A.

3. With the file name SURVEY.WPS highlighted, press the [Enter] key to "press" the <OK> button.

   You have just instructed the computer to (1) copy the survey document from disk into the computer's memory, and (2) start the word processor software so that you may see and edit the survey document.

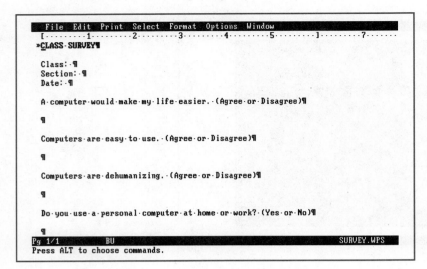

```
 File  Edit  Print  Select  Format  Options  Window
[·······1·········2·········3·········4·········5·····]········7······
»CLASS·SURVEY¶

 Class:··¶
 Section:··¶
 Date:··¶

 A·computer·would·make·my·life·easier.·(Agree·or·Disagree)¶

 ¶

 Computers·are·easy·to·use.·(Agree·or·Disagree)¶

 ¶

 Computers·are·dehumanizing.··(Agree·or·Disagree)¶

 ¶

 Do·you·use·a·personal·computer·at·home·or·work?·(Yes·or·No)¶

 ¶
Pg 1/1          BU                                      SURVEY.WPS
Press ALT to choose commands.
```

Figure 2.12
Initial Survey document screen.

---

4. The Works main menu bar and the OPEN dialog box will disappear from the screen, and the display shown in Figure 2.12 will appear.

Like all Works applications, the screen of the word processor is divided into five parts: a menu bar, a formula/ruler line, the work area, a status line, and a message line.

The **menu bar** runs across the top line of the screen and is always highlighted. In the word processor, the menu bar contains menus titled File, Edit, Print, Select, Format, Options, and Window.

The **formula/ruler bar** appears just under the menu bar. In the word processor, it is called a *ruler* and shows the locations of the margins and tab settings.

The **status line** is the next-to-last line on the screen. In the word processor, the status line displays the page number of the text you are viewing in the work area, as well as the name of the file you are editing.

The **message line** is the last line on the screen. It is used to display descriptions of what commands and dialog boxes do, and occasionally instructions on how to finish a command in progress.

The work area is that part of the screen between the menu and formula bars above and the status and message lines below. It is used to display the information that a particular program is designed to manage. In the word processor, the text you edit is displayed in the work area.

In the work area, notice that the word processor uses some familiar symbols in unfamiliar ways. A paragraph sign — the character that proofreaders use to designate the beginning of a paragraph — is visible on the screen. Word processors use the paragraph sign to mark the end of a paragraph. You can point to, select, and edit paragraph symbols as you can any other character. You can join two paragraphs into one simply by deleting the paragraph mark that separates them. Many of the word processor commands, such as commands that double-space lines of text or those that center lines of text between the margins, apply to whole paragraphs.

Spaces between words are displayed as tiny dots. This makes it easier to see when you have accidentally typed two spaces in a row. Neither the tiny dots nor the paragraph marks appear on the paper when you print a document. They appear only on the computer screen, to make editing the text easier. If you prefer, you can turn off the display of these special characters by using a command in the Options menu. You will learn more about this in Chapter 4.

The double right arrow character (>>) in the upper left-hand corner is the beginning-of-page symbol. It is displayed in the left margin and cannot be selected like other characters.

Editing with the Word Processor

In the upper left-hand corner of the work area, next to the beginning-of-page symbol, is the **blinking cursor**. It indicates the active location on the screen — in the case of the word processor, the location where the next character you type will appear. The blinking cursor is always movable; you can move it over the characters displayed in the work area by using the arrow keys. (Try it.)

Use the arrow keys to move the blinking cursor to the line where the word "Class" appears. Then move it so that it falls underneath the paragraph symbol one position beyond the colon. Take a look at Figure 2.13. Type your class name and number, just as you would on a typewriter. You don't need to use the [Enter] key when you are finished typing.

Use the down arrow key to move the blinking cursor down one line and the left arrow key to move it to the paragraph sign following the word "Section." If your class is divided into sections, type your section number or the section leader's name. Then move the blinking cursor to the next line and type today's date.

If you make a spelling mistake, use the [Backspace] key to erase characters. Each time you press the [Backspace] key, the letter to the left of the blinking cursor will disappear, and you can type in your correction. Using the [Backspace] key to delete characters allows you to edit all the text in the work area. Be careful, though, since you can easily delete characters by accident.

You will notice that there is one paragraph symbol at the left margin below each question in the survey. Use the arrow keys to move the blinking cursor to that paragraph symbol; then type in your answer. When you finish, move the blinking cursor to the paragraph symbol following the next question, and go on.

The last question at the bottom of the work area appears to have no paragraph symbols following it. Actually, they are just hidden from view. The survey is too long to show in the work area all at once. To view the remainder of the survey, hold down the down arrow key. When the blinking cursor reaches the bottom line of the display, the text will move up. This maneuver, called *scrolling*, causes new lines of text to appear at one edge of the work area while other lines of text disappear from

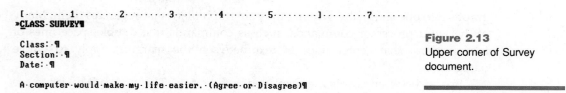

Figure 2.13
Upper corner of Survey document.

the opposite edge. Figure 2.14 shows the new display of the rest of the survey document. In the word processor, you can scroll up and down by using the up and down arrow keys or the [PgUp], [PgDn], [Home], and [End] keys. Note that the end-of-document symbol is a diamond. When you see the diamond, you know that you have reached the last character in the document.

When you have finished responding to the survey, scan the document for typing mistakes. If you discover a misspelled word, use the arrow keys to position the blinking cursor to the right of the mistake. Pressing the [Backspace] key will cause characters to disappear and the space to close up. Type in your correction, and the word processor will insert it in the proper location.

Saving

When you have finished your proofreading and corrections, the first thing you will want to do is save your document. In order to do so, you will need to use the menu bar to activate the **Save command** on the File menu.

First activate the menu bar by pressing the [Alt] key once; the word "File" on the menu bar will highlight. Press the down arrow key to display the File menu. Now press the up and down arrow keys to move the highlight up and down the File menu. Each item on the file menu is a command that can be activated if you press the [Enter] key while it is highlighted.

You can press the left and right arrow keys to display the other menus on the menu bar. Try it now and take a few minutes to explore all the menus, but don't press the [Enter] key yet. Notice that, as you highlight each command, an explanation of what the command does appears in the message line at the bottom of the screen.

Notice, too, that each command has one letter highlighted when it is displayed. For instance, the letter "N" is highlighted in the word NEW in the File menu. Instead of pressing the arrow keys to highlight a command and then pressing the [Enter] key to activate it, you can press the highlighted letter instead. This is a shortcut that makes activating a command faster; it works on the menu bar itself, in each menu, and in dialog boxes. If you have a mouse, you can use it to choose commands from menus and fields in a dialog box. See Appendix B, "Special Mouse Shortcuts," for instructions.

Now use the arrow keys to redisplay the File menu, and then highlight the Save command on the File menu. When the word "Save" is highlighted, press the

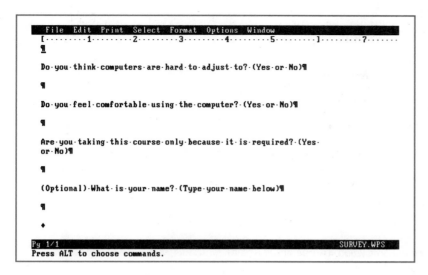

Figure 2.14
The rest of the Survey document.

[Enter] key to activate the command. The File menu will retract, and the word processor will spend several seconds copying your survey document to disk.

Now try the shortcut method to perform the Save command. Press the [Alt] key to activate the menu bar; press F to display the File menu and then press S to activate the Save command. Don't worry; saving the file twice in a row is a harmless operation.

Printing

To print your completed survey document, hold down the [Alt] key to activate the menu bar; press P to display the Print menu and then press P again to activate the **Print command.** The Print menu will retract and the PRINT dialog box will appear.

The default values of the dialog box fields are to print one copy of the document on the printer; this is what you want to do. Make sure that the printer is connected to the computer and that the power switch is turned on. The paper should be positioned in the printer so that the top edge is just above the rollers. Most printers have a button labeled "line-feed" that will advance the paper in one-line increments and another button labeled "form-feed" that will eject an entire page of paper. Another button marked "on-line" must be *off* for the form-feed and line-feed buttons to work. After you have adjusted the paper position, turn the "on-line" button back on. Then press the [Enter] key to "press" the <Print> button on the dialog box.

You don't have to use the [Tab] key to move the blinking cursor to the <Print> button. When a dialog box is displayed you may press the [Enter] key at any time to finish performing the command. Similarly, pressing the [Esc] key will activate the <Cancel> button and cause the dialog to disappear, and the command will not be performed.

CLASS SURVEY

Class: Introduction to Computers
Section: 4
Date: September 15

A computer would make my life easier. (Agree or Disagree)

Agree

Computers are easy to use. (Agree or Disagree)

Disagree

Computers are dehumanizing. (Agree or Disagree)

Agree

Do you use a personal computer at home or work? (Yes or No)

Yes

If yes, what kind is it? (Type the computer's brand name)

IBM Personal Computer

Do you use a computer more or less than once a week? (More or Less)

Less

Do you think computers are hard to adjust to? (Yes or No)

Yes

Do you feel comfortable using the computer? (Yes or No)

Yes

Are you taking this course only because it is required? (Yes or No)

No

(Optional) What is your name? (Type your name below)

Roland Alden

Sample printed version of the Class Survey.

Before transmitting your document to the printer, the software will determine whether the printer is properly connected to the computer. If the printer is improperly connected or isn't turned on, the program will display an alert dialog titled FILE ERROR or PRINT ERROR. If this happens, you may have to use the "Select Text Printer" dialog box in the Print menu to tell Works about your printer.

After you have finished printing your class survey, hold down the [Alt] key to activate the menu bar; press F to display the File menu and then press X to activate the **Exit command**. You will exit Works and return to the operating system.

The operating system will display the A> prompt on the left side of the screen. If you wanted to reenter the Works environment at this point, you could do so by typing in the command B:WORKS and pressing the [Enter] key. If you want to quit using the computer entirely, remove any diskettes you inserted into the computer and check to see whether the computer should be turned off.

As you become more familiar with the Works software, by completing the exercises that follow, you will find that practice translates directly into the ability to use the software to solve problems.

Review

Key Terms

Integrated program	Menu	[Ins] key
Word processor	Window	[Del] key
Document	Dialog	Option box
Spreadsheet	Reverse video	Text box
Charting	Scrolling	List box
Database	Function key	Menu bar
Record	[Esc] key	Formula/ruler bar
Field	[Tab] key	Status line
Query facility	[Alt] key	Message line
Communications	[Ctrl] key	Blinking cursor
User interface	Cursor-movement key	

Discussion Questions

1. How do computers differ from cars and other industrial products?
2. How does two-way communication between a computer and a user take place?
3. Name two video techniques that a display uses to make interacting with software more visible.
4. What is the most common use of the [Tab] key in the Works software?
5. What is the purpose of a system restart command?
6. In the Works environment, what is the name of the area of the screen where a document is displayed?
7. What is the purpose of a mouse?
8. Outline the steps in opening an existing document in the word processing program.
9. What is the function of the blinking cursor?
10. How do you move the blinking cursor on the display?
11. Name two ways to access portions of a document that are not visible on the display screen.
12. What are the necessary conditions for printing a document?
13. How do you "leave" the word processing environment?

Software Exercises

1. Browse through all the menus in the Works word processor and study the explanations displayed on the message line. Each command that ends with ellipses (...) causes a dialog box to be displayed. Activate each dialog box command to cause the dialog box to be displayed. Study each dialog box and press [Esc] to cancel the dialog box. See how much you can learn about the word processor by studying the menus and dialog boxes before you go on to Chapter 3.

2. Experiment with the following commands on the Format menu: Left, Center, and Justified. What effect do they have on the paragraph that contains the blinking cursor? Try ending a line with the [Shift] and [Enter] keys pressed together; how does the [Shift] and [Enter] combination differ from the [Enter] key alone?

3

Computers and Problem Solving

Preview   No problem can be solved — with or without the aid of a computer — until it is understood and well thought out beforehand. This is so because computers do not solve problems as we do; computers are simply tools with which to perform tasks.

In this chapter, we'll show you a step-by-step method that you can use to organize your thinking about problems. Then we'll show you some general-purpose tools that will help you to look at problems in a logical and systematic way.

You'll get some hands-on practice by using the Works spreadsheet program to help solve a problem. That way, you'll begin to learn how application software can be used as an effective problem-solving tool.

In this chapter, you'll learn:

- What a problem and a solution consist of
- The role of computers as general-purpose tools for problem solving
- A method for organizing the flow of problem solving
- New points of view for approaching problems
- How to break a large problem into smaller, more manageable steps
- Approaches to solving problems when writing, calculating, and analyzing
- How to get started with a spreadsheet program

Problem Solving

Problem solving is a **process** — a systematic series of actions aimed at a specific goal. Novices often approach problems in a random, trial-and-error, or hit-or-miss fashion. More experienced problem solvers develop logical and orderly approaches to problems. There are two reasons why the latter kind of approach is preferable: (1) it helps you to organize your thinking about the problem, and (2) it helps you to visualize a solution.

It's easier to solve a problem when you use a step-by-step method. Writing, analyzing, and organizing and retrieving information are problem-solving activities for which a logical method is particularly well suited. But before we show you such a step-by-step method, let's define what a problem and a solution are.

What Is a Problem?

A **problem** is any question or matter characterized by doubt, uncertainty, or difficulty. This broad definition facilitates a positive view of problems as unmet needs or as the difference between where you are and where you want to be. People often classify problems as personal, economic, social, political, and so on. But whatever the category, calling something a problem implies that it isn't the way it should be.

A person's attitude is a very important aspect of problem solving. Many people view problems as irritations. Of course, some problems *are* irritating: the car that won't start, the door that sticks, the check that bounces. These are problems that we avoid if we can.

But another way to look at problems is to view them as opportunities. Entrepreneurs tend to interpret problems as unmet needs, and thus as opportunities to make money. A problem can also be an opportunity to advance your thinking to a new level or to make a useful contribution to society. If you take a positive attitude toward the problems you are going to be solving in this class, they can be opportunities to further your learning, develop your skills, and gain confidence in your own problem-solving skills.

What Is a Solution?

A **solution** is an answer to or explanation for a problem. It is often the result of some course of action taken by an individual or an organization that wants to bring about a change.

It is an interesting exercise to think about your circumstances and the material objects that surround you as *prior solutions to problems*. Stop reading for a moment and glance around you. If you are in a dormitory or a classroom, the room you are sitting in is a prior solution to the problem of educating people. The clothes you wear, the house you live in, the car you drive, the food you eat, the book you are reading — all can be perceived as prior solutions to problems.

Just as they do with problems, people also tend to classify and categorize solutions. Solutions to social problems are sometimes called *laws*; solutions to mental or mathematical problems are often called *rules* or *axioms*. Solutions to physical problems may be called *tools, artifacts, products, buildings,* and so on. In the classroom, it is often necessary or preferable to simulate the events in the real world; thus, teachers construct models they call *case studies, practice sets, exercises,* or *exams,* whose solution takes the form of a written or oral answer.

In this book, you'll learn about problems and their solutions in more or less the same way you learned to play sports or games. First, you'll practice with exercises that have already been worked out. As you have already done with the word processor, you'll learn the rules of the game and what you can and cannot do. Then we'll give you some variations on the worked-out problems so that you can practice and explore a little further. Finally, you'll move on to problems that you choose yourself, whose solutions haven't already been found.

Computers as Problem-Solving Tools

A computer is an ideal problem-solving medium, since it is capable of *modeling* or *simulating* almost any kind of event or process that can occur in the real world. A **model** or **simulation** duplicates the interesting properties of its real-world counterpart, usually at a lower cost. Rather than giving students a real business to run, a business teacher can have students practice with a financial model of the business before venturing out on their own. A physics teacher can simulate the effects of a nuclear explosion and leave the actual event to the imagination of the students. General-purpose software that uses word processing, spreadsheet, database, and communication capability, is an ideal medium with which to practice solving a wide variety of problems. It can teach you important concepts while you learn by doing.

However, there are many problems that a personal computer won't help solve. It won't help you to write creatively, although it may free up time for you to use to explore writing. It won't help you to remember your relatives' birthdays, although it can store and retrieve a list of birthdays in a database. What kinds of problems are computers good at helping people to solve?

What Computers Do Best

Though a word processor can help you to write a love letter or a poem, a personal computer system is particularly well suited to the kinds of problems that yield to

rationality and logic. What characteristics of computer systems make them such useful tools for problem solving?

- *Speed.* A computer system can give you immediate feedback. It can store and organize information and recall it quicker than you can. It can add a list of numbers or do other calculations faster than you can.

- *Accuracy.* A computer system calculates much more reliably and accurately than you can. In fact, when computer systems are applied to well-thought-out, repetitive operations, such as calculating a payroll or processing income tax returns, they can virtually eliminate the errors that people are prone to when they do repetitive calculating.

- *Reduced drudgery.* Exploring problems becomes more fun. Because menial tasks like calculating are handled by the computer system, you can concentrate on analyzing alternative solutions.

■ *Neatness.*   Writing and calculating by hand usually involve scribbling notes, deciphering illegible inserts, wadding up aborted drafts, erasing, crossing out, and retyping. A word processor can help you to polish your reports and term papers for a clearer, cleaner, and perhaps more informative presentation than is possible with other methods.

■ *Logic.*   Because a computer system can only perform routine tasks in obedience to your instructions, it requires you to do an orderly analysis of the problem and the relationships between its parts.

What People Do Best

A computer is a useful tool, but it can't think. Computers only do what you tell them to do: no more, no less. Computers don't solve problems; they carry out solutions that people devise. The people who formulate the problem and devise a procedure for solving it are the problem solvers. The key to using a computer as a problem-solving tool is to become familiar with the computer system and figure out what it can do for you. Among the aspects of problem solving that people are best equipped for are the following:

■ *Judgment.*   People know when a problem is outside their sphere of expertise. They know when the best answer is to ask someone else for help. A computer will keep plugging away, processing "the facts," even if the facts don't add up to anything. People know where to look for prior solutions to similar problems, when an imperfect solution is preferable to waiting for a perfect one, and when to hold off and wait for that missing piece of information.

■ *Flexibility.*   People are good at anticipating and responding to change. They aren't locked into their environment. They might accept it, but they can also change it. They learn that there are many exceptions to any rule. They figure out when to break the rules. On the other hand, the more unstructured a problem becomes, the more difficult it is to use a computer to solve it.

■ *Intuition.*   Insight into a problem can take the place of formal logic or reasoning. What we call *intuition* is actually a kind of condensed reasoning or recognition process, made possible by experience. Card players don't stop to count the spots on the cards; they simply recognize the patterns from past experience.

■ *Feeling.*   People approach problems with eagerness, curiosity, competitiveness, tension, excitement, anxiety, love, affection, or hate. These feelings often stimulate creative solutions that aren't possible when problem solving is reduced to "the facts."

■ *Knowledge representation.*   Computers don't really understand what they are doing. If they did, they could behave in a more intelligent manner. People have a far richer repertoire of representations (or meanings) for ideas, notions, and images, and they store and recall them on demand.

The Problem-Solving Process

To apply a computer system to problem solving, you need to organize the problem to be solved. For this, you need a set of guidelines to help you think about a problem in a systematic, orderly way. This is where a step-by-step method comes in handy. Solving a problem from beginning to end requires you to approach the solution systematically by organizing your thinking about the problem.

A **procedure** is a sequence of steps, each of which specifies one or more actions and the order in which they are to be taken. You already use procedures as problem-solving tools in everyday life. You find your way to a new friend's house by following a set of directions. You cook an interesting dinner for a new boyfriend or girlfriend by following a recipe. You preregister for classes or assemble a new appliance by following step-by-step instructions.

We can characterize the steps in a general-purpose approach to problem solving as follows:

1. Get to know the problem.
2. Define the problem.
3. Identify alternative solutions.
4. Choose the best alternative.
5. Implement the solution.
6. Evaluate the results.

These six steps provide you with a consistent procedure for (1) turning problem solving into a systematic series of events and (2) breaking up a large or complex problem into smaller pieces. It is a method that can be applied to a wide variety of problems.

Of course, some problems are more complex and overwhelming than others. A good rule of thumb is: Complex problems require complex strategies, whereas simpler problems call for less formal tools and strategies. The problem-solving process that we describe in this chapter may not fit every problem you ever have to solve. It is not meant as a prescription for the right answer. It is a general set of guidelines. Before resorting to a trial-and-error approach, investigate its use to see if it fits the problem.

The problem-solving process is also dynamic; it doesn't always proceed step-by-step from step 1 to step 6. As Figure 3.1 demonstrates, the process can loop back on itself at any time. Suppose, for example, that, while you are searching for alternative solutions, you discover something that sheds new light on the problem

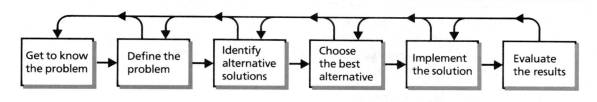

Figure 3.1
Flow chart of the problem-solving process.

definition. You can and should go back to the previous step and incorporate that new information into your problem definition. At other times, you may find yourself working on two or three of the steps at the same time.

Get to Know the Problem

Most problems require you to make assumptions. Information about a problem is often implicit or subtle. For example, if a friend doesn't return your repeated phone calls, you may assume that something is wrong. Often, the simple analytical technique of asking questions is all you need to solve a problem. At other times, getting to know a problem may mean examining your assumptions about it.

Checklist for Getting to Know the Problem

- Does a problem actually exist?
- Have you encountered a similar problem before?
- Do you know of a similar problem someone else has encountered?
- Whom can you ask, and/or what can you read about the problem?
- What assumptions are you making about the problem?

For example, suppose you own a music store and make a small profit at it. How do you know whether you are managing the business well? You might try making a list of your assumptions about the nature of the retail music business and then asking a consultant about similar stores' pricing policies, advertising, merchandising, promotions, and so on. It may turn out, for example, that your assumptions about merchandising are mistaken. Perhaps you could increase your profit considerably by discounting your prices, staying open at night, or selling compact disks as well.

Sometimes students expect real-world problems to present themselves like the examples in textbooks: clearly organized, well articulated, and accompanied by a ready-made solution. Problem solving rarely begins this way. If you suspect that a problem exists, listing your assumptions about it can help you to (1) decide whether a problem actually exists, (2) figure out what you could do about it, and (3) actually do something to solve it.

Define the Problem

Formulating a problem is usually the most crucial step in solving it. Defining a problem can be time consuming. Often what we call problems are only *symptoms* — the visible effects of an underlying problem. A fever, a runny nose, and an upset stomach are all symptoms of a real problem — the flu. Distinguishing between symptoms and problems is important in accurately defining the problem you want to resolve. Thus, a doctor tries to determine the exact reasons for a patient's symptoms because different problem definitions would lead to different treatments.

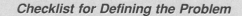

Checklist for Defining the Problem

- What facts do you know about the problem?
- What exactly is the problem?
- What are the pertinent surrounding circumstances?
- What are my objectives?

If you don't understand a problem, you can't solve it. Take the time to clarify the problem in an unambiguous way. The best way to do this is to ask yourself continually, "What is the problem?" It is easy to overlook that question. Instead, most people jump to the question, "What can I do about the problem?" For example, consider the problem of purchasing a personal computer. Many people begin by asking, "Which computer should I buy?" But they are bypassing a more important question: "What do I want to do with a personal computer?"

If the problem you are trying to solve is particularly difficult — if it involves a lot of ambiguity — it's worth the time to refine the problem definition until you have developed a set of clear, complete objectives, or statements of intent. This does not mean that you need to know everything in advance. It simply means translating your problem into formal statements of intent, which will serve as guidelines for subsequent steps in the problem-solving process.

For example, when a problem calls for designing a system, the problem definition is often called a **functional specification.** It specifies the functions that the system must perform. Suppose your problem is to design a computer-based system to help people prepare their income tax returns. Your functional specification would probably list the kinds of information that will go into the system (income and expense data, tax regulations, and instructions for calculating the amount of

Input and Output

To get results, you must first input data into a computer. Different tasks call for different input devices. A single type of input activity, such as entering text, can require varied methods for varied circumstances. Having the right input tools makes the work go more efficiently. Of course, once you've provided input, you want output. Perhaps you want to look at a file or print a chart. In any case, you need an output device to convert the computer's digital data into a useful form. This photo essay illustrates the variety of devices computers use to handle input and output.

1. New input devices are dramatically changing the way many types of work are done. Information compiled by this electronic meter reading system is transferred to a mainframe computer, which produces the customer's electric bill the same day.

Input

Besides the traditional keyboard and mouse, there are many input devices designed to meet the special needs of business, industry, and even the arts.

2. Wherever the movement of products must be recorded quickly and accurately, hand-held optical character readers (OCRs) are useful. These devices help with inventory control in stores, libraries, and assembly lines.

3,4. Replenishing store shelves is a simpler, quicker task using this device, called an Econoscan. The device that gathers information from the shelves can be connected to a telephone, through which it transmits orders at a rate of 800 items per minute.

5. Supermarket checkout laser scanners are specialized input devices familiar to the general public.

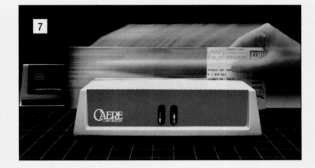

6. Touch screens enable fingers to do work usually done by a mouse or keyboard. This screen uses sensors to determine where a finger or pencil is touching it.

7. This compact optical character reader makes short work of entering data from utility bills.

8. You don't have to know how to type to use this pressure-sensitive, battery-operated tablet. Just insert a standard 8½- by 11-inch printed form, and fill it out with a ballpoint pen. The tablet recognizes handwritten characters, displays them on the one-line liquid crystal screen, and stores them in memory. Later the information can be loaded into any computer.

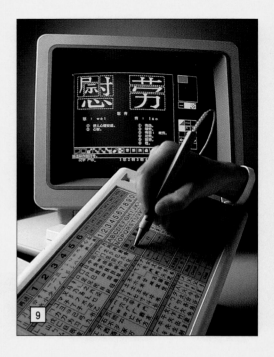

11. With the appropriate interface, you can attach a piano-style keyboard to a personal computer. Here an optional interface card allows an IBM personal computer to control a Musical Instrument Digital Interface (MIDI) keyboard and function as a versatile music synthesizer system.

9,10. Just as computers "speak" many languages—BASIC, FORTRAN, etc.—so do computer users. These two very different input devices perform similar functions, enabling the user to enter Hanzi characters of the Chinese written language into the computer.

12. Voice input systems are used in applications where the operator's hands are occupied with tasks other than data entry. These systems allow the computer to "listen" to a limited vocabulary of spoken words.

Graphical Data Entry

Computers equipped with special input devices to handle artwork are valuable graphic design tools.

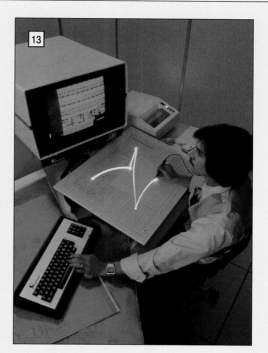

13. This computer-aided design system supports a wide range of design, drafting, and manufacturing operations on large-scale integrated (LSI) chips. The user enters data from either the keyboard or a graphics tablet.

14. A light pen can accurately sense where it touches a CRT screen. The upper and right edges of this screen represent a menu of commands. With a light pen, you can quickly choose commands as well as draw on the screen.

15. A design can be input by placing artwork on a graphics tablet and tracing it with the puck. The keypad on the puck is used to enter specific points and to issue commands.

Screen and Print Output

Every personal computer user is familiar with monitors, but the output that these devices are capable of may surprise many users. Computer printouts used to mean hard-to-read letters on special paper. Today, computer printers can produce high quality typography and graphic images. Printers can generate special forms, and they can print in color, too.

16. High-resolution color monitors satisfy both personal and professional needs. Recreational users can display vivid game graphics and a versatile "canvas" for paint and draw programs. Business users can review complex data in attractive and easy-to-decipher formats.

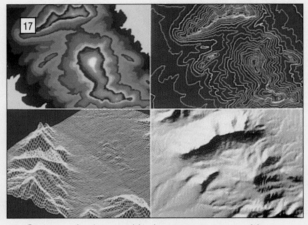

17. Cartography (mapmaking) represents an exciting use of computer technology. Creating maps by computer starts with capturing large geographical data sets in a map database. Once inside the computer, data can be displayed in many ways. Here terrain is depicted on a monitor by using (clockwise from upper left) color-coded elevations, contour lines, shaded relief, and rotated profiles.

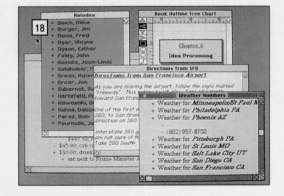

18. Windows appear to sit on this Apple Macintosh screen in the same way pieces of paper can pile up on a desktop. Overlapping windows can be created, moved, or resized without affecting existing windows. You can bring any window to the top of the stack by pointing to it and clicking the mouse button.

19. Liquid crystal displays are popular for portable computers because they consume little power. For example, the battery in this portable computer can operate up to eight hours without recharging. Hidden in the side of the computer are two 3.5-inch 720K diskette drives.

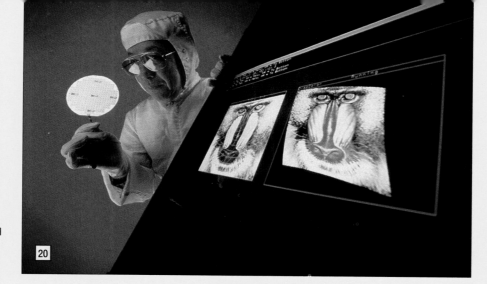

20. This TRW technician is inspecting a chip that can manipulate video images, as is demonstrated on the monitors to the right. The chip is suited for applications ranging from personal computer graphics to medical ultrasound technology and guided missiles.

21. When used with sophisticated software, some high-resolution monitors can produce images that approach photography in sharpness and range of colors.

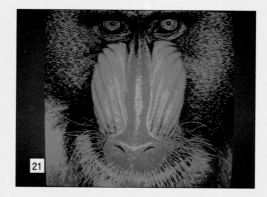

22. Pen plotters produce smoother lines than dot-matrix printers, but they operate much more slowly. This inexpensive six-pen plotter prints by moving the paper back and forth while moving the pen from side to side, with 250 steps per inch. To fill a region with color, the pen must run back and forth many times, which is a slow process. The six pens allow the plotter to draw in six colors without stopping.

23. This pen holder is part of a large commercial flat-bed plotter.

24. These large drafting plotters are used for computer-aided design (CAD) projects. They provide highly accurate and detailed output for mechanical, electronic, and architectural design work.

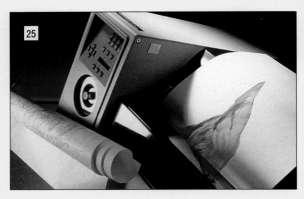

25. A particularly valuable function of plotters is the ability to convert three-dimensional models from a computer screen into two-dimensional hard copy, as is being done here.

26. This hand-held printer prints and dispenses gummed labels. The labels can be printed with bar codes such as UPC (Universal Product Code), as well as alphabetic characters. Information for the labels can be entered through the keypad on the printer, or the printer can be connected to a computer.

27. Laser printers like this one combine text and graphics to produce publication-quality printing for office needs. They print quickly and quietly, and they offer numerous typefaces and typesizes.

Window 2

tax due) and the tax return forms that must come out of the system. By stating clear, complete, definitive functions, the functional specification defines the problem in an unambiguous way. It also serves as a guideline for designing the system.

Identify Alternative Solutions

The first step in identifying alternative solutions is to clarify your goals. Once you have defined what success would consist of, the available alternatives are the various ways of achieving that goal. At this point, it is a good idea to come up with as many ideas as possible about ways to reach the goal. Then you will have a wide range of alternatives from which to choose.

The technique called **brainstorming** — unrestrained thought or discussion, without prejudging or rejecting any ideas — is a good way to generate many different (1) viewpoints on the problem, (2) approaches to the goal, and (3) alternative solutions. Imagine, for example, that you are in Boston and your goal is to get to southern California. Time and money are not constraints. Stop reading for two minutes, and brainstorm all the possible ways you can imagine to get to California.

Checklist for Identifying Alternatives

- What are the most obvious ways to reach the goal?
- Are there any alternative approaches?
- Have I left anything out?

Did you restrict yourself to conventional forms of transportation, such as plane, train, bus, and car? How about walking, riding the rails, hitchhiking, or ballooning? Did you consider alternative routes, such as across Canada or via the Panama Canal? What about combinations of alternatives, such as flying to Chicago and then renting a car? Brainstorming can stimulate some creative ideas that you might not allow yourself if you stick to conventional solutions and common sense. Your list of alternatives may grow and evolve as you explore new ways of seeing the problem.

Choose the Best Alternative

How do you choose the best alternative? You evaluate the possibilities, using criteria that enable you to assess various characteristics of each. Then you can rank the list of alternatives from most to least desirable.

Your evaluation criteria should include such constraints as time, money, and personal knowledge of what you can and cannot do. For example, let us restate the problem of the Boston-to-California trip as follows: you attend school in Boston, and you want to go to California for your one-week spring break. You have $300 saved for the trip. Given these constraints, you can rank the alternative modes of transportation rather quickly.

Checklist for Choosing the Best Alternative

- What are the criteria for choosing?
- What are the constraints?
- Which criteria should I emphasize most?
- How would I rank the alternatives in light of the criteria?
- Is the best alternative obvious?

Implement the Solution

Implementing the solution means taking the course of action (establishing the procedure or process) you have chosen. Later in this chapter, you will solve a budget problem using a spreadsheet and hand in your answer to the instructor. In real life, however, implementing the solution would mean going out and living on your proposed budget.

Checklist for Implementing the Solution

- What tasks are involved?
- What steps must be taken to carry out the tasks?
- How much time will each step take?
- How long will the entire implementation process take?
- What help do I need?

In essence, you will be using the computer to model the real world. Real-world problems require you to take a course of action to implement your solution. For example, solving the problem of deciding which personal computer to buy involves trying out different personal computers, comparison-shopping, and eventually purchasing the one of your choice.

Evaluate the Results

In a classroom setting, your instructor gives you feedback in the form of a grade and perhaps comments or encouragement. But experienced problem solvers learn

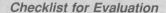

> *Checklist for Evaluation*
>
> ■ Does the solution work?
> ■ Are the results what I hoped for?
> ■ Are there any obvious improvements I could make?
> ■ Is there time to try out a different approach?

to look at the strengths and weaknesses of their own finished products, decisions, or solutions, as well as at the process of arriving there. A good coach goes over each game, evaluating the team's performance and asking such questions as "What did they do best?" "What areas need improvement?" and "What parts of the game need more work?" Evaluation is a learning tool. It allows you to make the most of the problem you have just solved, so that you can put your experience to use in solving future problems.

Variations on Problem Solving

Many different fields have generated valuable strategies and approaches to problem solving. As you enlarge your problem-solving repertoire, you may want to explore these approaches in greater depth.

Decision Making

In business, one of the most valued skills that a good manager can have is decision-making ability. **Decision making** is a problem-solving approach for situations in which only partial information is available about a problem or situation. Decision-making skill is also important in situations in which the information is incomplete. Incomplete information introduces the element of uncertainty and requires the decision maker to form opinions and exercise judgment. Decision making incorporates the following steps:

1. Start the decision-making process by considering any information that sheds light on the problem. How do you know when you have enough information? There is no easy answer. Time is usually a constraint, and a search for all the relevant information could go on indefinitely. For example, suppose you are graduating from college, and you have to make a decision about taking a job. Of course, you want the perfect job, but your finances dictate that you find one rather quickly. You will begin the job search by considering the available jobs, applying, and interviewing. You

certainly cannot know everything about all of the possible jobs. What jobs should you apply for?

2. Form an opinion; then ask other people what they think. Under conditions of incomplete information, it is important to seek intelligent criticism and feedback from external sources. For example, if you are making a decision about choosing a job, you might ask classmates who are in a similar situation for their opinions on which job they would take.

3. Identify a list of alternatives. In the case of deciding which job to take, you might make a list of alternative salaries, working conditions, job locations, potential for advancement, and potential for creative work.

4. Identify a list of criteria on which the alternatives should be judged. For example, the commute to work should not take more than 30 minutes, the salary should not be below $20,000 per year, and the job should involve some writing skills.

5. Judge how well each alternative meets each criterion. For example, you have two job offers, one of which pays better but has a longer commute, whereas the other offers more opportunity for advancement.

6. Select the best alternative.

Decision making is essentially the art of dealing with uncertainty. Rarely does a decision maker have all the required information at hand. Often, all the options are less than ideal. Also, the bigger the decision, the greater the risk. With practice, you can develop skill in the art of judging the "right" choices and the "right" risks.

Top-down Design

Computer programmers, systems analysts, and software engineers often use a top-down approach to solving programming and design problems. In **top-down design**, the solution to a problem is first specified in general terms and then broken down into finer and finer detail until further detail becomes unnecessary.

Computer professionals are not the only people who use a top-down approach. Consider the problems an architect faces when designing an office building. Because an office building is a highly complex system, the architect first develops a rough overall solution to guide his or her thinking. This might involve sketches or drawings and a list of specific requirements that the building must satisfy. Then the architect breaks the problem down into subcategories, such as lighting, plumbing, heating and cooling, public spaces (lobbies and halls), and private spaces (offices). The result of this process is a functional specification, which developers and engineers use to construct the building.

Writers too sometimes use top-down design. They start with an outline, then add more and more detail until the document is complete.

Top-down design essentially means starting with the whole and working toward the parts. To put it another way, top-down design takes a big problem and makes a lot of little problems out of it.

A WORD ABOUT
Artificial Intelligence

You have seen how a personal computer can become a much more capable problem–solving assistant, but how could it become a more *intelligent* assistant?

Artificial intelligence (AI) is the branch of computer science that attempts to understand the nature of human intelligence and to produce intelligent computers by programming them to perform tasks that require humanlike qualities, such as reasoning and perception.

Examples include systems that play games like checkers and chess, robots that work in factories, and systems that can use the knowledge and rules of thumb that experts use to solve problems.

The long-term goal is to understand human intelligence well enough to develop software that exhibits intelligent behavior. Besides AI's being an emotionally charged issue, anyone looking closely at current experimental programs could not fail to see a great gap between human self-awareness and intelligence and programs that are artificially intelligent. The problem is that nobody really knows exactly how people think. Like psychologists, AI researchers want to understand how people think. But instead of experimenting with humans, AI researchers experiment with computer programs.

AI researchers have not been very successful in getting computers to do simple things that require intelligence, but they have had some success in getting computers to solve problems in highly structured, highly specialized areas. *Expert systems* are computer programs that solve specialized problems at the level of a human expert. They are used in medical diagnostics, chemistry, geology, and business. Their major drawback is their inability to handle unique situations. They only work in extremely limited cases, and only after they have been fed information from human experts and fine tuned. But expert systems, unlike their human counterparts, don't make judgments or jump to conclusions. And they never have a bad day.

The Design Process

The arts and the design professions add the element of creativity to the problem-solving process. Creative problem solvers are usually unafraid of mistakes, because they expect to learn from them and to incorporate that experience into the solution of the next problem. They are not afraid of being unusual, having been rewarded for unconventionality in the past. Nor are they afraid to take risks, because they associate large risks with large rewards.

As a process of creative problem solving, design can be described as a sequence of events or phases that the problem solver has to pass through. In *The Universal Traveler*, Don Koberg and Jim Bagnall characterize the phases of the creative problem-solving process as follows:

1. *Acceptance.* Stating your initial intentions and seeing the problem as a challenge.
2. *Analysis.* Finding out what the world of the problem looks like.

3. *Definition*. Conceptualizing and clarifying your major goals in addressing the problem.

4. *Ideation*. Searching for all the different ways of getting to the goal.

5. *Selection*. Comparing the goal with the possible ways of getting there.

6. *Implementation*. Taking action or giving physical substance to the alternative you have chosen.

7. *Evaluation*. Charting the progress of the design, and ultimately assessing its effect.

The ability to think creatively about problems is largely a matter of overcoming blocks to creativity. We all bring ingrained habits and attitudes to the problem-solving process. Creative people often expend a lot of effort on examining their own thought processes, to prevent old patterns from becoming obstacles to change and new learning.

It is important to become aware of when and how your habits of thinking operate and to notice how they affect the way you solve problems. Ingrained mental habits can be useful shortcuts (for instance, there's no need to come up with a fresh approach every time you do your laundry or make a cup of coffee), but you must take care that they do not inhibit or predetermine how you solve important problems.

Writing

Writing is a creative problem-solving process in which we all engage at one time or another. For most people, the problem that writing poses is uncertainty about what to say. It is useful to view the process of composition as consisting of three broad steps:

1. *Prewriting*, during which the writer reads, discusses, reflects, and begins to put his or her ideas into the form of jotted notes, informal outlines and memory aids, and short bursts of prose.

2. *Writing*, the actual composition of a sustained narrative.

3. *Revising*, when the writer reorganizes, condenses, elaborates, polishes, proofreads, and asks other people for their comments.

The Process Applied to Résumé Writing

When you have a problem that calls for writing, you might want to investigate the tools offered by a word processor. In Chapter 2, you used a word processor to fill out a questionnaire. Now let's assume that you've just made an appointment with an employment agency to help you find a new job. They have asked you to bring several copies of your résumé with you, for them to distribute to potential employers.

A word processor is an ideal tool for creating a résumé, because it enables you to revise quickly and effortlessly. You can try out different formats without retyp-

Prewriting

Notes
— How to use a word processor
— steps
— mechanics of entering, editing, revising, changing, saving, printing documents

Writing

This chapter will examine the steps necessary to use a word processor to write various types of documents, and how to use a word processor to accomplish the mechanics of entering and editing text, and the functions of revising, changing, saving, and printing a document.

Revising

This chapter will examine the steps necessary to use a word processor to write various types of documents, and how to use a word processor to accomplish the mechanics of entering and editing text, and the functions of revising, changing, saving, and printing a document.

A word processor is a helpful tool when writing is viewed as a problem-solving process.

ing. You can create specialized versions to emphasize specific strengths for specific jobs. Later, you can update your résumé without retyping.

The following guidelines will show you how to apply the steps in the problem-solving process to word processing and résumé writing.

1. *Get to know the problem.* Familiarize yourself with what a résumé is and what it is supposed to accomplish. Take the time to look at examples of other people's résumés, particularly those in the field you want to enter. Notice differences in their formats and the different impressions that different formats convey.

2. *Define the problem.* Ask yourself what impression you want your résumé to convey. Think about what you want the output to be. For instance, do you want your résumé to fit on a single page?

3. *Identify alternative solutions.* There are many different formats for résumés. Yours could be single- or double-spaced; you could list your previous jobs in retrospective or prospective order; you could use underlining, capitals, centering, or a combination of styles for headings. You could include or omit a statement of your career goals. You could use full sentences or participles, present tense or past tense, and so forth.

4. *Choose the best alternative.* The word processor enables you to try out different combinations of style elements and format options. Analyze the different approaches and select the best combinations, based on your goals and possibly on the suggestions of the employment agency.

RESUME

Roland Alden
123 Main Street
Anytown, CA 90026
(818) 555-1212

Job Objective: Summer employment or internship in computer
programming before attending University of California Irvine in
the fall to major in Computer Science.

EDUCATION

1990 Will graduate in June from Altair Community College with an
Associate Arts degree.
Major: Computer Information Systems, Minor: Art, GPA 3.76
Activities: President—Student Chapter—Association for Computing
Machinery.

WORK EXPERIENCE

Spring, 1989 Lab Assistant, Altair Community College Computer
Laboratory. Assisted students in running and debugging programs.

Summer, 1988 Technical Support, Computerworld Computer Store.
Assisted with configuring and testing hardware and software for
computer systems.

Summer, 1987 Typesetter (intern), Daily Planet. Proofread copy
and entered text for advertising using a Compugraphic
typesetting system.

PERSONAL DATA

Age, 21; height, 5'9"; weight, 165 lbs.; health, excellent;
unmarried; hobbies are writing applications on my
Macintosh personal computer and photography.

REFERENCES

Dr. Ellen Goodright
Professor of Computer Information
Altair Community College

Mr. Noel McGinni
Professor of Art
Altair Community College

Mr. George Verant
Owner, Computerworld
Anytown, CA

Sample résumé.

5. *Implement the solution.* Write and revise your résumé until you are satisfied with it. Then print several copies for the employment agency to send to prospective employers.

6. *Evaluate the results.* In the case of a résumé, of course, the ultimate test is whether or not you get the job you want. But many other factors can affect that outcome, some of them beyond your control. The number of job interviews your résumé generates may be a better measure of its effectiveness. The employment agency may be able to help you evaluate your résumé.

The Spreadsheet Tool

Although surveys have shown that word processing is the most widely used personal computer application, many businesspeople begin with spreadsheets. For problems that are mathematical in nature, you might want to investigate a spreadsheet program. It can be extraordinarily useful for problems that involve the analysis of numbers. We are about to do an exercise using the Works spreadsheet program.

A Spreadsheet Example

Assume that you are about to graduate from college and have accepted a job in another city. It pays $20,000 per year. You currently live with your parents while attending school, but you will have to rent an apartment when you move. You will also need to buy a car when you move. Your parents are going to give you $2,000 as a graduation present.

Your goal is to move into your own apartment, work hard, live comfortably, save a little money, and become self-sufficient. Your parents have always taught you to be frugal, so you think it would be wise, before striking out on your own, to figure out how much you can afford to pay for your car, rent, and monthly expenses and still have a little left over.

Assumptions and Considerations

1. Your monthly net income is your gross income of $20,000 a year minus 25 percent taxes, divided by 12. Your one-time net income is the $2,000 gift from your parents.

2. It costs you one month's deposit on the rent to move in. You will have to estimate how much an apartment will cost in your new city, and you will need to estimate other expenses, such as the cost of a telephone, food, utilities, and so on.

3. Since you must buy a car, you will need to use some of your parents' $2,000 gift as a down payment. You will have to borrow the rest of the money. The monthly cost of the car depends on its actual price, how large

your down payment is, how long you finance the car, the interest rate for the loan, and the cost of insurance and gas.

4. Savings are net income minus total expenses. If expenses exceed income, the number is negative.

In this example, you are going to modify a spreadsheet. We have already designed and built the spreadsheet, so you can concentrate on exploring the spreadsheet tool before learning to create one of your own. (You will learn those techniques in Chapter 6.) You are going to use the Works spreadsheet to:

1. Select and open the spreadsheet called Budget.
2. Use the spreadsheet to perform a *what-if* analysis of the sample budget.
3. Modify the monthly expenses listed in the budget until you have achieved the goal of saving at least $200 a month. You can also change the spreadsheet to more accurately reflect your personal situation.
4. Save the revised spreadsheet on your disk.
5. Print the completed budget.

To complete this assignment and to become familiar with the spreadsheet environment, use the step-by-step instructions that follow. Use the procedure you learned in Chapter 2 to load Works into your personal computer. From the opening screen, perform the following steps:

1. First, use the NEW dialog to start the spreadsheet and open the file called BUDGET.WKS.

   A blinking cursor appears under the bullet next to the label "Word Processor." Press the down arrow key once to move the bullet next to the label "Spreadsheet." Now press the [Tab] key once to move the blinking cursor to the <New> button, and once again to move it to the <Open> button.

   Now "press" the <Open> button by pressing the [Enter] key on the keyboard.

2. The NEW dialog disappears and is replaced by the OPEN dialog box. You will use this dialog box to locate and open the spreadsheet file.

   Now press the [Tab] key to move the blinking cursor to the box labeled "Files in: A:\". Use the up and down arrow keys to browse through the list and highlight the file name BUDGET.WKS. Notice that the blinking cursor disappears and is replaced by the highlight.

3. With the file name BUDGET.WKS highlighted, press the [Enter] key to "press" the <OK> button.

4. In a few seconds, the display shown in Figure 3.2 will appear.

```
  File  Edit  Print  Select  Format  Options  Chart  Window
"Budget Plan
          A          B          C        D        E          F
  Budget Plan
1 Budget Plan
2
3 General Expenses                             New Car
4 ─────────────────────────────────          ──────────────────────────
5                 Monthly    One-time          Sale Price      16,000.00
6 ─────────────────────────────────           Down Pmt         1,600.00
7 Rent            550.00     550.00            Amt Financed    14,400.00
8 Utilities        45.00      45.00            Term in Months         36
9 Phone            50.00      65.00            Interest Rate       12.0%
10 Food           125.00                       Monthly Pmt        478.29
11 Car            628.29    1,600.00           Insurance           95.00
12 ─────────────────────────────────          Gas                 55.00
13 Total Exp    1,398.29    2,260.00           ──────────────────────────
14 ─────────────────────────────────
15 Net Income   1,250.00    2,000.00           Total car costs    628.29
16 ─────────────────────────────────
17 Sav or (Loss) (148.29)    (260.00)
18
19
20
A1                                                          BUDGET.WKS
Press ALT to choose commands.
```

Figure 3.2
Budget spreadsheet.

What-If Budget Analysis

The first thing you will want to do is to get acquainted with the spreadsheet environment. We have already filled the spreadsheet with numbers and formulas representing assumptions about your spending. As you can see, if you followed our optimistic budget, you would be living far beyond your means. Not only would you be unable to pay your monthly bills; you wouldn't have any money left over for large purchases, emergencies, or savings. You'll have to make a few budget cuts to achieve your goal of saving $200 a month.

Before you get started solving the problem, take the time to familiarize yourself with the spreadsheet. First, notice that it is a grid of lettered columns and numbered rows. The intersection of each column and row on the grid is called a **cell**. Each cell has a name, which consists of the column letter and the row number. The cursor is currently highlighting cell A1. To move the cursor around, use the arrow keys as you did with the word processor.

The screen display is 6 columns wide (A through F) and 19 rows deep. The *entire* spreadsheet is 32 columns wide and 256 rows deep. To view other parts of the spreadsheet, you can use various keys to scroll the spreadsheet. For example, to see more rows, press the [PgDn] key. The [PgUp] key will return the cursor to cell A1. The arrow keys will also scroll the spreadsheet. Before going on, scroll the spreadsheet back to its original position, with the cursor highlighting cell A1.

Now look at the line directly below the menu bar. It is called the **formula bar**. A cell can contain text, numbers, or a formula or it can be empty. When a cell contains a formula, it displays the results of computing the formula; the formula itself is displayed in the formula bar. For example, move the cursor to cell B17. In the formula bar, you will see the following formula:

    =B15-B13

This formula subtracts the contents of cell B13 from the contents of cell B15. The advantage of using such **cell references** rather than actual numbers will become apparent when you begin to modify the Budget spreadsheet in the next section. This exercise will not ask you to change or modify any of the formulas. You will only be modifying cells that contain numbers. The Budget spreadsheet is protected; if you accidentally try to change a formula, Works will display a dialog box explaining that locked cells cannot be changed.

Now stop exploring the spreadsheet and go back to the problem. A spreadsheet is an ideal tool for what is called *what-if* **analysis**. You can change one cell in the spreadsheet and watch the results of that change ripple through the entire spreadsheet.

For example, assume that you cut back on your food expenses. You can analyze the effects of lower food expenditures by asking a *what-if* question: "What if my food expenses decrease to $100 a month?" To try this, move the cursor to cell B10 and type in the number 100. Then press the [Enter] key. The program will automatically recalculate all the numbers in the spreadsheet that are affected by the food expenditure. What numbers do you think have changed? The total in cell B13 has changed, since it is the sum of the monthly expenses, and one of those (food) has changed. The savings or loss in cell B17 has changed, because it is dependent on the total in cell B13.

It should be noted that the [Enter] key isn't the only key that causes a cell to be updated. Pressing the [Tab] key after changing a number updates the cell and causes the cursor to move to the cell immediately to the right of it.

Try reducing your expenses until you have reached the goal of saving $200 per month (cell B17 should read 200.00 or more). Notice that cell B17 is in parentheses now. Following standard practice for financial statements, negative numbers are displayed in parentheses. Later you will learn how to change the appearance of numbers in cells; you could, for instance, make negative numbers appear with a minus sign instead of parentheses. Assuming that you just cut your monthly food budget to $100, cell B17 will display (123.29), meaning that this budget calls for you to spend $123.29 more than your income. In the category of one-time expenses, cell C17 will show a value of (260.00), indicating that your one-time expenses are also too high.

The expenses over which you probably have the most control are rent, food, and your new car. Intuition might tell you that your budgeted car is costing a lot, as is rent. However, there are many detailed numbers in this budget, and one way to get the "big picture" is with a chart that displays a series of numbers as a picture. The Budget spreadsheet includes a charting option which displays a bar graph of all monthly expenses.

To activate the Chart menu and use the View command on it, use the [Alt] key method. Press the [Alt] key and then C and V. The display shown in Figure 3.3 will appear.

This chart is called a *bar graph*. Each number in the expense column is displayed as a vertical bar. The larger the number, the taller the bar. As you can easily see, rent and the car are by far your largest expenses. Now press the space bar to return to the spreadsheet.

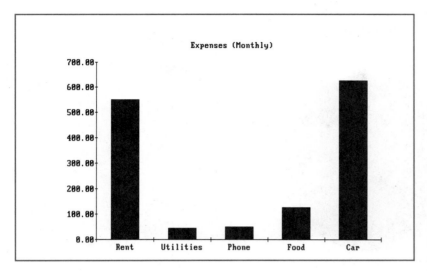

Figure 3.3
Budget bar graph.

Depending on what city your new job will be in, you may be able to reduce the amount you pay for rent. When you reduce the amount in cell B7, you automatically reduce the amount in cell C7. Thus, both the monthly savings or loss in cell B17 and the one-time figure in C17 are affected. However, just reducing your rent won't be enough to meet the goal of saving $200 per month.

As the bar graph showed, the car is your biggest expense. The monthly cost of your car, $628.29, appears in cell B11. However, you cannot just change the value in this cell. It is the result of a series of complex calculations from the cells in column F. In order to reduce the amount you are spending for a car, you will have to analyze what the car is costing and why. Again, a chart may help.

To switch to the second chart built into the Budget spreadsheet, press the [Alt] key, then C, and then 2; the display does not change immediately. Now, to view the chart, press [Alt], C, and V. The display shown in Figure 3.4 will appear.

This chart is called a *pie chart* because of its shape. Each number is displayed as a "slice" of the pie. Pie charts let you see how much each number contributes to the whole. In this case we are charting three numbers from column F: the cost of insurance, the monthly payment for the car loan, and the cost of gas. These numbers added together represent the total monthly cost of the car. As you can see, the payment for the car loan is over 75 percent of the cost of the car. Now press the space bar to return to the spreadsheet.

Move the cursor to cell F10. This is the formula for the monthly payment on the car. In the formula bar, you should see the formula

    =PMT(F7,F9/12,F8)

The letters PMT represent a **function**, which is built into the Works software. A function is a procedure that takes some input, called *parameters*, and returns an answer. PMT is called the payment function; it computes the payment for a loan and takes three parameters, which appear between parentheses and are separated

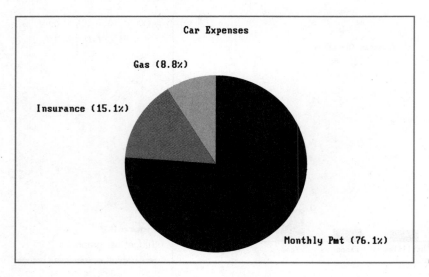

Figure 3.4
Budget pie chart.

by commas. The parameters are the amount of money borrowed (F7), the interest rate (F9/12), and the length of time the money is borrowed (called the *term*; F8). You can also think of the payment function like this:

```
=PMT(amount,interest,term)
```

Cell F7 contains the amount of money you will be borrowing. It is a formula, too: the cost of the car less the down payment. You can reduce the amount in two ways. You can buy a less expensive car (change the number in cell F5), or you can make a bigger down payment on the car (change the number in cell F6). Remember that the down payment figure also shows up in cell C11 and contributes to the total of one-time expenses in cell C13. Your down payment can't be too large, because you need to use some money to pay deposits on your apartment and utilities.

Cell F9 is the annual interest rate you will have to pay for the car loan. In the monthly payment calculation, you see F9/12. The "/" symbol indicates division; so the value is the contents of F9 divided by 12. The annual figure is divided by 12, because we are computing a monthly payment. You may want to check in the newspaper or call your bank to see if 12 percent would be a reasonable figure for you. If you want to enter a different figure, be sure to type the % character so that Works will recognize the number you enter as a percentage.

Cell F8 holds the term of the loan in months; the longer the term, the lower the monthly payment. Auto loans are typically for 24, 36, or 48 months. Try different figures to see how the monthly payment is affected.

Experiment with changing the expenses in your budget, but be realistic. If you buy an expensive car and manage to get a low monthly payment by using a term of 48 months, remember that an expensive car will cost more to insure, and it may use more gas. With each change you make, the spreadsheet automatically recalculates the totals. Try to understand the effect each change has on your overall budget. You can switch between the two charts (chart 1 and 2) using the Chart menu, and you can quickly view the current chart by pressing [Alt], C, and V.

After you have successfully completed the exercise, enter your name into cell A2. To do so, move the cursor to cell A2, type your name, and press the [Enter] or [Tab] key.

Printing the Spreadsheet

To print your spreadsheet, press the [Alt] key and P to display the Print menu, and then press P again to activate the Print command.

The PRINT dialog box will appear. Make sure that the printer is connected to the computer and turned on, and then press the [Enter] key to "press" the <Print> button on the dialog box.

After printing, press the [Alt] key, F, and S to activate the Save command on the File menu. This will save the changes you have made to the spreadsheet. Next press the [Alt] key, F, and X to activate the Exit command.

The operating system will display the A> prompt on the left side of the screen. If you wanted to reenter the Works environment at this point, you could do so by typing in the command B:WORKS and pressing the [Enter] key. If you want to quit using the computer entirely, remove any diskettes you inserted into the computer and check to see whether the computer should be turned off.

Review

Key Terms

Problem	Decision making
Solution	Top-down design
Model	Cell
Simulation	Formula bar
Procedure	Cell reference
Functional specification	*What-if* analysis
Brainstorming	Function

Discussion Questions

1. Give two reasons for treating problem solving as a logical and orderly process.
2. Why do most problems require you to make assumptions?
3. What fields of study might you draw on to learn about problem solving?
4. Describe two behaviors that are typical of creative problem solvers.
5. What is the first step in identifying alternatives?
6. Explain one way to choose the best among a list of alternatives.
7. How is the design process similar to the steps in the problem-solving process?
8. What is the key element in decision making?
9. Why are decision-making skills useful in problem solving?
10. List three advantages of using application software to solve problems.
11. Assume that one of your long-term goals is to communicate more effectively with a wider range of people. How might the software we have been discussing help you to accomplish that goal?
12. List two potential uses you might have for a spreadsheet program. Then discuss why they would be good spreadsheet applications.
13. Imagine that you are in charge of preparing the annual budget for the federal government. How might a spreadsheet help you? Would using charts, such as bar graphs, help?

Software Exercises

1. In the spreadsheet example, suppose you have been offered a job that pays $22,000 a year. Use the spreadsheet to do a *what-if* analysis of how this would affect the budget calculations.
2. You are considering accepting a job that pays $24,000 a year in New York City, where you may have to pay as much as $1,500 a month for an apartment. Assuming that you don't need a car in New York, can you still meet your goal of saving $200 per month?

3. Suppose an auto manufacturer is offering a special promotion on an $8,000 economy car. They will "give" you a $500 down payment if you buy the car using their financing: a one-year loan at only 8 percent interest or a two-year loan at 12 percent. Can you afford it?

PART II

Applications

How should you learn to use computers? By rolling up your sleeves and getting some hands-on experience with application software. Words cannot adequately describe software like word processing, spreadsheet, database, and chart programs. But with a little help you can acquire the skills needed to use them.

Learning how to operate a program isn't the same thing as knowing what to do with it. Part II also provides you with examples to help you discover how to use application software to solve relevant problems.

Chapters 4 and 5 introduce you to word processing. Here you'll learn how to use a word processor to compose, edit, revise, and print documents. Chapters 6 and 7 introduce you to spreadsheets. You'll design spreadsheets and use them to solve number-oriented problems. Chapters 8 and 9 introduce you to databases. We'll show you how to structure, organize, and retrieve information. Finally, Chapter 10 shows how charts are used to study numbers and relationships between them.

- After you complete Chapter 4, you will have used the word processor to compose, revise, save, and print several sample documents.
- After you complete Chapter 5, you will have used the word processor to enhance documents with a variety of character and paragraph formats.
- After you complete Chapter 6, you will have used the spreadsheet program to design a spreadsheet; enter numbers, formulas, and text; and solve some simple number-oriented problems.
- After you complete Chapter 7, you will have built several number-oriented spreadsheets and explored some decision-making alternatives via *what-if* analysis.
- After you complete Chapter 8, you will have built a database, entered and edited the data, and searched and sorted the data for selected records.
- After you complete Chapter 9, you will have created and implemented a database application and used the reporting feature to print a report.
- After you complete Chapter 10, you will have created several kinds of charts from data contained in a spreadsheet you produced in Chapter 7. You will also have created a chart from information contained in a database.

4

Introducing Word Processing

Preview   A word processor is a computer program that you can use to write, print, and store most of the written communication that you need in your personal and professional life.

In this chapter, you'll learn step by step how to use a word processor to compose, edit, revise, and print documents. This chapter will examine how to write various types of documents. It will also teach you how to use a word processor to enter and edit text, and to revise, save, and print a document.

Along the way, we'll discuss how writing with a word processor differs from writing manually or with a typewriter. We'll also provide you with plenty of examples, so that you can explore some of the features of the Works word processor.

In this chapter, you'll learn:

- ■ The use of word processors as general-purpose problem-solving tools
- ■ The different types of documents
- ■ The process of editing
- ■ How to select, copy, and move text
- ■ How documents look on the display screen
- ■ How to write a sample letter
- ■ How to correct and revise text
- ■ How to save and print documents

Word Processing and Problem Solving

Word processing is the use of software that aids in the composition, revision, filing, and printing of text. The term *word processing* was coined at IBM in 1964 to describe electronic means of handling standard office functions and to distinguish those functions from *data* processing. In those days, a word processor was an entire computer dedicated to the task of word processing. Because of their cost and the special training needed to use them, these early word processors were largely limited to secretarial use in medium- and large-scale offices.

Although these **dedicated systems** are still found in offices where heavy-volume word processing is the norm, word processor today commonly means software, rather than a dedicated computer. It has become one of the most popular applications for personal computers. Some uses of word processing software on personal computers are by:

- Authors and editors writing articles and books
- Businesspeople writing memos, correspondence, proposals, and reports
- Scientists and engineers writing professional journal articles
- Teachers writing tests, course outlines, and assignments
- Charities and political organizations writing fund-raising proposals and form letters
- Students writing homework assignments and term papers

Word processors are general-purpose problem-solving tools. They are used in situations in which the user defines the problem (decides what to write and how to write it) and then prepares a solution (composes the written text), drawing on his or her knowledge and problem-solving skills. As a general-purpose tool, a word processor is not restricted to any particular kind of writing. It can be used to help make any written communication clear, effective, neat, and error free, as well as to streamline the writing process.

Writing is a problem-solving skill whose fundamentals you have already acquired. Whether you write manually or with a typewriter, you will find the transition to word processing relatively easy. The mechanics of using word processing software are straightforward. The text that you type on the keyboard is temporarily stored in the computer's memory and displayed on the screen. While the text is in memory, you can change it in any number of ways and immediately see your changes on the display screen. If you aren't satisfied with your changes, it's relatively easy to try another alternative.

You can easily make such changes as:

- Inserting and deleting text

- Copying text from one location to another
- Moving text from one location to another
- Choosing different formats for printing

You can view all of these changes on the display screen; you don't have to retype any drafts. Whenever you're ready, you can save the text onto disk. And, of course, you can print it at any time.

Some Word Processing Basics

Once you become accustomed to using a word processor, its benefits — easier, faster, and neater writing — will become more apparent to you. Before learning to use one, though, it is helpful to learn the terminology of the software you are using. Then you can practice the functions and commands that the word processor uses to prepare, revise, format, and print text.

What Is a Document?

The end product of word processing is a printed **document**. A *document* is any text or collection of characters (letters, numbers, spaces, punctuation marks, and other symbols). The Works word processor has a limit of approximately 25,000 of these characters. At 250 characters per typewritten page, that would translate into 100 pages, but as you will see, special characters and formats reduce the total number of pages that it is possible to create.

It is useful to categorize documents by type, because some word processors place limitations on the types of documents they can produce. Broadly, the categories of documents are (as illustrated in Figure 4.1):

- Simple, sequential, uninterrupted text, such as a letter, note, memo, or rough draft
- A structured document, such as a report, term paper, or book. The structure is provided by such elements as pages, sections and chapters.
- A document whose layout determines its form, such as a résumé, chart, or diagram. The elements of layout include centering, indentation, tabs, and multiple margins.
- A complex arrangement of layout and typographical elements — such as multiple columns, super- and subscripting, boldface, italic, and underlining — and different styles and sizes of type. This kind of document might also include footnotes, an index, and a table of contents.

The User Interface The user interface to the TriPac software will borrow from several concepts common to the Apple Macintosh, and garden-variety IBM PC software like Lotus 1-2-3. The concepts and models are chosen because they are easy to use or illustrate a behavior common to most personal computer software.

Concepts which have been excluded include those that are characteristic only of older generations of software, which new users can avoid by smart shopping, and those that only pertain to very advanced personal computer applications that are not of immediate concern to a novice user.

As a practical matter, the user interface must be usable on an IBM PC or compatible with no graphics capability, and an Apple II/c under UCSD Pascal with 80 column video. The user interface must also provide at least the minimum support needed for the three major applications of the TriPac series: the Word Processor, the Spreadsheet, and the Database.

General Principles The user interface will be based on three key concepts: the menu bar, the workspace, and dialog boxes.

The menu bar appears on the top line of the screen (line 1). It is separated from the rest of the screen by a rule across the second line (line 2). The menu bar, like the Macintosh menu bar, consists of one-word titles that each identify a "drop down" menu. The words can be nouns or verbs that identify the general category of functions that the menu provides. The rest of the screen (line 3 to the end) is called the "workspace".

Functional Specification   2/14/85

The User Interface

The user interface to the TriPac software will borrow from several concepts common to the Apple Macintosh, and garden-variety IBM PC software like Lotus 1-2-3. The concepts and models are chosen because they are easy to use or illustrate a behavior common to most personal computer software.

Concepts which have been excluded include those that are characteristic only of older generations of software, which new users can avoid by smart shopping, and those that only pertain to very advanced personal computer applications that are not of immediate concern to a novice user.

As a practical matter, the user interface must be usable on an IBM PC or compatible with no graphics capability, and an Apple II/c under UCSD Pascal with 80 column video. The user interface must also provide at least the minimum support needed for the three major applications of the TriPac series: the Word Processor, the Spreadsheet, and the Database.

General Principles

The user interface will be based on three key concepts: the menu bar, the workspace, and dialog boxes.

The menu bar appears on the top line of the screen (line 1). It is separated from the rest of the screen by a rule across the second line (line 2). The menu bar, like the Macintosh menu bar, consists of one-word titles that each identify a "drop down" menu. The words can be nouns or verbs that identify the general category of functions that the menu provides. The rest of the screen (line 3 to the end) is called the "workspace".

Because in our implementation the menu bar cannot be reached using a mouse, we will use a mode that is toggled by the "escape" key. Striking the escape key will cause the cursor to leave the workspace and go to the

Page 1

Table 39
Estimated and Actual Figures

Number	Estimate	Actual	Percentage
#143	1,600	1,743	108.9%
#287	2,000	1,573	78.7%
#319	750	921	122.8%
#439	1,300	1,289	99.2%
#539	1,500	1,652	110.1%
#649	1,700	1,422	83.6%
#722	1,700	1,555	91.5%
#811	900	523	58.1%
#948	2,500	2,775	110.0%
Totals	13,950	13,453	96.4%

FUNCTIONAL SPECIFICATION FOR THE TriPac SOFTWARE

THE TRIPAC WORD PROCESSOR™
THE TRIPAC SPREADSHEET™
THE TRIPAC DATABASE™

BY
ROLAND ALDEN
AND
ROBERT BLISSMER

[DATED: FEBRUARY 14, 1985]

The User Interface

The user interface to the TriPac software will borrow from several concepts common to the Apple Macintosh, and garden-variety IBM PC software like Lotus 1-2-3. The concepts and models are chosen because they:

are easy to use
or
illustrate a behavior common to most personal computer software.

Concepts which have been excluded include those that are characteristic only of older generations of software, which new users can avoid by smart shopping, and those that only pertain to very advanced personal computer applications that are not of immediate concern to a novice user.

As a practical matter, the user interface must be useable on an IBM PC or compatible with no graphics capability, and an Apple IIe/c under UCSD Pascal with 80 column video. The user interface must also provide at least the minimum support needed for the three major applications of the TriPac series: the Word Processor, the Spreadsheet, and the Database.

General Principles

The user interface will be based on three key concepts: the menu bar, the workspace, and dialog boxes.

The menu bar appears on the top line of the screen (line 1). It is separated from the rest of the screen by a rule across the second line (line 2). The menu bar, like the Macintosh menu bar, consists of one-word titles that each identify a "drop down" menu. The words can be nouns or verbs that identify the general category of functions that the menu provides. The rest of the screen (line 3 to the end) is called the "workspace".

Because in our implementation the menu bar cannot be reached using a mouse, we will use a mode that is toggled by the "escape" key. Striking the escape key will cause the cursor to leave the workspace and go to the menu bar; hitting the

---

FIGURE 4.1
Four categories of documents.

The sophistication of the word processing program determines which types of documents you can produce. The Works word processor can produce the first three types of documents. Typographically complex documents usually also require special hardware devices, such as a graphics printer, a laser printer, or a typesetter.

How to Create a New Document

This is a hands-on exercise. To begin, you should have the Works software up and running on the computer. If you are not yet familiar with the DOS commands demonstrated in Chapter 1 and the Works commands demonstrated in Chapter 2, it would be a good idea to review them before beginning. To create a new document:

---

1. Make sure the NEW dialog box is on your screen and the Word Processor option is chosen; that is, it has the bullet character beside it.

2. Press the [Enter] key to activate the <New> button.

3. Note that, when you create a new file, Works automatically names it. For example, Works names word processing files WORD1.WPS, WORD2.WPS, and so on. When you save the file for the first time, you will want to give it a more descriptive name.

What You Will See

Figure 4.2 shows the newly opened document. Below the menu bar, you will see a ruler line. The *blinking cursor* is in the upper left-hand corner. The cursor is positioned under a paragraph mark. To the left of the cursor is the double right arrow character (>>) used to mark page breaks. A diamond-shaped symbol below the cursor marks the end of the document.

When writing manually or on a typewriter, the mechanics of writing begin with a blank piece of paper. In word processing, the equivalent of a blank page is the empty document into which you insert text. In the vocabulary of word processing, going from an empty file to a completed document is known as **editing**. Editing includes composing the original text, revising (inserting, deleting, correcting, and formatting text), and periodically saving copies of the document onto disk.

The blinking cursor can be moved to any point in the document by using the cursor-movement keys. However, since your document is empty, you cannot yet move the blinking cursor. To practice using the basic editing features, we will start you off with some exercises that involve the format of the document rather than its content.

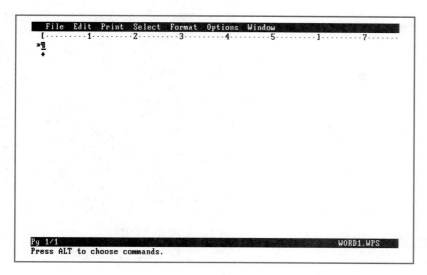

FIGURE 4.2
Newly opened document.

Experimenting with Word Processing

When you use a word processor, you will constantly be performing two operations: inserting new text into the document and manipulating the text that is already there. To begin practicing, insert some text into the document. Type

    This is a test.

Note that the blinking cursor has shifted to the end of the sentence. Your document is now one sentence long. Since the blinking cursor can be moved anywhere in the document, you can now use the left and right arrow keys to move the blinking cursor anywhere in the sentence.

Now move the blinking cursor to the initial *t* in *test* and type the deliberately misspelled words

    word porcessing

followed by a space. Note that the new text is automatically inserted beginning at the location of the blinking cursor and that the text that follows it is pushed to the right. You don't have to worry about deleting text by typing over it.

Next, you would like to correct the spelling of *porcessing*. To do that, you must command the word processor to manipulate the text that is already there. (In this case, the command will be to delete the *o* in the misspelled word and then correct the spelling.) To do so:

1. Move the blinking cursor under the letter *o* in *porcessing*, as shown in Figure 4.3, and press the [Del] (delete) key.

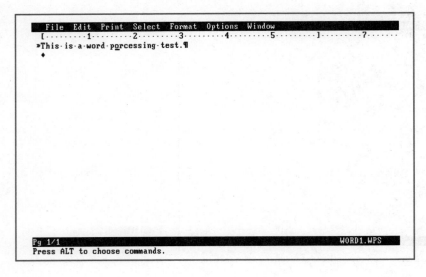

File Edit Print Select Format Options Window
```
[·········1·········2·········3·········4·········5·······]·········7·····]
»This·is·a·word·porcessing·test.¶
    ◆
```

```
Pg 1/1                                            WORD1.WPS
Press ALT to choose commands.
```

FIGURE 4.3
Test document.

2. The delete function erases the character on which the cursor is positioned. The space left by the deleted character is closed up.

3. To correct the spelling, move the blinking cursor one position to the right (under the *c*) and type the letter *o*. When inserting a character or characters, position the blinking cursor at the point where you want the insertion to begin.

By moving the blinking cursor, using the [Del] key, and inserting additional text, you can correct spelling and other errors in a document. Pressing the [Del] key several times deletes several characters in sequence. Try positioning the blinking cursor under the *w* in *word* and pressing the [Del] key four times. The characters will disappear one at a time, and the space left by the deletions will automatically close up. Then, without moving the blinking cursor, retype the letters *word*.

Another way to delete characters is to use the [Backspace] key. Ordinarily, the [Backspace] key is used to correct typing mistakes as you make them. When you press the [Backspace] key, it deletes the character to the left of the cursor. Pressing it several times deletes several characters in a row. For example, position the blinking cursor on the space between *word* and *processing*. Press the [Backspace] key four times. Like the [Del] key, the [Backspace] key causes the text to the right of the blinking cursor to close up. Without moving the blinking cursor, retype the letters *word*.

Selection

Selection is an important principle of word processing. It is used to choose a set of characters to be manipulated, such as by:

File Edit Print Select Format Options Window
[········1········2········3········4········5········]········7······
»This·is·a·word·processing·test.¶
 ◆

Pg 1/1   WORD1.WPS
Press ALT to choose commands.

FIGURE 4.4
Highlighting text.

- Copying the characters elsewhere in the document
- Moving the characters elsewhere in the document
- Deleting the characters

Note that selection is always used in conjunction with another command. To practice selecting:

1. Move the blinking cursor to the beginning of the document (to the *T* in *This*).

2. Hold down the [Shift] key and press the right arrow key continuously until you have highlighted the entire sentence, as shown in Figure 4.4. Highlighting will appear on the display screen as reverse video. Note that the blinking cursor has disappeared.

3. You can cancel the selection by pressing any one of the arrow keys without holding the [Shift] key down. The blinking cursor will return, and the selection highlighting will disappear.

4. Selection can proceed in either direction. Repeat the steps to select the sentence by moving the cursor to the paragraph mark after the end of the sentence. This time, hold down the [Shift] key and press the left arrow key continuously. The highlighting will proceed to the left. Before going on, cancel the selection.

You should remember the following important points about selection:

■ A selection begins at the left edge of the blinking cursor. In other words, when you press the right arrow key, the highlighting begins on the character where the blinking cursor was last located. If you press the left arrow key, the highlighting begins on the character to the immediate left of where the blinking cursor was last located.

■ A selection replaces the blinking cursor. Think of the blinking cursor as a one-character selection, or think of a selection as an extra-wide cursor.

■ A selection will be replaced by an insertion. For example, if you select a sentence and press Y, the highlighted sentence will be deleted and replaced by the insertion of the letter *y*. If you do this accidentally, you can reverse your most recent action by using *Undo*. The **Undo command** restores text you've deleted or reverses formatting changes.

To use the Undo command:

1. Select a sentence in your document. Then press Y. The highlighted sentence will be deleted and replaced by the insertion of the letter *y*.

2. To reverse the deletion and replacement, activate the Undo command by pressing the [Alt] key. Move the highlight to the Edit menu and then to the Undo command. Press the [Enter] key. Your original sentence will reappear.

3. Note that the Undo command only restores the most recent change or deletion. You can't use it to restore earlier changes or deletions. For example, if you delete some text, execute another command, and then wish to retrieve the deleted selection, you will have to retype it.

Now we will show you some commands to use with selection when you want to edit a document.

Copy

The **Copy command** is used to copy a passage of text from one location in a document to another, leaving the original intact. To practice using the Copy command to copy the sentence you selected earlier:

1. Move the cursor to the beginning of the document. Repeat the procedure outlined in the last section to select the entire sentence.

FIGURE 4.5
Edit menu with copy command highlighted.

2. Press the [Alt] key to activate the menu bar. Move the highlight right, to the Edit menu, then down to the Copy command. The screen will look like Figure 4.5. Press the [Enter] key.

3. The status line at the bottom of the screen will now ask you to "Select new location and press ENTER or press ESC to cancel."

4. Press the right arrow key to move the blinking cursor to the paragraph mark at the end of the sentence. Note that the selection highlight disappears when you press the arrow key to move the cursor. When the cursor is positioned, press the [Enter] key. A copy of the sentence selected will appear, starting at the cursor position.

Type in another sentence or two, and practice the Copy command.

Move

The **Move command** is used to move selected characters from one location in a document to another. The Move command deletes the text from its original location and moves it to a new location.

As an analogy, imagine that you want to reverse the order of two paragraphs using scissors and tape. You would cut one paragraph out of its original location and tape it in at the new location. The Move function in the Works word processor accomplishes the same thing. By contrast, Copy copies a selection but leaves the original intact.

To practice moving:

1. Move the cursor to the beginning of the second sentence in your document and type:

   ```
   Move this sentence to the end.
   ```

2. Select the sentence you just typed, using the selection process described on page 103.

3. Press the [Alt] key to activate the menu bar. Move the highlight to the Edit menu and then to the Move command. Press the [Enter] key. The status line at the bottom of the screen will remind you to "Select new location and press ENTER or press ESC to cancel."

4. Press the right arrow key to move the blinking cursor to the end of the document. Note that the selection highlight disappears when you press the arrow key to move the cursor. When the blinking cursor is positioned, press the [Enter] key.

5. The selected text will appear, starting at the blinking cursor's position.

Editing Shortcuts

Once you have learned the uses of some of the commands in the Edit menu, you can use a shortcut method for invoking those commands. Recall that one letter in each menu and one letter in each command is highlighted. You activate a command using the shortcut method by pressing the [Alt] key, then pressing the highlighted menu letter (such as *E* for *Edit*), and then pressing the highlighted letter for the specific command on that menu. This technique can be used with all of the Works menus and dialog boxes. To practice using the shortcuts in conjunction with commands on the Edit menu:

1. Select the second sentence in your document. Then press the [Alt] key, E, and C in that order. This activates the Copy command.

2. Now move the cursor to the paragraph mark at the end of the document, press the [Enter] key, and watch as the sentence is copied at the end of your document.

3. To move a selection, select a sentence, but this time press [Alt], E, and M in sequence.

4. Now move the cursor to the paragraph mark at the end of the document, press the [Enter] key, and watch as the sentence is moved to the end of your document.

5. To delete a selection, select a sentence, then press [Alt], E, and D in sequence. The selection will be deleted. This works much as pressing the [Del] key does.

6. To undo the deletion, press [Alt], E, and U in sequence. The selection will reappear exactly where it was.

So far, you have chosen only sentences. A selection can also be a single character, a word, a sentence, a group of sentences, a paragraph, or the entire document. To practice selecting a passage of text larger than a sentence, type a few additional sentences into your document, so that at least three new lines of text appear on your display.

---

1. Move the cursor somewhere near the middle of the top line on the display and hold down the [Shift] key.

2. Now press the down arrow key. The text to the right of the cursor on the top line and the text to the left of the cursor on the next line will be selected.

3. Still holding down the [Shift] key, press the down arrow key again. Another line of text will be highlighted. Now press the up arrow key; the previously highlighted line of text will no longer be selected. Now hold down the [Shift] key and press the down arrow key twice to select a passage of text.

Using selection in combination with the [Del] key deletes a block of selected text. If you choose a word or a passage of text and then press the [Del] key, the selected text will be deleted from the document. As previously mentioned, the Undo command allows you to reverse your most recent command. If you delete a selection by mistake, the Undo command can be used to recover it.

Now select and copy all of the text in your document. Then keep copying the entire document over and over, filling up the display screen with text so that you can observe the feature called *scrolling*.

Scrolling

When a document is too large to be displayed on the screen all at once, **scrolling** — moving text up, down, left, or right on the screen — brings different parts of the document into view. For this discussion, we will confine ourselves to vertical or up and down scrolling. Later, in Chapter 6, "Introducing Spreadsheets," we will discuss horizontal or left and right scrolling.

Pressing the down arrow key continuously moves the blinking cursor down the display line by line. When it reaches the bottom line, a new line of text appears at the bottom of the display. All the text on the display moves up one line, and the line at the top of the display disappears.

Pressing the up arrow key causes the same process to occur in reverse. The blinking cursor moves line by line up the display; when it reaches the top line, a new line of text appears at the top, the remaining text moves down one line, and the line at the bottom disappears.

You can scroll faster by using the [PgUp] and [PgDn] keys to move the blinking cursor page by page, up or down the display. The keys marked [Home] and [End] are often used to move the blinking cursor to the beginning (home) or end of a line of text or document. All four of these keys are often used in combination with the [Ctrl] and [Shift] keys. The combination usually signifies a variation on the key's basic meaning. For instance, pressing the [Home] key moves the blinking cursor to the beginning of a *line*. Holding down the [Ctrl] key while pressing the [Home] key moves the blinking cursor to the beginning of the *document*. Holding down the [Shift] key while pressing the [Home] key selects all characters between the blinking cursor and the beginning of a line.

Editing and the Display

The **format** of the text is the way it is physically organized on the display screen. Whenever text is inserted or deleted, the word processor automatically reformats the display to accommodate the insertion or deletion.

To visualize this, think of a document as a continuous stream of text that flows from the beginning to the diamond-shaped end-of-document symbol. The word processor's display screen is a rectangle consisting of 20 lines, each 60 characters long. The ruler line under the menu bar shows you the line length with a right bracket character ( ]) in the 60th position.

As you type, the cursor continues advancing to the right to indicate the location of the next character. When the cursor reaches the end of a line, it automatically drops down to the first position in the next line. If you're in the middle of a word when the cursor reaches the end of a line, the word is carried down to the next line, along with the cursor. This feature, called **word wrap**, allows you to continue typing without using the [Enter] key, as you would have to use a carriage return on a typewriter. The [Enter] key has a special function, which we will discuss in the next section.

Word wrap occurs when you insert or delete text, to eliminate crowding or gaps in the stream of text. To see word wrap in action, move your cursor to the middle of the first line of text and add the sentence:

```
This is a test of the word wrap feature.
```

Watch how the text at the end of the line drops down to the next line. Then use the [Del] key to delete part of the sentence you just added, and watch how word wrap works in reverse.

Word wrap also occurs when you hyphenate a word at the end of a line. To observe this feature, choose a line that is filled with text and move the cursor within the last word in the line. If you insert a hyphen within the word, you will see the remainder of the word drop to the beginning of the next line. If you delete the hyphen, you will see word wrap work in reverse. You will notice that the word must end at the last position in the line for word wrap to work.

A WORD ABOUT
The Future of Word Processing

Word processors trace much of their current design to their typing heritage — aiding in the mechanical aspects of composing, revising, and formatting text.

Today word processors are used to produce simple printed documents. In the next few years, word processing technology will be extended to help in the production of elaborate publications and complex technical documents. Such word processors will easily combine illustrations and text and be able to analyze the structure of documents well enough to organize tables of contents, indexes, and other document components automatically.

In the past, word processing was nearly the last step in the production of written material. The original author rarely used the word processor to create an initial rough draft. Tomorrow's word processors will have many author-oriented features, which will enhance the more creative aspects of writing. For instance, features like the ability to organize and reorganize a large document in outline form are being added to word processors. In the future, word processing will be part of a larger system of data organization that can keep track of research notes, diagrams, and photos — all supporting the author's need to synthesize information before a document can be created.

As more and more documents are created on computers, there is less need for them to be printed. Today's electronic mail systems deliver millions of messages that are read on a computer and never printed. Future word processors will abandon the metaphor of the printed page entirely and allow authors to organize text in ways that are impossible when a document must be printed. Today such systems are called *hypertext*, but tomorrow they may be taken for granted and simply included in the category of word processors.

Hypertext allows a document or a collection of documents to be organized in different ways at the same time. The reader can follow a concept along a given path of information, while another reader can follow a different concept. The reader can push different buttons embedded in the document to turn the pages, but the information on the next page can be different every time. Although such an organization is not suitable for presenting a single concept in a well-defined way, it is ideal for complex documents, such as technical manuals, and reference works, such as encyclopedias. Tomorrow's authors will require new kinds of word processing software to create such documents.

A logical extension of the hypertext concept is called *hypermedia*. In hypermedia, communication is not limited to text; it can also include illustrations, sounds, animation, even television. For instance, an auto repair manual may feature many pages of written instructions, tables of specifications, and part diagrams. But it could also feature illustrations that are really short movies. When a button near the illustration is pressed, the illustration comes to life, with moving pictures and sound explaining how to remove and repair a part.

Such systems exist today in various commercial and experimental forms. Using them to communicate the ideas of the future is the goal of word processing.

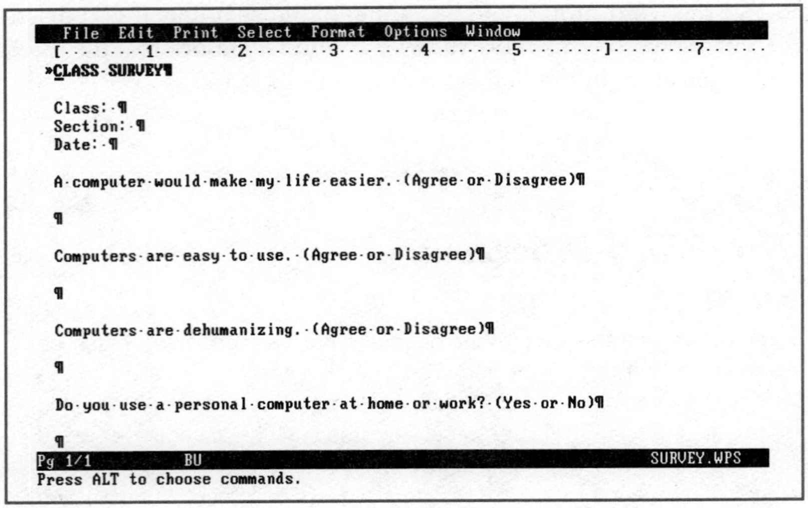

```
   File  Edit  Print  Select  Format  Options  Window
  [.........1.........2.........3.........4.........5.........].........7.....
  »CLASS·SURVEY¶

   Class:·¶
   Section:·¶
   Date:·¶

   A·computer·would·make·my·life·easier.·(Agree·or·Disagree)¶

   ¶

   Computers·are·easy·to·use.·(Agree·or·Disagree)¶

   ¶

   Computers·are·dehumanizing.·(Agree·or·Disagree)¶

   ¶

   Do·you·use·a·personal·computer·at·home·or·work?·(Yes·or·No)¶

   ¶
  Pg 1/1         BU                                    SURVEY.WPS
  Press ALT to choose commands.
```

FIGURE 4.6
Survey screen showing
paragraph marks.

Paragraphs

Breaks occur in the continuous stream of text only when you create a paragraph. Recall from Chapter 2 that the end of a paragraph is indicated by a **paragraph mark** (¶). In the survey shown in Figure 4.6, paragraph marks appear at the end of each line. To create a paragraph in your document, move the cursor to the end of the first sentence. Then press the [Enter] key. A paragraph mark will appear where the cursor was, and the text to the right of the cursor will move down to the next line. The first line has become a paragraph.

To insert a blank line between paragraphs, you can simply create a paragraph without any text in it. Press the [Enter] key again. A blank line will be created, with a paragraph mark at the left margin, and the remainder of the text will drop down one line. In the next chapter, you will learn how to format paragraphs to achieve various special effects.

Note that the paragraph mark, along with the spacing dots between words, is optionally visible. To make these characters invisible, press the [Alt] key and go to the Options menu. Choose the "Show All Characters" command (it currently has a bullet next to it to indicate that this feature is on) and press the [Enter] key. To toggle back to making the characters visible, use the shortcut method: press [Alt], O, and A in sequence to activate the "Show All Characters" command again.

When you feel comfortable using these commands, press the [Alt] key to activate the menu bar. Then press F to view the File menu and A to save your file. The SAVE AS dialog box will appear. Note that the "File Name" field contains the highlighted text WORDS1.WPS. To rename the file TEST, simply type the word *test*. Because the file name was selected, your insertion will replace the selected text, as in the word processor. Press the [Enter] key and continue with the next lesson.

Do this & turn it in

```
123 Main Street
Anytown, CA 90026
September 23, 19 XX

Mr. Robert H. Blissmer
Houghton Mifflin Company
One Beacon Street
Boston, MA 02108

Dear Mr. Blissmer:

The blocked paragraph style is widely used in business
correspondance. This version is called a full-blocked style
because each line begins at the left-hand margin. Using full-
blocked style is also the fastest way to type.

New paragraphs are indicated by double spacing rather than
indenting. The format for a blocked letter consists of: the
return address, the date, the recipient's address, then the
salutation. The body of the letter is followed by a complimentery
close, and the sender's name.


Sincerely yours,



John Doe
```

FIGURE 4.7
Sample letter.

Writing a Sample Letter

To let you apply the editing concepts you have just learned, we have composed a sample letter for your practice. Press [Alt], F, N, and [Enter] in sequence to open a new file.

Then type the letter exactly as shown in Figure 4.7 (including the spelling mistakes). Use the [Enter] key to create new paragraphs. For example, type in the first address line — *123 Main Street* — then press the [Enter] key, type in the second address line, then press the [Enter] key, and so on. Also use the [Enter] key to insert a blank line between the date and the recipient's address, and between the

```
┌─────────────────────────────────────────────────────────┐
│  File Edit Print Select Format Options Window             │
│ [·········1·········2·········3·········4·········5·····]·······7······ │
│ »123·Main·Street¶                                         │
│ Anytown,·CA·90026¶                                        │
│ September·23,·1986¶                                       │
│ ¶                                                         │
│ Mr.·Robert·H.·Blissmer¶                                   │
│ Houghton·Mifflin·Company¶                                 │
│ One·Beacon·Street¶                                        │
│ Boston,·MA·02108¶                                         │
│ ¶                                                         │
│ Dear·Mr.·Blissmer:¶                                       │
│ ¶                                                         │
│ The·blocked·paragraph·style·is·widely·used·in·business·   │
│ correspondance.··This·version·is·called·a·full-blocked·style· │
│ because·each·line·begins·at·the·left-hand·margin.·Using·  │
│ full-blocked·style·is·also·the·fastest·way·to·type.¶      │
│ ¶                                                         │
│ New·paragraphs·are·indicated·by·double·spacing·rather·than· │
│ indenting.··The·format·for·a·blocked·letter·consists·of:··the· │
│ return·address,··the·date,··the·recipient's·address,··then·the· │
│ salutation.·The·body·of·the·letter·is·followed·by·a·     │
│ complimentery·close,·and·the·sender's·name.¶             │
│ Pg·1/1                                    WORD1.WPS       │
│ Press ALT to choose commands.                             │
└─────────────────────────────────────────────────────────┘
```

FIGURE 4.8
Sample business letter.

recipient's address and the salutation. You'll find that the letter doesn't fit on one screen.

Editing: Correcting Mistakes

After you've finished typing in the business letter, you will want to (1) correct the deliberate mistakes in the letter and (2) proofread the letter for any additional mistakes of your own. Scroll back to the beginning of the letter. The screen will look like Figure 4.8. Use the arrow keys to move around in the document.

In the letter, the words *correspondence* and *complimentary* are misspelled. To correct each spelling, first select the character you want to change. Use the arrow keys to position the cursor on the *a* in the misspelled word *correspondance*. Press the [Del] key to delete it. Then type in the correct letter *e*. Do the same for the misspelled word *complimentery* by deleting the second *e* and replacing it with an *a*.

Revising: Adding New Text

Now you can practice inserting additional words and sentences into the business letter. At the beginning of the second paragraph, add the following text to the first sentence:

```
With this style,
```

Notice how the text to the right of the cursor moves and how the word processor uses word wrap to reformat the entire paragraph. Don't forget to add a space and to make the uppercase *N* lowercase. Then change the last sentence in the second paragraph to read:

```
After the body of the letter, end with a complimentary
close and your name.
```

```
 File  Edit  Print  Select  Format  Options  Window
[········1·········2·········3·········4·········5·········]········7······
Dear·Mr.·Blissmer:¶
¶
The·blocked·paragraph·style·is·widely·used·in·business·
correspondance.·This·version·is·called·a·full-blocked·style·
because·each·line·begins·at·the·left-hand·margin.·Using·
full-blocked·style·is·also·the·fastest·way·to·type.¶
¶
With·this·style,·new·paragraphs·are·indicated·by·double·
spacing·rather·than·indenting.·The·format·for·a·blocked·
letter·consists·of:·the·return·address,·the·date,·the·
recipient's·address,·then·the·salutation.·After·the·body·of·
the·letter,·end·with·a·complimentery·close·and·your·name.¶
¶
¶
Sincerely·yours,¶
¶
¶
John·Doe¶
◆


Pg 1/1                                            WORD1.WPS
Press ALT to choose commands.
```

FIGURE 4.9
Revised business letter.

You can do this in either of two ways: (1) select the existing sentence and delete it, then type in the new sentence; or (2) type in the new sentence, and then delete the old sentence. You can delete the old text before inserting the new text, but remember that, once deleted, it is gone. If you're replacing a long passage of text, such as rewriting a sentence, it makes sense to add the new text before deleting the old, in case you change your mind. Figure 4.9 shows the revised business letter.

For additional practice in deleting and inserting text, make the following changes in the business letter:

---

1. Replace the three address lines with your own home address.

2. Replace the date with today's date.

3. Replace the name John Doe with your own name.

Saving the Document

After you've finished the revisions, you will want to save the document onto disk so that you can refer to it in the future and won't have to type it over again. To save the document, press the [Alt] key and go to the menu bar. Press F, then A, to activate the "Save As" command. The SAVE AS dialog box will appear. Name the document BLETTER (short for *business letter*). Then press the [Enter] key. The red light on the disk drive will go on, and a copy of the document will be stored on the disk.

Particularly if you are working on a long document, there is a very important reason to save copies of it periodically. A document stored in memory is temporary,

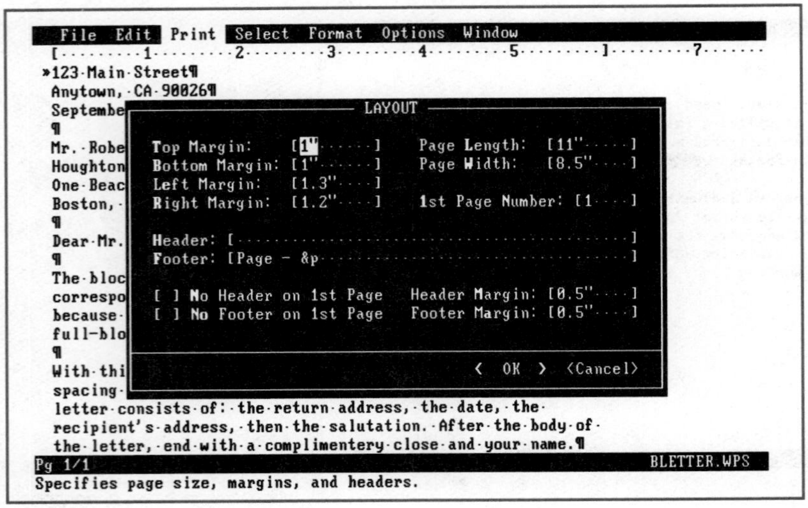

```
  File Edit  Print  Select  Format  Options  Window
 [.........1.........2.........3.........4.........5.........].........7.......
»123·Main·Street¶
Anytown,·CA·98026¶
Septembe┌─────────────────── LAYOUT ───────────────────┐
¶        │                                              │
Mr.·Robe │ Top Margin:    [1"·····]  Page Length:  [11"·····]│
Houghton │ Bottom Margin: [1"·····]  Page Width:   [8.5"····]│
One·Beac │ Left Margin:   [1.3"····]                     │
Boston,· │ Right Margin:  [1.2"····]  1st Page Number: [1····]│
¶        │                                              │
Dear·Mr. │ Header: [..................................]│
¶        │ Footer: [Page — &p······················]│
The·bloc │                                              │
correspo │ [ ] No Header on 1st Page  Header Margin: [0.5"···]│
because· │ [ ] No Footer on 1st Page  Footer Margin: [0.5"···]│
full-blo │                                              │
¶        │                                              │
With·thi │                    < OK >  <Cancel>          │
spacing· └──────────────────────────────────────────────┘
letter·consists·of:·the·return·address,·the·date,·the·
recipient's·address,·then·the·salutation.·After·the·body·of·
the·letter,·end·with·a·complimentery·close·and·your·name.¶
Pg 1/1                                          BLETTER.WPS
Specifies page size, margins, and headers.
```

FIGURE 4.10
LAYOUT dialog box.

because memory itself is temporary. If you turn off the power switch or the plug is knocked out of the socket, the contents of memory will be lost. If something happens to the program while you are editing a document, and you have to restart the computer, the contents of memory will be lost as a result of the restart. This is only a minor annoyance if it causes the loss of a brief or unimportant document, but it could mean losing hours of work. A good rule of thumb when working with a word processor is to save your document every 15 or 20 minutes. That way, if something should go wrong, only a small amount of work is lost.

Printing the Document

Printing a document also involves deciding on the format, or layout, of the printed page. Page layout is a matter of page size, left and right margins, page numbering, and headers and footers.

To see the **default** layout for printing your documents, press [Alt], P, and L in sequence. The LAYOUT dialog box will appear, as shown in Figure 4.10. A default value is one that Works uses if you don't specifically change it. Most of the time, you will print on 8½-by-11-inch paper. Some printers are capable of printing on 14- or 17-inch-wide paper, and it is possible to change the page size in Works.

The Layout Dialog

The Layout command always displays a LAYOUT dialog box. Most layout dialogs feature many options. For this discussion, we will simply give you an overview of the options. In later chapters, you will learn more about these options. Figure 4.11 shows a diagram of a page illustrating where each measurement applies. The options fall into several groups: margins, page size, page numbering, and header/footer control.

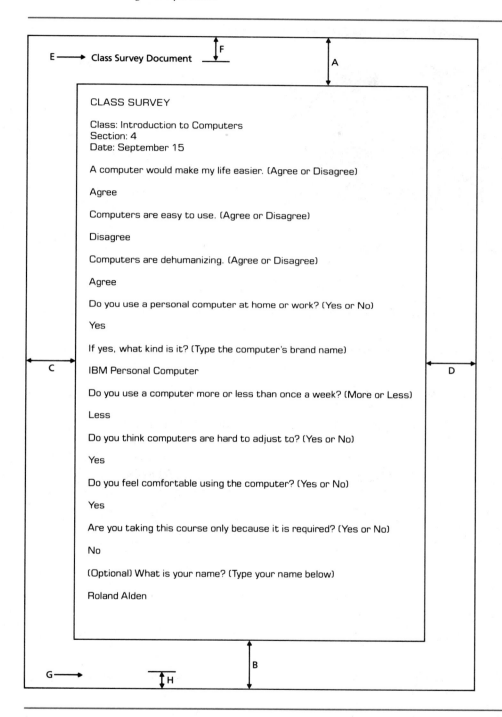

CLASS SURVEY

Class: Introduction to Computers
Section: 4
Date: September 15

A computer would make my life easier. (Agree or Disagree)

Agree

Computers are easy to use. (Agree or Disagree)

Disagree

Computers are dehumanizing. (Agree or Disagree)

Agree

Do you use a personal computer at home or work? (Yes or No)

Yes

If yes, what kind is it? (Type the computer's brand name)

IBM Personal Computer

Do you use a computer more or less than once a week? (More or Less)

Less

Do you think computers are hard to adjust to? (Yes or No)

Yes

Do you feel comfortable using the computer? (Yes or No)

Yes

Are you taking this course only because it is required? (Yes or No)

No

(Optional) What is your name? (Type your name below)

Roland Alden

FIGURE 4.11
Page layout. A: Top margin; B: bottom margin; C: left margin; D: right
margin; E: header; F: header margin; G: footer; H: footer margin.

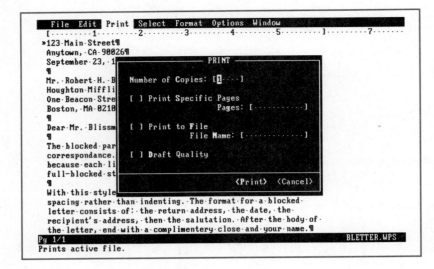

```
 File  Edit  Print  Select  Format  Options  Window
[.........1.........2.........3.........4.........5.........].........7......
»123·Main·Street¶
Anytown,·CA·90026¶
September·23,·1┌─────────────── PRINT ───────────────┐
¶              │                                     │
Mr.·Robert·H.·B│ Number of Copies: [1·····]          │
Houghton·Miffli│                                     │
One·Beacon·Stre│ [ ] Print Specific Pages            │
Boston,·MA·0210│              Pages: [···········]   │
¶              │                                     │
Dear·Mr.·Blissm│ [ ] Print to File                   │
¶              │          File Name: [···········]   │
The·blocked·par│                                     │
correspondance.│ [ ] Draft Quality                   │
because·each·li│                                     │
full-blocked·st│                                     │
¶              │              <Print>  <Cancel>      │
With·this·style└─────────────────────────────────────┘
spacing·rather·than·indenting.·The·format·for·a·blocked·
letter·consists·of:·the·return·address,·the·date,·the·
recipient's·address,·then·the·salutation.·After·the·body·of·
the·letter,·end·with·a·complimentery·close·and·your·name.¶
Pg·1/1                                        BLETTER.WPS
Prints active file.
```

FIGURE 4.12
PRINT dialog box.

- The margins are controlled by four text boxes that allow you to specify a measurement for the top, bottom, left, and right margins.
- The page size is controlled by the "Page Length" and "Page Width" text boxes. The default is 8½-by-11-inch paper.
- The page numbering starts with the value entered into the "1st Page Number" text box. The default is 1.
- Headers and footers will be discussed in the next chapter.

The Works word processor also lets you indent individual paragraphs from the left and right margins. The margins, set with the LAYOUT dialog box, apply to the entire document. Indents apply to each paragraph individually. Many specialized documents, such as screenplays, poetry, and résumés, have style requirements for which special indentation can be a useful feature.

To print your business letter document without special formatting:

1. Press [Esc] to cancel the LAYOUT dialog box.

2. Press the [Alt] key to activate the menu bar, press P to move to the Print menu, and press P again. A PRINT dialog box, like the one in Figure 4.12, will appear.

3. Make sure the printer is plugged in and turned on and that the top edge of the paper is positioned underneath the print head.

4. To print the document, press the [Enter] key.

In the next chapter, you will learn how to change formats in a document before printing it.

Review

Key Terms

Word processing
Dedicated system
Document
Editing
Selection
Undo command
Copy command

Move command
Scrolling
Format
Word wrap
Paragraph mark
Default

Discussion Questions

1. What office functions was word processing originally intended to perform?
2. Briefly explain why word processors are general-purpose problem-solving tools.
3. Briefly outline the mechanics of using a word processor.
4. What is the simplest type of document?
5. What is the most complex type of document?
6. What two operations will you constantly be performing when using a word processor?
7. Describe the function of the [Del] key.
8. How is the function of the [Backspace] key similar to the [Del] key?
9. What is the purpose of selecting text?
10. What is the difference between Copy and Move?
11. What is the function of word wrap?
12. Why should you periodically save copies of the document you are writing on a word processor?

Software Exercises

1. Use the word processor to write a one-page, single-spaced essay on the benefits of word processing.
2. Experiment with inserting text by using the arrow keys to move around in your test document and typing in additional text. Then practice using the [Del] and [Backspace] keys to delete text.
3. Practice copying and moving various blocks of text. Try using the editing shortcuts — the [Alt] key in conjunction with the letter keys.
4. Use the [Enter] key to create paragraphs in the document. Experiment with deleting sentences, lines, paragraphs, and paragraph marks by selecting and then deleting with the [Del] key.
5. After revising the business letter, print a copy and hand it in to your instructor.

6. Use the word processor to write a one-page letter to your instructor describing how easy or difficult it was to complete the word processing exercises.

7. Research another word processor, by using it or by reading its documentation or articles about it. Use the Works word processor to write a report on the differences between Works and the other word processor.

5

Working with Word Processing

Preview   In this chapter you'll see how word processing can simplify the creation of more complex documents. Word processing can help you write research papers, term papers, and reports. You'll learn step by step how to electronically compose, edit, and revise various drafts of a sample report.

You can also use your word processor to format your documents so that they will be easier to read and more aesthetically pleasing. We'll show you how a variety of paragraph and character formats can be used to create more interesting and informative written communication.

At the end of the chapter we'll discuss more advanced features of word processors and show you how these features can further enhance written communication. We'll also discuss how desktop publishing software running on personal computers can be used to prepare and print a wide variety of typeset- or near-typeset-quality documents.

In this chapter, you'll learn:

- How to revise drafts of a document electronically
- The use of search and replace
- Options for the format of printed documents
- How to format characters
- Advanced features of word processing
- Features of desktop publishing

Writing the First Draft

In Chapter 3, we discussed writing as a problem-solving process. Word processors have many features that can help you with this. The best way to show you those features is to practice on a draft document. Begin by creating a new document which will be saved with the name REPORT. Then type in the first draft of the report, exactly as shown in Figure 5.1. Save the document as REPORT.

```
The birth of the type-writer

In 1868, Christopher Latham Sholes, with the assistance of Carlos
Glidden, invented the first type-writer. The prototype model used
a piano-style keyboard and was the size of a kitchen table. The
type-writer was redesigned several times, and in 1873, Remington
and Sons, gunsmiths, agreed to manufacture and sell it.

In 1874, the Remington Model I type-writer was introduced. It had
no lower-case letters, and typed words were not visible until
several lines had been typed in. When it was exhibited at the
Philadelphia Centennial Exposition in 1876, many people were
willing to pay 25 cents to type a note to show their friends, but
few were willing to purchase the device.

One of the early problems with the Sholes and Glidden type-writer
was jamming of the keys. Even the earliest typists were too fast
for the machine. The solution was to fix the keyboard layout in
order to get the typists to slow down. By chance, the keyboard
arrangement spelled out Qwerty on the top row of letters, so the
keyboard is often called a Qwerty layout. Because rearranging
the keys placed freqeuntly used letters all over the keyboard,
jamming of the keys was reduced.

In the early years the feeling that correspondence should be
written in longhand, plus the poor quality of the type-writer,
kept sales low. But by the mid 1880s, the type-writer was found
in many modern offices, and the word "secretary" came to mean a
woman at a type-writer. Today, the office type-writer is being
replaced by the word processor, and typing has become a survival
skill for nearly everyone.
```

FIGURE 5.1
Text for the REPORT document.

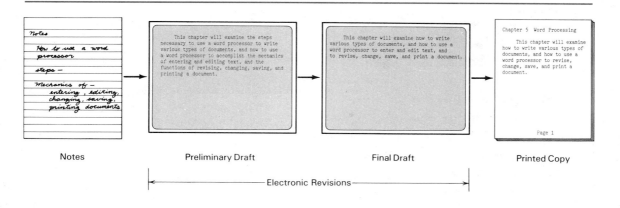

Notes Preliminary Draft Final Draft Printed Copy

Electronic Revisions

With a word processor, you do not have to retype the entire text in order to change or revise it. Revisions can be accomplished electronically.

Revising the First Draft

A word processor is an ideal tool for writing the kinds of documents that you first compose in draft form, then revise several times, and eventually print in final form. A word processor makes it possible to polish draft after draft — making changes, viewing the results of those changes, and occasionally changing your mind and turning to an earlier draft.

In this chapter, you'll see how much of the process of revising can be accomplished electronically, without physically typing draft after draft, as you would on a typewriter. We'll take you through various drafts of the report you just typed. Remember to save the document after each draft.

Search and Replace

Search and replace is a set of commands that searches a document for a particular word or phrase and replaces it wherever it occurs with another word or phrase which you wish to substitute for it. A common use for search and replace is to correct a consistently misspelled word. In addition, Search used by itself is sometimes more convenient than using the cursor-movement commands to jump quickly to a specific point in a document.

Another common use for search and replace is to reduce the tedium of typing many repetitions of a frequently used phrase. For example, this chapter uses the term *word processor* over and over. In early drafts of the manuscript, we used the abbreviation *wp*. Later, we used the replace command to substitute the full phrase for the abbreviation.

In the report you just entered, we purposely used the old-fashioned spelling of the word *type-writer*. To replace it with the more modern spelling, *typewriter*, use the following set of instructions:

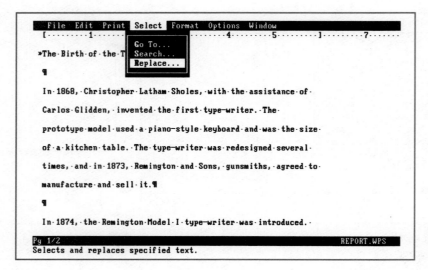

Figure 5.2
Select Menu.

1. Return the cursor to the beginning of the report by holding down [Ctrl] and pressing [Home].

2. Press [Alt] and S in sequence to activate the Select menu, as shown in Figure 5.2.

3. Now press R to activate the Replace command. A dialog box will appear. Type in *type-writer* in the "Search For" text box. Then press the [Tab] key.

4. The cursor will move to the "Replace With" text box. Type in *typewriter* and press the [Enter] key.

5. The Replace command searches forward from the cursor — that is, to the right of the cursor — until it finds the first occurrence of *type-writer*. When that text is found, it is highlighted. Figure 5.3 shows you what you will see.

6. To replace the highlighted text, press the [Enter] key. The highlighted text will be replaced by *typewriter*, and the next occurrence of *type-writer* will then be highlighted.

7. Repeat the process to change all occurrences of *type-writer* to *typewriter*.

Note that Replace searches forward from the position of the cursor. We asked you to start with the cursor at the beginning of the document to make sure the entire document was searched.

The Search command is similar to the Replace command, except that the text is only searched for, not replaced.

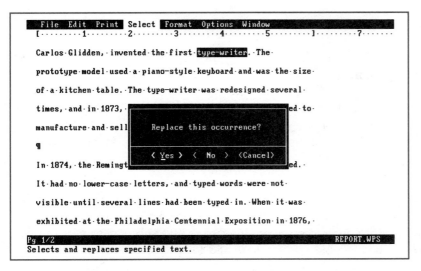

```
 File  Edit  Print  Select  Format  Options  Window
[·········1·········2·········3·········4·········5·········]·········7······
Carlos·Glidden,·invented·the·first·type-writer.·The·
prototype·model·used·a·piano-style·keyboard·and·was·the·size·
of·a·kitchen·table.·The·type-writer·was·redesigned·several·
times,·and·in·1873,·                    ed·to·
manufacture·and·sell   Replace this occurrence?
¶
                         < Yes >  <  No  >  <Cancel>
In·1874,·the·Remingt                          ed.··
It·had·no·lower-case·letters,·and·typed·words·were·not·
visible·until·several·lines·had·been·typed·in.·When·it·was·
exhibited·at·the·Philadelphia·Centennial·Exposition·in·1876,·
Pg 1/2                                              REPORT.WPS
Selects and replaces specified text.
```

Figure 5.3
Finding type-writer.

When either command locates a word or phrase, it is highlighted as a selection. You can quit executing Search or Replace commands at any time by using the <Cancel> button in the SEARCH dialog box. The highlighting will disappear, and the cursor will reappear in the position following the highlighting.

You can use the Search command to search for a word or phrase and then simply type in a replacement word or phrase, instead of using the Replace command.

You can also use the Replace command to automatically replace all instances of the sought after text. For example, to replace *typewriter* with *type-writer*, move the cursor to the beginning of the document, fill in the appropriate text boxes, and choose the <Replace All> button. After all instances of *typewriter* have been replaced, a message will appear, telling you how many instances were replaced.

There are several matching options when using Search or Replace commands. You can:

- Match text even when it is embedded in another word. For example, try searching for *key*. The Search command will highlight any word that contains *key*, such as *keyboard* and *keys*, as well as the word *key* by itself.

- Match whole words only. Repeating the above example when searching for *key* will produce no matches at *keyboard* and *keys*. Only the word *key* by itself will be found.

- Match an exact arrangement of upper and lowercase letters. For example, had you typed in *Type-writer* with an uppercase *T*, the Search command would have searched for that exact form and found only the instance in your title.

Writing Additional Drafts

A word processor makes it easy to change the appearance of text in order to enhance a document. In Works, you use commands in the Format menu to change the appearance of characters and paragraphs. For example, it is common to write a first draft double-spaced, so that you can proofread it and make corrections, then single-space the final version.

There are several ways to use the Format commands to double-space your report:

1. *By individual paragraphs.* Move the cursor anywhere in the first paragraph. Press [Alt], T, and D in sequence to double-space a paragraph. To double-space the rest of your report, move the cursor into subsequent paragraphs and execute the "Double Space" command for each paragraph.

2. *Copying paragraph formats.* After double-spacing the first paragraph, press [Alt], go to the Edit menu, and choose the "Copy Special" command. Move the cursor to the second paragraph and press [Enter]. A dialog box will appear. Choose the "Paragraph Format" option and press the [Enter] key. Continue moving the cursor and repeating the Copy Special command to double-space the remaining paragraphs.

3. *Entire documents.* To select the entire document, move the cursor to the first character in the document, hold down the [Shift] key, and press the [PgDn] key (as well as the down arrow key if necessary) until the document is highlighted right up to the end-of-document symbol. Then use the [Alt], T, and S sequence to single-space the entire document again.

Format Menu

The Format menu is divided into three groups of commands, as shown in Figure 5.4. The first group of commands applies to characters; the second to paragraphs; and the third to tabs. The paragraph group includes six commands for common styles, such as flush-to-the-left lines or double-spacing. In addition, the Paragraph command displays the PARAGRAPH dialog box, which allows you to change several paragraph formats at once.

This dialog box contains fields to set the left and right indenting of the paragraph, as well as the indenting of the first line of the paragraph. You may also set the line spacing of the paragraph and indicate how many blank lines should appear before and after the paragraph. The "Alignment" choice box allows you to choose whether the lines of the paragraph are to be set flush to the left, centered between the margins, flush to the right, or flush to both margins (justified).

In addition, one check box indicates whether the lines of the paragraph can be split across a page boundary. This allows you to keep special lines of text that

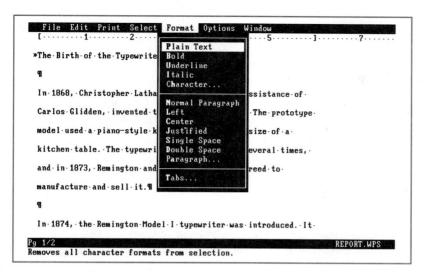

Figure 5.4
Format Menu.

should appear together on a single page. For instance, a table should not be broken across a page boundary.

Another check box indicates that a paragraph must appear on the same page as the paragraph immediately following. This is commonly used to ensure that a headline stays with the paragraph that it describes.

Page Breaks

Word processors have fixed-length pages, which usually correspond to the 11-inch-long standard sheet of paper. When a page becomes filled with text, a new page is automatically created. You can start a new page before the existing page is filled with text by inserting a **manual page break** into the document.

There are many circumstances in which you will want to begin a new page, rather than filling up the preceding page. For example, in a document that contains chapters, you will want each chapter to begin at the top of a new page. You can do this by inserting a manual page break before the chapter title.

Figure 5.5 shows two conditions called *orphans* and *widows* that can occur when using a word processor. An **orphan** occurs when the first line of a paragraph falls at the bottom of a page. A **widow** occurs when the last line of a paragraph falls at the top of a page. Works has built-in widow and orphan elimination.

After you have double-spaced your report, you can scroll through it and observe where the page break symbol occurs. The first one always appears at the beginning of a document. When the document was single-spaced, no further page break symbol occurred, because the short report wasn't longer than one printed page. When the short report is double-spaced, a page break occurs in the middle of the last paragraph. To insert a manual page break after the third paragraph of your report:

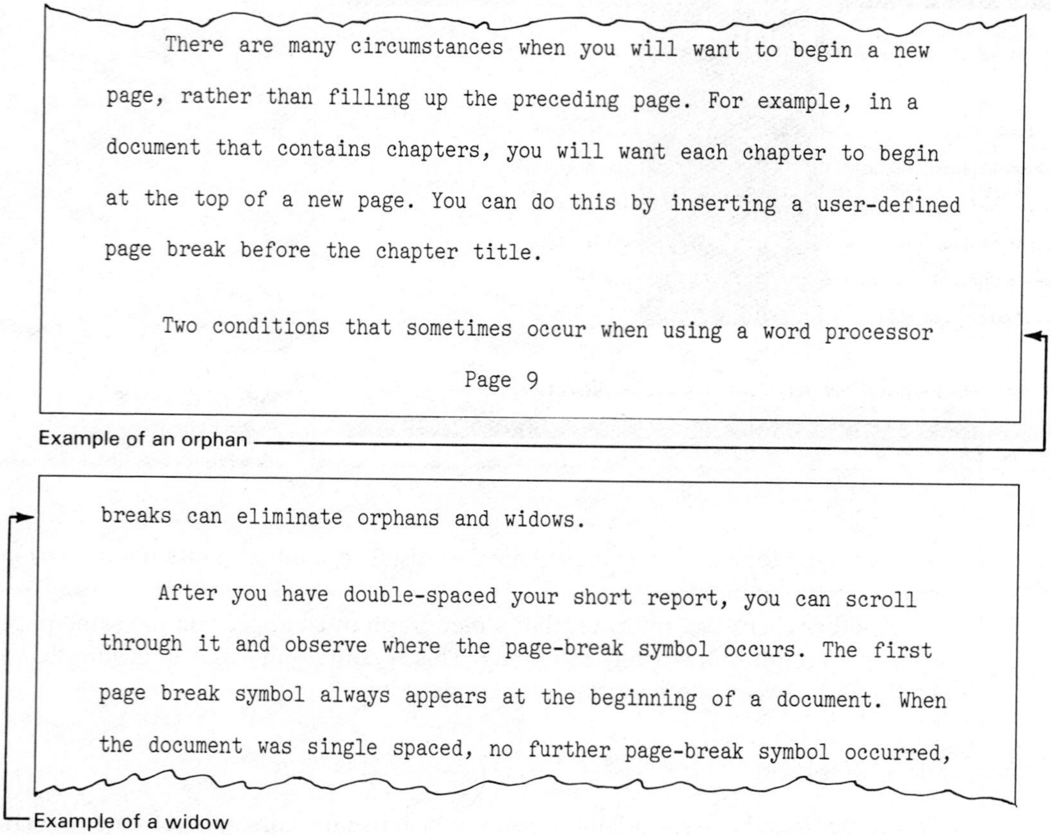

There are many circumstances when you will want to begin a new
page, rather than filling up the preceding page. For example, in a
document that contains chapters, you will want each chapter to begin
at the top of a new page. You can do this by inserting a user-defined
page break before the chapter title.

Two conditions that sometimes occur when using a word processor

Page 9

Example of an orphan

breaks can eliminate orphans and widows.

After you have double-spaced your short report, you can scroll
through it and observe where the page-break symbol occurs. The first
page break symbol always appears at the beginning of a document. When
the document was single spaced, no further page-break symbol occurred,

Example of a widow

FIGURE 5.5
Sample widow and orphans.

1. Move the cursor to the paragraph mark that separates the third and fourth paragraphs of your report. Press [Alt], E, and P in sequence to display the INSERT SPECIAL dialog box from the Edit menu, as shown in Figure 5.6. Choose the "Manual Page Break" option and press the <OK> button. A manual page break will appear as a dotted line across the screen, as in Figure 5.7.

2. A manual page break can be deleted, if you change your mind. To delete it, move the cursor to the dotted line. Then press the [Del] key. The display will appear as it was before the page break was inserted.

Figure 5.6
INSERT SPECIAL dialog box.

3. The shortcut method for inserting a page break is to position the cursor where you want the page break to occur and hold down the [Ctrl] key while pressing the [Enter] key.

Tabs

Tabs are stopping points along the horizontal dimension of a document. Used in conjunction with the [Tab] key, they mark the spot where the cursor will stop

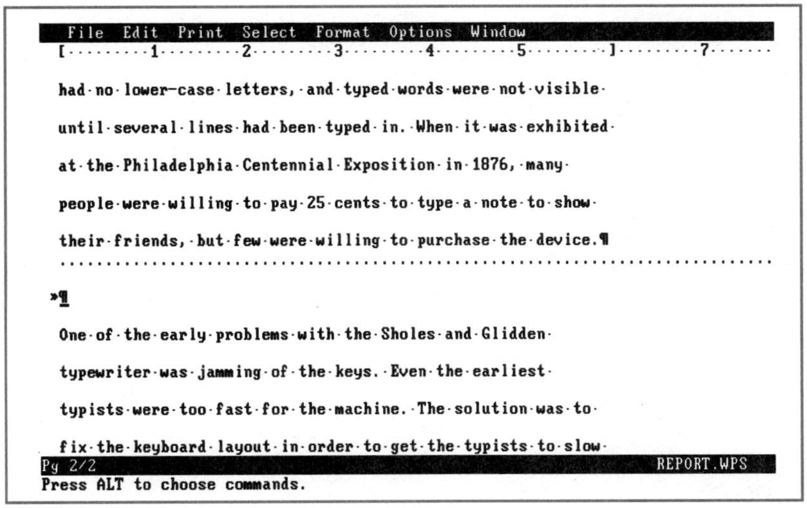

Figure 5.7
Manual page break.

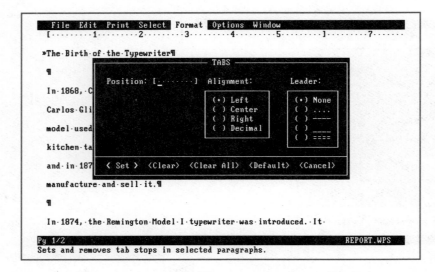

Figure 5.8
TABS dialog box.

when the [Tab] key is pressed. Tabs are used to indent outlines and align columns in a table. They are set using the TABS dialog box on the Format menu. Press [Alt], T, and T in sequence to display the TABS dialog, as shown in Figure 5.8.

In the text box captioned "Position", you can enter the character position where you want the tab stop set. If you enter 5, then a tab will be set 5 spaces from the left margin. If you enter a measurement like 1" (inch), then a tab stop will be set one inch from the left margin.

The choice box captioned "Alignment" allows you to specify whether text will be set flush left, right, or centered on the tab stop. If the alignment is decimal, then numbers will have their decimal points aligned on the tab. The ruler line across the top of the screen displays an L at each flush left tab stop, an R and C at flush right and centered tab stops, and a D at each decimal tab stop.

The choice box captioned "Leader" allows you to specify a character that will be repeated from one tab stop to the next. These leaders are used to draw the eye across a wide column to the next tab stop, as in a table of contents.

Name	Phone number	GPA	Major
Robert Blissmer	213-555-1212	3.72	Business
Roland Alden	617-444-1212	4.00	Engineering
Joyce Conte	413-621-8772	3.50	Psychology
Emily Woods	219-331-6134	2.75	Math
George Garcia	516-883-3210	3.00	Psychology

Figure 5.9
Sample information for table.

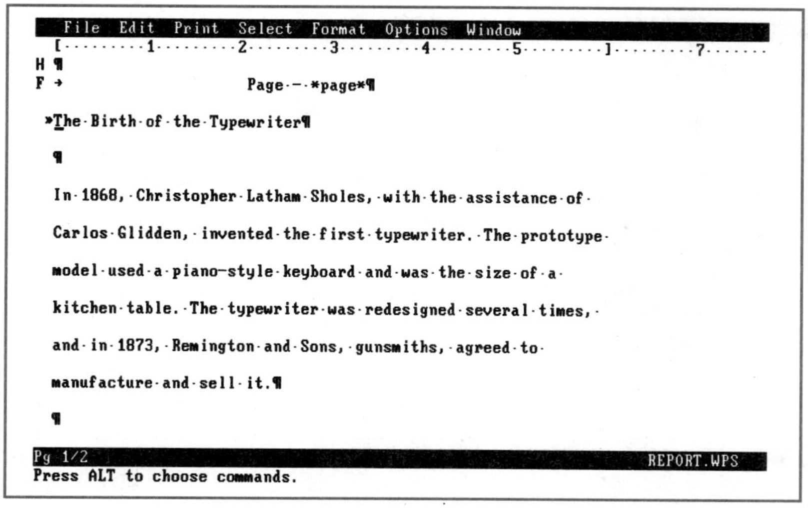

```
 File  Edit  Print  Select  Format  Options  Window
 [··········1·········2·········3·········4·········5········]·········7·······
H ¶
F  →                       Page·-·*page*¶

»The·Birth·of·the·Typewriter¶

  ¶

In·1868,·Christopher·Latham·Sholes,·with·the·assistance·of·

Carlos·Glidden,·invented·the·first·typewriter.·The·prototype·

model·used·a·piano-style·keyboard·and·was·the·size·of·a·

kitchen·table.··The·typewriter·was·redesigned·several·times,·

and·in·1873,·Remington·and·Sons,·gunsmiths,·agreed·to·

manufacture·and·sell·it.¶

  ¶

Pg 1/2                                         REPORT.WPS
Press ALT to choose commands.
```

Figure 5.10
Header and footer paragraphs.

The <Set> button causes the tab to be set, and the <Clear> button causes any tab at the position to be removed. The <Clear All> button will remove all tabs, and the <Default> button will install the default tabs, which fall every one-half inch.

To practice using tabs, create a document using the sample information shown in Figure 5.9. The names that begin in position 1 will form a left-aligned column. Use a right-aligned tab stop to right-align the column of phone numbers, a decimal tab stop to decimal-align the column of grade point averages, and a centered tab stop to center-align the major column.

Headers and Footers

A **header** is text that appears at the top of each printed page. A **footer** is text that appears at the bottom of each printed page. Headers and footers are entered into the document only once. The word processor inserts them on each page when the document is printed. You create the text for headers and footers by using the "Headers & Footers" command in the Options menu. To create a header for your sample report:

1. Press [Alt], O, and H in sequence to activate the "Headers & Footers" command in the Options menu.

2. At the beginning of your document, you will see two paragraphs displayed: one marked with an "H" and one with an "F" in the left margin. These are your header and footer paragraphs. They look like the example in Figure 5.10.

3. The default header is a blank paragraph; the footer contains the text "Page - *page*". It is often sensible to use page numbers as footers. The text

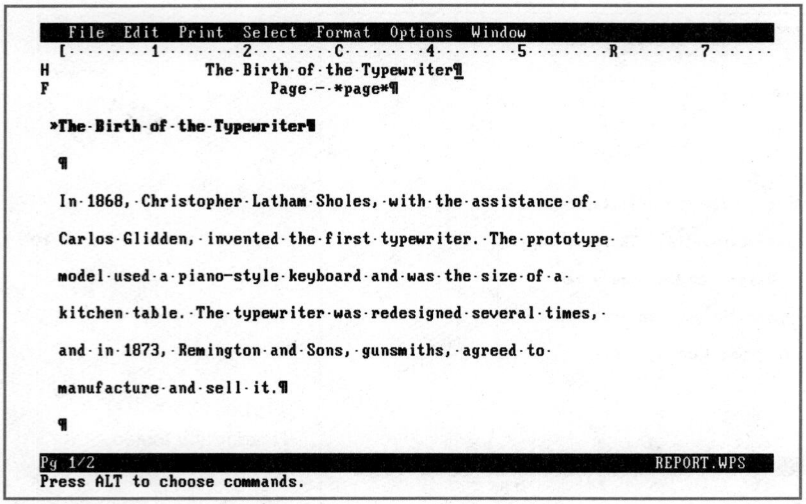

```
  File  Edit  Print  Select  Format  Options  Window
[·········1·········2·········C·········4·········5········R········7······
H                    The·Birth·of·the·Typewriter¶
F                        Page·—·*page*¶

»The·Birth·of·the·Typewriter¶

  ¶

In·1868,·Christopher·Latham·Sholes,·with·the·assistance·of·

Carlos·Glidden,·invented·the·first·typewriter.··The·prototype·

model·used·a·piano-style·keyboard·and·was·the·size·of·a·

kitchen·table.··The·typewriter·was·redesigned·several·times,·

and·in·1873,·Remington·and·Sons,·gunsmiths,·agreed·to·

manufacture·and·sell·it.¶

  ¶
Pg 1/2                                              REPORT.WPS
Press ALT to choose commands.
```

Figure 5.11
Sample header and footer.

"*page*" is really a special character, inserted using the "Insert Special" command from the Edit menu. It causes the page number to be printed. You can insert other special characters into the header or footer text, such as one that automatically prints the current date or time.

_____

All the usual paragraph formatting commands apply to the header and footer paragraphs. However, only one paragraph can be used as a header, and only one can be used as a footer. If you want a header or footer paragraph to be more than one line, you can press the [Ctrl] and [Enter] keys together to cause a line to break within a paragraph.

You specify header and footer options by using the Layout command in the Print menu. Press [Alt], P, and L in sequence to display the LAYOUT dialog box.

The "Header Margin" and "Footer Margin" text boxes specify the distance from the top and bottom of the paper that the header and footer text will print. The default is one-half inch. The "No Header on 1st Page" and "No Footer on 1st Page" check boxes allow you to prevent the header and footer from printing on the first page. This is usually done when the first page is a cover sheet.

The "Header" and "Footer" text boxes provide a place for you to type in a short sentence or phrase to be used as the header or footer. If you define a header or footer by editing the special paragraphs displayed by the Headers & Footers command you can ignore these text boxes.

The headers and footers do not appear in the screen display at the point where each page ends, only at the top of the document as the first two paragraphs. However, they will appear at the top and bottom of each page when the document is printed. Figure 5.11 shows a pair of header and footer paragraphs on the screen, and Figure 5.12 shows how they appear when printed.

The Birth of the Typewriter

In 1868, Christopher Latham Sholes, with the assistance of Carlos Glidden, invented the first typewriter. The prototype model used a piano-style keyboard and was the size of a kitchen table. The typewriter was redesigned several times, and in 1873, Remington and Sons, gunsmiths, agreed to manufacture and sell it.

In 1874, the Remington Model I typewriter was introduced. It had no lower-case letters, and typed words were not visible until several lines had been typed in. When it was exhibited at the Philadelphia Centennial Exposition in 1876, many people were willing to pay 25 cents to type a note to show their friends, but few were willing to purchase the device.

Page 1

Figure 5.12
Printed sample of headers and footers.

Switching Between Documents

It can be useful when drafting a document to be able to take information from an existing document and copy it into the draft you are currently working on. The Copy or Move commands can be used to transfer information from one document to another.

Works allows you to have up to eight files (documents, spreadsheets, or databases) open at one time. That means that you can work on one file and, without closing that file, work on another. However, Works displays only one file at a time on your screen.

To open another file, use the Open command in the File menu. The file you open becomes the active file and will replace the existing file on the screen.

For example, suppose you want to copy your own name and address and the date from the letter you wrote in the previous chapter into the report. If you are currently working with the report, open the letter document. To do so:

1. Press [Alt], F, and O in sequence to open the letter document. When the dialog box appears, choose the BLETTER.WPS file. That document will replace the report file on the screen.

2. Select your name and address, then press [Alt], E, and C in sequence to start the Copy command in the Edit menu.

3. Then press [Alt] and W to activate the Window menu. There should be two files at the bottom of the menu: 1 BLETTER.WPS and 2 REPORT.WPS. Press 2 to switch back to your report.

4. Move the cursor to the beginning of the document and press the [Enter] key to finish the Copy command. The name and address will be copied into your report.

In upcoming chapters, you will see how information can be transferred from a spreadsheet or database into a word processing document.

Additional Formatting

So far, we have been discussing how to change the appearance of paragraphs. You can also use the commands in the Format menu to change the appearance and placement of characters as well.

Recall from Chapter 3 the sample résumé. We showed you how to solve the problem of creating one. Now let's use the word processor to dress it up. First create a new document called RESUME. Then type in the sample text, but don't worry about formatting it yet. Everything you type should be flush left.

Now use the Format commands to center the appropriate paragraphs, as shown in the sample résumé. Next, select the title RESUME and make it boldface. You can apply more than one format to a character. For example, a word can be both boldface and underlined, so add underlining to the title RESUME.

Note that on the screen, Works always displays characters in one style and size; plain characters appear normal, and characters that will be printed with any special attributes appear slightly highlighted. You can't tell if a highlighted character is bold, underlined, italic, or some combination of these by its appearance on the screen. However, you can check exactly which formats are in effect for your current selection by looking at the status line at the bottom of the screen. In the case of the word RESUME, the status line shows BU for **b**old and **u**nderlined.

Now apply boldface to your name and to the subheadings EDUCATION, WORK EXPERIENCE, PERSONAL DATA, and REFERENCES. To finish off your formatting, underline "Job Objectives" in the first paragraph, as well as the dates under the WORK EXPERIENCE subheading, and save your document.

When you print your document, you'll see the correct styles, sizes, and positions, with one exception: some printers can't print italic characters. If your printer can't, it may print them with an underline to signify italic. You might want to print a sample of bold, italic, and underlined characters to see exactly what your printer is capable of printing.

Note that you can format before typing, so that when you type, the text has those formats. And whenever you insert new characters into already existing text, they will take on the same attributes as those to the left of the cursor.

Advanced Word Processing Features

So far, we have been discussing the features basic to virtually all word processors. These features provide enough functionality, flexibility, and ease of use to meet most users' needs. However, there are several advanced features that enhance the process of creating and revising documents:

- Some documents are very complex and require features like automatic footnoting, indexing, proportional spacing, multiple columns, and differing typefaces and styles.
- Other advanced word processing features are conveniences, such as spelling and style checkers, what-you-see-is-what-you-get displays, and windows.

Word processing.

The way in which these advanced features are implemented in various word processors varies enormously. You can determine whether or not any of these features are useful for your word processing tasks by going to a computer or software store and trying out word processors that offer them.

Writing Enhancements

Writing enhancements consist of (1) "electronic proofreaders" that help you to produce error-free documents, and (2) programs that automate the production of document components, such as footnotes, a table of contents, and an index. Some word processors come with built-in enhancements. If an enhancement is not built in, it can sometimes be purchased as a separate program which processes the document created by the word processor.

Spelling Checkers

A spelling checker, or spelling correcter, is a program that checks documents for spelling errors. It works by comparing the words in your document with words in a built-in dictionary. Wherever it finds a word that is not in the dictionary, it will stop and allow you to decide if an error was made and, if so, how it should be fixed.

Style Checkers

More sophisticated electronic proofreaders, often called **style checkers**, automatically hyphenate words, point out punctuation and grammar errors, and check your writing style for awkward or redundant usage and wordy phrases. These programs work like spelling checkers. They highlight the problem text and give you the choice of accepting or rejecting a proposed correction.

Contents, Footnotes, and Indexes

Other advanced writing enhancements enable you to create footnotes, tables of contents, and indexes. Most word processors offer footnoting capability. You simply type the number and the footnote as you type the text. Depending on your choice, the word processor automatically moves the footnote to the bottom of the appropriate page, the end of the chapter, or the end of the document. If you change the document, such as by adding or deleting text, the footnotes are automatically moved to the proper position.

A *table of contents* is a list of the major headings in a document, in order of appearance, along with their page numbers. Some word processors can automatically generate a table of contents with appropriate page numbers if you mark the entries you want to include.

An *index* is an alphabetically arranged list of topics with page numbers located at the end of a document. Some word processors allow you to mark words in the text for automatic indexing. Others automatically index every word in the document and allow you to exclude those that don't belong (such as *a, and, the*, and so on). The latter technique is much faster than marking each word individually.

Printing Enhancements

In the 1960s and 1970s, the design of word processors was strongly influenced by the electric typewriter. In those days, the market for word processors was in business offices; most users were secretaries. A "good" word processor's printed output emulated the output of an electric typewriter. In fact, a whole class of computer printers are called **letter-quality**, because their printing resembles the output of an electric typewriter.

If you compare typewritten and typeset text (such as the text you are now reading), you will see that typeset words are easier to read and more aesthetically pleasing. An appropriate mixture of typefaces and sizes can be used to create more interesting and informative written communications. However, typesetting is expensive. It is only practical when a large number of copies will be printed.

Advances in personal computer printer technology, first in dot-matrix printers and then in laser printers, have made it possible to approach the quality of typesetting at a comparatively modest cost. With a word processor that supports advanced printing features, it is possible to consider the following:

- Mixing styles and sizes of type to give greater impact to the printed word
- Changing the layout of the printed page; for instance, printing two or three columns of text
- Mixing graphics, such as photos, drawings, and computer-generated charts, with text

When typography, layout, and graphics are combined, the possible expressive power is far greater than can be achieved with the printed word alone.

Display Enhancements

Though the end product of word processing is a printed document, writing with a word processor also involves interaction with the display screen. Many word processors can print such graphic elements as boldfacing and underlining but cannot show these features on the display screen. However, advances in graphic-display hardware, such as add-on graphic adapter boards and special video processors, are now capable of enhancing a display.

What You See Is What You Get

The newest word processors offer **what-you-see-is-what-you-get,** or **WYSIWYG,** display. WYSIWYG means that the display on the screen is a very close representation of what will be printed on paper. Word processors that use this approach use graphics software to display text. For example, Microsoft Word accurately displays **boldface**, *italics*, SMALL CAPS, <u>underlining</u>, and superscripts and subscripts on the display screen.

Windows

Windows are a technique that word processors use to divide the display screen into variable-sized rectangles in order to view different parts of a document, or two or more documents, simultaneously. Windows make it easier to move text within a large document. With two windows, you can see two different parts of the document at the same time while deciding how you want to rearrange the text. Similarly, windows make it easy to simultaneously view and move text between two different documents.

Desktop Publishing

Even though advanced word processing features are quite useful, there is another group of users whose needs transcend word processing. As you learned in Chapter 4, word processing evolved to meet the needs of secretaries and writers to handle standard office functions. Similarly, desktop publishing evolved to meet the needs of publishers and graphic designers.

A WORD ABOUT
Laser Printers

The end result of word processing is usually a printed document. The quality of that printed document is directly related to the kind of printer used.

Laser printers offer near-typeset-quality text, the ability to print drawings, and higher speed than conventional printers. In the past, laser printers were limited to minicomputer and mainframe applications that needed fast, high-volume printing. These high-cost laser printers will continue to be used for such applications, but low-cost laser printers are now available for personal computer applications.

Personal computer laser printers can produce eight pages per minute, at a resolution of 300 dots per inch. They mix type styles and sizes, as well as graphic images, on the same page. By comparison, a letter-quality printer can print only one page per minute, can print only one type style and size, and cannot print graphics at all.

Laser printers create images by means of a laser beam that scans an electrically charged drum. As in a copier, toner or ink with an opposite charge sticks to the drum and is then transferred to paper by pressure and heat to create the finished image.

Laser printers are quite different from conventional printers. They are actually powerful, special-purpose computers designed for printing. They contain a microprocessor and large RAM and ROM memories, all needed to produce high print speed and resolution. For example, to print one page of graphic images at a resolution of 300 dots per inch, each square inch requires 90,000 dots. An 8-by-10-inch image requires 7.2 million dots. Since each dot is equivalent to one bit, it takes about a megabyte of memory to store a single page.

In its simplest form, **desktop publishing** involves the use of personal computers and page composition software to prepare and print a wide variety of typeset- or near-typeset-quality documents.

Desktop publishing is an attractive alternative to the traditional process of using graphic designers, typesetters, layout and production artists, and printers for a wide variety of organizational publishing activities. These include the publishing of:

- Books and technical documentation
- Newsletters, proposals, and résumés
- Financial statements
- Business forms
- Proof copies for commercial typesetting and printing

In these applications, the potential advantages of desktop publishing include:

- Reducing the number of steps and the time required to publish printed pages
- The ability to print on demand (when and where needed)
- The ability to produce customized documents
- A dramatic reduction in publishing costs

You are already familiar with the cycle of composing, revising, saving, and printing documents in word processing. Desktop publishing simply adds another dimension by changing the way documents are generated, formatted, manipulated, styled, and printed.

Word processing involves making decisions about the quality of the language: grammar, spelling, and the structure of sentences and paragraphs. Word processing makes writing easier, faster, and better. It isn't restricted to any particular kind of writing; it is used to help make *any* written communication clear, effective, neat, and error free. Word processors are full of features, such as search and replace, move, copy, and undo, which allow the author to revise the verbal content of a publication: words.

Desktop publishing, on the other hand, involves making decisions about the quality of the design: typography, the layout of words on the printed page, and the size and placement of graphics and illustrations in the text. Desktop publishing software allows the graphic designer to revise and change the visual content of a publication: its illustrations, layout, and overall style.

A typical desktop publishing program turns the computer into an electronic drafting table. Figure 5.13 shows the screen of Aldus PageMaker, a popular program. Text and graphic images from a variety of sources are inserted into electronic pages. The flow of text into columns and from page to page is controlled by the

Figure 5.13
Aldus PageMaker, a desktop publishing
program, uses a desktop metaphor for
its screen display.

user. Unlike a simple word processor, desktop publishing software can arrange text in multiple columns. Typography affects the size of the text. The size of illustrations, such as photos and graphs, can be adjusted, and decisions about where they will appear can be made. Electronic "grids" help the user to align images easily. Design elements, such as lines and boxes, can be fabricated on demand.

In addition to outstanding graphics capability, desktop publishing requires a mouse or its close relative, the electronic pen, in addition to a keyboard. The mouse allows the user to "point" at parts of the screen, giving graphically oriented commands, such as "move that text there."

Desktop publishing can also make use of another kind of graphic device, called a *scanner*. A **scanner** "scans" a drawing or photo and translates it into information that the desktop publishing software can use. The technology is quite similar to that involved in the wire photos seen in a newspaper. Without a scanner, desktop publishing software is limited to images that the computer generates itself; with a scanner, photos and artwork from many different sources can be incorporated into a design.

Although most desktop publishing programs do not yet allow color photographs to be handled effectively, many allow so-called *spot color* to be specified. For instance, if a headline is to be blue, with the remainder of an article in black, the software will print two separate pages: one with the headline only and one with the remaining text. A printer can then use these two pages to make two printing plates, to print with two different colors of ink.

Because desktop publishing requires so much graphics capability of the computer, it didn't develop until personal computers with advanced graphics became popular. For example, PageMaker first became available on the Apple Macintosh and is also available on MS-DOS personal computers with the Microsoft Windows Presentation Manager graphics software.

Table 5.1 summarizes just a few of the many differences between word processing and desktop publishing. Since almost everyone needs to communicate ideas by writing them down, almost every computer user will want to use word processing software. Simply printing a document prepared with a word processor, making a few copies, and then distributing them to friends or associates can be viewed as a form of small-scale publishing. When such publishing is no longer so

TABLE 5.1
Differences between word processing and desktop publishing.

Word Processing	Desktop Publishing
writing	publishing
editing	design
letters, term-papers	magazines, books, brochures
advanced typewriter	advanced drafting table
word wrap	automatic hyphenation
bold, italic	many type styles and sizes
text only	text and elaborate graphics
single flow of text	multiple columns, articles

simple or on such a small scale, desktop publishing software becomes useful. Such situations are commonplace in business, where formal and highly effective printed communications are often needed.

Although an individual author, using only words to communicate ideas, may never need to be involved with desktop publishing directly, it's not unusual for those words to go through the process of desktop publishing, at the hands of a graphic designer, before they finally reach the printed page. However, some authors need to use pictures, as well as words, to communicate a message. For instance, in the field of technical writing, graphics that accompany text are often needed to communicate complex information clearly. In such situations, the author needs to formulate ideas for illustrations while the text is being written.

Thus, the distinction between desktop publishing and advanced word processing software can be somewhat artificial. Of course, not everyone who uses a computer for writing will become a professional graphic designer; yet everyone can be an *amateur* graphic designer. Indeed, as desktop publishing gives more and more people the opportunity to communicate ideas with graphics, as well as with words, a kind of visual literacy may become almost as important to published communications as verbal literacy is today.

Review

Key Terms

Search and replace
Manual page break
Orphan
Widow
Tab
Spelling checker
Style checker

Letter-quality
What-you-see-is-what-you-get
  (WYSIWYG)
Window
Desktop publishing
Scanner

Discussion Questions

1. Why is a word processor a good tool for revising drafts of documents?
2. Name two occasions when you might use search and replace while revising a document with a word processor.
3. When might you want to insert a manual page break in a document?
4. Where are headers and footers located on a printed page?
5. What is the difference between a spelling checker and a style checker?
6. What advances allow word processors to emulate the printing quality of typesetting?
7. Name some of the ways in which printing enhancements can give the printed word more impact.
8. Why might desktop publishing software be useful to the author of a technical document?

Software Exercises

1. Write and print a two-page, double-spaced paper on the benefits of word processing. Include headers and footers.
2. Rearrange the report you entered in this chapter by moving the second paragraph to follow the third.
3. Search the same report for the term *Qwerty* and replace it with QWERTY.
4. Print a double-spaced copy of the same report. Before printing, make sure you have formatted the document so that no paragraphs are broken across a page boundary. In other words, look for the page break symbol. If it appears in the middle of a paragraph, use the PARAGRAPH dialog to keep the paragraph on one page.
5. Create a table like Figure 5.9. Use the Tab menu to set the tab stops for the table.

Computers in the Workplace

Few businesses remain untouched by computer technology. Today, many products are designed with the aid of computers and are built in factories with the help of computers. Some products are even built by computers in the form of robots. Many products have computers inside. Most large companies would drown in a sea of paperwork were it not for the computers in their offices.

1. Large offices rely on networks of computers for a variety of information management services such as electronic mail, database access, word processing, and decision support.

In the Office

In the past, programmers were the primary computer users in corporations. But now office workers use computers for retrieving information, budgeting and forecasting, and word processing.

2. Personal computers have made it possible for even very small companies to perform tasks like payroll, inventory control, and order entry using computers. These functions once required computers only large companies could afford.

2

3

3,4. Office workers used to share mainframe or minicomputers to perform computerized tasks. Today, most office workers use personal computers.

5. Although spreadsheet programs are extremely popular among office workers, most office surveys find that word processing is the single most important office use of computers.

4

5

Computer-Aided Design

Offering precision and speed possible only with computers, CAD systems have become essential tools for many engineers.

6. Aided by computers, design engineers can determine what modifications need to be made to a product before manufacturing begins, thus reducing production costs. Here engineers collaborate in the design of a coffeemaker.

7. In the fast-changing fashion industry, CAD systems enable companies to keep abreast of trends. This system can produce three-dimensional simulations and up to 16 million colors. It can also permanently store information about fabrics, colors, and designs.

8. Products large and small rely on CAD. This system is used in the design of recreational vehicles.

9. Shoe designs can be scaled from one size to another quickly when the designs are stored electronically.

Industry

From research to parts maintenance to automated assembly lines, computers in industry are
making a difference.

10. This Westinghouse worker is assembling a microprocessor-based hydraulic elevator control. The control
relies on a network of custom-designed, large-scale integrated circuit chips.

11. Computers are almost
as well suited to working in
the noise and bustle of a
warehouse as in the quiet
confines of an office. Although dust, temperature
extremes, and magnetic
fields can damage com-
puters and storage devices,
today's machines can be
made durable enough to
function in most ordinary
work environments.

12. Using a touch screen, a machine operator can enter
product part numbers. The computer is linked to a central factory automation computer that controls production for approximately 500 parts.

13. Scientific research benefits tremendously from computer technology. Researchers use personal computers to produce precise and almost instantaneous measurements, calculations, and analyses.

14. This "clean room" robot is designed for use in semiconductor fabrication, and features six axes of motion for precise movement. Specially designed robots like this minimize contamination and breakage of manufactured products, and reduce human exposure to hazardous materials.

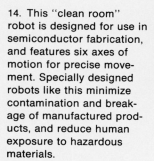

15. Numerically controlled (NC) machines can cut, stamp, drill, or grind nearly any material. For most manufacturing operations, NC machines are faster and more accurate than people. This NC cutting system is designed to cut fabric for the apparel, aerospace, automotive, and related industries. It can cut through many plies (layers) of fabric at once.

16. Quality control is another area where computers shine. Here a personal computer is used in the Krug winery in the Napa Valley, California to measure the chemical content of wines.

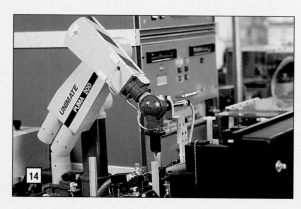

For Businesses and Professionals

17. This 173-store pharmacy chain uses computers for inventory control, prescription processing, customer records, billing, price updates, and to prepare reports for corporate headquarters.

18-20. With their capacity for tracking, storing, and instantly updating data, computers have become essential partners in fields ranging from law and finance to the oil industry.

21. Computerized merchandise management is a virtual necessity for today's retail stores. In addition to tracking inventory, computer programs can assist in placing orders, charting sales, preparing accounting statements, and much more.

22,23. Because of their tremendous versatility, computers provide start-to-finish assistance for many types of projects. Both the conceptual work of the architect and the ''nuts and bolts'' work of construction crews depend on computers.

24. A worker enters data to speed a shipment from this automated parts distribution center.

Publishing

Computers have not replaced the printed page. But they've done a great deal to enhance it.

25. Integrated publishing systems like this one combine text with photos and line art.

26. Computers have long been used to publish newspapers and magazines. The widespread use of computers at the Orlando, Florida *Sentinel* is typical of most large newspapers.

27. A complete desktop publishing system is likely to include a laser printer (foreground), a scanner (middle), and a fast personal computer with a high-quality display.

28. SnapShot, a software package from Aldus Corporation, can capture both live and recorded images from video cameras, VCRs, and video laser disks for later use in published documents. Captured images can be retouched or altered with special effects, placed on a page, and printed.

6

Introducing Spreadsheets

Preview   As you already know, spreadsheet programs are software packages that help you perform calculations you would otherwise do with a pencil and paper or with a calculator. A spreadsheet program is a general-purpose problem-solving tool: it does for calculating what a word processor does for writing. You enter the numbers and formulas, and the program shows you the results on the screen and in printed form.

A spreadsheet program also gives you instant feedback on the effects of any changes you decide to make. By recalculating the results automatically, it eliminates time-consuming revisions.

This chapter will show you both how to design a spreadsheet and how to enter numbers, formulas, and text. In the next chapter we'll look at how to use the spreadsheet as an analytical tool for solving number-oriented problems.

In this chapter, you'll learn:

- The concepts embodied in electronic spreadsheets
- Some uses for spreadsheets
- How to design and edit a spreadsheet
- How to build a spreadsheet model
- The process of entering text, formulas, and numbers
- How to change the appearance of a spreadsheet
- How to edit and correct mistakes
- How to save and print a spreadsheet

Spreadsheets and Problem Solving

Spreadsheet programs help solve problems that can be represented with numbers and formulas. A spreadsheet program creates an **electronic spreadsheet** — a computerized version of the traditional accountant's worksheet, which organizes numerical information in rows and columns. The spreadsheet can store numbers, formulas, and words; perform automatic calculations; and save the results for future reference.

Similar numerical analysis software has long been available for larger computer systems, but it required a programmer to define the structure of the problem and to enter the numbers and formulas. This meant that people like managers and accountants had to rely on their programming staffs to create and manipulate the programs. Because spreadsheets are interactive and fairly easy to use, they put analysis back into the hands of the individual. Anyone can simply run the spreadsheet program and begin solving a problem without having to learn a complex programming language.

Using a spreadsheet program.

		RECORD ALL TRANSACTIONS THAT AFFECT YOUR ACCOUNT							
NUMBER	DATE	DESCRIPTION OF TRANSACTION	TAX ITEM (√)	AMOUNT OF PAYMENT-DEBIT OR FEE (−)			AMOUNT OF DEPOSIT OR CREDIT (+)	BALANCE FORWARD	

Figure 6.1
Sample check register.

The first step in solving a problem, whether on paper or with a spreadsheet program, is to structure the problem and its solution. In the case of number-based problems, this involves building a **numeric model** of the problem. For example, to balance your checking account, you gather the existing data — the deposit slips and the canceled checks — and sort them in sequence. Then you add the amount of the deposits and subtract the amount of the canceled checks. Most people do this in a checkbook register, which consists of vertical columns for addition, subtraction, and the balance and horizontal rows for listing each check and deposit, as in Figure 6.1. But you could also build a spreadsheet model of your checking account. To do this, you type numbers, formulas, and labels into the electronic spreadsheet. Once the model is built and the data entered, the spreadsheet program takes care of performing the calculations.

What other kinds of models might a spreadsheet user build?

■ Financial planners use spreadsheets to make forecasts. For example, a manager could enter this year's sales figures and a formula for projected growth over the next five years. The program could then compute the sales forecast and adjust figures accordingly.

■ Managers use spreadsheets to help prepare budgets. As you saw in Chapter 3, alternative budgets can be analyzed by simply changing budget values.

■ Accountants use spreadsheets to do tax planning and to prepare income statements, profit-and-loss statements, and balance sheets.

■ Scientists use spreadsheets to analyze the results of experiments.

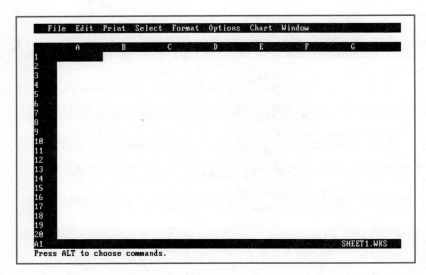

Figure 6.2
Initial spreadsheet screen.

A spreadsheet program is a general-purpose problem-solving tool because it is an excellent medium for:

1. Building a numeric model.
2. Asking "What if a value, or several values, in the model change(s)?"
3. Entering the new value(s) and watching the program recalculate the model.

The interactive nature of the spreadsheet program allows you to compare the results of alternative models.

The Electronic Spreadsheet

Let's look at a spreadsheet now, to see how the spreadsheet program works. This is a hands-on exercise. To begin, you should have the Works software up and running on the computer. To create a new spreadsheet:

1. Make sure that the NEW dialog box is on your screen and that the Spreadsheet option is chosen; that is, it has the bullet character beside it.

2. Press the [Enter] key to activate the <New> button.

What You Will See

Take a look at Figure 6.2. The electronic spreadsheet is displayed on the screen as horizontal rows and vertical columns. The intersection of each row and column is called a **cell**. In most spreadsheets, like this one, the columns are labeled with letters on the top margin, and the rows are numbered on the left margin. The cell where column *A* and row *1* intersect is called cell *A1*. The column letter is always specified first.

On the first line of the display you will see the menu bar for the spreadsheet program. Directly below the menu bar is the **formula bar**. The formula bar is used to enter and edit numbers, formulas, and words, or text. Near the bottom of the screen is the status line. The left side of the status line contains the **cell reference**, which tells you the location of the **active cell** (in this case, A1). The active cell is the cell that will be changed when you edit its contents in the formula bar.

Moving Around in the Spreadsheet

The Works spreadsheet is 32 columns wide by 256 rows long. Some spreadsheet programs have hundreds of columns and thousands of rows to accommodate very large models, such as the financial workings of an entire corporation. For instance, the spreadsheet of Microsoft Excel has 256 columns by 16,384 rows.

But even a small spreadsheet is too large to be displayed on the screen all at once. **Scrolling** brings hidden portions of the spreadsheet into view. There are several ways to scroll around the spreadsheet:

1. The up, down, left, and right arrow keys move the cursor around the spreadsheet.

2. To scroll vertically, press the [PgDn] key. The spreadsheet will scroll down one page and the cursor will appear in cell A21. Then press the [PgUp] key. The cursor will scroll back up to cell A1. (Note that the cell reference in the status line also identifies the location of the cursor.)

3. To scroll horizontally, hold down the [Ctrl] key and press the [PgDn] key. The spreadsheet will scroll one page to the right. If you started at cell A1, the cursor will jump to cell H1. Then hold down the [Ctrl] key and press the [PgUp] key. The spreadsheet will scroll one page to the left, and the cursor will jump back to cell A1.

An alternative to manual scrolling is the "Go To" command in the Select menu. It moves the cursor to a specific location in the spreadsheet. To use the "Go To" command:

---

1. Press [Alt], S, and G in sequence. A dialog box will appear. Type *AF256* and press the [Enter] key.

2. The cursor will jump to the bottom cell in the last column, cell AF256.

3. Now press the [F5] function key. That is the shortcut method for accessing the Go To command. Type *A1* in the dialog box and press the [Enter] key.

The Go To command has other uses, which we will explain later in the book.

When the cursor is located on a cell, that cell is active, meaning that you can enter a number, a formula, or text into it. The active cell is highlighted in reverse video.

Figure 6.3 is a summary of all the spreadsheet scrolling commands. Most of these are not used in the example problems, but feel free to try them out now, or later as you do the exercises in this book.

Entering Information Into the Spreadsheet

Suppose you want to use a spreadsheet to solve the problem of adding two numbers. A general-purpose solution to this problem would be to place the first number in cell A1, the second number in cell A2, and the sum in cell A3. Cells A1 and A2 contain the numbers to be added, and cell A3 contains the formula A1+A2.

1. Position the cursor to highlight cell A1. Then type the number *4* and press the down arrow key. The cursor will drop to cell A2, and the number 4 will appear in cell A1. (Note that numbers are displayed as whole numbers. We will show you how to change the display of numbers later in the chapter.)

2. With the cursor on cell A2, type the number *5* and press the down arrow key. The number 5 will appear in cell A2, and the cursor will drop to cell A3.

3. In cell A3, type the formula *=A1+A2*. The "=" character tells Works to interpret A1+A2 as a formula; it doesn't matter whether the letters you type are capital or lowercase. Now press the [Enter] key. The number 9 will appear in cell A3. Note that pressing the [Enter] key in this case does not move the cursor.

The spreadsheet program automatically calculates the sum, 9, and displays it in cell A3. However, the spreadsheet is more than just an electronic calculator. It keeps track of all the relationships between the various numbers and formulas. If a number changes, all the formulas that use that number are automatically recalculated. For example, move the cursor to cell A1. Notice that the number 4 appears in the formula bar. Now type the number *5* and press the [Enter] key. Notice that the number in cell A3 also changes, from 9 to 10. Changing the number in cell A1 causes the number displayed in cell A3 to change automatically.

Entering *numbers* into a spreadsheet creates **static values**. In other words, the values don't change unless you manually enter a new number. Entering *formulas*, by contrast, creates **dynamic values**. Dynamic values change automatically if the values that created them change. Formulas combine standard arithmetic operations (+, +, *, /), functions, numbers, and references to other cells.

We used cells A1, A2, and A3 in the previous example because it is conventional to add numbers in vertical columns. But we could just as easily use cell A2

To move	Press
Left one cell in range	[Shift] + [Tab]
Right one cell in range	[Tab]
Up one cell in range	[Shift] + [Enter]
Down one cell in range	[Enter]
Next unlocked cell	[Tab]
One block left	[Ctrl] + left arrow
One block right	[Ctrl] + right arrow
One block up	[Ctrl] + up arrow
One block down	[Ctrl] + down arrow
One screen left	[Ctrl] + [Pg Up]
One screen right	[Ctrl] + [Pg Dn]
One screen up	[Pg Up]
One screen down	[Pg Dn]
To beginning of row	[Home]
To end of row	[End]
To beginning of file	[Ctrl] + [Home]
To end of file	[Ctrl] + [End]
Quit Extend/Collapse selection	[Esc]

Figure 6.3
Spreadsheet scrolling keys.

for the first number, cell B2 for the second number, and cell C2 for the formula A2+B2. Horizontal arithmetic is often used in spreadsheets when the data are chronological. For example, a monthly budget might label 12 columns in a spreadsheet with the names of the months. In fact, horizontal and vertical arithmetic are often used together. To see how this works:

1. Move the cursor to cell B1 and type the number *5*. This time press the right arrow key. The number 5 will appear in cell B1, and the cursor will move right to cell C1.

2. With the cursor on cell C1, type the formula *=A1+B1* and press the [Enter] key. The number 10 will appear in cell C1.

3. Now press the left arrow key twice to move the cursor back to cell A1. Type the number *4* and press the [Enter] key. Note that both cells A3 and C1 are automatically recalculated, from 10 to 9.

Editing the Spreadsheet

The information you type isn't entered immediately into a cell. Until you press the [Enter] key or move the cursor to another cell, it remains in the formula bar. As long as a cell is the active cell, you can edit its contents in the formula bar. If you

Press	To
left arrow	Move the cursor left one character
right arrow	Move the cursor right one character
[Home]	Move the cursor to the beginning of the cell contents
[End]	Move the cursor to the end of the cell contents
[Shift] + arrow key	Select characters in the direction of the arrow
[Backspace]	Delete the character to the left of the cursor or the selected characters
[Del]	Delete the characters under the cursor or the selected characters
[F2]	Switch between edit and point mode

FIGURE 6.4
Spreadsheet editing keys.

want to change the information in the active cell, the process is like that of editing with the word processor.

Position the cursor on cell A1. To activate the formula bar, press the [F2] function key. The message line at the bottom of the screen will display "Edit formula." You can now correct an error in the active cell by using the left and right arrow keys, the [Backspace] key, and the [Del] key. For example, try pressing the [Backspace] key to erase a character and then press the [Enter] key. Note that, after you press the [Enter] key, the formula bar is empty and cells A3 and C1 change. The spreadsheet considers a blank as a zero for calculation purposes.

Figure 6.4 summarizes the spreadsheet editing functions. Most of these editing commands are not used in the example problems, but feel free to try them out now, or later as you do the exercises in this book.

Information is entered into the active cell (sometimes called **updating** the active cell), when you press the [Enter] key or move the cursor to select another cell. Recall from Figure 6.3 that there are several ways to do this:

■ Pressing the [Enter] key causes no cursor movement.

■ Pressing the up arrow key causes the cursor to jump up one cell. Pressing the down arrow key causes the cursor to jump down one cell. The left and right arrow keys will not cause cursor movement when the editing function has been activated.

■ Pressing the [Tab] key moves the cursor one cell to the right. (When the active cell is A1, pressing the [Tab] key jumps the cursor to cell B1.)

- Pressing the [Shift] and [Tab] keys simultaneously moves the cursor one cell to the left. (When the active cell is B1, the [Shift] and [Tab] combination moves the cursor to cell A1.)

- Pressing the [PgUp] or [PgDn] cursor-movement keys will cause the cursor to jump to the top or bottom of a column (unless it's already there).

Any cell can contain text instead of a number or a formula. Text is used in a spreadsheet for labels, such as row and column headings; to block off certain areas, such as by inserting a row of dashes between a column of numbers and a total; or to include explanations or other remarks.

The column width of the Works spreadsheet has been preset to 10 positions. (Later in the chapter, we will show you how to change the column width.) If you enter text that is wider than the width of the active cell, the remaining text will be displayed in the cell or cells to the right if they are empty. For example:

1. Move the cursor to cell A4 and type the letters *abcdefghijklmno*. Press the right arrow key. The first ten letters (*a* through *j*) will be displayed in cell A4; the rest will be displayed in cell B4 (if it is empty).

2. Now move the cursor to cell A1 and type the same letters *abcdefghijklmno*. Press the right arrow key. Note that only the first ten letters are displayed (assuming cell B1 is full).

3. Even though all of the letters you typed are not displayed, they are still stored in the appropriate cell. For example, if you move the cursor back to cell A1, you will see all of the letters you typed displayed in the formula bar. They are preceded by the quotation mark (") character which tells the spreadsheet that the text contains no numbers or formulas.

4. To leave the spreadsheet, press [Alt], F, and X in sequence. A dialog box will appear, asking if you want to save changes to SHEET1.WKS. Answer <No> and then press the [Enter] key to leave the spreadsheet and exit Works.

A Sample Spreadsheet Problem

Now let's use these fundamental operations to build a spreadsheet model. You are already familiar with the receipts that accompany consumer purchases. The general format of such receipts is illustrated in Figure 6.5.

In this example, you will practice the mechanics of designing a spreadsheet model; entering text, formulas, and numbers into a spreadsheet; changing

Quantity Description	Price	Amount
2 Box Disks	$29.95	$59.90
1 Box Paper	$39.95	$39.95
2 Magazines	$2.50	$5.00
Sub Total		$104.85
Tax (5%)		$5.24
TOTAL		$110.09

Figure 6.5
Sample receipt.

the values; watching the program recalculate the values; and saving and printing the spreadsheet.

Designing the Layout

The first step in building a receipt spreadsheet model is to design the layout of the model. Then, by figuring out the relationships within the data, you can specify the formulas in the model. Begin by using a paper worksheet to lay out the model. You can use the one in Figure 6.6 if you wish.

Although a paper worksheet is useful at the beginning of the design process, by the end of this section you will learn just how flexible the electronic spreadsheet is. Because the layout of the spreadsheet is already given in Figure 6.6, you can begin developing the formulas to calculate the Amount, Subtotal, Tax, and Total cells.

When working with spreadsheet programs, it is important to distinguish the *name* of a cell (its column and row coordinates, such as A1) from the *value*, or contents, of the cell (such as the number 4). In a cell that contains a formula, the value of the cell is the number that the formula results in. (When a formula references an empty cell or a text cell, the value of the cell is 0.)

Formulas use names of cells, numeric values, and arithmetic operations. Some of the arithmetic symbols they use may be unfamiliar to you. Spreadsheet programs use * instead of × to signify multiplication and / instead of ÷ to represent division.

When working with formulas, it is also important to remember the hierarchy of arithmetic operations. The rules are as follows:

- Operations inside parentheses are performed first.
- Multiplication and division are performed next.
- Addition and subtraction are performed last.

	A	B	C	D	E	F	G
1	Quantity	Description		Price	Amount		
2	– – – –	– – – –	– – – –	– – – –	– – – –		
3							
4							
5							
6	– – – –	– – – –	– – – –	– – – –	– – – –		
7				Subtotal			
8				Tax			
9				– – – –	– – – –		
10				Total			
11							
12							
13							
14							
15							
16							
17							
18							
19							

Figure 6.6
Paper receipt worksheet.

As the following examples show, the order in which operations are performed can affect the outcome:

$10 - 5 * 2 = 0$

$(10 - 5) * 2 = 10$

If you want an operation or a series of operations to be performed first, enclose it in parentheses. When one set of parentheses occurs inside another set of parentheses, the inner set of operations is performed first. Now let's go back to Figure 6.6.

To determine the amount multiply Quantity by Price. For the first item sold, the Amount will appear in cell E3. The formula for cell E3 is =A3*D3. (Although we will consistently use capital letters in cell references, the spreadsheet program will convert any lowercase letters you type into capital letters.) There are corresponding formulas for Amount in cells E4 and E5, but let's hold off on those for now.

The Subtotal in cell E7 is determined by adding or summing the individual amounts. An easy way to add in a spreadsheet program is to use the Sum function. Recall the brief description and use of functions in Chapter 3. A **function** is a built-in calculation. It consists of a function name followed by one or more arguments in parentheses.

To sum the individual amounts use the formula =SUM(E3:E6) for cell E7. The reason for including cell E6 in the SUM function will become apparent in an upcoming section called "Adding to the Spreadsheet." Note that in this case the Sum function contains only one argument; the colon is used to separate the beginning and ending range of cells.

Tax is computed by multiplying the Subtotal by 0.05, so the formula for cell E8 is =E7*0.05.

Finally, the Total (cell E10) is the sum of the Subtotal and the Tax, represented by the formula =SUM(E7:E8).

Building a Spreadsheet Model

Once you have figured out the layout and the formulas, you are ready to begin building the actual spreadsheet. Use the paper worksheet as a guide in setting up the on-screen spreadsheet.

---

1. Make sure the NEW dialog box is on your screen and the Spreadsheet option is chosen; that is, it has the bullet character beside it.

2. Press the [Enter] key to activate the <New> button.

Entering Text

To begin building the receipt, type *Quantity* in cell A1. Note that the word appears on the formula bar; nothing appears yet in cell A1 itself. A value will appear in the active cell only when you have either finished the entry by pressing the [Enter] key or moved to the next cell.

If you make any spelling errors, use the [Backspace] key to back up and delete the mistake, then continue typing. When you have finished typing in your first entry, press the right arrow key to move the cursor to the right. The word "Quantity" will appear in cell A1, and the cursor will move to cell B1.

Type *Description* and press the right arrow key. Your entry will appear in cell B1, and the cursor will move to cell C1. Bypass cell C1 by pressing the right arrow key again, and position the cursor on cell D1. Type *Price*. Continue on to cell E1, and type *Amount*.

To insert a dotted line in row 2, move the cursor to cell A2, type a quotation mark (") followed by 50 hyphens, and press the [Enter] key. Entering the quotation mark tells the spreadsheet that the hyphens are text characters, not minus signs.

To insert another dotted line in row 6, you could move the cursor to cell A6 and repeat the procedure, but an easier way to do it is to select row 2 and copy it into row 6. To copy cells A2 through E2 into row 6:

---

1. Position the cursor on cell A2.

2. Press the [F8] function key and use the right arrow key to extend the selection through cell E2.

3. Press [Alt], E, and C in sequence to choose the Copy command in the Edit menu.

4. Position the cursor on cell A6 and press the [Enter] key.

Enter the labels for cells D7, D8, and D10, as shown in Figure 6.6.

Entering Formulas

Move the cursor to cell E3 and type the formula *=A3*D3*. This formula tells the spreadsheet program to multiply the contents of cells A3 and D3 and display the results in cell E3. Recall that the "=" sign informs the program that the active cell will contain a formula, not text or a number.

After checking the formula bar for errors, press the right arrow key. Since cell E3 displays the result of the formula (rather than the formula itself) and there are not yet values in cells A3 and D3 to multiply, the value displayed is 0.

You could type similar formulas for cells E4 and E5, but that might lead to typing errors. Instead, let's observe the flexibility of the spreadsheet program in action and use the Copy command to copy the formula in cell E3 to cells E4 and E5.

To do this, select cell E3, then choose "Copy" from the Edit menu, as you did in the previous section. Move the cursor to cell E4 and press the [Enter] key. Note that you have not "cloned" or made an absolute copy of the formula in cell E3. Works automatically changes the cell references in the new formula to =A4*D4, because it uses **relative references** to locate cells. To put it another way, the original formula in cell E3 is telling Works to multiply the contents one cell to the left of E3 by the contents four cells to the left of E3. When you copy the formula to cell E4, Works still looks one cell to the left of E4 and four cells to the left of E4 to derive the correct formula.

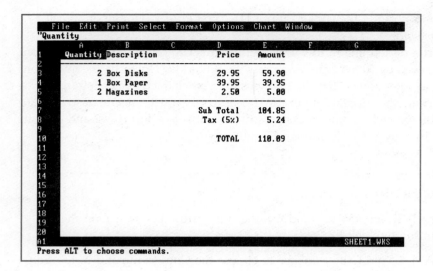

Figure 6.7
Receipt spreadsheet.

Copying relative references saves considerable time when you need several formulas that all use the same horizontal or vertical relationships. You simply enter the formula once, then copy it to the other cells that use the same formula.

Now repeat the command and copy cell E3 into cell E5.

Type the appropriate formulas for cells E7, E8, and E10. Note that the formula for cell E8 is slightly different from the others: it contains the number 0.05, in addition to a cell reference.

Entering Numbers

Entering a number into a cell is very straightforward. Use the sample data supplied in Figure 6.5. Move the cursor to cell A3 and type the number 2. Press the right arrow key and cell A3 will be updated to reflect your entry.

In cell B3 type the text *Box Disks*. Then move the cursor to cell D3 and type the number *29.95*. Press the [Enter] key. Now that enough data have been entered, numbers will appear in the Amount, Subtotal, Tax, and Total cells.

Move the cursor to cell A4 and type the number *1*; then move the cursor to cell B4 and type the text *Box Paper*. Next move the cursor to cell D4 and type the number *39.95*. Each time you change a cell, every dependent cell in the spreadsheet will be recalculated. Finish typing in the sample data from Figure 6.5. The receipt spreadsheet is shown in Figure 6.7.

Changing Formats

The analytical and calculating capabilities of a spreadsheet are certainly its most powerful and compelling features. But unadorned columns and rows of text and

Figure 6.8
Format menu.

numbers can be very tedious to look at. Like a letter or a paper done on a word processor, a finished spreadsheet is meant to communicate information to other people. Thus, the ability to create an attractive spreadsheet is becoming an increasingly important skill.

Before we complete the sample receipt, we will want to make a few changes to the format of several cells. In addition, some of the column headings do not appear to be correctly positioned over the numbers in the columns.

You can change the format (appearance) of cells by using the Format menu. Refer to Figure 6.8 as you make the following changes.

To change the format of cell D3 to dollars:

1. Position the cursor on cell D3, then press [Alt], T (for Format), and D in sequence.

2. The dialog box shows the default as two decimal places, so all you have to do is press [Enter], and the format of cell D3 will change to dollars.

Now, using the same procedure, change cells E3, E7, and E10 to dollars.

The dollar format displays a dollar sign, inserts commas in large numbers, and gives control over the decimal point. The comma format works like the dollar format, except the dollar sign is omitted.

Now change the format of cell D5 to commas:

1. Position the cursor on cell D5, then press [Alt], T, and C in sequence.

2. The dialog box shows the default as two decimal places, so all you have to do is press [Enter].

Using the same procedure, change cells E5 and E8 to commas.

Now you will want to use the Style command in the Format menu to right-align cells A1, D1, E1, D7, D8, and D10. To right-align cell A1:

---

1. Position the cursor on cell A1, then press [Alt], T, and S in sequence.

2. Use the down arrow key to move the bullet down to the Right option in the "Alignment" box, then press [Enter].

Continue using the Style command to right-align the previously mentioned cells. Note that the Right option leaves a blank space in the rightmost position of the cell. That way, information in a right-aligned cell won't run into information in the adjacent cell to the right.

Adding to the Spreadsheet

The receipt spreadsheet we have constructed appears to have no more room. What if we want to add more items? Again, the flexibility of the spreadsheet makes it easy to do so.

The Insert command in the Edit menu allows you to insert entire blank columns or rows anywhere in the spreadsheet.

Let's use the Insert command to add another detail line. First, select all the cells in row 6 by moving the cursor into cell A6. Now press [Alt], S, and R to choose the Row command from the Select menu. Next press [Alt], E, and I to choose the Insert command from the Edit menu. Note that inserting a new row causes the remaining rows to move down. All formula references in the moved rows are adjusted accordingly.

The new row needs a copy of the formula used to calculate the Amount cell.

---

1. Position the cursor on cell E5, then press [Alt], E, and C in sequence.

2. Move the cursor to cell E6, then press [Enter].

Recalculating the Spreadsheet

To see how the spreadsheet changes when new information is added, enter the following data in the appropriate cells in row 6:

4 Ribbons   7.95

Note that when the new price is entered, the figures in the Amount, Subtotal, Tax, and Total cells are recalculated.

Receipts of this nature usually also contain the name and address of the person to whom the sale is being made, as well as a date. To complete our receipt spreadsheet, let's add that information in the top four rows.

---

1. Move the cursor to cell A1. Hold down the [Shift] key and move the cursor to cell A5; this selects cells A1 through A5.

2. Press [Alt], S, and R to choose the Row command from the Select menu; this selects rows 1 through 5.

3. Next press [Alt], E, and I to choose the Insert command from the Edit menu. This will move the spreadsheet down, leaving five new blank rows.

4. In cell A1 type *Sold to* and in cell A4 type *Date*. Right-align both cells using the Format menu.

5. Use the Copy command to copy the dotted lines in row 7 to row 5.

6. Move the cursor to cell B4. While holding down the [Ctrl] key, simultaneously press + and ;. The current date will appear in the formula bar. When you press the [Enter] key, the current date will appear in cell B4. Remember that your computer must have either an automatic clock/calendar, or you must have entered the correct date at the Date prompt when you started the computer.

Another way to enter the current date or time in a cell is to use the Now function by typing =NOW() in the cell. Now returns a number for the current date and time. You must use the Format menu's "Time/Date" command to format the number.

Using the Now function causes the time and date to be updated automatically each time the spreadsheet recalculates, so its use is not appropriate for a receipt date.

Now type the name and address of Houghton Mifflin Company as shown in Figure 6.9

Saving and Printing the Spreadsheet

To save the spreadsheet before leaving the spreadsheet program:

---

1. Press [Alt] and F in sequence.

2. Choose the "Save As" command and press the [Enter] key.

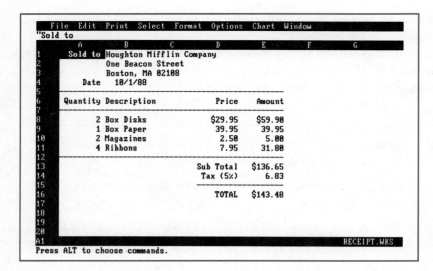

Figure 6.9
Redesigned receipt spreadsheet.

3. A dialog box will appear. Type in RECEIPT and press the [Enter] key.

The cursor will return to the previous position in the spreadsheet.

Before printing, make sure that a printer is connected to the computer and running. If you have forgotten how to set up your printer, review the section on printing in Chapter 2.

To print the spreadsheet, press [Alt], P, and P to choose the Print command from the Print menu. A PRINT dialog box will appear. To print one copy, press the [Enter] key.

Additional Printing Features

Using the commands in the last section, Works will print your entire spreadsheet. This is fine, because the Receipt spreadsheet is less than one page. However, for larger spreadsheets, you may want to consider some formatting alternatives before printing.

Often it is desirable to print just a portion of a spreadsheet. To do this, use the "Set Print Area" command. First select the range of cells you want to print. Then use the Print menu's Set Print Area command *before* executing the Print command. Once you have set a print area, it stays in effect. For example, to print the entire spreadsheet once again, you must first select the entire spreadsheet, then reset the print area.

Works divides a large spreadsheet into pages and prints the pages top to bottom and left to right. Pages break according to the usual 8½-by-11-inch page size. This doesn't necessarily produce a page break at a convenient location, so you

A WORD ABOUT
The History of the Spreadsheet

The spreadsheet has been one of the most important personal computer applications. In fact, the personal computer and the spreadsheet program were invented at about the same time, in the late 1970s. Although software that performed the same general tasks as the spreadsheet was available for mainframe computers long before the invention of the personal computer, the first interactive spreadsheet, called VisiCalc, became available in 1979 for the Apple II, one of the first personal computers.

VisiCalc was initially developed by Dan Bricklin and Bob Frankston as a graduate school project. VisiCalc took the computer world by storm because it offered one of the first practical reasons for ordinary people to buy and use personal computers. It also played a large role in helping Apple Computer, Inc. sell its computers to business.

VisiCalc was one of the first examples of business applications software for personal computers, but it was naturally constrained by the technical limitations of the Apple II. In 1981 IBM introduced its Personal Computer (PC), a computer that could have 10 times as much memory as an Apple II. Although VisiCalc was redesigned to run on the PC, it wasn't redesigned enough. By 1982 another early personal computer pioneer, Mitch Kapor, had developed a spreadsheet program called 1-2-3. 1-2-3 was very similar to VisiCalc but was designed especially for the PC and was fundamentally different in one important respect: graphics. 1-2-3 was designed to instantly display a chart from spreadsheet numbers. The ability to chart numbers and move back to the spreadsheet without losing one's concentration made 1-2-3 very attractive to professional finan-cial analysts (who were about the only people using spreadsheets in 1982).

It didn't take long for 1-2-3 to dominate the market for spreadsheet software. Mitch Kapor and the company he founded, Lotus Development Corp., were among the first examples of a new computer industry phenomenon. Each new generation of hardware, exemplified by the transition from the Apple II to the IBM PC, is accompanied by a new generation of software that often eclipses its predecessors.

By 1984 history was preparing to repeat itself when Apple introduced the Macintosh. Lotus did not want a competitor to do to 1-2-3 what 1-2-3 had done to VisiCalc, so Lotus prepared a new program, called Jazz, for the Macintosh. Jazz was more than a spreadsheet; it included a word processor, a database, and telecommunications software. Unfortunately its spreadsheet was less capable than 1-2-3. Meanwhile, another company, Microsoft Corp., was developing a spreadsheet called Excel. Excel was designed for the most powerful computers in the Macintosh family, and it offered many new features that 1-2-3, designed for an earlier generation of personal computers, did not. Lotus tried hard, but Excel has come to dominate the market for spreadsheet software on the Macintosh.

Now a new generation of personal computers is becoming available, based on Operating System/2 (OS/2) from Microsoft and IBM. Both Lotus and Microsoft would like to dominate the market for spreadsheet software on OS/2, but if history repeats itself, the most popular program for OS/2 may come from a company we have yet to hear from.

TABLE 6.1

Function keys. This table shows which function keys to press to perform various tasks. Many of the keys are shortcuts for menu commands.

Function	Key(s)
Edit	[F2]
Move	[F3]
Copy	[Shift] + [F3]
Reference	[F4]
Go To	[F5]
Next window	[F6]
Previous window	[Shift] + [F6]
Repeat Search	[F7]
Repeat Copy or Format command	[Shift] + [F7]
Extend selection	[F8]
Select row	[Ctrl] + [F8]
Select column	[Shift] + [F8]
Select spreadsheet	[Shift] + [Ctrl] + [F8]
Calculate Now	[F9]
Exit Charting	[F10]
View Chart	[Shift] + [F10]

can create your own horizontal and vertical page breaks. To create a horizontal page break, select the entire row at which you want the page break to occur. Then use the Print menu's "Insert Page Break" command. A page break mark (>>) will appear next to the selected row. Rows below the page break will print on the following page.

To create a vertical page break, select the entire column at which you want it to occur, then use the Insert Page Break command. Columns to the right of the page break will print on the following page.

You can also delete any page break you create by using the "Delete Page Break" command.

Additional Format Features

You have already learned how to change the alignment and format of cells in a spreadsheet. There are other ways to change the appearance of the spreadsheet.

Columns that contain different types of information often require different widths. For example, the leftmost column in a spreadsheet is usually used to label the rows. If it consists of a list of names, it is likely to require more space than columns of numbers. Also, instead of leaving an empty column to the right of "Description" as we did in the Receipt spreadsheet, we could have changed the width of the Description column.

Works defaults to a column width of 10. To change the width of a column, simply select any cell in the column you wish to change and go to the Format menu's Width command. In the dialog box, type in the desired column width and press the [Enter] key.

Column width can vary from 0 to 79 characters. When a column has a width of 0, it is called a *hidden column* and is not displayed or printed. You can redisplay hidden columns by using the Select menu's Go To command. In the "Reference" text box, enter the first cell name for the hidden column (if column B is hidden, enter B1) and press [Enter]. Then use the Format menu's Width command to widen the column.

Review _____

Key Terms

Spreadsheet program	Scrolling
Electronic spreadsheet	Static value
Numeric model	Dynamic value
Cell	Updating
Formula bar	Function
Cell reference	Relative reference
Active cell	

Discussion Questions

1. What is the main difference between numerical analysis programs for large computers and spreadsheet programs for personal computers?

2. Why is a spreadsheet program a general-purpose problem-solving tool?

3. How would you scroll quickly from any cell in the spreadsheet back to cell A1?

4. What keys would you use to move the cursor to the left after entering data into a cell?

5. Why is a formula said to contain dynamic values?

6. What key activates the editing function in the formula bar?

7. What is the first step in the process of building a spreadsheet model?

8. What is the hierarchy of arithmetic operations?

9. How does the spreadsheet program "know" that a cell contains a formula?

Software Exercises

1. On the Receipt spreadsheet, type your name and address into cells B1, B2, and B3 to the right of the "Sold to" in cell A1.

2. Change the format of the spreadsheet to calculate a 10 percent discount on all purchases. To do so, replace cell D13 with the text "Less 10%"; then replace cell E13 with a formula that subtracts 10 percent of the subtotal amount. Then change the rest of the spreadsheet so that the tax is calculated on the discounted amount and Total reflects the discount.

3. Change the spreadsheet to give a 10 percent discount only for purchases that total $100 or more. You can use the If function to test the value of Subtotal in cell E12. For instance, in the formula =IF(E12>100,E12*.90,E12), the first parameter, E12>100, tests if E12 is greater than 100 and, if so, the second parameter becomes the value of the function. E12*.90 computes a 10 percent discount. If E12 is not greater than 100, then the third parameter, E12, becomes the value of the function.

4. When you have finished making these changes, print and submit a copy of your Receipt spreadsheet.

7

Working with Spreadsheets

Preview   In Chapter 6, we introduced some basic productivity-promoting features of spreadsheets. This chapter will explore another facet of spreadsheets: using them as analytical tools for building and solving number-oriented problems. We will show you how a spreadsheet can help you explore business decision alternatives through *what-if* analysis. We will also characterize some common business problems in which intuition and judgment are more important than analytical thinking.

You'll also learn the technique for integrating information contained in a spreadsheet into other spreadsheets and into word processing documents.

At the end of this chapter, we'll discuss some additional features of spreadsheets that are useful for more sophisticated applications.

In this chapter, you'll learn:

- How to build analytical spreadsheet models
- Uses for *what-if* analysis
- How to transfer data to a word processing document
- How to build a forecast spreadsheet
- How to transfer data between spreadsheets
- Uses for templates
- Windowing techniques
- Linking spreadsheets
- Uses for macros

Putting the Spreadsheet to Work

Recall from Chapter 3 the problem we posed about managing a music store. How would you know whether you were managing the business well? Managing a business is a skill that involves intuition, judgment, and analysis. A spreadsheet can't help you with intuition and judgment, but it can help you with many of the tasks that are necessary to make analytical business decisions.

Suppose that, after graduating from college in January, you take a job as assistant manager of Music to Go — a small store in the local shopping mall that sells records, tapes, and compact disks. Although your job title is assistant manager, your boss is going to give you most of the responsibility for running the store, since she is a regional manager for seven Music to Go stores and can visit your store only once a week.

Music to Go started as a chain of stores in urban areas, and it has grown very fast. This rapid growth will provide an opportunity for you to manage an entire store. Unfortunately, Music to Go's corporate MIS (management information systems) department hasn't yet been able to expand enough to provide each store with the customized inventory and sales information needed to manage a retail store.

As you learned in Chapter 6, one of the benefits of using a spreadsheet is the ability to build **models**, or simplified pictures of real-world events. Models can help you forecast, analyze, budget, and plan. They can also provide insight into the relationships among such key variables as units, sales, and prices.

Building a Sales Analysis Model

Music to Go's corporate headquarters provides you with computer printouts, but it does not provide you with the kind of data with which you can compare alternatives. For example, the inventory printout you get from corporate headquarters has sales broken down by record label and by individual record (LP), cassette tape (CA), or compact disk (CD).

The problem with this printout is that the data are organized by record company and unit sales, which is useful for reordering and inventory control, but not for sales analysis by category and musical style. To come up with a new sales strategy, you need to answer the following questions:

- What kinds of music do my customers want?
- Do they want records, cassette tapes, or compact disks?

The information is in the printout, but it will take some work to extract it. You decide to take the printout and use your spreadsheet to summarize and analyze the data. Figure 7.1 shows the results of some unit sales figures that you derive from the printout for the month of January. Music to Go uses a unified pricing

	CD	LP	CA
Rock	440	120	360
Classical	240	200	240
Jazz	120	80	360

Figure 7.1
Music to Go unit sales figures.

strategy: all compact disks are priced at $13.99; records, at $8.99; and cassette tapes, at $7.99.

Ideally, your model should be built so that a simple change in one number changes all related numbers. Since you know that a spreadsheet can quickly and easily sum columns and rows, you decide to design the model as a grid similar in concept to Figure 7.1.

To create your sales analysis spreadsheet, make sure the NEW dialog box is on your screen and the Spreadsheet option is chosen (has the bullet beside it). Press the [Enter] key to activate the <New> button. Use the paper worksheet in Figure 7.2 as a guide in building your on-screen model.

Sales by Units

Before typing in any text, use the Format menu's Width command to change the width of column A to 15 characters. Then type in the appropriate headings in the cells indicated in Figure 7.2, and type in the prices in cells B2, C2, and D2.

Because you are going to be working with numbers in the spreadsheet, use the Format menu's commands to do the following:

1. Use the Style command to right-align cell B1 and cells B3 through E3.

2. Change the format of cells B2, C2, and D2 to dollars with two decimal places.

3. Select the range of cells B6 through E10 by positioning the cursor on cell B6, holding down the [Shift] key, then pressing the arrow keys. Change the format of the selection to General.

To insert a line of dashes in row 4, we will show you an alternative to the technique you used in Chapter 6.

1. Move the cursor to cell A4, type in a quotation mark (") followed by 15 hyphens, and press the [Enter] key. Then move the cursor to cell B4 and select cells B4 through E4 by pressing the [Shift] and right arrow keys. Type in a quotation mark followed by 10 hyphens and press the [Ctrl] and [Enter] keys. Then use the Copy command in the Edit menu to copy row 4 to rows 9 and 11. (Recall from Chapter 6 that you first select a group of cells, press [Alt], E, and C to activate the Copy command, then move the cursor to the new location and press [Enter].)

	A	B	C	D	E	F	G
1	Music To Go	Prices					
2	Sales Analysis	$13.99	$8.99	$7.99			
3		CD	LP	CA	Total		
4	– – – – –	– – – – –	– – – – –	– – – – –	– – – – –		
5		In Units					
6	Rock						
7	Classical						
8	Jazz						
9	– – – – –	– – – – –	– – – – –	– – – – –	– – – – –		
10	Total						
11	– – – – –	– – – – –	– – – – –	– – – – –	– – – – –		
12							
13							
14							
15							
16							
17							
18							
19							

Figure 7.2
Worksheet for sales analysis.

2. Now let's enter some formulas to sum the rows and columns. Cell B10 is the sum of cells B6 through B8; type =SUM(B6:B8) in cell B10. Use the Copy command to copy cell B10 to cells C10, D10, and E10.

   Similarly, cell E6 is the sum of cells B6 through D6, and the Copy command can be used to replicate that formula in cells E7 and E8.

3. Use the sample data supplied in Figure 7.1 to enter data for cells B6 through D8. When you are finished, check to make sure that the appropriate sums appear in the totals rows and columns.

	A	B	C	D	E	F	G
1	Music To Go	Prices					
2	Sales Analysis	$13.99	$8.99	$7.99			
3		CD	LP	CA	Total		
4	— — — —	— — — —	— — — —	— — — —	— — — —		
5		In Units					
6	Rock	440	120	360	920		
7	Classical	240	200	240	680		
8	Jazz	120	80	360	560		
9	— — — —	— — — —	— — — —	— — — —	— — — —		
10	Total	800	400	960	2,160		
11	— — — —	— — — —	— — — —	— — — —	— — — —		
12		In Dollars					
13	Rock						
14	Classical						
15	Jazz						
16	— — — —	— — — —	— — — —	— — — —	— — — —		
17	Total						
18	— — — —	— — — —	— — — —	— — — —	— — — —		
19							

Figure 7.3
Sales by dollar amount.

With the resulting design, you can see that it is easy to change any number in the spreadsheet (such as an individual category of units sold) and have the related numbers adjust automatically.

Before continuing, be sure to save the spreadsheet and name it MUSIC1.

Sales by Dollar Amount

Now you are ready to translate unit sales into dollar sales. To simplify building and using the spreadsheet, you will add another set of data to MUSIC1. Take a look at Figure 7.3.

Notice that using this layout, you don't have to re-enter certain column headings, just add "In Dollars" in cell B12. You can also copy certain information from existing cells. For example, move the cursor to cell A6, select cells A6 through A11, and activate the Copy command in the Edit menu.

Move the cursor to cell A13 and press the [Enter] key. The titles in cells A6 through A11 will be copied to their new locations.

Instead of numbers in the rectangular grid of cells B13 through E17, you need to enter formulas. For example, the dollar sales for rock CDs equal price multiplied by unit sales. You could type 13.99 in all your formulas, but what if you need to change the price in the future?

Now you can see the reason for entering prices in cells B2, C2, and D2. Doing so gives you the flexibility to change the price without having to rewrite the formula. Instead of using a constant number, such as 13.99, in formulas, you can use a cell reference. Thus, the formula for cell B13 is cell B6 multiplied by cell B2.

Before you enter the formula =B6*B2 into cell B13, ask yourself, "What if I want to copy that formula into cell B7?" If you copied it as is, Works would adjust the formula to cell B7 multiplied by cell B3 (=B7*B3), because Works assumes that the cell names in the formula are relative references. But the price is in cell B2, *not* in cell B3.

Absolute References

There is another type of reference called an **absolute reference** — a cell reference that does not change. You can use absolute references to tell Works *not* to adjust the formula when it is copied. You create an absolute reference by placing a dollar sign ($) before the cell letter, number, or both.

1. So, for cell B13, enter the formula =B6*B2. Now copy cell B13 into cell B14. Works will adjust the first cell reference (B6) but leave the second cell reference (B2) absolute. The resulting formula in cell B14 will be =B7*B2.

2. Copy the formula again into cell B15. Then enter similar formulas with absolute references into cells C13 and D13, and copy those formulas into cells C14, C15, D14, and D15.

3. For the totals, you can copy the totals formulas used in the "In Units" section of the spreadsheet. First, move the cursor to cell E6, select cells E6 through E8, and copy those cells into cells E13 through E15. Then copy cells B10 through E10 into cells B17 through E17.

4. Also, because you are working with dollar amounts instead of integer numbers, as you did in the last section, select the rectangular grid of cells B13 through E17, and use the Format menu's Dollar command to change the format of the cells to dollar with zero decimal places.

Remember, periodically saving your spreadsheet is always a good idea.

What-If Analysis

Not only can you now compare various figures in both unit and dollar sales, you can also compare alternatives. Using a spreadsheet to compare alternatives is often called *what-if* **analysis**. Because the spreadsheet keeps track of the relationships among the numbers, you can look at alternatives by asking, "What if a certain number changes?" and letting the program recalculate your spreadsheet.

For example, what if Music to Go raised the price of compact disks to $15.99? All you need to do in this case is to change the CD price in cell B2 to 15.99 and watch the spreadsheet recalculate all the relevant numbers.

Sales by Percentage

Although the dollar amounts are useful, you'd really like to answer questions like "What percentage of sales is made up of compact disks?" or "What percentage of sales is made up of jazz LPs?" As you might have already guessed, it's easy to add yet another section to your spreadsheet. Take a look at Figure 7.4.

---

1. Copy cells A13 through A18 into cells A20 through A25. Then format cells B20 through E24 as percentages with zero decimal places. Percentages of sales calculations are the individual dollar amounts in each category (such as classical LPs) divided by total sales. In this case, total sales (cell E17) becomes an absolute reference, so it should be written as E17 in your formulas.

2. Start with the formula =B13/E17 in cell B20. Then use the Copy command to replicate the formula through the remainder of the cells. Finally, copy the totals formulas as you did in the last section. Don't forget to format the copied cells as percentages.

Freezing Titles

After completing the last section, you will notice that it's impossible to see your column heads when you scroll vertically. A way to keep the titles in view while scrolling is called **freezing titles**. The "Freeze Titles" command in the Options menu lets you lock selected rows or columns while you scroll. In the MUSIC1 spreadsheet, move the cursor to cell A5, then activate the "Freeze Titles" command. Now when you scroll down, the column heads will stay stationary, and you can view any of the three sections of your spreadsheet.

Building a sales analysis model allows you to do two things: (1) eliminate the tedium of manual calculations and (2) ask *what-if* questions by comparing alternative models. In breaking down sales by category and musical style, you can more easily answer the questions we posed earlier, such as "What kinds of music do my customers want?" and "Do they want records, cassette tapes, or compact disks?"

	A	B	C	D	E	F	G
1	Music To Go	Prices					
2	Sales Analysis	$13.99	$8.99	$7.99			
3		CD	LP	CA	Total		
4	– – – –	– – – –	– – – –	– – – –	– – – –		
5		In Units					
6	Rock	440	120	360	920		
7	Classical	240	200	240	680		
8	Jazz	120	80	360	560		
9	– – – –	– – – –	– – – –	– – – –	– – – –		
10	Total	800	400	960	2,160		
11		– – – –	– – – –	– – – –	– – – –		
12		In Dollars					
13	Rock	$6,156	$1,079	$2,876	$10,111		
14	Classical	$3,358	$1,798	$1,918	$7,037		
15	Jazz	$1,679	$719	$2,876	$5,274		
16		– – – –	– – – –	– – – –	– – – –		
17	Total	$11,192	$3,596	$7,670	$22,485		
18	– – – –	– – – –	– – – –	– – – –	– – – –		
19		In Percent	(of Sales)				
20	Rock						
21	Classical						
22	Jazz						
23	– – – –	– – – –	– – – –	– – – –	– – – –		
24	Total						
25		– – – –	– – – –	– – – –	– – – –		

Figure 7.4
Sales by percent.

Spreadsheets and Integration

Recall from Chapter 1 that Works is an integrated program. This means that you can easily copy data from one of the programs to another. For example, the Works spreadsheet allows you to copy information from one spreadsheet to another or to a word processing document. Before beginning the next section, save MUSIC1 and exit Works.

Writing a Memo

Suppose you wanted to send a memo to the regional manager showing her the breakdown of sales in dollar amounts by product type and music category. It's easy to copy the sales information from the MUSIC1 spreadsheet to a word processing document. Here's how:

1. Use the word processor to write your memo (use Figure 7.5 as a sample). Call your file MEMO and save it.

2. While you are still in the word processor, use the Open command in the File menu to open MUSIC1. The memo on the screen will be replaced by the spreadsheet.

3. Select the rectangular grid of cells A13 through E17, then copy the cells with the Copy command in the Edit menu.

4. Go to the Window menu. At the bottom of the menu you will see a list of file names that should include MUSIC1 and MEMO. Switch to MEMO by highlighting its name and pressing the [Enter] key.

When you copy data from the spreadsheet to the word processor, Works arranges the data into a table of rows and columns. The program separates each column with a tab stop character and places a paragraph mark at the end of each row. The tab stops should correspond to the width of the spreadsheet cells. Position the cursor at the left margin just below the statement "Following are the sales results for January:" and press [Enter]. You may have to do some rearranging to properly align the sales figures into a rectangular grid.

Building a Sales Forecast Model

The regional manager was quite impressed with your sales figures. After all, she has never seen a memo quite so elegant. When she makes her weekly trip to your store, she asks, "Can you do a monthly sales forecast for the rest of the year? In our sales meeting last week, the vice president of marketing was forecasting a 2 percent per month growth rate for the remainder of the year. I'd like to see what

Date: (Today's date)
To: Regional Manager
From: (your name)
Subject: Sales for January

Following are the sales results for January

(Data from spreadsheet copied here.)

Based on these results, I'm looking forward to a great February.

Figure 7.5
Sample memo.

Personnel	Sales
Asst. Mgr. $1,250/mo.	Sales Growth 2%/mo.
Clerks 3 @ 1,000/mo.	Cost of Sales 60%

Rent: $1,400/mo. or 6% of sales, whichever is higher.

Figure 7.6
Assumptions.

that looks like for this store." She hands over her notes (Figure 7.6) on the vice president's assumptions and assigns you the task of forecasting your store's overall sales-and-profit picture for the remainder of the year.

The assumptions include the number of employees and average wages, a rent formula ($1,400, or 6 percent of sales, whichever is higher), and the growth rate forecast. According to the vice president's best estimates, sales should increase by 2 percent a month for the remainder of the year; meanwhile, the cost of sales is estimated to remain constant at 60 percent of sales.

As in the last chapter, building the model begins by figuring out the layout of the spreadsheet, then developing the formulas. Figure 7.7 shows a partial layout of the spreadsheet forecast model. The model will project dollar amounts for each month, as well as a total for the year, and you will use it to look at the effects of variations in sales and expenses. Notice that it is divided into two main sections: "Assumptions" and "Categories."

The Assumptions section allows you to change numbers easily without having to rewrite the formulas, as you did in the last spreadsheet. For example, instead of using an absolute number, such as 2 percent in the formulas for calculating growth in sales, you can use a cell reference. This enables you to write a general-purpose formula that can accommodate any change in growth. If the estimated growth rate should change to 1.5 percent, for example, you have only one cell to change, and all cells containing references to it are automatically changed.

Begin building your spreadsheet (call it MUSIC2) by copying the titles and information shown in Figure 7.7. When you type the wage formulas into cells E5 and E6, use the number of employees multiplied by the wage in Figure 7.6.

Don't forget to enter all 12 months plus a Total column in row 9. When you enter a date, such as a month name like January, Works automatically converts it to the short form (Jan) and right-aligns it in the cell. When you enter a percentage figure, such as 2%, Works converts it to the fractional form (0.02) for calculations; however, Works still displays 2% in the cell.

Now let's concentrate on filling in column B. Then we'll develop the formulas for the rest of the columns.

Sales for January (cell B12) come from the MUSIC1 spreadsheet. You can copy them into the forecast in much the same way you copied data into the word processing document. However, there is a difference. The cell that stores the sales total is a formula, and you want to copy only the *value* of the cell, not the formula itself. To copy the value, use the "Copy Special" command in the Edit menu.

If MUSIC1 is already open, use the Window menu to switch to it. Otherwise, use the Open command in the File menu. In the MUSIC1 spreadsheet, select cell E17, then activate the "Copy Special" command. Now switch back to MUSIC2, move the cursor to cell B12, and press [Enter]. A dialog box will appear; press [Enter] to choose the "Values Only" option, and the value for the January sales figure will be copied into the cell.

Gross profit equals sales minus the cost of sales; the cost of sales is equal to sales multiplied by the cost of sales percentage figure (60 percent). In other words,

	A	B	C	D	E
1	Music To Go				
2	Sales Forecast				
3					
4	Assumptions		Employees	No	Wages
5	Growth (per mo.)	2%	Asst. Mgr.	1	$1,250
6	Cost of Sales	60%	Clerks	3	$3,000
7			Total	4	$4,250
8	Rent is 6% of	Sales or $1,800	whichever is	greater.	
9	Category	Jan	Feb	Mar	Apr
10	------	------	------	------	------
11	Revenue				
12	Sales				
13	Cost of Sales				
14	------	------	------	------	------
15	Gross Profit				
16	------	------	------	------	------
17	Expenses				
18	Rent				
19	Wages				
20	Telephone				
21	Advertising				
22	Supplies				
23	------	------	------	------	------
24	Total Expenses				
25	------	------	------	------	------
26	Net Profit				

Figure 7.7
Sales forecast model.

the formula for cell B13 is =B12*B6. The formula for cell B15 is =B12-B13.

Except for rent (which will be based on a formula) and wages (derived from cell E7), the expense categories are straightforward numbers, as follows:

Telephone	$400
Advertising	500
Supplies	800

Enter these numbers into the appropriate cells.

Recall the use of functions from Chapter 3. The formula for rent is $1,400 per month, or 6 percent of sales, whichever is greater. To write this formula, we use the **IF function**, which tests a value and then generates one of two possible results based on the test.

Write the formula for cell B18 as =IF(B12*6%<=1400,1400,B12*6%). This formula says: if 6 percent of sales are less than or equal to 1,400, use 1,400; otherwise use 6 percent of sales.

Total expenses are the sum of cells B18 through B22; net profit is gross profit (cell B15) minus total expenses (cell B24).

February's sales in cell C12 are computed by increasing January's sales in cell B12 by the 2 percent figure in cell B5. In general, to increase a number n by a percentage p, we can multiply $n*p$ and add the result to n. Thus, the formula for calculating cell C12 is =(B12*B5)+B12.

The same general formula can be applied to forecasting increases in sales for March, April, May, and so on. In fact, because we've written the formula with a relative cell reference for B12, we can copy the formula into those cells, and Works will adjust the cell reference.

In addition, because we've used an absolute reference to the percentage cell B5, we can change the value in cell B5 without changing the formula for the percentage increase.

By now you should have built and formatted the MUSIC2 spreadsheet. If you have not done so, go back and make sure your spreadsheet is completed before proceeding to the next section.

What If You Change the Forecast?

What-if analysis lets you play with the numbers in the spreadsheet to explore alternative outcomes, such as best and worst cases. You can ask such questions as "What if sales increase by only 1.5 percent per month?" or "What if sales increase by 3 percent per month?" The answers to such questions are simple enough to find out.

1. Increase the cost of sales figure in cell B6 from 60 percent to 65 percent. What happens to the net profit figures in row 26?

2. Assume your growth rate is really 4 percent instead of 2 percent, by entering 4% into cell B5. If the growth rate were that high, you would probably need three more employees to work at the store.

3. Change cell D6 to 6 and see what happens to the net profit figures in row 26. What happens if you can get by with only five employees?

As you can see, the speed of the spreadsheet allows you to easily explore many variations on how to run your music store. Today many businesses use *what-if* analysis to look further into the future than might otherwise be possible. Managers use spreadsheets to anticipate different business conditions and develop suitable long-range strategies.

What the Spreadsheet Can't Do

Of course, as assistant manager of Music to Go, you should have a feel for music and the music business. To be successful, you will need to listen to the radio, go to concerts, and understand what is new and fashionable. And you must also

---

A WORD ABOUT
Spreadsheets and Documentation

Does the following look familiar to you? (Hint: Look back at column F of the BUDGET spreadsheet you used in Chapter 3.)

```
=F5-F6
=PMT(F7,F9/12,F8)
```

What does it mean? That's exactly the problem. Some spreadsheets will be used for years to come. If a spreadsheet is difficult to read and understand, it's difficult to change. It may be difficult to determine exactly what it calculates and to verify that the spreadsheet produces the right answers.

Works and most other spreadsheet programs offer a way to help clarify formulas, by giving a cell or range of cells a meaningful name. Instead of using cell references in formulas, these names are used. As a result, the formulas become very readable.

The Name command in the Edit menu creates a name for the selected cell or cells. For example, suppose you gave the names Sale Price and Down Pmt to cells F5 and F6.[1] Then the formula =F5-F6 would become

```
=Sale Price-Down Pmt
```

If you follow through and name F7 Amt Financed, F8 Term in Months, and F9 Interest Rate, the payment formula in F10 becomes

```
=PMT(Amt Financed,Interest
Rate/12,Term in Months)
```

When developing formulas, names help you concentrate on the problem at hand, help document the spreadsheet, and they help others locate specific information.

In very simple examples, or when someone develops a spreadsheet for his or her own use, naming cells may not be important. But when people create spreadsheets for other people to use, good documentation is essential for understanding and communication.

[1] If you try this with the Budget spreadsheet, don't forget to first turn off protection (the Protect command in the Options menu).

understand the musical tastes of your customers. Sometimes you will be responsible for predicting whether or not a new record will be popular.

These are decisions that are based largely on intuition and judgment. You have to make these decisions well, or you won't be very good at managing Music to Go. Yet while your intuition might tell you what kind of music your store should sell, each time you order new merchandise, you must translate your intuition into exact numbers.

Of course, no one can predict the future, but when the speed and precision of a spreadsheet are combined with *what-if* analysis guided by intuition and good judgment, the quality of management decision making can be greatly enhanced.

Additional Spreadsheet Features

Templates

A **template** is a partially completed spreadsheet. Templates are often designed by specialists for use by nonspecialists. For example, a tax accountant might construct an IRS Form 1040 spreadsheet template to help novice users compute their income taxes. The tax-form template would take care of planning the spreadsheet and deciding what formulas to enter. The user would simply copy the template into the spreadsheet program and begin solving the tax calculation problem.

Because there are so many potential applications for spreadsheets, many special-purpose templates have been created. You can obtain packaged templates on disk for such applications as budgeting, bookkeeping, investment analysis, and real estate transactions. Many books about specific applications also supply designs for templates that you can type into your spreadsheet program.

Some templates are specially designed to be used by people unfamiliar with how a spreadsheet works. These templates hide the formulas and use built-in prompts and forms to guide the user through the process of entering data. For example, a data-entry template can automatically move the cursor to the proper location for data entry; when all items have been entered, it automatically saves and prints the completed spreadsheet without any intervention by the user.

Very Large Spreadsheets

As spreadsheets have evolved, they have become larger. For example, the original personal computer spreadsheet, VisiCalc, had 254 rows. Another popular spreadsheet, Lotus 1-2-3, raised that number to 2,048 rows. Next, SuperCalc III offered 9,999 rows. Recently, Microsoft's Excel raised the number of rows to 16,384.

Working with a very large spreadsheet differs in several ways from working with a small one. One difference is the manner in which recalculation is handled. In the Works spreadsheet, recalculation is normally automatic. Whenever a new value is entered, every formula in the spreadsheet is immediately evaluated and, if necessary, recalculated.

In spreadsheets with thousands of cells, recalculating formulas can take considerable time. When making new entries, the time spent waiting for recalculation can become unacceptably long. For this reason, Works and other spreadsheets offer a **manual recalculation** option. With this option, formulas are recalculated only when you enter the "Calculate Now" command.

Another feature is the ability to split the screen so that you can view different portions of a large spreadsheet simultaneously. This feature is often called **windowing**. For example, suppose you wanted to compare the data in rows 2 through 4 with data in rows 124 through 126. The split-screen windowing feature allows you to divide the spreadsheet horizontally at a specified row. Splitting the screen vertically is also possible.

In some spreadsheet programs, windows enable you to view two or more spreadsheets simultaneously.

Linking Multiple Spreadsheets

Often, one spreadsheet will use information calculated by another spreadsheet. **Linking spreadsheets** is a technique for consolidating information from two or more spreadsheets, to avoid having to continuously reenter or copy information.

Linking is slightly different from copying information. Linking establishes a permanent relationship between spreadsheets. For example, if linking were available in the Works spreadsheet, you could have specified a link between the sales figures in the MUSIC1 and MUSIC2 spreadsheets. When the figures changed in MUSIC1, MUSIC2 would be automatically updated.

As another example, suppose several departments are revising their budgets. Each department creates a spreadsheet. Then, a consolidated budget linked to each departmental budget is created. Linking ensures that the latest figures from the department budgets are incorporated into the consolidated budget.

Macros

A **macro** is a single command that invokes a sequence of other commands. Macros are often used to automate repetitive tasks. For example, when preparing budgets, you might have to enter the same heading across the top of every budget spreadsheet. In this case, you could use a macro to avoid typing the headings over and over.

More complicated macros can be used to create new functions that augment those already provided by the spreadsheet. Some spreadsheets contain a **macro language**, which resembles a programming language, but in which users can create sequences of long and complicated instructions which are embedded in the spreadsheet program and activated like any other command. For example, a user might have the weekly task of transferring information from one spreadsheet into a company-wide model and printing a report of the results. This entire procedure could be automated by using an interactive macro, which would not only perform the tasks but also prompt the user for input and make decisions based on the input.

Review

Key Terms

Model   Manual recalculation
Absolute reference   Windowing
What-if analysis   Linking spreadsheets
Freezing titles   Macro
IF function   Macro language
Template

Discussion Questions

1. What is the difference between a relative and absolute cell reference?
2. Why would you use an IF function in a formula?
3. What is the purpose of the "Freeze Titles" command?
4. How can linking be used to break a large problem down into several smaller spreadsheets?
5. How can macros be used to customize a spreadsheet application?
6. How might templates and macros be used to standardize spreadsheets within a company?
7. How can *what-if* analysis lead to more creative problem solving?

Software Exercises

1. Type your name and the name and number of your class into the upper left-hand corner of the MUSIC2 spreadsheet. After you finish each of the following exercises, print the results for your instructor.
   a. Revise the model by substituting a 3 percent increase in sales.
   b. What if sales increase only 1.5 percent? What would your estimated net profit at the end of the year be?
   c. What if cost of sales increases to 70 percent of sales, while sales growth slows down to 1.5 percent per month? What would your estimated profit for the year be?

Table 7.1 Grade book data			
Pat Abbot	73	89	96
Michael DeLuca	98	96	76
Silvia Ramos	66	76	73
Anthony Smith	67	87	98

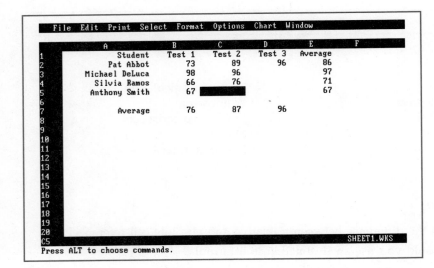

```
 File  Edit  Print  Select  Format  Options  Chart  Window

           A          B        C        D        E        F
 1             Student    Test 1   Test 2   Test 3   Average
 2            Pat Abbot       73       89       96        86
 3        Michael DeLuca      98       96                 97
 4         Silvia Ramos       66       76                 71
 5        Anthony Smith       67    ███████               67
 6
 7             Average        76       87       96
 8
 9
10
11
12
13
14
15
16
17
18
19
20
C5                                                    SHEET1.WKS
Press ALT to choose commands.
```

Figure 7.8
Partially completed Grade Book spreadsheet.

2. Revise the spreadsheet to model a different increase in sales each month. What happens if sales increase dramatically in December?

3. Revise the spreadsheet to allow a different figure for advertising expenses each month. What happens if advertising expenses are higher in November and December?

4. *Grade book.* Create a sample grade book, using the data in Table 7.1 on the previous page. Figure 7.8 shows the partially completed grade book. Fill in the data, column by column, and keep a running average score. *Hint:* The AVG function gives an average of values in a range reference and ignores blank cells, so AVG(B2:D2) will yield the correct average test score for the first student.

5. *Savings account.* Build a savings account spreadsheet, using the data in Figure 7.9. Assume an interest rate of 5 percent per year, compounded annually. Calculate various interest rates for various initial deposits.

```
A9                                                          Empty
           A              B        C    D    E
1      Interest Rate       0.05
2      Initial Deposit   100.00
3
4      After 1 year      105.00
5      After 2 years     110.25
6      After 3 years     115.76
7      After 4 years     121.55
8      After 5 years     127.63
```

Figure 7.9
Sample savings account data.

8

Introducing Databases

Preview   The ability to store data is one of the most powerful features of today's computer systems. Databases are a computerized solution to the problem of storing collections of data. In the broadest sense, they are computerized record-keeping systems. Just as word processors improve on the typewriter and spreadsheet programs extend the principle of a manual ledger, database programs are an elaboration on the filing cabinet.

But simply storing data is not enough. Anyone whose desk is cluttered with books and stacks of papers knows that storing data does not guarantee being able to find relevant information later on. For that, you need structure. Database programs provide the means to structure and organize data to create information.

Finally, there isn't much point in organizing information unless it can be easily manipulated and retrieved. A database program also takes advantage of the computer's ability to sort data, make comparisons, and select specific information.

In this chapter, you'll learn:

- How database programs help solve problems
- The functions of a database program
- How to design a database
- How to enter and edit data
- How to query for and select records
- How to sort records in a database
- How to print selected data

Database Programs and Problem Solving

A **database program** is software that stores, organizes, manipulates, retrieves, and summarizes data. In short, it is a computerized record-keeping program. A **database** is a collection of various types of data, organized according to a logical structure.

In the late 1960s, centralized computers in large organizations processed data for all of their organizations' departments or divisions. It turned out to be wasteful and time consuming to maintain separate and often duplicate sets of files for different applications. The database approach made it possible to create a centralized data repository, on which each department or division could draw for its needs. Database management software was developed to create and maintain the database and to link it to the application programs that used it.

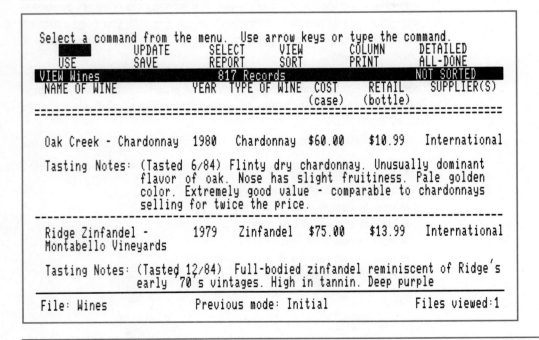

Hobbyists can use database programs to keep track of their collections. Shown here is a display from a wine collection database.

The first database programs required technical support staffs. Their output was also limited to sophisticated, but static reports. With the advent of on-line systems, however, they began to evolve into highly interactive end-user tools. When databases for personal computers came on the market, nontechnical users (such as small business owners) began to develop their own database applications. No longer was it necessary to hire programmers, or even to learn how to program, in order to use a database.

Database programs are applicable to any kind of project that involves creating a repository of data and then manipulating that data to extract useful information. For instance, some typical uses of database programs on personal computers include:

- Salespeople keep track of sales leads, prospects, customers, orders, and payment records.
- Hospitals keep track of patients' histories, symptoms, test results, doctors, and diets.
- Writers create bibliographies and indexes for books and papers.
- Real estate agents match property listings with potential clients.
- Hobbyists keep track of collections of coins, stamps, music, or wine.
- Magazine publishers maintain lists of subscribers and advertisers.

Database programs manage information by allowing the user to structure the data, add and delete items as needed, manipulate the data, and select information from the database. These functions make databases a useful tool for almost any problem that involves retrieving and analyzing past and current data.

A Sample Database Application

A common database application is keeping track of an inventory. An inventory might be as simple as a stamp collection or as extensive as the merchandise in a retail department store or the thousands of parts used to build an automobile or airplane.

Assume that you're going to lend a hand to your uncle who buys used cars at wholesale auctions, repairs them, and then sells them to dealers. His inventory of used cars isn't large, but business is brisk and turnover is rapid. Your uncle has a good reputation, and buyers call daily with requests for specific makes and models of cars. He receives inquiries like, "Do you have a late-model Cadillac?" and "I need a 1980 Volvo four-door with air conditioning and standard transmission. Have you got one?"

You're going to design a database called Car to keep track of your uncle's inventory of used cars and to help answer customers' questions about the cars in stock.

A WORD ABOUT
Databases and Libraries

If you'd like to walk around inside a giant database, you need only visit your nearest library. Libraries are databases; they store information, organize it, and make it possible for you to use that information.

To organize information, libraries use either the Dewey decimal system or the Library of Congress system to catalog books and other documents. A library card catalog is a simple form of database index. The card catalog provides a method of organizing books in the library. However, once you have identified a book you want, you or a librarian must still search through rooms filled with shelves to locate the book.

Today, many libraries are starting to utilize computer database technology to deliver new kinds of information services that are not possible without computers. For instance, the card catalog itself has been automated and coupled with other on-line circulation systems. Books, periodicals, and even library cards now have bar codes, just like products in the grocery store. Libraries use these tools to keep track of their inventory of information. If a library doesn't have a particular book in its stacks, it can send a message to another library, requesting that the book be delivered. By combining resources electronically, several libraries together can offer a wider range of information than each could otherwise afford.

Libraries are also starting to offer access to electronically published information. In principle, anyone with a personal computer and a modem can access an electronic information service. However, it takes a great deal of skill to navigate the vast sea of electronic data and find the exact information required. Librarians are trained to do just that, and they can help you take advantage of electronic as well as printed information sources.

Though some may be nostalgic for the old ways, computers allow today's libraries to be better managed. In addition, they help librarians and scholars take advantage of that unique "database" we call the library.

To create and use the database, you'll use all four functions of the database program to:

- Design the database.
- Enter and edit data.
- Query for, select, and sort data.
- Display, print, and save the selected data.

Designing a Database

The starting point for any database application is to design the database. First, you must think about what the Car database should look like. The Works database structures data in the form of a table almost identical to the spreadsheet, with horizontal rows and vertical columns. Each column designates a **field**, the smallest

Designing a Database

Each column holds a field—a particular category of information.

LAST NAME	FIRST NAME	PHONE	ADDRESS	CITY	STATE	ZIP
Berglund,	Steven	603-347-1092	85 Summer St.	Keene	NH	03431
Conte,	Joyce	712-593-8471	195 Granite Ave.	Sioux City	IA	51104
Garcia,	George	206-279-5710	1225 Pond Rd.	Seattle	WA	98102
Kahn,	Stanley	518-732-8059	203 East Main St.	Aurora	NY	13026
MacAdam,	Joan	606-932-4628	9 School Ln.	Ashland	KY	41101
Pacella,	Nicholas	619-935-7214	400 Broadway	San Diego	CA	92110
Palmer,	Anthony	305-721-4980	16 Summit Ave.	Orlando	FL	32856
Richardson,	Paula	203-928-3608	1440 Riverside Rd.	Stamford	CT	06902
Sumner,	Chris	312-561-9527	56 Edge Hill Ave.	Chicago	IL	60604
Woods,	Emily	309-715-6007	42 Acorn Ln.	Peoria	IL	61625

Each row holds one record—a set of related fields pertaining to the same subject.

The headings provide field names.

Figure 8.1
Data structured in rows and columns.

unit of data stored in the database. Each row holds a **record,** a collection of related fields. Take a look at Figure 8.1. This particular view of a database is called a **list.** Works also lets you organize records into a **form.** A form shows one record; a list shows many records. It is easy to switch back and forth between the two views. The Textbook Edition of Works limits the size of the database to 256 records in total and 32 fields per record.

Designing a database means deciding on the **structure** of the records within it. The process includes the following steps:

- Determine what categories of information (fields) the records should contain.
- Determine the order of the fields.
- Name each field.

You want the Car database to answer the kinds of questions people typically ask when shopping for a used car. Each record should contain all the relevant data about a particular car. What should those data be?

Reviewing your uncle's records of past phone requests, you find that potential buyers want to know the make, model, color, year, price, mileage, and a few other details about each car. Each item in that list will become a field in a Car record.

Next, you need to decide the order in which the fields should appear. Since we are accustomed to reading from left to right, the most important data should be on the left. Let's make the order of fields in the record the same as your informal list of the things potential buyers want to know. To name the fields, you will give each field a short descriptive heading, as in Figure 8.2.

Starting the Database Program

Let's take a look at the database program now. To create a new database:

1. Make sure that the NEW dialog box is on your screen and that the Database option is chosen; that is, it has the bullet beside it.

2. Press the [Enter] key to activate the <New> button.

   Works automatically displays the form design screen. The word DESIGN will appear in the middle of the status line at the bottom of the screen. This form helps you visualize the structure of the record and the correspondence between field names and the data. You will use the form design screen to lay out and enter the names and fields that make up your database form.

The Form Design Screen

The form design screen is like a blank sheet of paper. To create a form, you position fields anywhere on the screen. If you need more room, you can use up to eight screens to design a form. After you've created the form, you will use it to enter data into your database.

A field name, such as Make, can be up to 15 characters long followed by a colon (:). The fields in the Car database should be named and entered in the following order:

> Make:
> Model:
> Color:
> Year:
> Cost:
> Price:
> Mileage:
> Remarks:

To create your form:

1. It would be nice for the form to be roughly in the middle of the screen. Use the down arrow key to move the cursor down 5 lines; then use the right arrow key to move the cursor 15 places to the right.

Figure 8.2
Data for the Car database.

Make	Model	Color	Year	Cost	Mileage	Remarks
Mercedes	380SL	Blue	1983	37999	14000	One owner
Volvo	244DL	Brown	1977	4100	65000	Sunroof
Porsche	944	Red	1984	22950	13800	Power windows
Ferrari	308GTS	Silver	1980	32500	29000	Luxury trim
Ford	Mustang	Green	1976	375	102000	Running well
Dodge	Colt	Silver	1981	1250	42000	4 speed AM/FM radio
Honda	Civic	Blue	1984	7200	16000	Hatchback
Porsche	928	Red	1983	33900	16600	Leather interior
Audi	4000S	White	1984	13950	12000	Full fact equipped
Jaguar	XJ6	Green	1985	31895	5000	Leather interior
Honda	Accord	Silver	1979	2100	50000	4 door
Buick	Park Ave	Green	1982	9500	30000	Velour interior
Buick	Skylark	Brown	1982	4800	18500	Air conditioning
Saab	900S	Blue	1983	11000	30000	Sunroof
Volvo	242DL	White	1983	9985	21000	Air conditioning
Audi	5000	Black	1981	8877	42000	Alloy wheels
Mercedes	380SL	Grey	1982	32900	38000	Perfect condition
Buick	LeSabre	Blue	1983	8995	38000	One owner
Saab	900S	Silver	1983	10000	19000	5 speed 4 door
VW	Rabbit	Beige	1980	1600	84000	Sunroof
Dodge	Colt	Red	1978	2500	48000	Excellent condition
Ford	Mustang	White	1982	3300	26000	Very clean
Porsche	911	Red	1982	24900	22000	Sunroof
Cadillac	Eldorado	Blue	1984	18900	8000	Leather interior
VW	Jetta	Silver	1984	7200	12000	Deluxe interior
Honda	Accord	Grey	1983	8000	30000	Electric roof
Ford	Granada	Red	1975	1500	120000	New paint
Volvo	244DL	Tan	1980	6950	53008	Air conditioning
Buick	Century	Ivory	1974	2200	90000	Mint condition
Jaguar	XKE	Grey	1964	7000	175000	6 cylinder
Buick	Regal	Grey	1982	6300	30000	Air conditioning
Audi	5000S	Silver	1981	5495	44000	Sunroof
Mercedes	280	Red	1985	26000	10000	Climate control
VW	Rabbit	White	1982	6500	32000	Rustproofed
Saab	Turbo	Red	1983	11500	60000	4 door
Ferrari	380GTB	Black	1977	28000	40000	Velour interior
Jaguar	XJS	Silver	1983	23000	30000	AM/FM stereo
Honda	Civic	Black	1983	5600	16000	5 speed
Buick	Park Ave	Maroon	1982	6950	34000	Mint condition
Saab	Turbo	Grey	1983	11900	21000	Alarm system

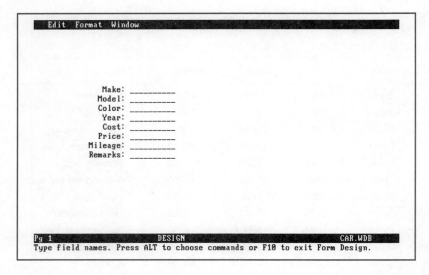

Figure 8.3
The completed forms screen for the CAR database.

2. Type *Make:* (don't forget the colon, because that is the signal for Works to create a data field). Then press the [Enter] key. Make: _____ will appear where you positioned the cursor.

3. Next, press the down arrow key to move the cursor directly underneath the "M" in "Make." Use the left arrow key to move the cursor one space to the left so the colons will line up; this will look nicer. Type *Model:* and press the [Enter] key.

4. Now move the cursor under the "M" in "Model" and type *Color:* then press the [Enter] key.

5. Repeat this procedure for all the field names in the database. When you are finished, you will have a right-aligned vertical column of field names on your screen, as shown in Figure 8.3.

6. Next, move the cursor two lines above "Make:," type *Car Database* and press the [Enter] key.

7. When you've finished defining your record, press the [F10] key to leave the form design screen and display the form screen. Then press [Alt], F, and A to save your database as CAR.

You are now ready to begin entering data, but first let's go over some database design tips.

Tips on Database Design

Because it's easy to create a database with Works, you may be tempted to set one up without thinking very far ahead. But it always pays to think through your record structure in advance. Here are some pointers on designing a database and specifying a record structure:

- Use a pencil and paper to consider various sequences, names, lengths, and types for the fields.

- Enter the most frequently used fields first. Even though you can scroll, it is best to have as much information as possible on the screen at once.

- The name of any field can be up to 15 characters long, though we have chosen shorter names for this example.

- In the List view, Works displays the database with the column widths set at 10. However, you can adjust column widths to fit any field lengths.

- Choose the appropriate format for a field by using the Format menu. For instance, if a field will contain a dollar value, use the Dollar command. If a field will contain a time or date, use the Time/Date command.

- Often, what appears to be a numeric field should be entered as text. For example, because Works always eliminates the leading zeros in a numeric field, zip codes should be entered as text even though they are all numbers. Thus, Works would display and print the Massachusetts zip code 01907 as 1907. To force Works to treat a number as text, you use one double quotation mark. For instance, typing "01907 will cause Works to display 01907.

- Use as many fields as you need to sort or select information. For example, if you are planning to sort names alphabetically according to the last name, use separate fields for first and last names.

Entering and Editing Data

Once the record has been defined, you can add data to the database. You'll do this by "filling in the blanks" in the form screen. Works adds new records to the database in the order in which you enter them. Records do not need to be complete; you can add a partial record to a database and fill in the empty fields later.

Entering Data

Make sure your Car database is open and you are in the form screen. The word FORM should appear in the middle of the status line at the bottom of the screen. Each field occupies a separate line, with the field's name on the left-hand side. A highlight corresponding to the field's length marks the field that is active.

The data for the car database are in Figure 8.2 on page 187. For now, enter just the first 20 records.

1. Enter *Mercedes* into the first field. Note that, during entry, data appear on the formula bar as they did in the spreadsheet. You can use the [Backspace] key to correct typing mistakes. Then press the down arrow key. Data will be entered into the field, and the cursor will move down to the next field.

2. Type *"380SI* in the Model field, then press the down arrow key. Remember that, as in the spreadsheet, any text starting with a number, such as certain car model numbers, should be preceded by a double quotation mark. Otherwise Works might interpret the data as a number or formula.

3. Next, type in the car's color and press the down arrow key to move to the Year field. Note that we don't use a time/date format for the year field, because that will force us to enter a month and day, which isn't useful for a car's model year number.

4. In the Cost field, use the Dollar command in the Format menu to change the field to dollar format with zero decimal places. Then type *37999* without a double quotation mark. A format command in a particular field applies to that field for all records in the database. Therefore, you don't have to use the format command for subsequent records, just for the first.

   The Price field is different from the other fields in the database. Its value is computed through the use of a **field formula,** an equation Works uses to calculate a field's value. Field formulas are like cell formulas in the spreadsheet. A formula in a field applies to that field for all records in the database. Your uncle marks up the price of his cars 50 percent over cost, so the formula to enter in the Price field is =Cost*1.50.

5. Use the Comma command in the Format menu with zero decimal places to format the Mileage field. Then type in the mileage number.

6. When you've finished entering data into the last field of the record, and you press the down arrow key, the record is stored in the database and a new blank form will be displayed on the screen. Type in the data for five records using the form screen.

You can scroll through the records you've just created by simultaneously pressing the [Ctrl] and [PgUp] or [PgDn] keys. [Ctrl] and [PgUp] moves to the previous record; [Ctrl] and [PgDn] moves to the next record. The status line at the bottom of the screen indicates the number of the record you are viewing.

Now let's take a look at the List view. To do so, press [Alt], O, and V to change to List view. Notice that fields line up in columns, records appear as rows, and each field name appears as a column title.

The List view is an easy way to view multiple records and scan through the database much more quickly than by using the Form view. A shortcut method for switching between the two views is to use the [F9] key. Press it now to switch to

Form view. Then press it again to switch back to List view. You can also enter data using the List view.

To do so, make sure that the cursor is positioned in the first column of the next empty row. Type in the data for the Make field, just as you did in the Form view, except press the right arrow key after typing in data to move the cursor horizontally to the next field. Continue typing in data until you have entered all 20 records.

Editing Data

As you enter records into the database, you can scroll the cursor up, down, left, and right to point to any field in the database. You can edit any field in the database by first selecting the field to be edited, then pressing the [F2] key. This activates the formula bar, just as it did in the spreadsheet. Also, the same editing keys that are used in the spreadsheet are used in the database. To review the editing keys, see Figure 6.4 on page 148.

Editing data serves two purposes. The first is to correct errors; the second is to update or replace the contents of a record with more current information.

In the Car database, the field most likely to be updated is "Remarks". For example, your uncle's sales strategy might be to make a note in the Remarks field of a particular car if it doesn't sell in a certain amount of time. You can update a remark by pointing to the field with the cursor, pressing the [F2] key, changing the remarks, and replacing the field in the record by pressing the [Enter] key.

Removing Data

Removing data is accomplished in the List view by simply selecting rows or columns (press [Alt], S, and R to select a record) and using the Delete command in the Edit menu.

For example, suppose the first three cars in the database were sold. You could remove them from your database by selecting the first three records and then using the Delete command to remove them from the database. Be careful; once the records are removed, you cannot retrieve them.

Querying for and Sorting Data

Database programs can perform several kinds of **data manipulation**. The usual reason for manipulating data is to answer a question. The user puts the request for information in the form of commands that cause the appropriate data manipulation to occur. The two most common types of data manipulation are:

- Searching, or querying for, and selecting records that match certain criteria and displaying those records.
- Sorting records according to one or more keys.

TABLE 8.1
Logical operators used to create criteria

Operator	Name
=	Equals
<>	Does not equal
<	Less than
>	Greater than
>=	Greater than or equal to
<=	Less than or equal to
|	Or
&	And
~	Not

Querying the Database

The database feature that enables you to ask questions of, or search through, the contents of the database is called **querying**, because queries, or questions, are the criteria used for searching through it. Let's consider searching or querying in the context of a customer calling in with some questions.

Suppose someone calls your uncle's car lot and asks, "Do you have a Porsche 928 in stock?" You need to translate that request into a query to the Car database.

Your query will specify the rules that the Works database should use to select records. You create a query by entering a rule into one or more fields. The rule specifies what the data in the field must be like in order for a record to be selected.

Rules are usually quite simple. They are similar to spreadsheet formulas, but instead of using arithmetic operators like + and *, rules use special operators called **logical operators**. Table 8.1 shows the logical operators you can use to create criteria.

The two most common rules use the equality operator (=) and the comparison operators (<, <=, >, >=). Equality tests for a perfect match. For example, if you enter ="*Porsche* in the Make field, Works will test all records and select only those in which the contents of the Make field are exactly *equal to* the text *Porsche.*

The comparison operators look for records that fall into ranges. For example, if you enter >30000 in the Price field, Works will find all records in which the price is *greater than* $30,000.

But now back to our specific question, "Do you have a Porsche 928 in stock?"

1. To translate that question into a specific query, press [Alt], Q, and D in sequence. The query screen will appear, listing the field names on the left-hand side in the same manner as in the form screen. The word QUERY should appear in the middle of the status line at the bottom of the screen.

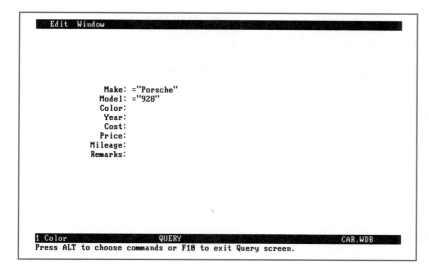

```
Edit  Window




           Make: ="Porsche"
          Model: ="928"
          Color:
           Year:
           Cost:
          Price:
        Mileage:
        Remarks:






1 Color                    QUERY                        CAR.WDB
Press ALT to choose commands or F10 to exit Query screen.
```

Figure 8.4
The completed query screen.
(Search for a Porsche 928.)

2. In the query screen, make sure the cursor is next to the Make field, type *="Porsche* and press the down arrow key.

3. The next consideration is the model. Move the cursor to the Model field. In the highlighted space, type *="928* (the double quote mark is necessary, because Model is a text field). Press the down arrow key again.

You have just translated the customer's question into the rules for a query. The query screen will look like Figure 8.4. To apply the query, choose the "Exit Query" command from the Edit menu by pressing [Alt], E, and X in sequence, or press the [F10] key to return to the list screen. The query screen will be replaced by the list screen, and any records that meet the query criteria will be displayed, as shown in Figure 8.5. All records that do not meet the query criteria will be hidden. You will discover that there is one Porsche 928 in stock.

If you want to see all of the records after a query, use the "Show All Records" command in the Query menu. The hidden records will reappear.

Should you specify a query for which no records match the criteria, a dialog box will appear, with the message "No records matched the query."

The next question the customer asks is, "Do you have a Porsche for less than $40,000?" Return to the query screen by typing [Alt], Q, and D in sequence. Notice that the query screen still contains the rules used for the last search. To delete the current query, choose "Delete" from the Edit menu. Then type *="Porsche* in the Make field and *<40000* in the Price field. After you enter the new rules, return to the list screen by pressing [F10].

Only one record in the first 20 you've entered meets these criteria. You can answer the customer's question by describing the one Porsche that sells for under

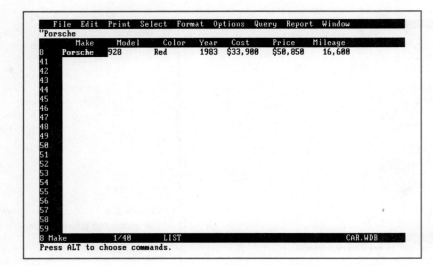

Figure 8.5
The one record (Porsche 928) that meets the criterion.

$40,000. Then return to your database by way of "Show All Records" in the Query menu.

When searching for data, keep in mind the following rules:

■ The equality operator works on the principle of matching. If there is any variation between the search criterion you type in and the contents of the field, no records will be selected. However, Works is case-insensitive. That means, for example, that if you had entered *porsche* with a lower-case *p*, instead of *Porsche* with an upper-case *P*, the records would still have been selected.

■ When more than one rule is used in a query, a record must satisfy all the rules to be selected. For example, if three rules are specified, a record is selected only if the first rule *and* the second rule *and* the third rule are satisfied.

Complex Searches

Sometimes more than one operator is required to answer a question. For example, suppose a customer asks, "What cars do you have between $20,000 and $30,000?"

In order to select all cars that fall within this price range, two operators must be specified in a single rule for the Price field. The rule >=20000 & <=30000 means that the price must be greater than or equal to (>=) $20,000 and (&) less than or equal to (<=) $30,000.

Complex searches can also be used to answer questions like "Do you have any Volvos or Audis?" The clue is the word *or*. Since both criteria refer to the same field (the Make field), the Make field rule should be = ="Volvo" | ="Audi" to select the records in which the make is equal to Volvo *or* (|) the make is equal to Audi.

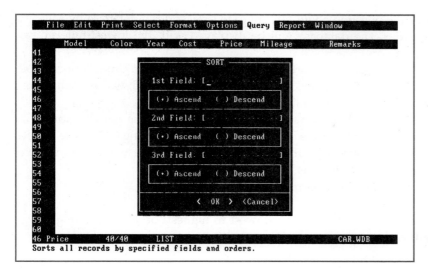

Figure 8.6
Sort dialog box.

Sorting Records

Sorting records means arranging them in a particular order. Examples of sorting include arranging alphabetically by name, numerically by price, or chronologically by date.

Sorting can greatly reduce the effort involved in searching. For example, consider a list of names sorted into alphabetical sequence, such as a telephone directory. If the names were not ordered alphabetically, you would spend a great deal of time trying to find a particular name. When items are sorted in a familiar sequence, you can rapidly (1) find a particular name, (2) determine whether a particular name is present or absent, and (3) scan or retrieve a group of similar names.

Sorting is often the best technique for answering general questions like "Do you have any low-priced cars?" or "Do you have any low-mileage cars?"

Sorting uses the Sort command in the Query menu. For practice, we will sort the records in the Car database to answer the two questions above.

1. A question like "Do you have any low-priced cars?" is rather broad, so you would like to provide the customer with the broadest possible answer. Press [Alt], Q, and S in sequence to select the Sort command.

2. A dialog box like that in Figure 8.6 will appear, listing field names and sort criteria. To answer the question, you want to sort the records by Price in *ascending order*. With the highlight on the word "Make" in the first field, type *Price*. Since "Ascend" is already selected with the bullet, press the [Enter] key. The dialog box will disappear, and the list screen will be displayed with the lowest-priced car listed first, the next-lowest-priced car second, and so on.

To answer the question about low-mileage cars, sort the database by Mileage in ascending order. The database will be displayed with the lowest-mileage car listed first, and so on.

Sorts can also be *nested* — sorted by up to three fields at a time. Suppose you want the Car database to be listed alphabetically by make and, within each make, to be arranged by price in ascending order.

First execute the Sort command. Then specify that Make is to be sorted in ascending order, and that Price is also to be sorted in ascending order. The resulting display will be grouped by the car's make. Within each make, cars will be listed by price in ascending order.

When sorting data, keep in mind the following rules:

■ Sorting can be done in *ascending* (lowest to highest) or *descending* (highest to lowest) order.

■ Sorting occurs from left to right.

■ Sorted characters are arranged according to the following sequences:

> Punctuation characters (.,#$)
> Numbers (0 – 9)
> Capital letters (A – Z)
> Lowercase letters (a – z)

■ In order to sort date and currency fields properly, the Time/Date and Dollar formats should be used.

Printing Data

To print all of your database, use the Print command in the Print menu. Make sure you deactivate any queries by using the "Show All Records" command in the Query menu. The PRINT dialog box is similar to that of the spreadsheet. Works prints a database as it appears on the list screen; however, there is often more information in each record than will fit on the width of one $8\frac{1}{2}$-inch-wide page.

To change the location of the Works-inserted page breaks, use the "Insert Page Break" command in the Print menu. You can specify horizontal or vertical page breaks anywhere in the database. You must first select the *entire* record (row) or column (field) where you want the break to occur.

The PRINT dialog box gives you the option of printing specific pages, and you can also print record and field labels if you wish. If you have the results of a query on the screen, the Print command will print only those records that satisfy the rules of the query.

Review

Key Terms

Database program

Database

Record

Field

List

Form

Structure

Field formula

Data manipulation

Querying

Logical operator

Sorting

Discussion Questions

1. For what use were databases originally designed?
2. Why are database programs useful for keeping track of inventory?
3. Name the four main functions of a database program.
4. In terms of content, what does a record consist of?
5. What are some considerations when defining fields?
6. What are the two purposes of editing data?
7. Why is sorting useful for answering questions of a general nature?

Software Exercises

1. Using the guidelines listed on pages 184 to 186, design and create a database to keep track of your music collection. Your collection consists of records, cassettes, and compact disks. You like to select sets of music by the same artist, no matter what the medium. Your tastes run the gamut of rock, jazz, classical, and reggae. You like to select groups of cassettes to take with you on long car trips. Create a database that would allow you to do all of this. Enter four sample records, print them, and hand the results in to your instructor.

2. Enter 20 more records from Figure 8.2, for a total of 40 records. Then use queries to answer the following questions, and the Print command to print the results:

   "Do you have any Saabs for under $12,000?"

   "What do you have in the way of Jaguars or Ferraris?"

   "Do you have any 1981, 1982, or 1983 Hondas?"

   "Do you have any Buick Park Aves for under $12,000?"

3. Use the Sort command to answer the following questions, and the Print command to print the results:

   "What do you have in the way of high-priced Ferraris?"

   "I don't care what it is, as long as it's black!"

   "Do you have any low-mileage, inexpensive cars?"

4. Create a personal address/phone book database. Create the following fields:

First Name:

Last Name:

Phone:

Street:

City:

State:

Zip:

Enter data in the database for five of your friends, sort the database alphabetically by last name, print the database, and hand it in to your instructor.

9

Working with Databases

Preview   In this chapter, you're going to use the Works database program to create a class schedule database for Altair Community College. In the process, you'll learn how to systematically analyze, design, and implement a database application. Then we'll show you how to use the Report function of the Works database to group, sort, and print a report document.

This chapter introduces a systematic problem-solving procedure for developing a database system. With Works, you can learn the basics of developing applications through hands-on experience. It also offers some guidelines to orient you to systems analysis and design.

Finally, we'll introduce you to some additional features of database programs.

In this chapter, you'll learn:

- How to develop a database application
- How to analyze a database problem
- How to specify requirements and identify constraints
- How to create a database
- How to copy data to the word processor
- How to generate reports
- About relational databases
- About security issues
- About data integrity issues

The Application Development Process

Application development is a problem-solving process that begins with the needs of the user and ends with a system that does what the user wants it to do. Between the two come the tasks of analyzing the need, designing the system, and implementing the application.

There are several ways to implement an application. You can buy a ready-made, off-the-shelf solution in the form of packaged application software. But a packaged program might not fit your needs exactly. You can develop your own custom program, to meet the exact requirements of your application. But this solution requires proficiency at designing and writing programs.

Between these two extremes lies the database program. It, too, might not fit your needs exactly, but it is an alternative worth examining. Because database programs are general-purpose programs, they are excellent tools for developing applications.

Using a database program to develop an application draws on the problem-solving method that we discussed in Chapter 3. In this case, getting to know the problem means getting to know the application, and defining the problem is a matter of specifying the functional requirements.

Getting to Know the Application

The application you are going to develop is a course registration system for a college. The database you'll create contains information on the courses offered, the scheduled times for each class, the number of credits a student receives for the class, and the number of students taking the class. You will then enter a set of test data for classes offered by Altair Community College.

When students register each semester, they need to select a personal schedule of classes. You will select classes from the database by using the database's Query function. You will then fill out a registration form by copying the data into a word processing document and printing a registration form.

Finally, you will define and print an "Enrollment by Department" report from the database by using the Report function.

As a builder-user, you will design and develop the system, enter the data, and also be its end user. A **systems analyst** is a person who interprets the user's needs in sufficient detail to develop the requirements, and then turns them over to a programmer who builds the system for the end user.

Specifying the Requirements

After you get to know the application and the user's needs and wants, the next step is to specify the requirements—to define the problem in a sufficiently well or-

```
Registration Form

Altair Community College

Date:

Name:
Address:
City:
State Zip:

Course   Description          Day    Time      Credits
----------------------------------------------------------


----------------------------------------------------------
                                   Total Credits:
```

Figure 9.1
Sample registration form.

ganized way to guide the development of an appropriate system. The result of specifying requirements is often called a **functional specification**. The steps in specifying requirements for a database application are as follows:

- Identify the outputs.
- Identify the inputs.
- Identify the types of queries and sorts used to question the database.
- Define the database.

For each step, you should assemble some documentation. In this case, that means writing down your thoughts, ideas, forms, and lists of questions and data fields. Under more formal circumstances, documenting the process is crucial in the design and development phases. When more than one person is involved in the process, written documentation serves as a communication tool among the people involved.

One of the outputs of your system will be a printed registration form that includes the date, the student's name and address, a schedule of classes, and credits. Figure 9.1 shows what it will look like.

To produce such a form, you'll need information from various sources besides the database. Identifying inputs involves thinking about the overall flow of data in the system. What data are entered into the system? Where do those data come from? The student's name and address and the date, for example, will be entered by the student using the system. The class titles, times, dates, and so on will come from the class schedule database.

Deciding what kinds of queries or sorts will be needed involves anticipating the kinds of questions people will want to ask about the class schedule. Here are some examples of questions that can be answered by querying or sorting the database:

- What if I can go to classes only after noon on Monday?
- I've heard that Professor Smith is a great teacher. How do I find out what classes she teaches?
- My work schedule limits me to Tuesday and Thursday afternoon classes. What classes can I take?
- I'm only interested in communications. What classes can I take?

Analyzing the output, input, and questioning requirements helps you decide what fields the database ought to contain. First, look at the sample output in Figure 9.1. It contains **fixed information,** such as the captions, and **variable information,** which changes on each registration form. Variable information includes the date, the student's name, and the class schedule.

The variable information that is entered by the student isn't included in the database. By ignoring it, as well as the titles and headers, you can isolate the data elements (fields) that must be stored in the database.

By process of elimination, the database consists of the following fields:

Dept:	department
Course:	course number
Description:	description of class
Days:	days of week class is held
Start:	class start time
End:	class end time
Instructor:	name of professor
Cr:	credits received for taking class
Enrollment:	number of students taking class

Identifying the Constraints

Any system will be constrained in certain ways. There are two broad categories of constraints: *organizational* and *technical*. **Organizational constraints** are environmental limitations, such as budgets, deadlines, and people's capabilities. While we cannot delve into these organizational constraints here, keep in mind that the project's budget and urgency, and the attitudes and skill of users, can play important roles.

Technical constraints are the limitations imposed by the hardware and the software themselves. If there were such a thing as a perfect database program, several steps in the development process could be eliminated. For purposes of explaining technical constraints, we will look at how they influence the process of choosing the record structure of the class schedule database.

You may want to glance back at Chapter 8, pages 186-190, about creating the record structure. We've already determined what fields each record should contain. We have also given each field a preliminary name. Now we have to specify their order and the size and type of each field. A good way to clarify your thinking about the order of the fields is to look at some course catalogs to see how other people have organized course data.

Now we've informally specified the requirements for a course registration application utilizing a class schedule database. For a database application, specifying requirements means assembling an overall picture of the outputs the application will produce, the inputs it must accept, the searches or sorts that must occur to produce the output, and the data that must be present in the database.

Implementing the Database Program

To create the database, use the procedure you learned in Chapter 8, pages 186-190. The record structure for the Class database should be as follows:

Field Name	Type	Width
Dept:	Text	4
Course:	Fixed (0 decimal places)	10
Description:	Text	20
Days:	Text	10
Start:	Time/Date	12 hour
End:	Time/Date	12 hour
Instructor:	Text	12
Cr:	Fixed (0 decimal places)	4
Enrollment:	Fixed (0 decimal places)	4

1. Use the form design screen to create the form for your Class database. (Make sure that the NEW dialog box is on your screen and that the Database option is chosen.) Enter the field names in the order shown above. Don't forget to enter a colon following each field name. As you did in Chapter 8 on page 188, move the cursor to create a right-aligned column of field names.

2. When you are finished entering the field names, move the cursor two lines above "Dept:" and type *Class Schedule Database*.

3. Next, press the [F10] key to go to the form screen, then press [F9] to switch to the List view. Before you begin entering the data, format the fields according to the specifications shown above, using the commands in the Format menu. For example, you will have to change the width of several

fields and use the Fixed command to format some of the number cells with 0 decimal places.

Note that the "Start" and "End" fields both use the Time/Date format. The Time/Date dialog box contains three option boxes. Choose "Hour, Minute" in the Show option box, then choose "12 Hour" in the Time option box. Regardless of which format you choose, you can always enter values like 13:00 or 1:00 PM, but the format determines whether it is 13:00 or 1:00 PM that is actually displayed. The examples in this book assume you are using 12-hour format.

4. Now you can add records to the database. This process is known as *data entry*. You're going to enter the sample data in Figure 9.2 into your database. Type in the data one record at a time. It doesn't matter whether you use the Form or the List view to do this. When you enter the start and end times, be sure to enter the times exactly as shown in Figure 9.2. When you've finished, press [Alt], F, and A to save your database as CLASS.

Evaluating the Results

Now let's translate the questions on page 202 into search and sort criteria, to test out the CLASS database.

1. *Question: What if I can go to classes only after noon on Monday?*   Press [Alt], Q, and D in sequence. The Query screen will appear, listing the field names on the left-hand side. This question translates into the query rules ="M for the Days field and >'12:00 PM for the Start field. Note that the time query is a special case in the Works database. It must be preceded by a single quotation mark ('), not the double quotation mark used in other query criteria.

   Type in the query criteria for "Days" and "Start," and press the [F10] key. The records that meet the selection criteria will be displayed on the screen; all other records will be hidden.

2. *Question: I've heard that Professor Smith is a great teacher. How do I find out what classes she teaches?*   This question translates into a query criterion of ="Smith in the Instructor field. Return to the Query screen, delete the last query by pressing [Alt], E, and D in sequence, then type in your new query and press the [F10] key. All the records that meet the query criterion will be displayed.

3. *Question: My work schedule limits me to Tuesday and Thursday afternoon classes. What classes can I take?*   Answering this question is very similar to an earlier query you performed. Search for ="TTh in the Days field and >'12:00 PM in the Start field. The records selected will represent the classes available on Tuesday and Thursday afternoons.

An Inside View

Computers are constructed from electrical parts—mainly transistors, capacitors, resistors, and wires. Because of intense competition, successful firms must use low-cost methods to build and connect electrical components. The fruit of this competition has been a number of fascinating and exotic manufacturing techniques. As you study this photo essay, you will gain insight into how these techniques work.

1. A composite drawing of circuit layers forms the backdrop for two finished wafers and an integrated circuit chip. Composite drawings of circuit layers for chips are 400 times larger than actual size.

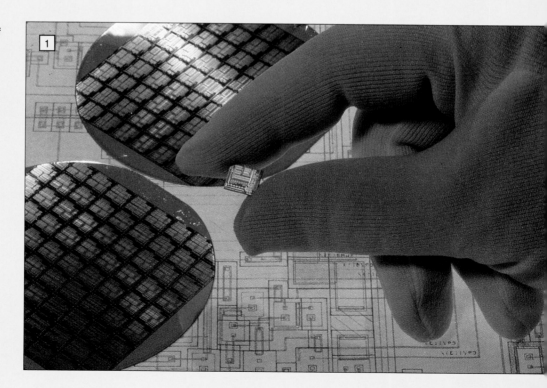

Manufacturing Chips

Microchips are the basic building blocks of the modern computer era. Here is how they are made.

2. Large silicon crystals are the raw material from which most integrated circuit chips are manufactured. Crystals 3 to 5 inches in diameter and several feet long are grown in a furnace containing an exceptionally pure bath of molten silicon.

3. Each silicon crystal is sliced with a diamond-edged saw into round wafers that are less than one-half millimeter thick. Because silicon crystals are harder than most metals, cutting them is expensive and slow.

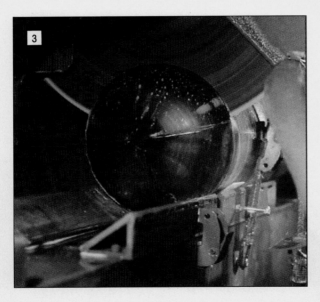

4. The first step in removing imperfections caused by cutting crystals is called *lapping*. Wafers are placed in carriers between two rotating plates that remove a prescribed amount of imperfections. Later the wafers are polished to a mirror finish.

5. During the manufacturing process, wafers are inspected many times. Here an IBM engineer inspects an experimental 8-inch silicon wafer that can accommodate more than 2,000 chips.

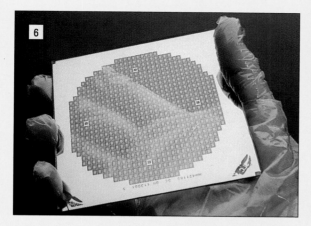

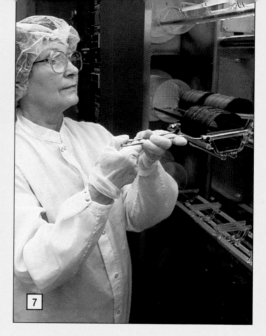

6. This photomask contains one layer of circuitry. The mask is created by an electron beam exposure system that etches tiny images on a metal-coated glass plate; the glass is transparent to ultraviolet rays, but the metal isn't. Before the mask can be used to create circuits, the wafers are dipped in a bath of ultraviolet-sensitive photoresist (a photographic-type emulsion). Then each wafer is exposed by shining ultraviolet light through the mask. Finally, the wafer is washed in a developing solution, leaving a pattern on the surface. This process deposits an image of a single circuit layer on the surface of the chip. A completed chip may require from 5 to 18 circuit layers.

7. During some processing steps, wafers are heated in ovens to produce an insulating layer of glass oxide on exposed silicon surfaces. Other steps use ovens to coat unoxidized surfaces with a thin layer of impurities, such as boron or phosphorous. The impurities create conductive and resistive regions in the silicon that form electronic circuits.

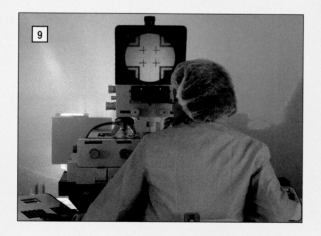

8. A wafer is washed after etching. This is a wafer of transducers to be used in read/write heads for hard disk drives.

9. Microscopes are necessary to align photomasks with the circuits on a partially completed wafer.

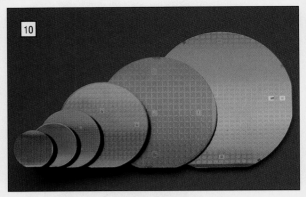

10. A finished wafer contains many integrated circuit chips organized like tiny postage stamps on a piece of paper. The wafers here range from 1 to 5 inches. The trend is toward larger wafers.

11. This National Semiconductor Corporation testing machine lowers 29 wires onto a chip and then runs it through a series of electrical tests. If the chip fails a test, a small ink spot is dropped on it to mark it as a reject.

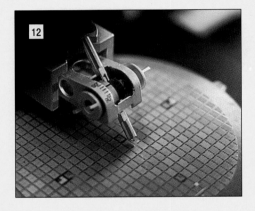

12. Eventually the wafer is ready to be diced into individual chips. Here a diamond-edged tool does the job.

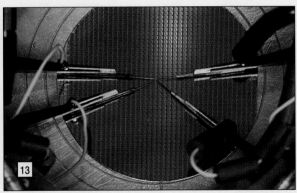
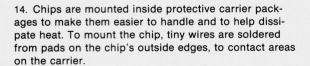

13. After the wafer is completed, each chip is tested by placing probes on tiny electrical contact pads around the outside of the chip.

14. Chips are mounted inside protective carrier packages to make them easier to handle and to help dissipate heat. To mount the chip, tiny wires are soldered from pads on the chip's outside edges, to contact areas on the carrier.

Circuit Boards

The most common way of linking chips electronically is to mount them on printed circuit boards made of fiberglass.

15. High-quality graphics terminals help lay out the design of circuit boards quickly and accurately.

16. Artwork masters can be produced directly from a computerized circuit board design aided by a computer-controlled photoplotter.

17. A Cray Research technician coats a printed circuit board with copper. This step follows an operation that covers areas of the board so that only the uncovered areas are plated with copper.

18. Integrated circuit chips have been installed in this completed Cray supercomputer circuit board.

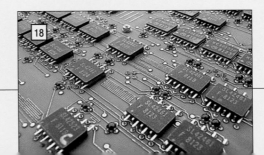

Memory and Storage

Memory devices are integral parts of a computer system. The speed, capacity and cost of memory are some of the factors that determine how useful a computer will be.

19. Hard disks store data on rapidly spinning metal platters. Each platter is polished to a mirror finish and then a thin coating of magnetic oxide is applied.

20. A disk drive assembly is loaded with contamination-free precision by a special function industrial robot.

21. The NeXT™ Computer System, introduced in October 1988, features a 256 MB optical disk that is the first removable, read/write/erasable optical storage disk. It can store the equivalent of 300 to 400 complete books and includes powerful searching and indexing capabilities.

22. This 4-million-bit chip provides dramatic evidence of the computer industry's continuing success at storing ever larger amounts of information in ever smaller spaces.

23. A CD-ROM (compact disk—read-only memory), like a musical compact disk, is read by laser light beams. One disk can store as much as 300,000 pages of text. Here CD-ROM technology is used by Hewlett-Packard to provide customers with up-to-date support information on certain models of HP computers.

24. Increasingly, mainframe computer centers are switching from reel-to-reel tape to magnetic tape cartridges, which are easier to load and require less storage space.

25. Magnetic tape is an excellent medium for inexpensive, long-term data storage. Because tapes cannot be accessed quickly, they are rarely used while data is being processed. Instead, they are used to back up hard disks and to store infrequently used data.

Manufacturing

26. This plant in Grenoble, France, assembles personal computers and terminals for the European market.

27. For low-volume manufacturing of circuit boards, electrical components are stuffed into the board by hand. All the components are mounted on one side of the board, leaving the back side bare. Then, the bare side of the board is passed over a flowing stream that solders all the pins in place in one operation.

28. Manufacturing jobs in the computer industry require a high level of skill, dexterity and patience. Work is done in a clean—sometimes ultraclean—environment.

	Figure 9.2							
	Data for class-schedule database.							

Dept	Co	Description	Days	Start	End	Instructor	Cr	En
EN	101	Intro to Engineering	MWF	9:00 am	10:00 am	McGinnis	3	32
CO	201	Public Rel. Writing	TTh	2:00 pm	3:30 pm	Simpson	3	45
PY	260	Experimental Psych	TTh	5:30 pm	7:00 pm	Kowalski	3	22
CS	101	Intro to Computers	MWF	9:00 am	10:00 am	Blissmer	3	44
LS	220	Human Physiology	MWF	3:00 pm	4:00 pm	Hagen	3	20
SA	101	Graphic Design I	TTh	9:30 am	11:00 am	Smith	3	12
MN	280	Studies in Finance	M	5:00 pm	7:00 pm	McMahon	2	34
FL	100	Beginning Italian	MWF	9:00 am	10:00 am	DeCollibus	3	21
PY	101	Intro to Psychology	TTh	9:30 am	11:00 am	Jamieson	3	125
CO	240	Feature Writing	M	6:00 pm	9:00 pm	Ryan	3	47
HI	121	The Sixties	MW	11:00 am	12:00 pm	Baker	2	33
CO	260	Broadcast Journalism	TTh	7:30 pm	9:00 pm	Hrynyk	3	15
LI	100	Freshman Composition	TTh	11:30 am	1:00 pm	Bassis	3	100
FL	114	Beginning French	MW	7:30 pm	9:00 pm	Vose	3	40
LI	218	American Short Story	MWF	8:00 am	9:00 am	Bassis	3	30
SA	232	Silkscreen Workshop	T	9:30 am	12:00 pm	Nitzberg	2	19
CS	101	Intro to Computers	M	4:00 pm	7:00 pm	Alden	3	55
CO	101	Intro to Advertising	TTh	7:30 pm	9:00 pm	Algaze	3	97
MA	112	Calculus Tutorial	Th	3:00 pm	4:00 pm	Leonardi	1	35
LS	111	Microbiology	MW	1:00 pm	3:00 pm	Verant	4	45
CS	220	Pascal Programming	MWF	11:00 am	12:00 pm	Blissmer	3	20
HI	180	Afro-American Hist	TTh	9:30 am	11:00 am	Lombard	3	55
EN	101	Intro to Engineering	TTh	5:30 pm	7:00 pm	McGinnis	3	32
LI	280	Poetry Workshop	Th	2:00 pm	4:00 pm	Bly	2	18
CO	101	Intro to Advertising	MWF	10:00 am	11:00 am	Algaze	3	88
CS	262	Artificial Intell	TTh	2:00 pm	4:00 pm	Alden	4	34
CO	220	Copywriting II	W	5:30 pm	7:00 pm	Simpson	3	25
FL	100	Beginning Italian	MW	5:30 pm	7:00 pm	DeCollibus	3	20
MN	280	Studies in France	TTh	9:30 am	10:30 am	McMahon	2	44
LS	221	Human Physiology Lab	T	2:00 pm	5:00 pm	Hagen	2	23
PY	101	Intro to Psychology	Th	7:00 pm	10:00 pm	Jamieson	3	125
HI	200	Russian History	MWF	10:00 am	11:00 am	Neidich	3	27
CS	220	Pascal Programming	Th	7:00 pm	10:00 pm	Blissmer	3	19
MN	212	Arts Management	MWF	10:00 am	1:00 pm	Schiffman	3	21
CO	201	Advertising Lab	Th	2:00 pm	5:00 pm	Algaze	2	25
CO	112	Photography Workshop	M	7:00 pm	9:00 pm	Quinn	2	58
MA	111	Calculus I	MWF	1:00 pm	2:00 pm	Leonardi	3	44
PY	220	Developmental Psych	W	4:00 pm	7:00 pm	Cook	3	29
CS	221	Pascal Tutorial	W	12:00 pm	1:00 pm	Blissmer	1	18
SA	280	Graphic Design II	TTh	11:30 am	1:00 pm	Smith	3	37
CO	220	Copywriting II	MWF	11:00 am	12:00 pm	Gellert	3	25
SA	101	Graphic Design I	W	4:00 pm	7:00 pm	Harnicar	3	44
FL	202	Intermediate Italian	MWF	8:00 am	9:00 am	DeCollibus	3	28
CS	101	Intro to Computers	W	6:00 pm	9:00 pm	Blissmer	3	67
LS	112	Microbiology Lab	Th	8:30 am	11:00 am	Verant	2	44
MN	101	Basic Accounting	MWF	2:00 pm	3:00 pm	McMahon	3	75
LS	220	Basic Nutrition	W	7:30 pm	9:30 pm	Callaghan	2	65
CO	112	Photography Workshop	T	2:00 pm	4:00 pm	Kestenbaum	2	53
CO	260	Broadcast Journalism	MWF	11:00 am	12:00 pm	Colburn	3	32

4. *Question: I'm only interested in communications. What classes can I take?* Answering this question translates into the following query: =*"CO* in the Dept field. The records selected will represent all the classes available in the Communications Department.

Generating the Registration Form

To register, you will create a registration form using the word processor and then select class records using the Query function. You will complete the registration form by copying each selected record into the form and then printing the form.

1. Use the word processor to create the registration form, using Figure 9.1 as a sample. Call the file REGFORM and save it.

2. While you are still in the word processor, use the Open command in the File menu to open the CLASS database. The document on the screen will be replaced by the database. Make sure you are in List view.

To select your classes, use the following query criteria: select one Literature course (Course = "LI) and two Computer Science courses (Course = "CS). The classes must meet on Monday, Wednesday, and Friday. Make sure there are no time conflicts in your schedule.

1. Each time you choose a class, use the Record command in the Select menu to select the class record. Then use the Copy command in the Edit menu to copy the record.

2. Go to the Window menu. At the bottom of the menu, you will see a list of file names that should include CLASS and REGFORM. Switch to REGFORM by highlighting its name and pressing the [Enter] key.

3. In REGFORM, move the cursor to the paragraph mark following the line of hyphens, and press the [Enter] key. The record from the database will be copied into your document. Don't worry that the record looks misaligned in the word processing document. You'll take care of *that* in a minute.

4. Use the Query command to select another class and repeat steps 1 through 3 until you have chosen three classes.

After you copy all three database records into the document, delete the tabs between the fields, and delete the Instructor and Enrollment fields. Then use the

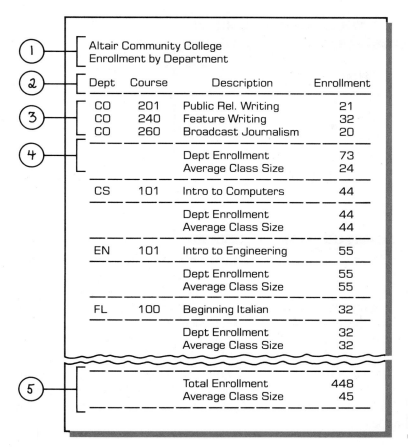

Figure 9.3
Sample report.

space bar to put spaces between the fields to align the records as a table of rows (one per record) and columns (one per field).

When you have arranged the course information on three lines between the rows of dotted lines, use the space bar to align the titles Course, Description, Day, Time, and Credits over the corresponding fields. Add today's date and your own name and address to the registration form, print a copy, and hand it in to your instructor.

Generating Reports

Reporting is a database program function that allows you to define and produce printed output.

You are going to use the Report function to create a report on enrollment by department. Figure 9.3 shows a sample of such a report. Notice that it has been sorted by department and course number.

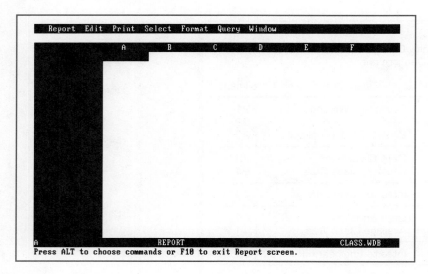

Figure 9.4
The Report screen.

This report contains five types of information that appear (1) at the beginning of the report; (2) at the beginning of a page; (3) each time a record from the database is used in the report; (4) at the end of each department; and (5) at the end of the report.

Defining the format of the report, like defining a database, is done with an on-screen form, which allows you to specify what to include in the report, where to put it, the source of the data, where the data should break, and the order in which the report is to appear.

Sorting and Grouping the Records

The first step is to sort the records into the order in which they are to appear in the report. The "Enrollment by Department" report needs to be sorted by department in ascending alphabetical order. In addition, you will sort courses in ascending order within each department.

Although we want to print all records in the database for this report, we want to break them into smaller groups of records representing classes in the same department.

Works creates groups with a **break,** which is made up of one or more lines inserted between groups of records. These lines can be blank or can contain text and statistics that summarize the information in the preceding group. To sort the database and set up the break fields:

1. Press [Alt], R, and D in sequence to bring up the Report screen, as shown in Figure 9.4. The screen is similar to the database List view, except that the leftmost column is used to display the row type.

2. Choose the Sort command from the Query menu. A dialog box will appear. In the "1st Field" text box, type *Dept*. Make sure "Ascend" has been selected as the sort order.

3. Leave the "Break" check box turned on (an X appears in it) to cause the sort field to be a break field as well. A break on the Dept field causes the records to be separated into groups according to department. The break lines are inserted at the end of each group.

4. In the "2nd Field" text box, type *Course*, make sure "Ascend" has been selected as the sort order, and turn off the "Break" check box. Press [Enter] to sort the database. You will return to the Report screen.

Defining the Report

Defining the report means designing the report. The report you are going to generate has already been designed as shown in Figure 9.3. Its structure consists of (1) two lines that appear at the beginning of the report, (2) a line that appears at the beginning of each page, (3) lines that appear each time a record from the database is printed, (4) lines that break up each department, and (5) total lines that appear at the end of the report. Keep in mind that the sample report in Figure 9.3 is not complete; it only shows the structure of the report not the content.

The Report screen is used to define the structure of the report. Each line on the Report screen is called a **row type;** it describes information that will be included in one or more lines (rows) of the report.

Some row types describe information that will appear at the beginning or end of the report; some row types describe information that will appear only at the top of each page. The Record row type describes a line that will appear for each record included in the report. Figure 9.5 shows the different row types available in Works.

To define your report:

1. Select the first four rows on the screen by holding down the [Shift] key and using the down arrow key so that the first four cells of column A are highlighted. Then press [Alt], S, and R in sequence. Now press [Alt], E, and I in sequence to choose the Insert command. A Type list box will appear. Select "Intr Report" from the list and press [Enter].

2. "Intr Report" will appear in the first four row types on the Report screen. Intr Report lines appear at the beginning of the report. Move the cursor to column A in the first row and type *Altair Community College*. Then move the cursor to column A in the second row and type *Enrollment by Department*. Leave the third and fourth rows blank.

Figure 9.5
Row Types available in Works.

Row type	Prints
Intr Report	At the beginning of a report
Intr Page	At the top of each page
Intr *1st breakfield*	At the beginning of each group created by the 1st breakfield
Intr *2nd breakfield*	At the beginning of each group created by the 2nd breakfield
Intr *3rd breakfield*	At the beginning of each group created by the 3rd breakfield
Record	Each record displayed in the database
Summ *3rd breakfield*	At the end of each group created by the 3rd breakfield
Summ *2nd breakfield*	At the end of each group created by the 2nd breakfield
Summ *1st breakfield*	At the end of each group created by the 1st breakfield
Summ Report	At the end of a report

Now we will define two lines that appear at the top of each page, using the "Intr Page" row type. The first Intr Page line defines the field names used to label the columns of our report.

1. Select the fifth and sixth rows on the screen, then choose the Insert command from the Edit menu. Select "Intr Page" from the type list and press [Enter].

2. You could manually type the field names in the columns, but we will use the "Field Name" command in the Edit menu. Move the cursor to column A in the fifth row and press [Alt], E, and N in sequence. A "Fields" list box will appear; select "Dept" from the list and press [Enter].

3. Move the cursor to column B in row five and activate the "Field Name" command again. This time select "Course" from the list and press [Enter].

4. Move the cursor to column C and select "Description" from the list, then move the cursor to column D and select "Enrollment." For the sixth row, enter 44 hyphens to create a dashed line.

Now we will create the record line to print individual records from the database.

1. Select the seventh row on the screen, then choose the Insert command from the Edit menu. Select "Record" from the list and press [Enter].

2. Move the cursor to column A in the seventh row, and press [Alt], E, and V in sequence to activate the "Field Value" command from the Edit menu. A "Fields" list box will appear. Select "Dept" from the list and press [Enter]. This command creates a formula that retrieves information from the Dept field in the database. The formula =Dept will appear in the formula bar.

3. Use the same procedure to place =Course, =Description, and =Enrollment into columns B, C, and D.

For this report, you want to group the records by department. You also want to provide summary statistics on each department, namely the sum of the enrollment by department and the average class size by department. To insert summary lines into the report:

1. Select rows 8 through 12 on the screen, then choose the Insert command from the Edit menu. Select "Summ Dept" from the type list and press [Enter].

2. Move the cursor to column D in row 9, and activate the "Field Summary" command in the Edit menu. A "Field Summary" list box will appear. Move the cursor to "Enrollment", then choose the SUM statistic by placing the bullet character next to it. Press the [Enter] key. The formula =SUM(Enrollment) will appear on the screen.

3. Move the cursor to column D in row 10, and repeat the procedure to insert the =AVG formula.

4. In column C, row 9, type in *Dept Enrollment* and, in column C, row 10, type in *Average Class Size*.

5. Rows 8 and 12 should have a row of hyphens like row 6. Copy row 6 to row 8 by selecting it and using the Copy command. Repeat these steps for row 12.

Finally, you want summary statistics at the end of the report, namely total enrollment and average class size for the whole school.

Select rows 13 through 15 on the screen, then choose the Insert command from the Edit menu. Select "Summ Report" from the type list and press [Enter]. Use the same procedure as above to create the summary statistics for your entire report on lines 13 and 14. Copy the row of hyphens from row 12 to row 15.

Viewing and Printing the Report

Before you print your report, take a look at it on the screen. To do so, use the View command in the Report menu. Of course, you can only view your report one screen at a time, so to view the next screen, press [Enter]. To view the entire report, screen by screen, repeatedly press [Enter].

Check the style of the report by comparing your on-screen view to Figure 9.3. (Remember the contents of your report will be different than Figure 9.3.) Have you forgotten to include any of the row types shown in Figure 9.3? You can return to the Report screen at any time by pressing [Esc] to make corrections or adjustments.

To print the report, use the Print command in the Report screen's Print menu. Then print a summary report by turning on the "All But Record Rows" check box in the Print command dialog box.

Don't forget to save your report file by using the Save As command in the Report menu. Any reports you design will be saved along with the database. Then use the "Exit Report" command in the Report menu to leave the report screen and return to the list or form screen in the database.

Additional Database Features

So far, it may seem easier to select records manually from a database, using your eyes, than to develop search and sort criteria for scanning the database. But a real class schedule database would contain thousands of records. If you had to scan through a database of this size, the advantages of letting software do the work would be obvious. Software won't overlook records, and it won't get tired.

Relational Databases

A **relational database** can relate records from separate databases through a field they have in common, as illustrated in Figure 9.6. Like many database programs, the Works database can directly manipulate only one database at a time. Multiple interrelated databases and relational data manipulation capabilities are the distinguishing characteristics of a relational database program.

If we were designing a large-scale course registration system, interrelated databases would be a great advantage. There could be a student database containing an ID number, name and address, transcript information, and financial information. Entering the ID number would automatically search the student database for the name and address. Linking an accounting database into the system would give

Course	Description	Day	AM/PM	Time	Instructor	CR.
CO 240	Feature Writing	M	PM	6-9	Ryan	3
.	.	.	.	.	.	.
.	.	.	.	.	.	.
.	.	.	.	.	.	.

Course	Student ID
CO 240	123456
CO 240	731657
CO 240	961121
CO 240	03567

Student ID	Name	Tuition Paid	Bal. Due
03567	Blissmer	500.00	-0-
.	.	.	.
.	.	.	.
.	.	.	.

Figure 9.6
Relationships among files can be
created through common fields.

direct access to tuition records. The registration process could produce class rosters, linking a database of classes and students into the system.

Database applications can quickly become quite complicated. The more complex the application, the more it pays to approach the problem systematically and plan ahead.

Database Size

The maximum size of a database is a technical constraint that must be taken into account in the design process. The limits of database packages can vary widely. A large-scale database program might advertise that it supports three open databases at once, up to 65,534 records per database, and 127 fields per record (with a maximum of 1,024 characters per record).

These numerical limitations can be better understood when they are compared to other numbers, such as the number of students in a college or items in an inventory. Such figures serve as a starting point for determining the number of records needed in a database. Estimates of characters per record, fields per record, and characters per field then serve as a base for defining the record size and structure. These types of calculations are important to ensure that the database program can handle the size requirements of a particular application.

Wildcard Searches

A **wildcard search** uses shorthand notation to fill in incomplete search criteria. For example, if you want to find a particular instructor's name in the database, but are unsure whether it is Smythe, Smithson, or Smith, you could type Sm********** in a query. Works would find all records that have an Instructor field beginning with *Sm*. The asterisks in the field name indicate that any acceptable characters may occupy those positions.

Data Security

Data security involves protecting the database against unauthorized access. Security is most important in a shared system, which gives many people access to the database. Often users are assigned a **password**, a code that identifies the user to the system. Figure 9.7 shows a typical password dialog.

Passwords can provide variable levels of access. A user can have complete access, access to selected records or fields, or read-only access, depending on the degree of confidentiality to be maintained.

For example, in a three-level, password-based course registration system, students would probably have level 1 (read-only) access to the database. Clerks in the registration office, whose responsibility is updating and maintaining the database, would have level 2 (read/write) access. Only the registrar would have level 3 access: the ability to read and write records and to modify the record structure.

Data Integrity

Data integrity concerns the accuracy and validity of the data in the database. In other words, it ensures that the data added to the database are correct. There are several ways to handle data integrity. Database programs can perform **edit checks** when data are entered into the database or updated.

More complex edit checks include range checking, in which upper and lower values are assigned to a field. For example, a field that designates the number of

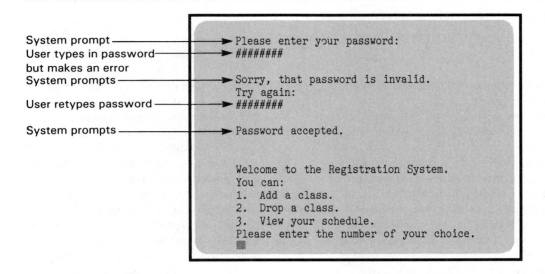

System prompt ─────────────▶ Please enter your password:
User types in password ─────▶ ########
but makes an error
System prompts ─────────────▶ Sorry, that password is invalid.
                             Try again:
User retypes password ──────▶ ########

System prompts ─────────────▶ Password accepted.

                             Welcome to the Registration System.
                             You can:
                             1. Add a class.
                             2. Drop a class.
                             3. View your schedule.
                             Please enter the number of your choice.

Figure 9.7
Sample password dialog.

hours worked per week might have a lower limit of 0 and an upper limit of 80. If you attempted to enter a number outside that range, the program would reject the entry.

A database is a significant and valuable resource, and there is always the danger that users could accidentally destroy data, delete the wrong data, or add the wrong data to a database. There is also a danger of losing or damaging the disk itself. For these reasons, it is crucial to back up the database. A **backup file** is a copy that is made just in case the original database is destroyed, lost, or damaged.

A WORD ABOUT
A New Breed of Databases

The concepts behind database management software originated on very large computers. Most large database systems are designed to support all the information needs of a corporation or government agency. This goal is important because such information is extremely valuable, and it is critical that all parts of the organization have access to the same up-to-date information.

Large databases are designed to deal with issues like access through networks, security and privacy, and reliability. In applications like airline reservations or banking, databases need to be available 24 hours a day, every day of the year, from countries all over the world.

When personal computers became popular, they borrowed many ideas from an earlier generation of computers. One of those ideas was database management. When a personal computer is used as if it were a miniature mainframe, to keep track of information for a small business or a small department in a large company, then a traditional approach to a database still makes sense. The requirements are scaled down, but the basic concepts remain the same.

However, when the personal computer is used as an information tool for a single individual, a completely different kind of database is appropriate. Recently a new concept, called *personal information management*, has become available on personal computers.

Personal information managers are very different from traditional database managers. They are more adept at dealing with a blizzard of unstructured information, such as the information a busy individual might accumulate during a workday, on a business trip, or while doing research. They juggle many sets of seemingly unrelated facts, and relationships may be discovered only later by browsing through the database.

A product called Agenda, from Lotus Development Corp., is one example of a personal information manager. Agenda allows a person to enter almost random items of information into a single, loosely structured database. There is no single structure for a record, as in a traditional database. Instead, information flows into the database and is automatically sorted into different categories, which may or may not seem to be related. They *are* all related, however, in the sense that the database is for the convenience of a single person, who can keep track of meetings, phone calls, shopping lists, and travel arrangements. Whatever structure does exist in an Agenda database can constantly change to meet the individual's immediate needs.

Another product, called Hypercard, from Apple Computer Inc., combines database software containing graphics, animation, and textual data with a programming language that allows the user to develop small, unique applications to suit personal needs. A Hypercard database might feature a map; pointing at a building on the map might lead to a floor plan; the floor plan might lead to a textual list of a furniture inventory for each office. Another database might behave like a personal Rolodex, featuring phone numbers and addresses. The difference is, with Hypercard, such a database would also feature a button that, when pressed, would dial the phone. Another button might display a picture of the person or a map of how to drive to that person's house or office.

But neither Hypercard nor Agenda can replace the existing database managers that are best suited for traditional applications. Neither can deal with hundreds of thousands of records of data. Instead, they are the first examples of a new generation of personal database software tailored to and adaptable to the needs of an individual.

Review

Key Terms

Application development	Row type
Systems analyst	Relational database
Functional specification	Wildcard search
Fixed information	Data security
Variable information	Password
Organizational constraint	Data integrity
Technical constraint	Edit check
Reporting	Backup file
Break	

Discussion Questions

1. What makes a database program a particularly useful application development tool?

2. How is the process of developing a database application similar to the general-purpose problem-solving method?

3. What is a *functional specification*?

4. Outline the steps involved in specifying requirements for a database application.

5. When is it easier to specify search criteria than to scan a database with your eyes?

6. How does a relational database differ from a database used by Works?

7. How might you use a wildcard search to query the class database for introductory courses?

8. What is the difference between data security and data integrity?

Software Exercises

1. Translate the following questions into search or sort criteria for the class schedule database, print the results, and hand them in to your instructor:

   a. I am only interested in two-credit classes. What are my options?

   b. Does Professor Alden teach any Monday morning classes?

   c. I can take classes only between 3:00 and 7:00 pm. What classes are available?

   d. What evening English classes are available on Wednesdays?

2. Use the Works Report feature to define, sort, and print a class schedule report arranged by time and day. Sort the CLASS database by time and day. Then, from left to right, print start time, end time, days, department, course, and description.

3. There is a database on your Works disk called COUNTRY. It contains a collection of statistics for twenty countries of the world. Use the Works Report feature to print a report from this database. From left to right print continent, country, and income; sort by country within continent. Break on the continent field and print the average income for each continent. Also, print the average income for the entire database on the last line of the report.

10
Working with Charts

Preview   The presentation of numbers usually has more impact if the numbers are converted into chart form. A large and complicated spreadsheet can be difficult to interpret. It can also be dull, since spreadsheets have little visual variety. A chart, on the other hand, can transform a sea of numbers into a single, unified picture.

When people use spreadsheets to present information to others, they want better ways of presenting numeric data. When people use spreadsheets to study numeric data, they need tools to help gain insight into the numbers. The Works charting software is a component of the spreadsheet, which simplifies the charting of the numbers contained in spreadsheet cells.

This chapter will show you how to create charts using the MUSIC1 spreadsheet developed in Chapter 7. Then we'll look at how to chart numbers from the COUNTRY database by copying the numbers from the database into a blank spreadsheet.

In this chapter, you'll learn:

■ What kinds of numeric data benefit from charting
■ Some uses for charting
■ Different types of charts and their appropriate use
■ How to chart data from the spreadsheet and the database
■ How to print charts

Visualizing Numbers

Charting is a technique for turning numbers into pictures. Simple charts can be used to illustrate a changing series of numbers. More complex charts show multiple series of numbers and their relationships. Charts are valuable when complex numeric data need to be communicated quickly and effectively. In the business world, charts are often used in presentations, technical literature, and financial reports.

Another use for charting is the discovery of unanticipated relationships in large groups of numbers. When numbers are properly charted, the unusual numbers or relationships will stand out. In a plain spreadsheet, all numbers look the same, and exceptions may go unnoticed. Charts are often used in scientific inquiry. A chart showing the relationship between cigarette smoking and lung cancer is one example.

Charts that track numbers over a period of time, such as months or years, can be used to spot trends that repeat over and over. For instance, a store might have

A chart can transform a sea of numbers into a single unified picture.

sales that go up near Christmas and down in the summer. Knowing about such trends is important to the store's management.

In both presentation and analysis, charting allows you to:

- Communicate quickly and precisely.
- More concretely represent relationships among data.
- Discover possibilities that might not be apparent in numeric form.
- Assimilate and remember data more easily.

Inside a Chart

All charts start with a grid. As Figure 10.1 shows, the grid is divided into an **X axis** running from left to right and a **Y axis** running from bottom to top.

The grid is evenly divided along both the X and the Y axes. However, the divisions can be, and usually are, different along each axis. The Y axis is used to

Figure 10.1
All charts start with a grid.

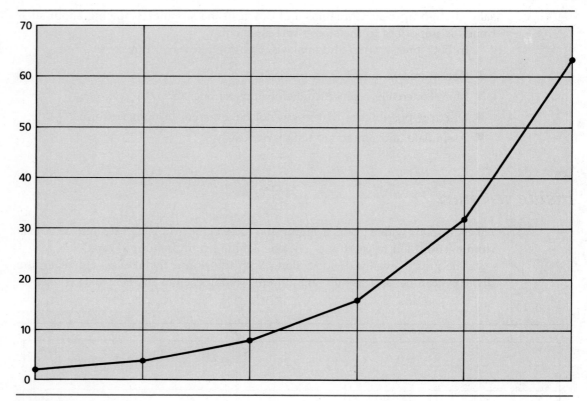

Figure 10.2
A line chart of the number series 2, 4, 8, 16, 32, 64.

plot a series of numbers called the *Y* series. Up to 6 different *Y* series can be plotted with Works. Figure 10.2 shows the *Y* series 2, 4, 8, 16, 32, 64 plotted as dots on a line. Notice that a **scale** runs from bottom to top along the *Y* axis. The scale is used to help the viewer of the chart understand the actual values of the numbers. Without the scale, we could see that each number is twice as large as the previous number; but the scale is needed to show exact values.

There can be only one *X* series along the *X* axis. Although the *X* series can also be a series of numbers, it is often a series of words used to label the corresponding numbers from the *Y* series. Figure 10.3 shows a chart with the *X* series Jan, Feb, Mar, Apr, May, Jun. The label Jan corresponds to the number 2, Feb to 4, and so on.

Figure 10.4 shows the same chart, but with another *Y* series: 1, 3, 9, 14, 30, 65. From the chart we can see that this second series of numbers correlates closely with the first. Since the chart now contains two *Y* series, a *legend* — a short descriptive phrase — has been added to label each one.

Chart Styles

Charts come in different styles that serve different purposes. The charts in Figure 10.3 and 10.4 are called **line charts** because they represent numbers as points on the grid connected by lines. To understand chart styles, it is important to appreciate the relationships that may exist between the numbers in a chart. Figure 10.4 charts the three following series:

2	4	8	16	32	64
1	3	9	14	30	65
Jan	Feb	Mar	Apr	May	Jun

Any chart will show the relationships between 2, 4, 8, and so on. However, a line chart will also show the relationship between 2 and 1, 4 and 3, 8 and 9, and so on.

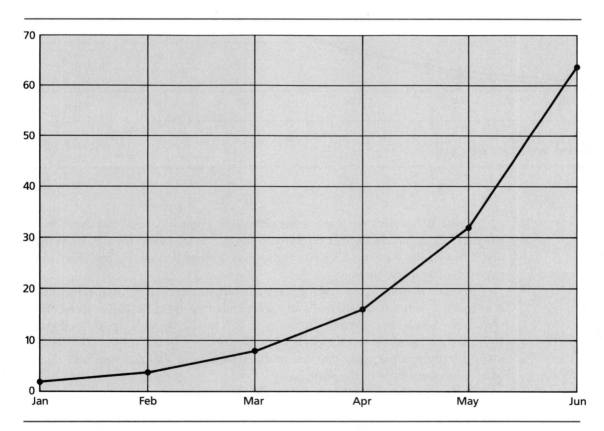

Figure 10.3

A series of words called the *X* series is used to label the corresponding numbers from the *Y* series.

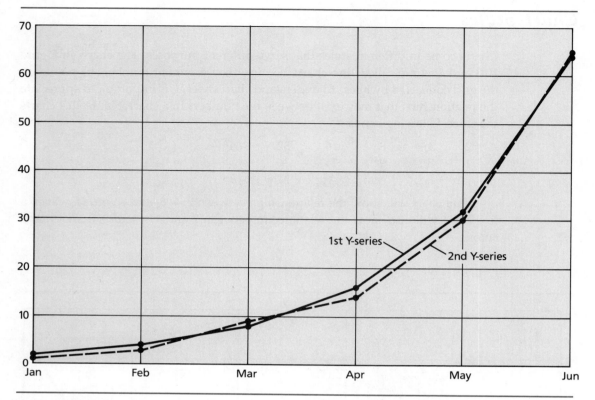

Figure 10.4
A sample chart with two *Y* series.

Figure 10.5 shows the same series charted in Figure 10.3 as a **bar chart**. Most simple charting needs are met nicely with the bar chart. When there is more than one *Y* series, the bars are divided into groups. Figure 10.6 shows the chart from Figure 10.4 as a bar chart.

Another popular chart style is the **pie chart**. A pie chart is used when there is only one *Y* series to be charted and each number needs to be shown in relationship to the whole. For instance, the series 2, 4, 8, 16, 32, 64 adds up to 126. Figure 10.7 shows a pie chart that displays each number as a "slice" of the pie. We can easily see from a pie chart that the number 64 is over half the sum and that 2 contributes very little to the sum.

There are other specialized chart styles, including

- The *XY* **chart** uses pairs of numbers from two *Y* series as *X* and *Y* values used to place dots at corresponding coordinates on the chart grid. Figure 10.8 shows an example of an *XY* chart. Because the dots are "scattered" over the chart, these charts are also called **scatter charts**. They are frequently used in scientific research because thousands of numbers can be packed into a single chart. Often it is not known whether the numbers form any pattern or not; if a pattern exists, the dots will form one or more clusters; the pattern of the clusters can provide significant insights into the data being studied.

■ The **hi-low chart** takes two *Y* series, one representing the highest value and one the lowest. Each pair is plotted along the *X* axis and connected by a vertical line. The top of the line is the high point and the bottom of the line the low. Moving from left to right along the *X* axis, the up and down wave of lines illustrates the changing difference between the high and low values. A related type of chart, the **hi-low-close chart,** plots three *Y* series. This type of chart is often used in stock market analysis to chart the daily highest, lowest, and closing prices of stocks. Figure 10.9 shows an example of a hi-low-close chart.

■ The **stacked bar chart** draws all the numbers in a series as a single bar. Figure 10.10 shows a stacked bar chart. The height of the bar represents the total of the values.

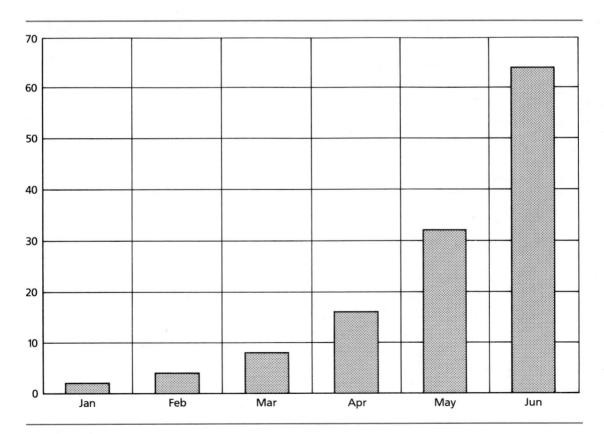

Figure 10.5
Figure 10.3 as a bar chart.

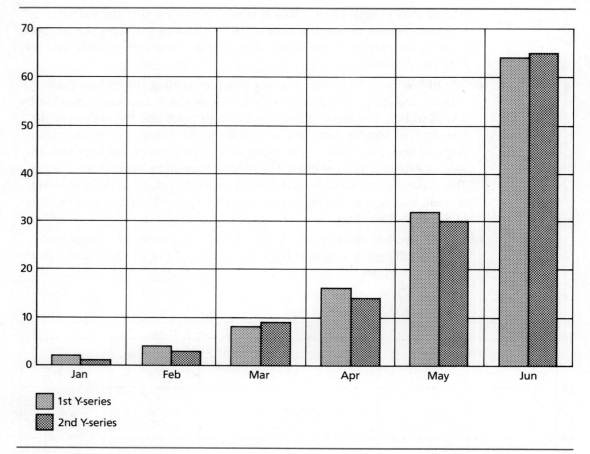

Figure 10.6
Figure 10.4 as a bar chart.

- The **100 percent bar chart** is like a stacked bar, except that the height of the bar represents 100 percent and the values charted represent the relative contribution to the whole, exactly as in a pie chart. Figure 10.11 shows a 100 percent bar chart.

Building a Chart

To build your own chart using Works, the first step is to open the spreadsheet file that contains the numbers to be charted. In this exercise, you will chart numbers from the spreadsheet MUSIC1 that you created in Chapter 7.

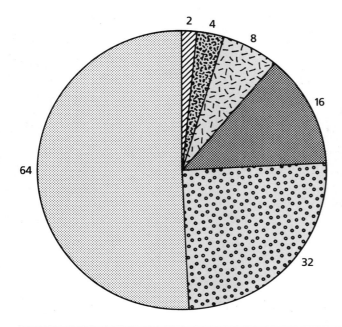

Figure 10.7
Figure 10.2 as a pie chart.

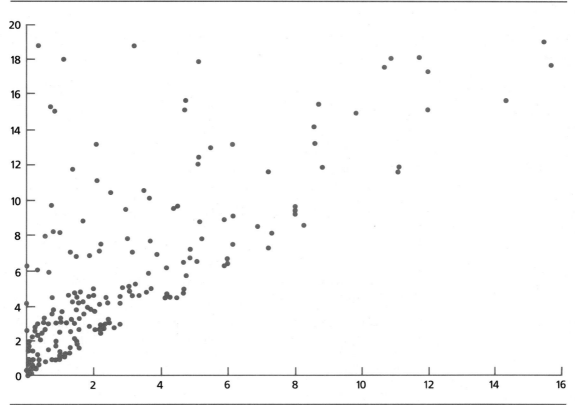

Figure 10.8
A sample *XY* chart.

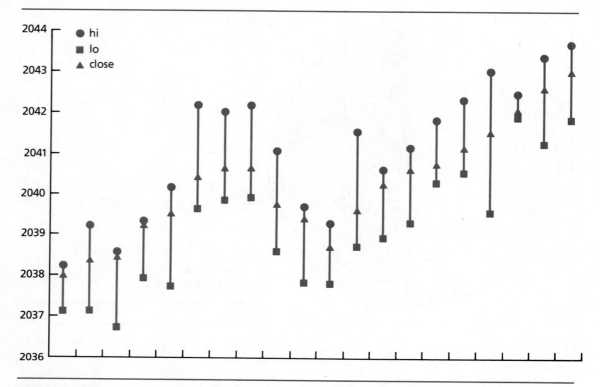

Figure 10.9
A sample hi-low-close chart.

1. Open the file MUSIC1.

2. Press [Alt], O, and U to unfreeze the titles so you can move the cursor to any cell. The "Freeze Titles" command was used on this spreadsheet in Chapter 7.

3. Move the cursor to cell A6.

4. Hold down the [Shift] key and move the cursor to cell D8. All the cells in the range A6:D8 should be selected.

5. Press [Alt], C, and N to activate the New command in the Chart menu and create a new chart. You are now in the charting component of the Works spreadsheet; notice that the menu titles have changed. Your screen should look like Figure 10.12.

You have just defined a new chart based on the data in the range A6:D8. Whenever you press [Alt], C, and N to create a new chart, Works creates a bar chart out of the selected cells.

1. Press [Alt], C, and V to activate the View command in the Chart menu. Your screen should look like Figure 10.13. If you don't see a chart, or if you see a dialog box with the message "Invalid or missing screen driver (SCREEN.GSD)," review the instructions in Chapter 1 regarding the file SCREEN.GSD.

As the legend at the bottom indicates, this chart shows the relationships between sales in the Rock, Classical, and Jazz music categories. There are three groups of three bars each. The three bars correspond to the three *Y* series from rows 6, 7, and 8. But why are there three groups, and what do they mean? The three groups arise from the fact that each *Y* series contains three numbers in columns B, C, and D. Because column A contained text, Works used it for the legend.

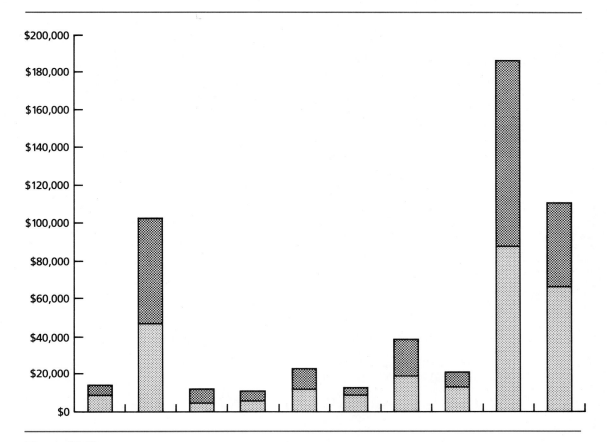

Figure 10.10
A sample stacked bar chart.

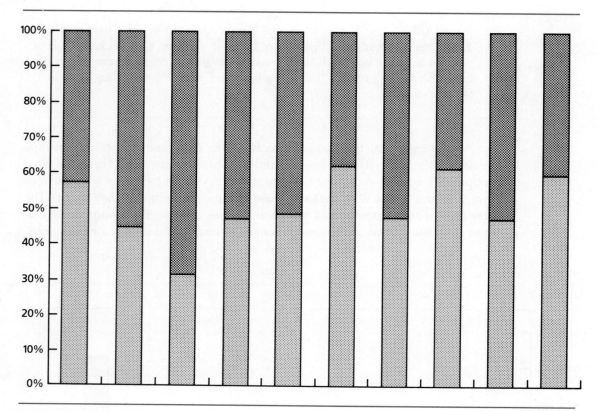

Figure 10.11
A sample 100% bar chart.

What is needed is an X series to properly label each number from the Y series. In this example, the X series corresponds to the three music formats, CD, LP, and CA, from cells B3:D3. To make these cells the X series:

1. Press the [Enter] key to return to the chart definition display.

2. Move the cursor to cell B3. Select cells B3 through D3.

3. Press [Alt], D, and X to activate the X-series command in the Data menu and make these cells the X series.

4. Press [Alt], C, and V to view the chart. The three groups should be captioned CD, LP, and CA.

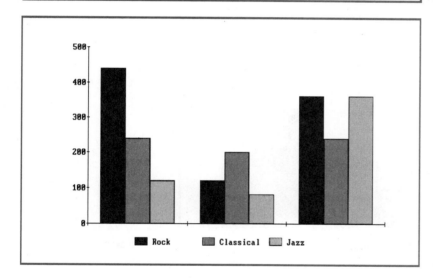

```
 Chart  Print  Data  Format  Options  Window
"Rock
           A          B         C         D         E        F        G
1   Music To Go    Prices
2   Sales Analysis  $13.99    $8.99     $7.99
3                      CD        LP        CA       Total
4   ─────────────────────────────────────────────────
5              In Units
6   Rock           440       120       360        920
7   Classical      240       200       240        680
8   Jazz           120        80       360        560
9
10  Total          800       400       960       2160
11  ─────────────────────────────────────────────────
12            In Dollars
13  Rock         $6,156    $1,079    $2,876    $10,111
14  Classical    $3,358    $1,798    $1,918     $7,073
15  Jazz         $1,679      $719    $2,876     $5,274
16  ─────────────────────────────────────────────────
17  Total       $11,192    $3,596    $7,670    $22,458
18
19           In Percent (of Sales)
20  Rock           27%        5%       13%        45%
A6:D8                 CHART                          MUSIC1.WKS
Press ALT to choose commands or F10 to exit Chart screen.
```

Figure 10.12
The initial Chart screen.

Figure 10.13
The Chart View command.

Now add a title to the chart to explain what it represents.

1. Press the [Enter] key to leave the Graph view; then press [Alt], D, and T to activate the Titles command in the Data menu. The TITLES dialog box will appear, as shown in Figure 10.14. Type *Unit Volume* in the "Chart Title" text box and *by Music Category* in the "Subtitle" text box; then press the [Enter] key.

2. Now press [Alt], C, and V to view your finished chart. It should look like Figure 10.15. Press [Enter].

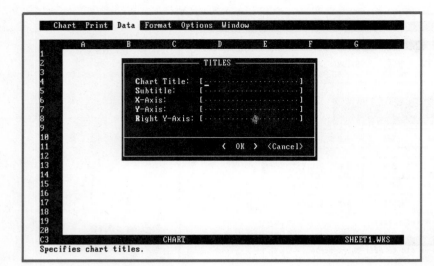

Figure 10.14
The TITLES dialog box.

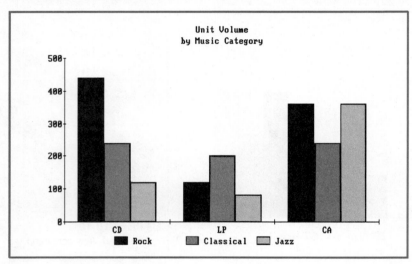

Figure 10.15
The Music chart.

You can use the Format menu to try out other chart styles.

1. Press [Alt], T, and S to activate the "Stacked Bar" command in the Format menu, then press [Alt], C, and V to view the chart. Notice that each of the three groups is represented by one bar, which is in turn divided into different shades that represent the *Y*-series categories Rock, Classical, and Jazz. The total height of each bar represents the combined sales of Rock, Classical, and Jazz in each *X* series of CD, LP, and CA.

2. Now press [Enter] to return to the chart definition display, and press [Alt], T, and P to activate the Pie command. Then press [Alt], C, and V to view the pie chart.

Notice that the Rock, Classical, and Jazz legend is gone and only the first *Y* series is shown in the three pie slices. Although Works is trying, these numbers cannot be correctly represented as a pie chart. Not all chart formats can be used meaningfully with a particular collection of data.

1. To restore the chart to the bar format, press [Enter] to return to the spreadsheet, then press [Alt], T, and B to activate the Bar command again.

2. To save this chart, press [Alt], C, and C to activate the Charts command in the Chart menu. Press the [Tab] key, type *CD LP CA Volume*, and press [Enter]. Note that the chart is saved as part of the spreadsheet, not in a separate file.

There are some numbers in the spreadsheet that can be meaningfully displayed as a pie chart. They are in the cells B10:D10, which contain the unit volume totals for CD, LP, and CA. A pie chart will show the proportions that CD, LP, and CA contribute to the total volume. To create this pie chart:

1. Press [Alt], C, and N to activate the "Chart New" command.

2. Select cells B3 through D3. Then press [Alt], D, and X to make the selected data the *X* series.

3. Select the cells B10 through D10. Then press [Alt], D, and 1 to make the selected data the first (and only) *Y* series.

4. Press [Alt], T, and P to activate the Pie command.

5. Press [Alt], D, and T to activate the Titles command. Enter *Unit Volume* into the "Chart Title" text box and press [Enter].

6. Press [Alt], C, and V to view the chart; it should look like the chart in Figure 10.16.

7. After you are finished viewing the chart, press [Alt], C, and C to activate the Charts command, and name the chart *Unit Volume*.

8. Press [Alt], C, and X to activate the Exit command, leaving the charting component of the spreadsheet.

9. Press [Alt], F, and C to activate the "File Close" command. Save the changes to the file.

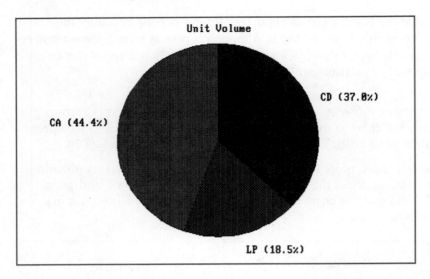

Figure 10.16
The Music pie chart.

Charting from the Database

Whenever large collections of numbers need to be computed, spreadsheets are useful, and whenever those numbers need to be studied, charts are useful. Thus, it is not surprising that the Works charting software is part of the spreadsheet. However, databases can contain numbers, too. In Chapters 8 and 9, you saw how queries can be used to study the information in a database. Queries allow you to select a small portion of the records in a database for a special purpose. But what if you want to study most, if not all, of the records in a database? If the information you want to study contains numbers, charting can help.

Although you cannot chart information directly in the Works database, you can copy database fields to spreadsheet cells and then chart those cells. In this exercise, you will copy fields from the COUNTRY database on your disk to an empty spreadsheet. This database contains population and economic data about selected countries in the world.

To create a line chart from these data:

1. First open the COUNTRY database file. Make sure you are in the "List" screen of the database.

2. Move the cursor into the second field, called "Country." You cannot select the field caption Country, but select the first country name.

3. Press [Alt], S, and F to activate the Field command in the Select menu. The entire column of country names will be selected. Now press [Alt], E, and C to activate the Copy command in the Edit menu, to copy the fields.

4. Press [Alt], F, and N to activate the New command in the File menu. The NEW dialog box will be displayed. Choose the Spreadsheet option, and press [Alt] and N to open an empty spreadsheet file.

5. Move the cursor to cell A2 and press [Enter] to copy the column of country names into the spreadsheet. Then move the cursor to cell A1 and type *Country* and [Enter] to give the column a caption.

6. Press [Alt], W, and 1 to activate the Window command and return to the database.

7. Move the cursor into field 11, captioned "Import$M." Now hold down the [Shift] key and press the right arrow key once to select field 12 (Export$M) as well.

8. Press [Alt], S, and F to activate the Field command in the Select menu. Both Import$M and Export$M columns will be selected.

9. Press [Alt], E, and C again to copy the fields.

10. Press [Alt], W, and 2 to activate the Window command and return to the spreadsheet.

11. Move the cursor into cell B2 and press [Enter] to copy the fields. Type the caption *Import$M* into cell B1 and *Export$M* into cell C1.

You have copied the data needed to chart imports versus exports from the database into a spreadsheet. Because there are 20 values for the *Y* series of this chart, we will create a line chart.

---

1. Move the cursor to cell A1, and while holding down the [Shift] key, move to cell C21. This selects all the cells from A1 through C21.

2. Press [Alt], C, and N to activate the New command in the Chart menu and switch to the chart component.

3. Press [Alt], T, and L to activate the Line command in the Format menu, to create a line chart.

4. Press [Alt], T, and D to activate the Data command. The DATA FORMAT dialog box, as shown in Figure 10.17, will be displayed.

5. Since this chart has two *Y* series, we will distinguish the first one, Import$M, with a dotted line. Press [Alt] and P, and press the down arrow key until "Dotted" is selected; then press [Enter].

6. Press [Alt], C, and V to view the finished chart shown in Figure 10.18.

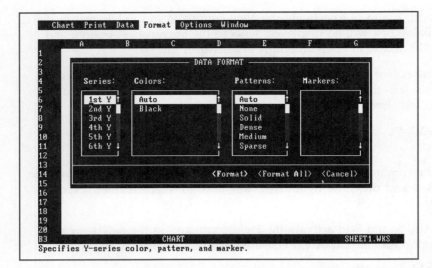

Figure 10.17
The DATA FORMAT dialog box.

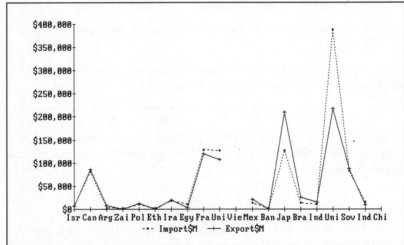

Figure 10.18
The Import Export chart.

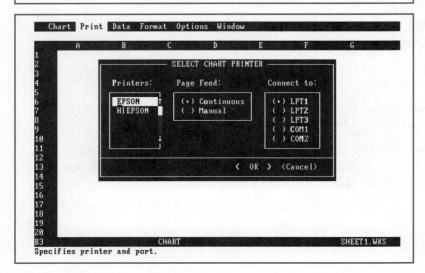

Figure 10.19
The SELECT CHART PRINTER dialog box.

This chart compares the exports of a country to its imports and compares them both to those of other countries. The height of the line on the *Y* axis indicates the dollar volume of the trade. The breaks in the lines are caused by the lack of data for China and Vietnam.

Notice how the lines run very close together for most countries. This means that these countries export about the same amount that they import. Their trade is balanced. Notice that Japan (Jap) and the United States (Uni) have the largest trade imbalances (the smaller value captioned Uni is for the United Kingdom). Not only do Japan and the United States have the largest trade imbalances, but the lines are switched. The "Export$M" line is on top for Japan, meaning Japan exports more than it imports; notice that the opposite is true for the United States, which imports a great deal more than it exports.

As you can see, this graph provides a great deal of insight into an ordinary column of numbers. It provides a dramatic picture of world trade that can be quickly grasped. And it is easy to see why the trade relationship between Japan and the United States so dominates economic news headlines.

Printing Graphs

You can print this graph if you have an appropriate printer attached to your computer.

1. Press [Alt], P, and S to display the SELECT CHART PRINTER dialog box shown in Figure 10.19. Use the arrow keys to select a printer displayed in the "Printers" list box. If you don't know which printer to use, ask for help, or try EPSON. Press [Enter].

2. Press [Alt], P, and P to display the PRINT dialog box. Make sure the printer is turned on, and press [Enter].

3. When printing is finished, you can press [Alt], C, and X to activate the Exit command, leaving the charting component of the spreadsheet. The new chart will keep the default name, CHART1.

4. Press [Alt], F, and A to activate the "Save As" command in the File menu. Give the file the name COUNTRY. This file will not replace the database file called COUNTRY. The database is named COUNTRY.WDB, and this file will be named COUNTRY.WKS.

A WORD ABOUT
Presentation Graphics

Virtually all spreadsheet programs offer some form of built-in charting capabilities. Through a few simple commands, these programs can transform data contained in their spreadsheet into charts, such as bar, line, and pie charts.

Although spreadsheet charts are relatively quick and easy to produce, they are not of very high quality. Presentation graphics software, coupled with a laser printer or a slidemaker, are used to produce high-quality charts and diagrams suitable for presentation to a large audience.

A popular medium for presentation graphics is the 35mm slide. Computerized slidemaking systems that attach to a personal computer can produce color 35mm slides quickly and inexpensively.

But the 35mm slide presentation faces stiff competition from portable liquid crystal display (LCD) projection pads that are placed on top of ordinary transparency projector units. These devices allow images on the computer screen to be displayed on the conference room wall. A remote control unit, similar to a slide projector's remote control, allows the presenter to interact with the presentation graphics software. Although not yet suitable for color presentations, this method eliminates the need to make 35mm slides. Also, since the images being projected come directly from the computer and presentation software, they can be quickly revised before, or even during, the presentation.

Projecting a chart with the Kodak *Datashow*.

Review

Key Terms

Charting	Bar chart
X axis	*XY* chart (scatter chart)
Y axis	Hi-low chart
Scale	Hi-low-close chart
Line chart	Stacked bar chart
Pie chart	100 percent bar chart

Discussion Questions

1. Why do newspapers use charts so frequently?
2. Name two things that charting allows you to do.
3. What is the difference between an *X* axis and a *Y* series?
4. How is it possible for a chart to be technically accurate but still misleading?
5. Describe three different chart styles.
6. Why is an *XY* chart often called a scatter chart?
7. Why would you use a hi-low-close chart for stock market analysis?
8. How can charts be used to explore a database?

Software Exercises

1. In the "Unit Volume" pie chart, use cells B17:D17 instead of B10:D10 to chart dollar volume instead of unit volume.
2. Use the Titles command in the Data menu to add a title to the import/export chart and then print it.
3. In the import/export chart, use the [Alt], O, Y command to activate the Y-AXIS dialog box. Change the minimum to 0, the maximum to 100,000, and the interval to 4,000. This changes the *Y*-axis scale. Notice how the rise and fall of the smaller values is accentuated and the large numbers, like those for the United States, fall off the top of the chart entirely.
4. Go back to the COUNTRY database and copy the "Literacy" and "%Urban" columns into the COUNTRY spreadsheet to chart these two *Y* series the same way imports and exports were charted. Notice if there is a strong correlation between the number of people living in urban areas and the literacy rate.
5. Find some statistics in your newspaper and create a chart to illustrate them. The weather report or the sports section are good places to look for tables of numbers.

PART III

Connections

Computers have had a dramatic impact on business, government, and society. Seen from this viewpoint, the computer is not so much a technical tool as it is a powerful agent of change. As a result, society has the ability to reorganize work in ways that benefit both organizations and people. Organizations can become more efficient and effective; people can become more creative. But such a promise does not come without problems. We still have to develop attitudes and skills that are consistent with the new technologies.

Part III provides you with a useful way to think about the fundamental relationships or connections between computers and society. The first connection is communications. Chapter 11 discusses the important role that communications has assumed in computing. Chapter 12 delves into office automation, management information systems, electronic banking, factory automation, and computers in the professions. Chapter 13 explores the uses of computers in government, education, the arts, and the sciences.

Chapter 14 covers the ethical issues surrounding computers. Finally, Chapter 15 discusses how you might go about buying your own personal computer.

- After you complete Chapter 11, you will have gained an understanding of how communications software is used to access information services like home banking and electronic mail.
- After you complete Chapter 12, you will understand how computers are used in the workplace.
- After you complete Chapter 13, you will have a better awareness of the role of computers in society's institutions.
- After you complete Chapter 14, you will be able to discuss the ethical implications of computer use in managing personal information.
- After you complete Chapter 15, you will understand the questions you should ask before shopping for a personal computer.

11

Introducing Communications

Preview   As you have learned throughout this book, a computer can help you perform many useful tasks. But a computer's capabilities are dramatically enhanced when it can communicate with other computers.

In this chapter, we'll discuss the many uses of computer-to-computer communication. You'll learn what hardware and software components are required for such communication. Then we'll explain some general steps that you can refer to when you begin using the Works communications tool. Although Works does include a communications tool, this chapter omits hands-on exercises, because you may not have access to the specific services used as examples.

Finally, this chapter will give you background on some of the volatile issues of the communications industry.

In this chapter, you'll learn:

■ Some basic communications concepts
■ What a communications network does
■ Types of communications networks
■ What an information utility provides
■ What a modem does
■ How to get started with the Works communications tool
■ Some communications industry issues

Communications Basics

Every time you make a telephone call, you are tapping into a vast worldwide communications system. But did you know that computers use the same telephone system to call other computers? In fact, much of the traffic over telephone lines today consists of computer-to-computer communication. Computer **communications** are the movement of information from one computer to another. Computer communications allow information to be moved from place to place and to be shared by many people.

Whereas the standalone personal computer allows an individual to work more efficiently in new and different ways, communications allow *groups* of people using computers to work together more effectively. By using computer-to-computer communications, it is possible to:

- Electronically communicate with friends and coworkers.
- Access your bank account to obtain statements, pay bills via electronic funds transfer, and transfer money between different accounts.
- Obtain the flight schedules of most airlines, make airline reservations, and purchase tickets.
- Search through libraries of bibliographic information.
- Read articles from news services.
- Obtain up-to-date financial information on stocks, bonds, and other securities.
- Access your broker's computer system to buy and sell stock.
- Work at home, moving information to and from your company's computer system.

The details of how computer-to-computer communications take place is a technical subject beyond the scope of this chapter. But the basic concepts of using computers to communicate are analogous to using the telephone and postal service, two systems with which almost everyone is familiar.

Computer Networks

Computers communicate through communications **networks**, special communications paths that allow information to be moved from place to place. The telephone

Using a local area network provided by 3Com Corp. and the HP Touchscreen personal computer, users in an office workgroup can share hard disks and printers. The network also allows users to send and receive electronic mail.

system is a communications network. You have probably heard of telephone companies like AT&T, MCI, and GTE. Other less familiar companies, like Telenet and Tymnet, provide communications networks designed especially for computers.

The largest networks are operated like the telephone system. Anyone can sign up for service and use the network. As with the telephone system, you are billed each month for the services you use. Large organizations sometimes have private networks to carry data only within the organization. However, most private networks make some use of public networks. For instance, a large bank in New York City might have a private network carrying data from branch to branch within the city itself. However, when data need to be moved across the country to Los Angeles, the bank uses a public network that has a communications satellite.

A **communications satellite** acts as a relay station in outer space. It receives data beamed at it from a ground station and relays those data to other ground stations. The satellite can carry the bank's data long distances at low cost. But the bank does not move enough data to Los Angeles to justify purchasing its own communications satellite.

Low-cost satellite dishes may soon enable personal computers to connect to a wide variety of services.

Electronic Mail

Public networks also serve an important role in providing computer communications between different organizations. A very important application of computer networks is electronic mail. **Electronic mail** is a cross between a letter and a phone call. Like a phone call, it is easy and quick; an electronic message is simple to prepare and usually arrives seconds or minutes after it is sent. Unlike a phone call, electronic mail does not require the recipient to be available when delivery is made.

Many companies have private electronic mail networks that improve the productivity of their employees. However, a private network serves only the employees of a single company. Those employees cannot send messages to their customers, suppliers, or anyone else outside the company. Public networks solve this problem by providing public electronic mail services.

Public electronic mail services work as follows. The service has a computer system large enough to hold thousands of **electronic mailboxes** — individual files stored on the computer system's disks. The service maintains the electronic mailboxes in much the same way that the postal service maintains a set of post office boxes. But instead of walking to the post office and picking up your mail, you simply use your computer to communicate with the electronic mail service. Your electronic mail can be read only by you, but other people can send mail to your mailbox. Like letters in a post office box, electronic mail messages are stored in your electronic mailbox until you decide to read them.

Public Electronic Mailboxes	
Service (Company)	Subscribers
Easy Plex (CompuServe)	275,000
EasyLink (Western Union)	130,000
Dialcom (British Telecom)	100,000
Telemail (US Sprint)	80,000
Quick Comm (GE)	80,000
MCI Mail (MCI)	75,000
On Tyme (McDonnell Douglas)	55,000
Info Plex (CompuServe)	40,000
RCA Mail (RCA)	25,000
AT&T Mail (AT&T)	25,000
Others	100,000
Total	985,000

A sample of the many electronic mail services available.

Electronic mail has a compelling advantage for the traveler. Unlike a phone number or a post office box, an electronic mail address is the same no matter where you go. If you are out of town and someone calls your home phone number, you won't be there. If someone mails you a letter, it will sit in the post office box until you return. However, if someone sends you electronic mail, you can read it (and reply) from anywhere in the world. It is for this reason that traveling employees, such as sales and service people, often use portable computers to send and receive electronic mail.

Information Utilities

Networks do more than make it possible for computers to communicate. They have made possible a completely new kind of service, often called an information utility. An **information utility** provides you with information and services through your personal computer. You subscribe to an information utility as you would subscribe to a magazine or sign up for telephone service. Your personal computer communicates, through networks, with computers owned by the utility. Together the computers provide you with access to information and services that your personal computer by itself could not possibly provide.

These services usually come in two categories, based on access to data and access to transactions.

Access to Data

Services based on access to data make sense when the value of the data is enhanced through computer delivery. Such data can be *time-critical*, or less valuable if you were to obtain it more slowly, say by reading a daily newspaper. The data may change so often that anything but the very latest information is almost useless.

```
                        No. 15701

                  Supreme Court of Idaho

              111 Idaho 759; 727 P.2d 1187

                  October 17, 1986, Filed

    Appeal from the District Court of the Sixth Judicial District of the State of
Idaho, Bannock County. Hon. Dell W. Smith, District Judge.

    Appeal from a jury verdict in favor of James R. Crane and Johnny L. King
against defendants, Fred Arthur Turner, Rollins Leasing Corp. and Sigman Meat
Co. Reversed in part and remanded for a determination on defendants motions for
a new trial or remittitur of damages. Affirmed on all other grounds.

    DONALDSON, C.J.

    William D. Faler, Esq., and Curt R. Thomsen, Esq., of Holden, Kidwell, Hahn &
Crapo, Idaho Falls, Idaho, attorneys for appellants, Turner, et al.

    James B. Green, Esq. and Steven V. Richert, Esq., of Green, Service, Gasser &
Kerl, Pocatello, Idaho, attorneys for respondent Crane.

    John C. Souza, Esq. of Whittier & Souza, Pocatello, Idaho, attorney for
respondent, King.

    DONALDSON
```

LEXIS is an information service used by lawyers which provides a database of all court cases and judicial opinions from federal and state courts.

Stock quotes and the price of airline tickets are examples of such data. Other services provide access to databases so large that it would not be feasible for a personal computer to hold one. The service allows you to browse through the data, using the query techniques you learned in Chapter 8. Then only the information you need is transferred, over the network, to your computer. An example is a popular service, called LEXIS, used by lawyers. It provides a database of all court cases and judicial opinions from all federal and state courts. Lawyers working on a particular kind of case use the service to get the records and legal opinions for similar cases. The information is more up to date than any printed law book could be, and the use of database query techniques to search for relevant cases is both easier and more accurate than browsing through a book.

Another service has been set up for investors specifically interested in stock market transactions. It is called Dow Jones News/Retrieval. This service includes financial and general news from *The Wall Street Journal* and *Barron's*. Subscribers can also obtain current stock price quotes, summaries of stock exchange transactions, and economic forecasts.

Access to Transactions

A *transaction* is an agreement, often an agreement to purchase something. Many information services are based on transactions. For instance, you can purchase shares of stock, pay a bill, and make an airline reservation and purchase the ticket using a credit card.

Introducing Communications

Home banking is a transaction-based service offered by many banks in conjunction with a checking account. Instead of writing paper checks, you use your personal computer to instruct the bank to transfer funds electronically to a specific business to pay a bill. Of course, you can see how much money you have in your account, and you can instruct the bank to pay a bill sometime in the future.

Many services combine transactions and access to data. For instance, when you purchase an airline ticket electronically, you also choose the airline and flight by browsing through a huge database of current airline flight information.

Local Area Networks

The communications networks that support electronic mail and other public services are examples of **wide-area networks**, networks that span a great geographic distance. Another way in which personal computers communicate with other computers is through a **local-area network**, or **LAN**, a network that is typically installed in a single office or building. All the computers that are connected to the local network can communicate with each other. Local networks allow computers to exchange local mail and share data and hardware devices, such as expensive printers. Local networks can be connected to wide-area networks so that mail can be exchanged and other local networks can be accessed.

Communication Hardware and Software

For computer-to-computer communication to occur, several components must work together. Each computer needs a hardware connection to the network, and software must take care of the many tasks necessary to communicate.

Terminals

The earliest form of computer-to-computer communication relied on **terminals** — devices used in a communication system to enter or receive data. Although terminals can still be found, personal computers are now more common. One method of computer communication is often called **terminal emulation**, in which software in a personal computer simulates a terminal. The keys you press on your personal computer keyboard are sent to the other computer, and what the other computer displays is shown on the screen of your personal computer. Terminal emulation is the most common method of accessing public information services. This is the type of communication provided by the Works software.

Modems

The hardware device that connects a personal computer to another computer over the telephone is called a **modem**. Figure 11.1 shows two personal computers linked

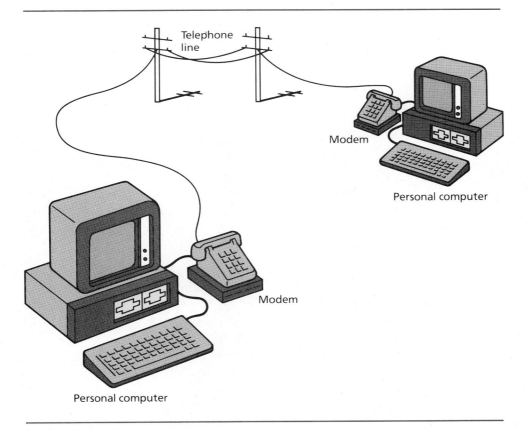

```
ENHANCED QUOTES BEING ACCESSED

ENTER QUERY
  ,ibm aapl


DOW JONES STOCK QUOTE REPORTER SERVICE
STOCK QUOTES DELAYED OVER 15 MINUTES
*=CLOSE PRICE ADJUSTED FOR EX-DIVIDEND


STOCK     BID       ASKED
          CLOSE     OPEN      HIGH      LOW       LAST      VOL(100'S)
IBM       124 5/8   125 1/2   126 3/8   125       126 1/8   5750
AAPL      19 5/8    19 3/4    21        19 1/2    20 5/8    6784

QUOTES HISTORICAL symbol:
          period:(Daily)Monthly Quarterly
          start date: 4/10/85  end date: 4/10/85
          today's date: 4/10/85
          type:(Stock)Warrant
Enter security symbol
DOW JONE          Scr              Access: DOWJONES 00:04:20 L2W1
```

With communications software and a modem, personal computer users can access information from an electronic library, such as the Dow Jones Stock Quote shown here.

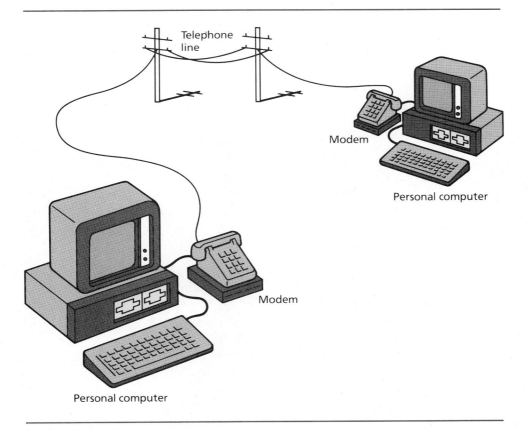

Figure 11.1
Personal computers linked by telephone lines.

A.

Comparison of (a) an external modem, and (b) an internal modem, which is shown with communications software and a user manual.

by their modems and the telephone lines. There are several types of modems available for personal computer users.

Internal modems fit inside the system unit of a personal computer.

Standalone modems are freestanding boxes with cables that plug into your computer. These modems must also plug into an AC power socket.

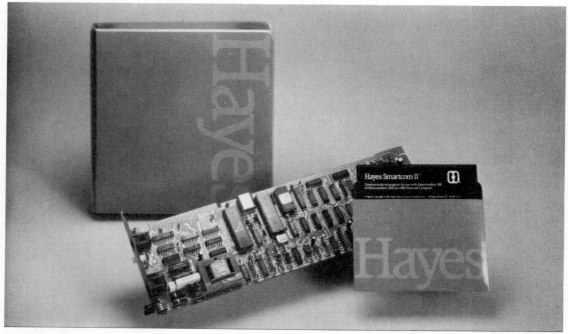

B.

Acoustic-coupled modems don't plug directly into a telephone jack. Instead, rubber cups are fitted over the telephone handset. They can be used in a hotel room or phone booth, where it might be inconvenient or impossible to use a direct connection.

Modems are often standard equipment for portable computers, such as the Tandy 100 and 200 and the Grid Compass. In other computers, they can be added later.

Communication Software

How do you tell a modem what to do? **Communications software** is the link between your computer and modem that performs the tasks necessary for computers to communicate with one another. The Works Communications tool is an example of communications software.

A Sample Works Communications File

Suppose you have decided to use the electronic mail service from MCI Corporation. MCI has sent you a subscriber's kit that includes a list of telephone numbers your computer can call to connect with their computers. You have also been assigned a *user ID* and a *password*. The user ID identifies you and your electronic mailbox. The password is a word or number that you must keep secret. When you call MCI mail, their computer will ask you to type in the password, to prove that you have the right to read the mail in your mailbox.

Creating a communications file with Works is just like creating a word processing, spreadsheet, or database file. You usually create a separate file for each computer you call. From the initial NEW dialog box, choose "Communications" and press the [Enter] key. The initial Communications screen will appear as shown in Figure 11.2.

Before you begin communicating, you must make some adjustments. At a minimum you must tell Works the telephone number that must be dialed to reach the other computer. Making a connection can be complicated by the fact that both computers must be "talking the same language" in order to communicate. There are three commands in the Options menu — Terminal, Communication, and Phone — that are used to configure a Works Communications file.

In order to connect to another computer, Works has to know the phone number of the computer to which you want to connect. With most modems, Works can dial the phone number for you.

1. Choose "Phone" from the Options menu. A dialog box will appear, as shown in Figure 11.3. Type in the local phone number for your city. If you are not in a major city, you may need to type a long distance number including 1 and the area code.

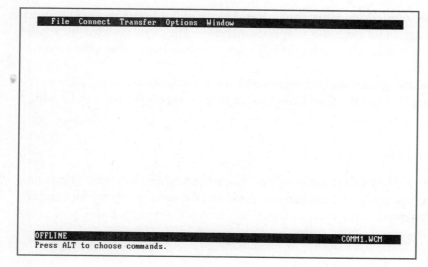

Figure 11.2
Initial Communications screen.

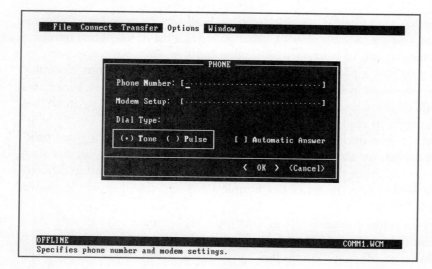

Figure 11.3
The PHONE dialog box.

2. Unless you have been given special instructions for your modem, ignore the "Modem Setup" text box. It is used to adjust some modems before dialing.

3. Select "Tone" or "Pulse". "Tone" means that you have touch-tone phone service (your phones have buttons). "Pulse" means that you have rotary service (your phones have dials).

4. Ignore the "Automatic Answer" check box. It is used when another computer will be calling yours.

The Communication command controls the speed and format of the data sent between two computers. The subscriber's kit will offer advice about what settings to use.

1. Choose "Communication" from the Options menu. A dialog box will appear, as shown in Figure 11.4.

2. "Baud Rate" tells the computer which of several standard speeds the modem will use to send and receive data. Common baud rates include 300, 1200, 2400, and 9600. Type in the baud rate specified in your subscriber's kit; for most services today, this is 1200.

3. The "Data Bits", "Stop Bits", "Handshake", and "Parity" options have to do with the format of data; use the settings your subscriber's kit recommends.

4. The "Port" choice box tells Works the communications port on your computer to which your modem is connected. Your subscriber's kit cannot tell you this; you will have to ask whoever assembled and configured your computer. If in doubt, you can try both settings and see which one works.

The Terminal command is used to change how characters are displayed on your screen and how the keys on your keyboard are interpreted by the other computer. You will rarely need to change the standard settings.

Once you have set these parameters, you can save the file and use it over and over. You can set up a file for each computer with which you frequently communicate.

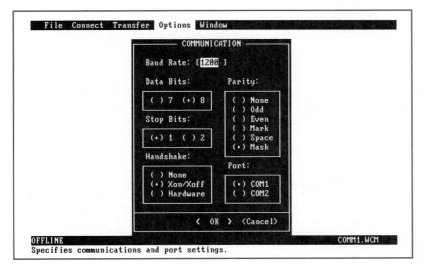

Figure 11.4
The COMMUNICATION dialog box.

Making the Connection

The Connect command on the Connect menu is used to actually dial the phone number and establish a connection with the other computer. Most modems have a speaker, so that you can hear the dialing and ringing sounds. When the other computer answers, you will hear a high-pitched tone and then the speaker will turn off; the connection has been made.

At this point, your subscriber's kit may have special instructions. For instance, you may have to press [Enter] several times to get the attention of the other computer.

Typically, the other computer will then ask you for your user ID and password before allowing you to access your mailbox or other services. These steps of identifying yourself (your user ID) and proving who you are (your password) are often called *signing on*. Finishing a communications session is called *signing off*. The time between sign on and sign off is often used to compute some or all of the charges you incur for using the service.

Advanced Features

An in-depth discussion of the more advanced uses of communications software is beyond the scope of this chapter. However, Works is capable of the following:

1. The process of signing on can be automated using the "Record Sign-On" command.

2. You can save the characters sent to your computer in a word processing file, using the "Capture Text" command in the Transfer menu. Later you can edit and print this file with the word processor.

3. You can send a file to the other computer, using the "Send Text" command in the Transfer menu.

4. If you need to send and receive files like spreadsheets and databases, which are more complex than plain text, you can use the "Send Protocol" command. This command requires close cooperation from the other computer.

If you need to use any of these advanced features, you may be able to get help from your instructor, your school's computer laboratory, and the information service you wish to use.

Communications Industry Issues

In the past, different segments of the communications industry were distinct. Printing and newspapers, telephone service, and cable television all evolved at different times as separate technologies within distinct business sectors.

Today these distinctions are less clear. The development of electronic technologies has created several problems and issues in distinguishing one medium from another. The telephone and computer industries are closely connected. Information in all media is stored electronically in databases and retrieved electronically by computer-to-computer communication over telephone lines. This makes it possible for information to be easily and inexpensively duplicated, sold, rented, or otherwise made available to millions of people.

Many applications of electronic technology are largely experimental. Knight Ridder Newspapers *(Miami Herald, Philadelphia Enquirer)*, the Times Mirror Company *(Los Angeles Times* and *Long Island Newsday)*, and the previously mentioned Dow Jones & Company *(The Wall Street Journal* and *Barron's)* have all experimented with various forms of electronic publishing. Similarly, the Bell companies, such as Pacific Bell and New York Telephone, are conducting marketing trials in which they offer electronic shopping, voice mail, and travel reservations. But such information utilities have become a bone of contention among various economic interests, particularly in the area of advertising.

A WORD ABOUT
Personal Computers as Agents

Traditionally, computers have been thought of as only computational engines that do what they are told when they are told. Now artificial intelligence (AI) techniques are being used to create a new kind of software service, called an *agent*, that can act independently without specific instructions.

The term *agent* originated with artificial intelligence researchers John McCarthy and Oliver G. Selfridge at MIT. They had in mind a system that, when given a general goal, could carry out the numerous computer operations needed to achieve that goal. The agent would stop and ask for instructions only when it was stuck. An agent could be a highly evolved communications tool, doing its business within a network of computers.

What might such an agent do? An agent acting as an intelligent personal electronic newspaper is one subject of current research. Such a newspaper would store a profile about the user's history of preferences, interests, and needs. It would then search through library databases and wire services looking for articles it knows the user is interested in. It would then present them for the user to browse through, read, or save for future reference.

Another possibility is that of an agent acting as a personal secretary. It would handle appointments and scheduling. Like the electronic newspaper, it would scan the databases and wire services and inform the user of events of importance or interest. It could even take over some routine chores: producing scheduled reports, periodically backing up files, and scanning sources for data to input to the user's programs.

There are many routine tasks that could be automated with the help of computers. However, if the computer requires the kind of step-by-step instructions that characterize most of today's software, such automation may not be worth the trouble. Agents can help free the user from the mundane and repetitive details needed to use complex computer environments, such as network-based information services.

Suppose, for example, that telephone companies were to offer information services that carried advertising and allowed consumers to place orders for merchandise electronically. What if you could use your personal computer to obtain classified advertising? Such forms of electronic advertising would definitely impact newspaper advertising revenues.

On the other hand, newspaper publishers and cable television companies have formed an alliance in which they propose to offer the electronic equivalent of the yellow pages. The telephone companies oppose such a venture, since publishing telephone directories (in print or electronically) is a lucrative component of their own business.

The matter is complicated because the federal government has long regulated the telephone industry and more recently the cable television industry. On the other hand, newspaper publishers are protected from government interference by the First Amendment to the Constitution; and private industries, like the computer industry, remain largely unregulated. The Federal Communications Commission (FCC), established to regulate interstate communication, has recently adopted a new regulatory framework that stimulates competition among the providers of information utility services, such as electronic yellow pages and classified advertisements, home shopping, electronic and voice mail, and travel reservations.

The original laws that granted telephone and cable television companies monopolies gave those companies tremendous advantages that private companies did not enjoy. At the same time, FCC regulations over the monopolies have prevented them from taking advantage of many new technologies that private companies are free to use. Vested interests on both sides want to protect their advantages, while technology continues to make new, innovative, and useful kinds of communication possible. Untangling the regulatory web that prevents innovative new services from reaching the public is a major goal of both the FCC and the industry.

Review _____

Key Terms

Communications   Terminal
Networks   Terminal emulation
Communications satellite   Modem
Electronic mail   Internal modem
Electronic mailbox   Standalone modem
Information utility   Acoustic-coupled modem
Wide-area network   Communications software
Local-area network (LAN)

Discussion Questions

1. Name three uses for computer-to-computer communication.

2. How is electronic mail similar to the postal service? To the telephone system?

3. What is a communications network?

4. What are some of the advantages of electronic mail? When is a phone call more useful?

5. Describe the difference between information utilities based on access to data and those based on access to transactions.

6. What is the difference between wide-area and local-area networks?

7. What is the purpose of a modem? How do you tell a modem what to do?

8. How is using the Works Communications tool similar to using the other tools?

9. What are the two primary steps involved in signing on to an electronic mail service or information utility?

10. Why are the distinctions between newspapers, telephone services, and cable television blurring?

Projects

1. Some experts argue that government regulation is necessary in the area of electronic information utilities. Others argue that regulations are obsolete and that the market should determine what is offered. Take a position on this dispute and defend it.

2. There are several vendors of electronic mail services. Obtain the names of three different vendors, and write to each of them to obtain literature concerning their services and prices. Prepare a report on your findings.

12
Computers at Work

Preview Every time you use a credit card, write a check, or eat at a fast-food restaurant, you initiate a computerized business transaction. The computer may not be visible, but at some point, it will register how much you paid or promised to pay, the date, and perhaps other details of your transaction. Once these data have been recorded, they can be used for many other purposes, from updating your account to compiling a market survey.

Today the computerization of basic business transactions is bringing us closer to popular fantasies of the "paperless office" and the "cashless society." To what extent have changes in office and business technology realized those dreams? In this chapter, we examine the impact of computers on the business and professional world. Beginning with office automation, we will see how computer systems begin to restructure organizations. Then we will study three specialized types of information systems in detail: transaction processing, management information systems, and decision support systems. Next we will briefly assess the ways in which computers and robots aid manufacturing. Then we will examine finance, banking, and retailing. After reviewing how computers have changed business organizations, we will shift our analysis to the professions, to see what kinds of changes they have been experiencing.

In this chapter, you'll learn:

- The functions of office automation
- The role of ergonomics in designing computer systems
- Uses for management information systems
- Uses for robots in manufacturing
- Uses for computers in finance, banking, and retailing
- How health care professionals use computers
- How lawyers use computers
- How journalists use computers

Computers in the Office

The idea behind **office automation (OA)** is simple: use the computer to assist in recording, filing, and communicating data and information. The payoff is increased efficiency, speedier record handling, and quicker response to the needs of the customer and to changes in the marketplace than may be possible under a manual system. In the world of business, early knowledge is power. Many a company has prospered by being the first to take advantage of a hot new fad or a trend in consumer buying. Any many a company has floundered for failing to anticipate a crucial change in customer taste or fundamental technology.

Consider a company that owned and operated three employment agencies in the suburbs of a large city. Aside from its accounting and payroll functions, the company's record keeping was devoted mainly to the complex task of matching job orders from employers with the qualifications of applicants. Under its manual system, the company kept its job orders in separate "tubs" identified by job description. There was one tub for secretaries, another for receptionists, a third for filers, a fourth for medical technologists, and so on. Each office separately maintained hundreds of such tubs for its own use. Once an applicant had been interviewed and qualified, the counselor would thumb through the orders in the appropriate tub for a job description that matched. The brain of the individual counselor was the CPU behind this manual system. Those counselors who were diligent searchers of the tubs or gifted with exceptional memories ("I remember a job description like this that came in last year! Now, where did I put it?") did well. Those who weren't persistent searchers or who had bad memories didn't do so well.

The chief aim of office automation should be to make a company more efficient by bringing out the best in its employees. And that was exactly the effect of OA in this case. The automated system consisted of microcomputers linked through a local area network and operating under custom software that classified every possible job order.

Instituting this OA system improved the efficiency of the business, because the computer instantly retrieved and matched job orders with applicants. A second result was speedier input of job descriptions. A job order logged into the system by a counselor at the North Office at 10:05 A.M. became available to a counselor at the Metro Office seconds later. A third result was that the company could now monitor its placements by counselor, job order, or even office. Thus, if management noticed that the South Office was swamped with data processing job orders, it could quickly transfer a counselor there who specialized in DP applicants. Eventually such a trend would also be spotted under a manual system, but much later. Like an army, the business that can deploy its people where they are most needed has a better chance of success.

Five Primary Functions

This case also illustrates the five major functions that make up OA: word processing, database management, spreadsheets, graphics, and communications. The following are snapshots of each function and its part in a typical OA scheme.

Word Processing

From Chapter 4 we know that *word processing* is the use of computers for preparing written documents. The term was coined by IBM in 1964 to distinguish its new line of typewriters from computer systems that do data processing. In the case of the employment agency, word processing was used to enter and log job orders; to acknowledge, by means of personalized form letters, the receipt of orders; and to allow counselors to correspond with each other as well as with applicants and employers.

Database Management

The intended use of the database in the employment agency was mainly to match job orders with applicants. But, once operational, the database also produced information vital for management of the whole company. For example, an exact profile of how individual counselors, offices, or regions were performing could be extracted from the database. Breakdowns of job orders by counselor, office, or region were instantly available from month to month, week to week, or even day to day. Management had its finger on the pulse of its daily business in a way impossible under a manual system.

Tied into the accounting system, the database also generated payroll records for individual counselors, billed commissions, made automatic entries into accounts receivable, and provided management with quarterly financial statements.

Spreadsheets

What if a DP counselor were added to the South Office? What if the Metro Office's decline in new business last month were sustained over the entire year? Playing *what-if* is the fundamental aim of spreadsheets. It is a game that management plays in earnest, with harsh financial penalties for poor forecasts or bad judgment. As you've seen from Chapter 7 on spreadsheets, the game of *what-if* is best played with accurate and up-to-date data. With OA, management has the most current figures at its fingers. If there has been a drastic dip in the North Office's business, for example, management knows the bad news nearly instantly and can respond quickly. Timely and accurate information is vital to any management decision.

Figure 12.1
A major aspect of contemporary office automation is the integration of computing
and communication technologies.

Graphics

As you learned in Chapter 10, graphics play an important role in the automated
office. A pie chart with an ominous chunk missing can dramatize a grim dip in
income in a way that numbers alone cannot.

Communications

If computers couldn't communicate with one another, their usefulness to humans
would be severely limited. But, thankfully, computers *can* "talk" to one another,
and business has been quick to grasp the benefits of this ability. Large companies
that issue portable computers to their field sales force can instantly communicate
any product or price change via modem. A stockbroker in Atlanta can have
immediate access to every nervous blip in the Dow Jones averages. An executive
on the 54th floor can send an important presentation via LAN hookup to an attorney on the 10th floor for scrutiny and addition of legal boilerplate. That three
offices could simultaneously share a common database of job orders and applicants
was the most useful feature of the automated office in our employment agency
example. It was the integration of computing and communication technologies (as
illustrated in Figure 12.1) that made this possible.

Computer communications also involve the widespread use of *electronic mail systems*. Two types of electronic mail systems have become popular: those within a single department or company and mail systems, such as MCI Mail, that use large-scale national or international networks.

Computer conferencing, in which groups of people communicate about a mutual problem through electronic mail, is also gaining in popularity. Studies have shown that such conferences require less time than face-to-face meetings. The conference may take place at a single sitting, with all participants on line, or it may extend over a period of time to allow for the drafting of replies and counter-arguments. But the bottom line of such electronic meetings is that they cost less than face-to-face sessions requiring long-distance travel and can often be used to iron out minor differences between departments and individuals.

A WORD ABOUT
Workgroup Computing

Personal computers allow *individuals* to work more efficiently. However, in organizational settings, *groups* of people need to work together efficiently. A new type of application software called *workgroup software* is designed to help groups — such as task forces, departments, or divisions — do just that.

Workgroup computing uses network technology to support applications that help group members communicate, like electronic mail. Other applications help automate specific types of group-related work. For instance, one workgroup word processing application allows multiple authors to collaborate in the writing of a single document. The software remembers who wrote what; when; and in what order. Other applications deal with meetings. Meetings are often difficult to schedule because it's hard for group members to gather together in one place at once. Electronic meeting software acts like an extended electronic mail conversation that happens over a period of days or weeks. Group members attend the meeting electronically, give presentations, make comments on presentations, and respond to the comments.

Another type of workgroup application automates the flow of work from one individual to another. For instance, a purchase order may need to be routed through several departments for approval and budget allocation. It is then routed to a purchasing department, where the order is actually placed. Or maybe an employee's expense report is routed to a manager and then on to payroll, where it is included automatically in the next pay cycle. The workgroup application knows that several people in purchasing and payroll can handle these reports, avoiding having routine paperwork held up because someone is sick or on vacation.

Workgroup computing is very new, but it may eventually have a large impact on the way office work is done. It is possible that conventional bureaucratic structures will be replaced by more fluidly organized workgroups, which can be created and dissolved to meet the needs at hand. Individual workers may belong to several workgroups at once, based on their interests and expertise. While some bureaucracy is necessary in a large enterprise, it can place a heavy burden on the people involved. Workgroup software shifts some of that burden onto computers, freeing *people* to do their best and most creative work.

Figure 12.2
Facsimile machines are popular for sending contracts with a handwritten signature from a branch office to a home office; for international mail when same-day mail is needed; and in countries where the language has an alphabet of several thousand characters.

Finally, *facsimile transmission (fax)* is the use of machines to transmit pictures of documents — whether handwritten, line-drawn, or typeset — over telephone lines (see Figure 12.2). Most fax machines can produce an image detailed enough to do justice to a photograph. Deluxe fax machines can send and receive documents unattended, store documents for later transmission when rates are lower, transmit the same document to different machines, and even protect the confidentiality of documents by demanding a password before printing.

Personal computers can now be equipped with a special fax-compatible modem. Figure 12.3 shows the organization of a PC fax system. The PC may transmit either to another specially equipped PC or to a fax machine.

Human Factors: Ergonomics

Ergonomics is the science of adapting the working environment to suit the worker. Its emphasis isn't on changing the worker, but on engineering products to meet human comforts.

In the beginning of office automation, it was assumed that the computer could simply be plunked down where the typewriter had been, and that would be that. But workers soon began grumbling about headaches, eyestrain, and aching necks.

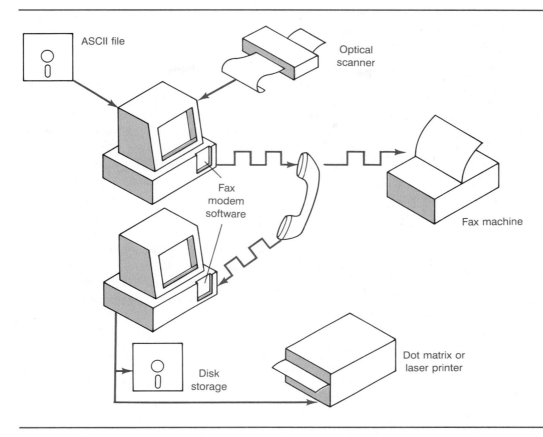

ASCII file

Optical scanner

Fax modem software

Fax machine

Disk storage

Dot matrix or laser printer

Figure 12.3
Personal computer fax configuration. The image can be transmitted to another personal computer or to a fax machine.

Allegations were made that the machines caused miscarriages, birth defects, and cataracts. These widespread complaints led to an in-depth study by the National Academy of Sciences on the effects of VDTs (video display terminals) on the health of workers. (The term *VDT* refers to any computer terminal, consisting of a CRT screen and a keyboard.) The academy issued its conclusions in 1983: no evidence existed to show that VDTs caused miscarriages, birth defects, or cataracts.

But that finding didn't quiet the chorus of worker complaints about eyestrain, weariness, and back problems. Scientists took a closer look and found significant reasons for worker discomfort. To begin with, there was a serious problem with lighting. *Task lighting* — which illuminates the surface area on which a worker is concentrating — is ideal for working at a typewriter, but terrible for a VDT, since it results in a glare reflected from the screen. Yet when the VDT replaced the typewriter, it inherited the typewriter's task lighting. Fluorescent lighting — exactly the kind one expert found illuminating nine out of ten offices — is likewise too glaring for a VDT screen.[1] Experiments indicated that nonreflective ambient background light is best for VDT work. Nor should a VDT ever be placed under a window, where the worker's eyes will be subjected to a double glare from the screen and the sun.

The problem of eyestrain caused by working before a VDT isn't imaginary. One study found that half of the estimated 15 million people who work at VDTs suffer blurry vision, eyestrain, and headaches.[2] Another researcher coined the term *technostress* to cover the symptoms of eye fatigue and other ailments reported by a target group of 100 VDT workers.[3] But these discomforts are easily remedied by adjustments to background lighting, the installation of glare shields, and other minor ergonomic adaptations. For example, workers who wear bifocals have an especially difficult time reading a VDT screen, because the upper lenses of such glasses typically have a focal length of 6 to 8 feet, whereas the lower ones have a focal length of 13 inches, making it nearly impossible for the wearer to comfortably read a screen 25 to 31 inches away. However, this potential source of discomfort can be reduced by outfitting the worker with special glasses.

The other principal source of worker complaints about VDTs is the physical layout of workstations. Some computers consist of a single unit with an undetachable keyboard and a fixed screen, which force all workers, regardless of height or girth, to sit in an identical position and stare straight ahead. Chairs were engineered for a rigid 90-degree posture. Studies later demonstrated that most workers prefer to sit at an angle of 104 degrees, which is apparently easier on the back, and to look down at the screen from an average angle of 31 degrees.[4] The detachable keyboards and tilt screens of later workstations in fact solved many of these initial problems.

You may think that these are small matters, but so is a grain of sand in the eye. One study found that, after ergonomic adjustments were made to a business's workstations, productivity increased between 4 and 8 percent.[5] Certainly, such gains are substantial enough to justify the minor expense of making workstations physically pleasing and comfortable to those who must staff them daily.

The computer industry has learned many lessons about the realities of humans in the workplace. One prime lesson is that a machine can't be abruptly imposed on an office unless it fits the habits and work styles of the people who will use it. For example, a new telephone system requiring the presence of at least three operators was installed in an office. The operators, who were used to taking their coffee break as a group, came to resent the machine and soon began clamoring that it didn't work. What's more, they "proved" their assertion.

Another important lesson is that experts can't discover what is comfortable and pleasing to workers without first studying the workers themselves. Such studies are under way at laboratories and will inevitably yield improvements in workstation and software design. For example, in one study conducted by Xerox at its Palo Alto Research Center (PARC), an experienced secretary was videotaped editing a document on a word processor. The secretary's 20-minute session behind the keyboard was broken down into 3,000 touching and typing events that were microscopically analyzed in increments as short as half a second.[6] Making programs that are better adapted to their human operators is the aim of this year-long study and others like it.

As one expert put it, "It is not enough for the system to provide a powerful and functional capability if the user cannot make use of it. The system should help the user without getting in his way, allowing him to concentrate on his task, not on the system; it should be efficient to use and easy to learn; it should be consistent, logical, natural."[7]

Information Systems

As we saw in our discussion of the employment agency's use of computers, computers not only make data entry quick and easy, they also allow managers and employees to analyze data and share or reorganize information. This section shows how businesses computerize basic business transactions and then transform those data into the information necessary to carry out the basic management functions of planning, organizing, staffing, directing, and controlling.

Computerization of Basic Business Transactions

Although, broadly speaking, office automation includes all computerization related to the office, traditional usage has limited the term to tasks related to word processing and telecommunications. Accounting functions, such as order entry and billing, are typically categorized under such labels as "general business applications" or "basic business transactions." These basic functions often consume most of the time and storage available on a company's computers. They constitute the central core of a business operation, but lacking glamor, they are sometimes neglected. As shown in Figure 12.4, the typical business accounting system has six main functional subsystems or components: general ledger, inventory, accounts receivable, accounts payable, payroll, and others, including orders and sales. Computerizing the accounting system consists of transferring tasks in each of these six areas from manual to software procedures. Businesses can choose separate software packages for each of the accounting functions or an *integrated* accounting system package, in which the individual components can share information easily.

Just as in a manual accounting system, the *general ledger* is a listing of business transactions by account. It is the heart of a computerized accounting system. Once a *chart of accounts*, which identifies the accounts used in the system, is defined, transactions can be entered in the ledger. How a transaction is entered or recorded depends on which of the six subsystems initiates it.

Let's assume, for example, that an order arrives at Bourke Manufacturing, a small furniture company with a computerized accounting system. A clerk enters detailed order information into the order-entry subsystem, which summarizes the order information and creates demand on the *inventory* subsystem. The inventory

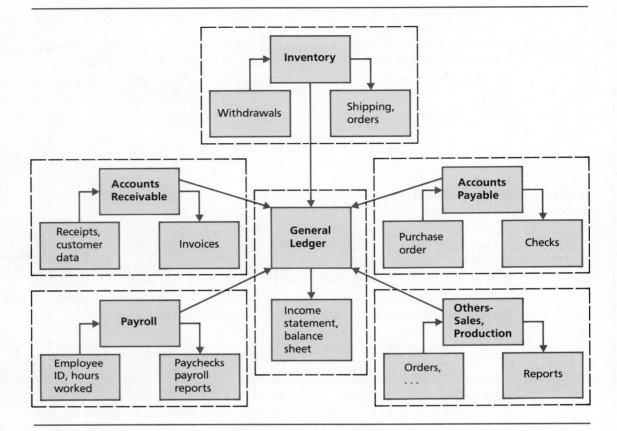

Figure 12.4
Overview of an accounting system for a small business, showing the six main types of transaction processing.

subsystem compares the order information with inventory status and does the following:

- Reserves inventory if available
- Creates demand on production or purchasing if inventory is insufficient to cover the order
- May initiate replenishment of inventory if fulfillment of the order will reduce available inventory below target levels

The inventory subsystem will then schedule fulfillment of the order according to the customer's requirements or shipping commitments contained in the order-entry subsystem.

When the order is filled, a shipping summary is entered into the computer. This summary removes that inventory from the inventory record, updates the shipping history, and initiates the billing cycle. The billing cycle, which involves the accounts receivable and sales subsystems, creates the sales history as well as the sales (revenue) and cost of sales (expense) entries that are ultimately summarized in the general ledger. In addition, the billing cycle produces the customer invoice, which notifies the customer of the fulfillment of the order and the obligation to pay, as well as the accounts receivable record, which identifies the amount due from the customer and completes the order-entry/order-fulfillment subsystem.

Accounts Receivable (AR) software manages the data that show how much individual customers owe for goods or services received. A good AR package will ensure prompt billing, simplify adjustments to customer accounts, and provide for effective collection on delinquent accounts. *Accounts payable (AP)*, on the other hand, record a business's outstanding obligations — what it owes — by assigning the arriving bills to appropriate categories and then initiating payment after determining that funds are available and appropriate authorization has been received. A computerized *payroll* package is particularly useful, because it facilitates accurate computation and reporting of wage adjustments, overtime, tax deductions, and other types of deductions used in preparing payroll checks.

The management of a company requires up-to-date reports from these various transaction subsystems, but additional information is needed for the tactical and strategic planning that is discussed in the next section. Specifically, managers and other top-level decision makers require regular overall summaries of the organization's operations. They also need forecasts of future operations under alternative policies or procedures, so that they can decide which course of action to take. Since these planning needs overlap with transaction processing requirements, integrated systems of organizing information have been developed.

Management Information Systems

Computers are used every day to process data into information. Less well known, but also a fact, is that much of the information processed by computers ultimately plays a part in management decisions. As you learned in Chapter 1, **management information system (MIS)** simply means the use of computer and other systems to generate the information necessary for management to perform its major functions of planning, organizing, staffing, directing, and controlling, which are shown in Figure 12.5. Each function is briefly described below.

- *Planning.* To plan means to set goals and objectives for the company. Management must know and understand the nature of the company, its competition, and its marketplace and be able to make accurate predictions about their future. Establishing the policies, procedures, programs, and business philosophy of a company is one important part of planning. Setting ambitious but achievable goals is another.

- *Organizing.* To organize means to develop and maintain the resources and structure of a company. Managers must be assigned, workers departmental-

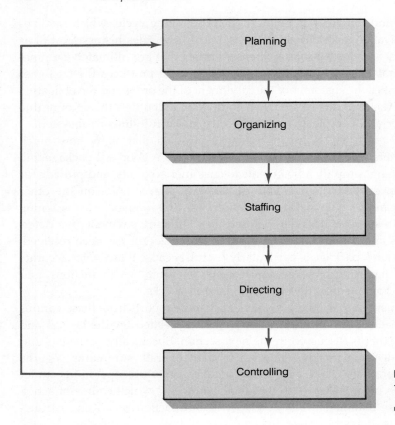

Figure 12.5
The five functions of management.

ized, and the company's resources effectively deployed in an attempt to meet desired goals.

■ *Staffing.*   Staffing is the continuous process of recruiting, hiring, and training employees.

■ *Directing.*   To direct means to coordinate the activities of a company and to delegate the authority necessary for carrying out those activities. Management directs by communicating with workers, channeling their energies, and motivating them to do their jobs well.

■ *Controlling.*   To control means to evaluate how well or poorly standards are being met and to take any action needed to correct deficiencies. Sometimes the necessary action requires returning to the planning function to revise goals or redefine policies.

Levels of Management

Management may be described according to three levels: operational, tactical, and strategic. As Figure 12.6 shows, each level requires a different kind of information that can be provided by an MIS. We will briefly describe the function of each management level, along with its information needs.

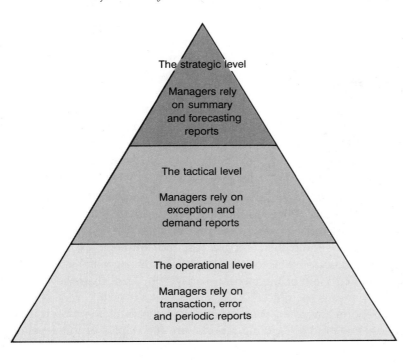

The strategic level

Managers rely on summary and forecasting reports

The tactical level

Managers rely on exception and demand reports

The operational level

Managers rely on transaction, error and periodic reports

Figure 12.6
The three levels of management. Managers at each level need different kinds of Information.

■ *Operational level.*   Also known as a front-line manager, a manager at the *operational level* is responsible for the day-to-day operations of a business. The manager of a single outlet of a hamburger chain is one example. Such a person is responsible for hiring help, maintaining inventories, supervising employee relations with customers, and verifying cash register totals.

Operational managers rely on transaction reports, error reports, and periodic reports to do their job. *Transaction reports*, also known as *detailed reports*, summarize line by line the daily transactions of the business. From a transaction report, the manager of a hamburger outlet can determine which worker operated register 3 between 11:00 A.M. and 2:30 P.M. *Error reports* warn the manager of a possible error. Preset limits programmed into the computer will signal an error when they are exceeded. For example, an employee's time card that shows 600 hours worked in a week will generate an error report — the preset limit may be a maximum of 60 hours for any one employee. *Periodic reports* aggregate and summarize information from transaction and error reports on a periodic basis — say, once a day, week, or month. These reports help the manager to see how well the business did in a given period.

■ *Tactical level.*   The *tactical level* of management, also known as middle management, is typically charged with the responsibility, not for a single unit, but for several units. A manager at this level in a fast-food restaurant chain might oversee the operations of 15 or 20 outlets, for example. Management here is concerned with assisting the separate units to achieve their goals and with correcting any exceptional situations. A unit that is flagging badly in sales or is the object of persistent consumer complaints will be singled out and draw the scrutiny of tactical management.

At the tactical level, management relies mainly on exception reports and demand reports. An *exception report* is generated by an MIS only when certain guidelines have either been violated or not met. For example, the computer may be programmed to issue an exception report if the sales at any one store fall by a certain percentage. Should this occur, management may call for a *demand report*, a report that is only generated by specific request, which might break down the overall decline by specific products.

■ *Strategic level.*   The *strategic level* of management is concerned primarily with long-range planning. Where is the company heading? How is it faring in a competitive marketplace? What new products has the competition introduced, and how should the company respond? Strategic managers don't have the microscopic view of the operational manager nor the selectively magnified view of the tactical manager. Instead, their view is of the big picture.

Summary reports and forecasting reports (sometimes broken down into planning, budgeting, and scheduling reports) are the staples of this level of management. *Summary reports*, as their name suggests, give management the big picture of how the company as a whole is doing. *Forecasting reports* predict future growth, resources, and profits. Depending on their content, these reports may also be called *planning, scheduling,* or *budgeting reports.* They help management measure the overall performance and health of the company.

The Basis of MIS

Behind every functional MIS is a database containing the millions of transactions that constitute a company's daily business. Every time a single hamburger is sold by a hamburger chain, for example, that sale is added to millions of others reported to the database. The marvel of the computer is that it is capable of aggregating such raw numbers and processing them into useful and varied kinds of information. As the engine behind this manipulation of data, the computer enables an operational manager to extract a transaction report from the same database from which a strategic manager derives a summary report.

External sources of data are also used to generate an MIS's reports. These sources will vary with the company's business. But many such external sources of data are available for computer processing by an MIS.

It would be a mistake if you concluded from this discussion that an MIS requires an enormous mainframe computer and the backing of a multimillion-dollar company. That may have been true in the 1960s and 1970s, when multinational conglomerates were the only users of management information systems. But with the explosion in microcomputers and minicomputers, a host of small businesses have adapted and evolved their own management information systems.

Government agencies use them, as do such nonprofit organizations as hospitals and charities.

Decision Support Systems

A subset of management information systems and a valuable tool for managers in its own right is a **decision support system (DSS)**. Decision support systems typically extend MIS through the addition of software that allows managers to simulate business conditions and play *what-if*. A significant feature of DSS that distinguishes them from MIS is the ability to deal with an *unstructured inquiry* —one for which no precedent exists — in making basic business decisions.

The heart of a DSS is a complex mathematical model that simulates the operating conditions of the company, as well as the business environment in which it exists. For example, the manager of a hamburger chain can use a DSS to price "kiddie burgers" for a nationwide sales promotion. Using the DSS, the manager can play *what-if* by anticipating probable sales volumes and profits for particular prices.

Consider another example. A printer who operates a large plant at nearly full capacity receives a special order to produce 1 million pamphlets. The MIS in place informs the printer about past business, backlogged orders, and anticipated deadlines but can't tell whether or not the new order may be filled if the present schedule is juggled. By playing *what-if* with the mathematical model that reflects the plant's actual operating conditions, the printer can calculate if, when, and how the new order can be filled.

Computers in Industry

Manufacturing and Robotics

The robot has had a curious history. Its origin is neither industrial nor mechanical, but literary. The term originated, not from the drawings of some mad scientist, but from a 1921 play, *R.U.R.* (Rossum's Universal Robots) by the Czech dramatist Karel Capek. Science fiction writer Isaac Asimov formulated a robotics law with the prime injunction that a robot shall do nothing to hurt its human master. But, fiction to the contrary, robotic uprisings or rebellions are neither probable nor realistic. **Robots** are nothing more than automated machinery under the control of a computer program — computers fitted with sensing devices, mechanical arms, and hydraulic appendages.

Today robots perform many useful but entirely innocuous and unrebellious tasks. A variety of businesses, from candy makers to pharmaceutical houses to plastic molders, use them to manufacture goods. But the largest user of robots is the auto industry in Detroit, with General Motors (GM) accounting for 35 percent

Figure 12.7
Robots on a GM assembly line weld the seams of a car body.

of all robots presently used in the United States (see Figure 12.7). Automobile makers initially used robots mainly for spot welding and painting, but lately "smarter" robots are tightening bolts, marking identification numbers on engines and transmissions by using laser beams, and gauging body dimensions with a combination of precision lasers and video cameras.[8]

The goal of robotics is to create machines that can manipulate materials and tools, react to unpredictable situations, and ultimately "see." Robots at some automobile assembly plants can already "see" with the help of multiple laser beams projected in a complex horizontal and vertical grid. Video cameras relay reflected data to light-sensing devices that digitize the information and transmit it to a computer. A system of laser beams and video cameras is used by auto makers to conduct precision measurements of automobiles rolling off the assembly line. Using this technology, the robot can "sense" whether the approaching half-assembled car statistically matches the ideal dimensions of the "perfect" car stored in computer memory. With one unit inspected every 30 seconds, the system results in cars with tighter-fitting doors and better-built bodies.

Many companies today are using *automatic guided vehicles (AGV)*. These self-propelled vehicles are widely used in factories to move materials between manufacturing stations. Some AGVs are guided by wires embedded in the floor; others follow an invisible fluorescent pathway. Companies like Sears, Roebuck use AGVs to pick up and deliver mail between departments.

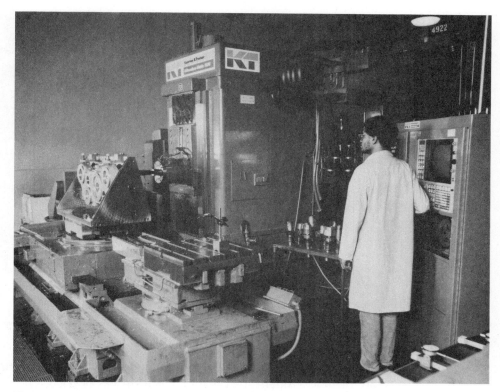

Figure 12.8
This lathe is a numerical control device.

These and similar manufacturing uses of robots fall under the heading of **programmable automation (PA)**. Common PA systems include *numerically controlled (NC) machine tools*, which can reshape or refine material used in a production process. Figure 12.8 shows an NC device used in production. When CAD/CAM robots and NC systems are linked together through a computerized database that plans, schedules, and controls a manufacturing process, the entire system is known as **computer-integrated manufacturing (CIM)**. Human beings must not only design and program these devices, they must "teach" robots how to carry out complex series of actions (Figure 12.9).

The adoption of PA systems has been somewhat slow because they require extensive planning and support. Not only do the machines need to be programmed and reprogrammed, but management must acquire expertise, establish training programs, and make sure that employees are receptive to the transformation that is required. The population of robots in the early 1980s was still only about 30,000 in Japan and 6,000 in the United States. As is clear from Table 12.1, welding and materials handling were the most common applications for industrial robots at that time.

Figure 12.9
Industrial robots are guided through a series of movements by human "teachers."

Other uses for robots are more exotic and even have a certain futuristic promise about them. Consider this scenario, which smacks of science fiction. A ranting man holed up in a basement apartment goes berserk and begins shooting at passersby. After communicating with the police on the telephone, the man promises to surrender and throws two handguns out into the hallway. But he has secretly hidden a third gun in his waistband and plans to kill the first police officer he encounters. The door creaks open; a robot whirls into the room, its high-intensity strobe lights temporarily blinding the man. The police rush in and subdue him.

A similar incident was played out recently in Manhattan. The star of the incident is known to New York police as a Remote Mobile Investigator, a machine equipped with steel claws, video-camera eyes, and two-way audio for communicating with suspects. With its human operator safely out of sight behind a bullet-proof shield, the machine is operated via a 360-foot cable. It's powered by two 12-volt batteries, capable of climbing a curb, and equipped with steel claws that can fire a gun, pick up a coffee cup, or drag a 350-pound victim to safety. Improved units now being developed will have color television cameras and be able to climb stairs, turn a key, and open a door. With some 100 police officers being killed every year in situations like the one described, authorities hope to save lives with these hazardous-duty machines.[9]

Other contemporary uses of robots are just as remarkable. Robotic arms capable of locating points within two-thousandths of an inch have been used in brain surgery to remove tissue samples of tumors for biopsy. Similar devices are used to drain abscesses, implant radioactive pellets directly into tumors, repair blood vessels,

TABLE 12.1
Installed Operating Industrial Robots, by Application

	Japan	United States	
	1982	1982	1990f*
Welding	25%	35%	23%
Materials handling	20%	20%	12%
Assembly	20%	2%	12%
Machine loading	8%	15%	19%
Painting	3%	10%	6%
Foundry	2%	15%	11%
Other	22%	3%	17%
Totals	100%	100%	100%

*f=forecast

and aim laser beams at diseased tissue with pinpoint accuracy. The sunken ocean liner *Titanic* was located in September 1985 by the *Argo*, a robot vehicle equipped with sonar and photographic equipment. Researchers are also developing robots for use in agriculture. "Agrimation" robots, now being engineered, will be able to pick apples, grapes, oranges, and other fruit. "Cowbots" being perfected in the Netherlands will use a system of heat sensors and visual guidance to mechanically milk cows.

Even so, human imaginings about robots far exceed the most fantastic uses to which they are presently put. We don't have units like C3PO, capable of translating a million intergalactic dialects. We have no Number 5s, like the star of the fanciful movie *Short Circuit*, which tells the story of a robot coming to life after being struck by lightning. Could such a thing ever really happen? Will the extraordinary robotic creatures of *Star Wars* fame ever really exist? And if they do come into being, how will they affect human workers? The first two questions will evoke wildly differing answers depending on whom you ask. No one knows what the future of robotics holds, what kinds of peculiar mechanical lifeforms might eventually be hatched in the research laboratory. As for the third question, some tentative answers are already possible about the effect robotics will have on the human workforce. Surprisingly little, says at least one researcher, who speculates that even with 100,000 robots at work in the 1990s, only 300,000 workers will find themselves displaced. This number represents only 0.3 percent of the present labor force. If such workers unhappily suffer a drop in earnings, it is projected that, within five years, they will have recouped the wages lost.[10]

Finance, Banking, and Retailing

Without computers, the banking and financial industries as we know them could not function. It has been estimated, for example, that over 19 billion personal checks are written and processed in this country each year. If all of these pieces of paper needed to be processed manually, with each check having to be handled an average of six times, up to one-third of the adult population of the United States would eventually be required to process checks. It seems clear that the computerization of check-processing procedures, which is accomplished by way of MICR (*m*agnetic *i*nk *c*haracter *r*ecognition) and OCR (*o*ptical *c*haracter *r*ecognition) equipment, has been more than just an enhancement to the banking industry. It has become an absolute necessity.

The computerization of the banking and financial industries hasn't stopped, however, with the automation of check-processing procedures. Relatively recent advances, such as electronic funds transfer, automated tellers, and point-of-sale (POS) systems, have brought us closer to the day when we might find ourselves living in a "cashless society." In the hypothetical cashless society, money is largely an abstraction that exists in the form of numbers passed from one computer system to another. Though we aren't yet close to this point, current technology gives us glimpses of the future.

Electronic Funds Transfer Systems (EFTS)

An **electronic funds transfer system (EFTS)** is a computerized system that processes information about financial transactions and facilitates exchanges of this information. When a business pays employees' salaries by transferring funds directly to their checking accounts it is using one type of EFTS. Making a payment on a loan or making an investment by having your bank deduct money from your account and transfer it directly to another bank or financial institution is another way of taking advantage of EFTS.

A typical EFTS uses computers, telephone lines, and satellites to link customers with banks and banks with other banks and institutions. This worldwide network weaves banks into computerized communities. It has been estimated that, in today's world, more funds are transferred each month via EFTS than were transferred in traditional ways in all the years before EFTS were introduced.[11]

Automated Teller Machines (ATMs)

One popular use of EFTS is the **automated teller machine (ATM)**, an interactive device that allows customers to access a bank's computer and complete transactions, such as cash withdrawals, without direct human intervention (see Figure 12.10).

Banks and other savings institutions issue a plastic card to a customer, who inserts the card into an ATM, in order to complete such banking transactions as cash withdrawals, deposits, and transfers of funds from one account to another.

Through networks such as CIRRUS, it is possible to get cash from an ATM in just about any part of the United States, even though the money is withdrawn from your account in your local bank. Headquartered in Detroit, the CIRRUS network links virtually all major cities in the country. CIRRUS and similar interstate networks have shown that it is technically possible for funds to be transferred from almost any point in the world to another. These networks consist of ATMS, which are connected to the local bank's computer, which in turn is interconnected with

Figure 12.10
An automated teller machine (ATM). Using
the keyboard a customer gains direct access
to her account and can then perform a
variety of banking functions.

national computer systems, which in turn could be interconnected with international computer systems. All one needs to participate in such networks is an identification card, such as a VISA card. In many ways, CIRRUS represents a glimpse at what would be possible with a nationwide computerized banking system. Such networks might one day allow any type of banking transaction to be completed from any point in the country.

Point-of-Sale (POS) Systems

A **point-of-sale (POS) system** consists of a series of computer terminals located where goods and services are paid for. Like an ATM, a POS terminal is connected to one or more computers. When a customer buys a product or service, the operator enters the amount of the purchase into a computer. In some POS systems, this amount is then deducted directly from the customer's account. POS systems can do more than simply transfer funds from one account to another, however. They can also be used by the seller of a product or service to keep sales or inventory records, to authorize checks, and to verify credit cards. POS systems enable goods and services to be sold without requiring the actual exchange of cash, increasing the degree to which business can operate on a cashless basis.

Figure 12.11
The universal product code (UPC) is appearing on more and more supermarket items.

You've undoubtedly seen the bar code called **universal product code (UPC)** on packaged goods in supermarkets and convenience stores (see Figure 12.11). Its extensive adoption has had a major effect on retailing, because it can be read by POS laser readers (Figure 12.12). The bar code printed on each package stores up to 12 decimal digits. You can see the 12 slots, or zones, of the code marked at the top of the sample in Figure 12.11. The 2 outer digits control and check the scanning, which makes it possible to scan the code forward, backwards, or sideways. The inner 10 digits contain two fields, one for the product number and the other for a unit price. A combination of thick and thin bars represents each of the 10 numbers from 1 through 9, which you can decipher by looking at the bars directly above those numbers in the diagram.

The UPC code has great flexibility and is being used for a variety of other functions, especially remote entry of data. Jobs that lend themselves to this technology include inventory control and patient monitoring, as well as standard POS functions.

Computers in the Professions

Professionals — doctors, lawyers, accountants, and others — use computers more than any other general occupational group, probably because they depend so much

Figure 12.12
Laser bar code readers are able to identify a code by scanning from several angles simultaneously. Here codes are read by a wand as part of an inventory-taking process.

on specialized information. Entry to a profession demands many years of education and training, and increasingly that education includes skills in computer applications. Personal computers and professionals coexist in our cultural consciousness, perhaps because so much software is well suited to the needs of the professional or perhaps because it is advertised as "for professional productivity." With allegiance both to an employer and to a profession, the professional has diverse information needs and operates fairly autonomously. Most professionals must write letters, organize files, prepare budgets, learn new techniques, and juggle priorities. Some professions, especially those that are health related, use specialized computer-based systems and techniques daily.

Health Care

Many doctors and nurses had early exposure to computers. Hospitals began putting patient records into computer systems in the early 1960s. In fact, the first studies of people's attitudes toward computerization were conducted among nurses at a New England mental hospital. These nurses felt quite positive about their work with computerized records, despite some fears about loss of their own job functions to the computer. This is still more or less the prevailing attitude toward computerization.

Bedside Information Systems

Computerized patient records today may include daily test results, diet information, and prescriptions. With hundreds of data items for each patient accumulating every day, medical databases offer a rich foundation for software designed to augment diagnostic decisions. A customized database package can help find case histories of previous patients with very similar medical profiles. After reviewing these cases, doctors can usually make more informed diagnoses and develop more effective treatment plans. And expert systems that can utilize the amassed data from daily hospital records have been applied to the diagnosis of illnesses on a limited basis. Among these expert systems are Stanford's MYCIN, which diagnoses blood infections; PUFF, which analyzes breath data to diagnose cardiopulmonary problems; and CADUCEUS, which can diagnose hundreds of different diseases.

Intensive care units have been equipped with computer-based patient-monitoring systems for years. These machines continuously measure the vital signs — heartbeat, breathing, brain waves, and temperature — and check for any irregular patterns in these streams of data. The computer automatically sounds an alarm if any of these signs falls outside a predetermined range. More complex patterns are scanned and checked by pattern-recognition software. Persons who are susceptible to seriously irregular heartbeats sometimes depend on these patient-monitoring systems after they leave the hospital. These persons can carry a recording device with them and periodically transmit their data over phone lines to the hospital's computer for analysis of their vital organs' performance.

Medical Imaging

Imaging involves reading and graphically displaying and analyzing data. *Medical imaging* collects and displays such data for medical purposes. The best-known medical imaging application is called **computer axial tomography (CAT)** and is commonly called a "CAT scan." *Tomography*, from the Greek word for "slice," is used in this context, because the method shows the doctor a cross-sectional "slice" of the human body (see Figure 12.13). CAT scanners first use x-rays to get many cross-sectional images, then the computer assembles a composite image that can be displayed in brilliant three-dimensional colors. This technology is particularly good at detecting brain tumors and consequently reduces the need for exploratory surgery.

Another, more recent form of scanning, called *nuclear magnetic resonance (NMR)*, produces even sharper images and doesn't require x-rays. The NMR machine houses a huge magnet that surrounds the patient and creates a very focused magnetic field that jostles molecules in body cells. The speed at which these molecules readjust their position, called *resonance*, makes it possible to differentiate various types of tissue. Both types of computer-controlled machines have made major contributions to cancer treatment by assisting in the early detection of malignancies.

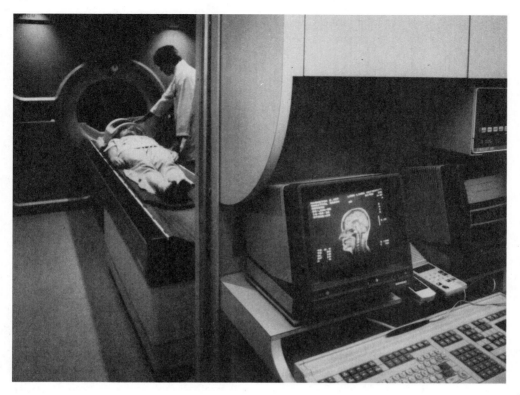

Figure 12.13
CAT scans are images generated by computer from an x-ray, which provide a cross-sectional view of the body.

Medical Education and Consulting

Some of the most popular instructional computer simulations have been designed to train students in medical procedures. For example, *Emergency Room*, from the University of Illinois PLATO system, teaches medical interns what to do when a seriously injured accident victim arrives in the emergency room. The simulated situations are captivating and challenging, providing many hours of potentially life-saving experience.

Nurses, doctors, dentists, and other medical professionals have an unusually heavy responsibility to keep their knowledge and skills up to date within their areas of expertise. Not only do they benefit from computer-assisted instructional approaches, but they increasingly rely on software rather than on human consultants to reach medical decisions. For example, drug conflict programs help professionals decide what drugs to prescribe by predicting complicating interactions between a drug and food or drugs that the patient has already consumed.

Computers play another important type of consulting role in organ matching. Finding organ transplant donors is often difficult because of the close match needed for successful transplants. Several organizations maintain computerized databases of registered organ recipient candidates. Through sophisticated electronic networks, the availability of an organ can be communicated, a satisfactory match found, and the organ shipped thousands of miles within a matter of hours.

Law

A 1984 survey found that attorneys typically spend about 25 percent of their time writing or drafting documents, about 23 percent in research, and about 7 percent planning and carrying out administrative duties. These are all tasks that can benefit from standard, off-the-shelf software, which implies that, if the average lawyer decided to take full advantage of contemporary computing, he or she might spend as much as 45 percent of his or her work time with a computer. Lawyers and criminal justice professionals use computers to produce documents, to access different kinds of databases, and to help organize the large volume of information associated with their daily work.

Law offices are small businesses, too. They have the same needs as other small businesses for planning, correspondence, accounting, payroll, billing, mailing lists, inventory, and scheduling. Very often, the computer first joins the law office to assist with these routine functions. But once it's in the door, people find other specialized things for the computer to do.

One such specialized application is the use of computers to search on-line databases. Westlaw, QL Systems, and LEXIS are the three best-known on-line services specializing in legal information. Legal professionals, who frequently must pore over a maze of court decisions for precedents and decisions that might influence the outcome of their own cases, regard these databases as indispensable sources of information. LEXIS, for example, catalogs some 500,000 court decisions in addition to some 60-odd years of administration rulings, trade regulations, and laws governing securities and tax issues. To summon up the landmark 1973 proabortion ruling made by the Supreme Court in *Roe vs. Wade*, for example, the attorney simply types in the name of the case. Less specific searches can be initiated by typing in the legal topic and appropriate codes — "grand theft," for example. Retrieval times on LEXIS, which is owned and operated by Mead Data Central of Dayton, Ohio, average no more than 20 seconds. Days, even weeks, of the attorney's time are saved, making legal services considerably less expensive.

For general information, other handy on-line systems, such as Dialog, are also available. Dialog is a collection of hundreds of databases on such crucial subjects as government, the physical sciences, humanities, and health. It also includes a massive Claims/Patent file that covers all patents ever filed in the United States. Trademarkscan, part of the Dialog offerings, catalogs information about U.S. registered or pending trademarks. Another database service, The New York Times Information Service, similarly catalogs and abstracts information from some 20 news services.

Journalism

Writing is the most essential and common job assigned to journalists, and word

Figure 12.14
With portable computers containing large fixed disk storage, it is increasingly possible to operate one's office from anywhere.

processing provides numerous features that enhance the productivity of writers, reporters, and editors of newspapers or magazines. It is very rare today to find journalists doing their writing and rewriting by hand or even by typewriter. Because journalists, especially freelance writers, are often on the go, word processing presented a number of problems before the advent of light, portable computers (see Figure 12.14). In 1983, Radio Shack began distributing Model 100, the first laptop computer that could be used for word processing. Within a couple of years, an estimated 50,000 journalists had acquired one. Even though this model had a screen display of only eight lines, with up to 40 characters in each line, it had a built-in modem that allowed quick and easy telephone connection to transmit story drafts back to the home office. Today many journalists rely on laptop computers wherever they are.

Whereas 15 years ago you couldn't find a large pressroom without typewriters, now you would be hard pressed to find a pressroom without computers and telephone jacks for modems. The new technology is not only convenient for reporters, it also gives their newspapers an edge in the race to print late-breaking news and scoop the competition.

The database of choice for the typical journalism student or professional is without a doubt NEXIS, offered by Mead Data Central. NEXIS indexes and files away every word written and printed in such periodicals as the *New York Times*,

Washington Post, Christian Science Monitor, Time magazine, and *Newsweek*, along with information from other less well-known sources, such as the BBC *Summary of World Broadcasts.* Information can be searched and retrieved by topic, writer, and even common phrases and expressions, such as "remains to be seen" or "obstacles to be overcome." Expense and complexity are the major drawbacks of using NEXIS. Finding and printing a dozen articles can run into hundreds of dollars. But, reckoned against the labor and time that must be expended to conduct such searches manually, NEXIS is clearly a valuable time saver.

Review

Key Terms

Office automation (OA)
Computer conferencing
Ergonomics
Management information systems
  (MIS)
Decision support system (DSS)
Robot
Programmable automation (PA)

Computer-integrated manufacturing
  (CIM)
Electronic funds transfer system
  (EFTS)
Automated teller machine (ATM)
Point-of-sale (POS) system
Universal product code (UPC)
Imaging
Computer axial tomography (CAT)

Discussion Questions

1. Considering that office automation often requires costly purchases and disruptive changes in procedure, why do so many offices move in that direction?

2. What is *technostress*, and how is it related to ergonomics?

3. Identify basic business transactions and explain how computerization improves the way an organization processes them.

4. What is a management information system? What distinguishes it from a decision support system?

5. What types of reports and information do different types (or levels) of managers need? Activate your imagination by considering specific businesses — a car dealership, for example.

6. What is an automated teller machine's primary function?

7. How can computers aid doctors in making diagnostic decisions?

8. Name two types of medical imaging. What is the difference between the two?

9. How do on-line databases assist the legal profession?

Projects

1. Select someone you know who works in a small business, such as a store, farm, or professional practice. Arrange to interview this individual about automation, information, and computers in his or her business. Before the interview, read the chapter and list appropriate questions you might ask. Write a summary of the interview using the terminology introduced in this chapter.

2. Go to several stores (or review catalogs of companies) that sell computer furniture. Make a list of all the features or settings that you would need to consider to select the best ergonomic workstation furniture.

3. Spend some time working at different types of computer-centered work areas. Describe (drawings are helpful) what you think would be the best workstation environment for you.

4. Select a profession, perhaps one for which you are preparing. Do some research and list the significant ways in which computers are used by persons in that profession.

Notes

1. Karen Berney, "The Cutting Edge," *Nation's Business*, April 1986, p. 54.

2. Karen Freifeld, "The VDT's," *Health*, March 1985, p. 75.

3. Craig Brody, *Technostress* (Reading, Mass.: Addison-Wesley, 1984).

4. Susan G. Hill and Karl Kroemer, "Preferred Declination in the Line of Sight," *Human Factors* 28, 2 (1986): 127-134.

5. Berney.

6. Daniel Goleman, "The Human-Computer Connection," *Psychology Today*, March 1984, p. 20.

7. Ibid.

8. Stuart F. Brown, "Building Cars with Machines That See," *Popular Science*, October 1985, p. 86.

9. Dennis Hevesi, "Steel Claws and Eyes: Robots Help the Police Take Place of Humans in Dangerous Situations," *New York Times*, 18 March 1987, sec. 2, p. 1.

10. Anthony Patrick Carnevale, *Jobs For the Nation: Challenges for a Society Based on Work* (Washington, D.C.: American Society for Training and Development, 1985).

11. Ahmed S. Zaki, "Regulation of EFT: Impact and Legal Issues," *Communications of the ACM*, February 1983, p. 112.

13

Computers and Society's Institutions

Preview   Computers have been in use for only five decades, but societies and cultures
have existed for many millennia. With such a brief history it seems remarkable that computers have already begun to change our basic social institutions. In this chapter we investigate the computer's effect on government,
education, the arts, and science.

Like the early days of the automobile, it is impossible to anticipate
many of the ways in which the computer will change society. The early signs
of social transformation, however, are described in this chapter. First you will
discover how computers allow large government agencies to deliver public
services such as law enforcement and emergency aid. After reviewing the
role of computers in defense and in local government, you will explore the
inroads computers are making in education.

While computers do not yet rival human artists, they are among the instruments with which people produce creative works. You will see examples
of art from motion pictures, drawing, painting, literature, and music — all
produced with the help of computers. Computers also support the rapid expansion of science. Simulation, complex mathematical models, and parallel
processors have opened up entire new fields for explorations — the space
program is but one example. The computer's role is not only immense, it is
integral to everyday life in our society.

In this chapter, you'll learn:

- How the federal government uses computers
- The implications of computers for law enforcement
- The pros and cons of computer-assisted instruction
- The use of computers in motion pictures
- The use of computers in art, literature, and music
- What a supercomputer is
- Applications for computers in space

Computers in Government

Government must forecast trends, plan services, enforce laws, and protect the welfare of citizens. Performing all these functions makes it almost totally dependent on computers. If the nation's population is aging, shrinking, expanding, or growing younger, the government must know, so that it can plan accordingly. Every change in the population curve means revised forecasts for housing, schools, health care services, social security, and national defense. And only computers are capable of doing the massive counting and statistical tabulating necessary to produce the needed information.

The extent to which federal, state, and local governments depend on computers is unknown. Large and small, thousands of government agencies depend on computer data processing.

The Federal Government

No one can definitely say how many files on private citizens are maintained by the federal government. Some estimates indicate that there are about 4 billion dossiers on citizens in the computer archives of government agencies — an average of 18 files for every living man, woman, and child.[1] Government agencies are so swamped with paperwork that no imaginable manual system of recording and retrieval can cope with it. The Patent Office has 27 million documents on hand, with 300,000 being temporarily lost at any given instant.[2] The Veterans Administration must administer the records of 13.5 million veterans. The Department of Housing and Urban Development keeps dossiers on 4.5 million Americans who have purchased homes through its loan guarantee program. Without computers, the storage space required by government agencies would transform the city of Washington, D.C., into an enormous warehouse for federal paperwork. Here we will discuss a few of the other agencies that rely most heavily on computers.

The Internal Revenue Service

The Internal Revenue Service (IRS) annually processes over 95 million tax returns. Returns are sorted by high-speed bar code readers capable of processing 1040 tax forms at the rate of 30,000 per hour, checked by computers for mathematical consistency, and stored on magnetic tape (Figure 13.1). Computers cross-check and analyze the returns against information received from employers on supporting documents, such as W-2 forms. Returns are also matched against a secret statistical profile and selected for manual checking depending on whether or not they conform or deviate from the expected norm. Computers randomly select another 30,000 returns for audit.

Figure 13.1
The IRS stores its huge volumes of tax returns on reels of magnetic tape.

The IRS has taken a stab at even further automating its return processing. In a 1986 pilot program conducted in selected cities, 25,000 returns were electronically filed by professional tax preparers, who were linked to the IRS computers by modems. Acknowledgment of the returns was made within a day, and refunds were issued within three weeks. If requested, refunds were credited directly to a taxpayer's bank account. The IRS plans to institute this program nationwide in the 1990s, using such major tax-preparing firms as H&R Block.[3]

The U.S. Census Bureau

Thanks to government computers operated by the U.S. Census Bureau, we know that, as of January 1, 1987, there were 243 million of us; that we experienced 8.7 deaths per 1,000 population the year before; and that the general fertility rate of 64.9 live births for every 1,000 women between the ages of 15 and 44 is the lowest recorded since 1930.[4] Figures this detailed would take human workers years to compile and calculate.

In fact, it was the U.S. Census Bureau's pressing need for an efficient method of counting that led Herman Hollerith (1860-1929) to invent the first commercial tabulating machine. Initially used in the 1890 census, the machine took only six weeks to tabulate what was then a population of 62,622,250 Americans.

Social Security

The Social Security Administration keeps records on 100 million workers and makes monthly disbursements to 36 million retirees. An equivalent manual system to accomplish this task would require hundreds of thousands of clerical workers and wouldn't be nearly as efficient.

The Securities and Exchange Commission

The Securities and Exchange Commission (SEC) receives and processes some 6 million pages of documents annually in regulating the affairs and transactions of public corporations. Before EDGAR, an acronym for *Electronic Data Gathering Analysis and Retrieval* system, went on line in 1985 to some 150 corporations, these public documents used to be stored on microfiche cards, and searching them required physical presence at an SEC office. EDGAR now offers instant retrieval of documents filed by any of the 10,000 corporations the SEC regulates. Documents electronically submitted to EDGAR via modem are available for on-line retrieval an hour later. EDGAR uses artificial intelligence software to translate corporate data on gross and net income into standard and readable formats and to allow complex word searches of corporate records. Officials estimate that EDGAR will save some $30 million in printing and postage costs when it becomes available to all public corporations in 1989.

The Legislative Branch

Computers are also being used in the legislative branch of the federal government. The LEGIS system provides members of Congress with information on the status and content of all legislative proposals. SOPAD (*Summary of Proceedings and Debates*) tracks the status of all legislative proceedings in the House and Senate. FAPRS (the *Federal Assistance Program Resource System*) informs members about assistance programs that might benefit their constituents. These systems simplify the complex process of passing laws and representing a constituency.

Defense and Security

The United States is guarded by tireless computer systems that are linked to infrared, atmospheric, space, and satellite sensors. This early warning system, with headquarters in the Cheyenne Mountain installation of the North American Aerospace Defense Command (NORAD), guards against nuclear missile attack (see Figure 13.2). Missile warning displays track the flight of incoming warheads and allow time for an appropriate response.

NORAD is presently the largest user of computers for defense, but that distinction promises to shift in favor of the proposed *Strategic Defense Initiative (SDI)*, popularly called *Star Wars*. Should it every become a reality, Star Wars will involve the use of computers to monitor sensors from thousands of satellites and to intercept incoming missiles. No one knows how the final system will work, but theoretically it will shoot down missiles by bouncing laser beams from orbiting satellites equipped with mirrors. The entire system, from detection of the incoming missiles, analysis of their trajectories, and destruction by laser beams bounced off "killer satellites," will be run by computers. Much debate swirls around whether or not the system as proposed is even feasible. But one thing is plain: existing programs and computers can't even begin to cope with the complexity of Star Wars. Significant advances in the design and development of hardware and software will have to be made before the envisioned system can work.

Figure 13.2

The NORAD control room. Here United States naval officers use the extensive NORAD computer surveillance system which will alert them immediately of any missile activity directed at the U.S.

One element of Star Wars that troubles critics is the amount of decision making the system will cede to computers. As a Department of Defense report puts it, "It seems clear . . . that some degree of automation in the decision to commit weapons is inevitable if a ballistic missile system is to be at all feasible."[5] In other words, a computer will decide when and whether to pull the trigger.

Especially troubling about this autonomy is the possibility that the computer might make a mistake. History tells us that such a possibility, even in the most sophisticated hardware, isn't far-fetched. In the early 1960s, for example, the U.S. early warning computer in Thule, Greenland, warned of incoming Russian missiles. The system had been activated by the rising moon. In June of 1984, the Strategic Air Command in Nebraska received two attack warnings caused by a faulty chip in a multiplexer.

Both false alarms were triggered by hardware failure, but similar miscues might also result from programming errors. Star Wars will require millions of lines of programming code, distributed among tracking radar, sensors, launchers, and missiles, and it will be vastly more complex than any existing computer system. Critics say that even the most painstaking efforts at debugging couldn't prevent some infinitesimal human error, which might trigger a false alarm and inadvertently fire a rocket. Examples of similar failures include the 1962 Mariner I probe to Venus, which had to be blown up after launch, because according to insiders, a programmer had inserted a period instead of a comma in a program. Another is the sinking of the H.M.S. *Sheffield* by an Exocet missile fired from an Argentine aircraft during the Falkland Islands War. The *Sheffield's* computer detected the attack of the French-built Exocet but didn't react, because it had been programmed to defend only against Soviet missiles. Its programmers hadn't anticipated the possibility that the *Sheffield* might one day come under attack by a French missile. Nor can the Star Wars programmers, say critics, anticipate every conceivable possibility.[6] And should an accident occur in an autonomous Star Wars system, the consequences for all humanity could be catastrophic. The debate continues.

Aside from these mammoth defense systems, all rockets and missiles rely on the use of miniature computers. For example, the U.S. TOW (*t*ube-launched, *o*ptically tracked, *w*ired guided) missile is designed to home in on an enemy tank with a laser beam aimed by the operator. As long as the operator keeps the laser beam focused on the tank, the missile will unerringly hit its target. Third-generation antitank missiles will carry several "submunition" warheads fitted with a computer capable of identifying an enemy tank and homing in on it with an infrared sensor.[7] Some sophisticated AMRAAM (*a*dvanced *m*edium-*r*ange *a*ir-to-*a*ir *m*issiles) have the so-called fire-and-forget capability, meaning that they can independently seek out a target without the aid of a human operator. But no existing system, no matter how sophisticated, cedes the decision to fire entirely to a computer.

Local Government

Local governments use computers for a variety of useful, if not exotic, purposes. Cities and neighborhoods use computers for budget monitoring and reporting, for police allocation, and for processing of traffic tickets, to name only a few mundane applications. They use them to prepare bills for water and power usage and to levy property taxes. In one example of people versus machine, the homeowners of Dekalb County, Georgia, rose up in protest when they learned that the county government intended to use computers to assess annual inflationary increases in property value. Homeowners had visions of an infallible machine automatically bumping up the assessments on their homes by a horrendously accurate percentage, leading to more and more taxes. The county government was pressured into abandoning its plan and reverting to the more inefficient and inexact system of manually assessing increases.

A significant and life-saving service offered by some local jurisdictions that use computers is the enhanced 911 emergency system. These systems use address *geocoding* that runs on a database containing the following information:

- The names and locations of all city streets, major buildings, parks, and landmarks
- Every working phone number, along with its listed address and map coordinates to pinpoint it

Figure 13.3
A police officer at a 911 answering point handles an incoming emergency call. The 911 computer system displays the caller's location on the screen, along with other important information.

■ The name, address, and location of every emergency service center

When a citizen calls needing help, both the name and the address of the caller appear on the operator's computer screen and are automatically routed to a dispatcher, who either radios an emergency unit or directs the computer to alert the nearest fire station, paramedic service, or police car (see Figure 13.3). The advantages of this system are obvious: even children who don't know their addresses can use it to summon help. Many lives have already been saved by enhanced 911.

Law Enforcement

The scene is a familiar one from television and movies. A police officer pulls over a traffic offender, reaches for the radio, and runs a "make" on the car's license number. What the viewer doesn't see is that the officer's query is relayed by computer to the database maintained at the FBI's *National Crime Information Center (NCIC)*. Over 8 million records are stored in this center, which receives calls from local police at the rate of 540,000 per day. Within seconds, the officer knows whether there are any outstanding warrants against the driver and whether the car has been reported stolen. Established by the FBI in 1967, the NCIC is one example of how computers are used in the fight against crime.

Figure 13.4

Fingerprint identification systems are changing the way police departments investigate crimes, giving them a new source of hot leads. This officer is studying one of the millions of fingerprints stored in the San Francisco police department files.

Consider another. A single fingerprint has been lifted from an orange Toyota used in a brutal crime in Los Angeles. Before computers, finding this lone fingerprint (known among law enforcement officials as a "cold make"), was common only on television police shows but unlikely in real life, since it would take an expert over 67 years to search the 1.7 million fingerprints in the files of the Los Angeles police for a match. But California had lately installed its new automated fingerprint identification system. Using a laser grid system to read and analyze fingerprints, the NEC computer scans the file at the rate of 650 prints per second. Three minutes later, it produces the names of ten suspects whose prints closely match the one from the Toyota. Richard Ramirez, the name heading the list, is later arrested and charged with being the Los Angeles "night stalker," suspected of 15 brutal murders.[8]

Automated fingerprint identification systems that digitize, store, compare, and retrieve fingerprints are the latest rage in law enforcement (see Figure 13.4). Before them, admitted one law enforcement official, "much of the dusting for prints" was done "for public relations."[9] But with the new machines, cold makes have become hot leads. Using optical disk storage and a memory of 1.6 gigabytes (1.6 billion bytes), the system was credited in its first four months of use in San Francisco with solving 34 crimes, including the 1978 murder of a San Francisco woman, which had consumed six years and 1,000 hours of police investigation.

Computer systems that monitor and enforce house arrest are also being proposed as one possible answer to overcrowded prisons. Prisoners sentenced to house arrest — usually first-time offenders or those convicted of minor crimes — keep their daytime jobs but must stay home at nights and on weekends. There are variations on the system, but they operate on a similar principle: the prisoner wears a device that sends a signal to a main computer when the wearer ventures past a specified distance from the house. If the device is disconnected, the computer is alerted, and the police are summoned. States including New Mexico and Florida are experimenting with this system.

As computer systems become more widely used in law enforcement, many worry about a vast potential for invasion of privacy. High on their list of concerns is the consolidation of government computers in a national scheme of data matching and searching. Safeguards built into the present system include a patchwork of computer jurisdictions — federal, state, and local — and the absence of any centralized data-gathering agency. In 1965 the Johnson administration proposed the creation of just such a Federal Data Agency, which would combine and collect all government data under one roof. The proposal had clear advantages in efficiency and expense over the existing system of separate and often duplicate data collection by different departments, but it was greeted with such a storm of protest that it was quickly withdrawn.

In June 1987, however, a variation on he same idea was revived. A proposal made by a federal advisory committee envisioned linking the computers of the SEC, NCIC, IRS, Social Security Administration, and other government agencies in a nationwide effort to track and locate crime suspects.[10] The federal panel also recommended the use of NCIC computers to list people suspected of committing crimes even if they hadn't been formally charged. Whether or not the proposal will be accepted is unclear; many legislators and citizens oppose any move to establish a centralized computer system that could potentially be used to monitor and invade the private lives of citizens.

Computers in Education

Computers never tire of the endless drills necessary to teach a basic principle or lesson. Thus, it's no surprise that early and enthusiastic prophesies about the computer included predictions that teaching would be among its primary functions. While computers are widely used to teach at nearly all levels of education, they haven't replaced the textbook, as some had predicted. Nor does it appear likely that they ever will.

Three out of five entering college freshmen have had at least half a year of computer science in high school. And nearly two-thirds of all colleges and universities have some programs designed to help students acquire computers through loans or at heavily discounted prices. It seems clear that American colleges and universities feel compelled to get in on the "computer revolution."

Figure 13.5
Drill–and–practice programs teach students through repetition of concepts. This girl is using a math program that teaches her addition.

Computer-Assisted Instruction

The use of computers to teach falls generically under the heading **computer-assisted instruction (CAI)**. Programs whose main task is teaching are known as **courseware**. Three main types of courseware are (1) drill-and-practice programs, (2) simulations, and (3) tutorials. Each type of program fulfills a specific educational need, which we will briefly discuss.

Drill-and-practice programs, like the one being used in Figure 13.5, reinforce lessons. Students must know, for example, the basic principle of multiplication before they can profit from a math program like CBS's Catch-a-Cake. In that particular program, an arithmetic problem appears on the screen, while a cake begins to fall to the accompaniment of a tinkling sound. The student "catches" the cake by solving the problem before the cake falls. Otherwise, the cake splatters, and the answer is displayed.

A wide variety of such drill-and-practice programs is available to teach skills from simple computation to the use of commas. Many use graphics to enliven their drills. In MasterType, for example, students zap letters menacing a space station by

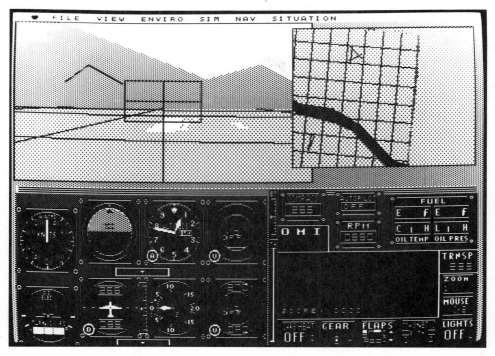

Figure 13.6
A flight simulator screen as it appears to the "pilot." This particular program by Microsoft is a game, simulating the experience of flying a plane.

quickly and accurately completing a typing drill. And research indicates that, for the most part, such programs work.

Programs that mimic the principles, causes, and effects found in reality are known as **simulations**. CATLAB, one example of a simulation, teaches the principles of genetics by having students breed cats of different colors. Players can select two cats for breeding, tell the computer how many offspring to produce, and instantly view the litter resulting from their genetic experiments. Run for the Money, Millionaire, and Bank President teach the principles of personal finance.

Simulations are clever at mimicking and compressing the principles behind an experience that might otherwise take students tedious months or years to witness. But they also have shortcomings. Used in an unsupervised setting, programs like CATLAB tend to bring out the mad scientist in students, who will indiscriminately breed grotesque litters of kittens while ignoring the principles of genetic selection that the program intends to teach.[11] Another drawback is the lack of realism in the controls of even the most effective simulations. Microsoft's Flight Simulator (see Figure 13.6) is one of the best programs of its kind, but a computer keyboard still isn't a realistic substitute for the controls of an aircraft.

Tutorials are programs intended to impart and actively teach principles and theories. In theory, the well-designed tutorial is programmed to detect the student's

Program: Hello! What would you like to explore today?
Student: We have to study math
Program: What math topic do you want?
Student: Fractions
Program: OK. Here is a practical problem to work on. You want a bike and Sally said she will sell you hers for $27.00. She said that this is only 1/3 of what you would pay for the bike in the store. If Sally is right, how much would it cost in the store?

You may use the calculator keys as shown in the upper right corner of the screen. Do you think you can get the answer?
Student: Yes
Program: Good, press the answer key when you think you have the answer.

Figure 13.7

This example illustrates features common in tutorial programs for elementary mathematics. While this one presumes some skill in using keyboards, the trend is toward systems that only expect the student to communicate to the program with touch-screen panels or pointing devices.

level of competence and adjust the difficulty of the material accordingly. The most extensive collection of on-line tutorials presently available is PLATO, offered through the services of Control Data. Subscribers to PLATO can take lessons in subjects that range from mastering the basic alphabet to quantum numbers in physics.

Some tutorials are imaginatively designed to engage students in a friendly exchange. Figure 13.7 is an example of the dialog between students and a computer used by young children.

But other programs are neither friendly nor well designed. Some fail to get the student actively involved. Screen after screen of instructional material is shown before the student is given a chance to take a stab at problem solving. In effect, the machine becomes a lecturer and the student a passive listener who is occasionally roused to answer a question.

Drawbacks to CAI

Does CAI work? That depends on whom you ask and what journals you read. Once study found that CAI was substantially less effective than peer and adult

Beyond the Desktop

Personal computers represent only one segment of the world of computing. Although these desktop devices now perform many tasks once reserved for much larger computers, big, powerful machines are still needed. These are the minicomputers, mainframes, and supercomputers used by government, big business, scientists, and engineers. Furthermore, these big computers—as well as their personal-sized counterparts —frequently need to communicate with still other computers and computer users. Hence the marriage of computing and communications that has taken place in recent years.

1. Business information is a precious commodity. It can be stored and shared effectively by centralized data processing centers in conjunction with telecommunications networks. This huge database in Orange, California, contains more than 130 million credit files and provides more than 75 million credit reports annually.

Mainframes and Minicomputers

Big brothers to PCs, these machines store and manipulate larger quantities of data than do PCs. They often share their data with PCs via a communication network.

2. The fastest computers are known as *supercomputers*. They perform millions or billions of calculations per second. Supercomputers generally are used to solve complex scientific or engineering problems.

3. These keyboards, along with the large red unit in the background, form part of a Cray X-MP supercomputer system. The X-MP can perform 600 million calculations per second. The 4 processors are immersed in a tank of frozen liquid to keep them cool.

4. Although a large hard disk drive stores from 100 megabytes to more than 5 gigabytes (100 million to 5 billion characters), large databases require many drives. Hard disk drives provide fast data retrieval; access times are measured in milliseconds (thousandths of a second).

5. The Hewlett-Packard 3000 Series minicomputers can directly support as many as 56 users. Here, a personal computer is linked to the minicomputer.

6. Minicomputers like this IBM System/38 can be linked with personal computers, workstations and other processors into a network to fulfill the multiple needs of a small or medium-sized business. The system offers the flexibility to design a network specifically for each customer.

7. Telex's MIS (management information systems) Center in Tulsa expedites communication between corporate headquarters and other Telex operations.

Communications

8,9. Orbital satellites and their earthbound counterparts, satellite ground stations, form an indispensable part of the computer communications network. Ground stations can be found in an ever widening variety of settings.

10. Computers are used to monitor and control orbiting communications satellites. Without earthbound control, the satellites would wander out of position and become useless.

11. Large communications networks are run from control centers like this one in Dallas.

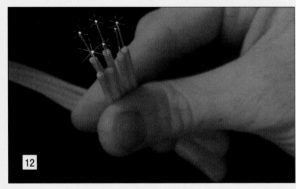

12. Optical fibers transmit data as pulses of laser light instead of electrical signals. They are extremely fast, compact, immune to electrical disturbances, and secure from eavesdropping. The tiny glass fibers in this picture can transmit hundreds of telephone conversations at once.

13. Researchers at RCA Labs are shown here testing teletext systems. These systems can be used to display news and weather information, present stock market quotations, or advertise shopping specials. A teletext system transmits to television sets by encoding data in the vertical blanking interval (the black bar visible when vertical hold isn't working) of a video frame. Then a teletext decoder in the television decodes the data into text and graphics to be displayed on the screen.

14. This facsimile (fax) machine can transmit a page of data over telephone lines in fifteen seconds. It can also transmit data to dozens of locations automatically, and delay the start of transmission until after business hours when telephone rates are lower.

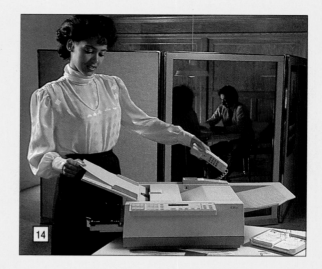

15. New telephone systems encode and transmit voice messages as digital signals rather than analog signals. As a result, both voice and data can be transmitted conveniently by one communications system.

16. Modems make it possible for computer data to be transmitted via telephone. Here the Navy employs a modem for ship-to-shore communication.

Sales and Support

The computer itself is only part of a package that includes software, service, and support.

17. Designing computer systems so that they are convenient to use involves ergonomics, the study of how human beings relate to their environments.

18. Software developers go to great effort to make their programs as "friendly" to the user as possible. At this IBM software usability laboratory, the actions and responses of software testers are carefully monitored.

19. Many organizations purchase service contracts that deliver quick, on-site repairs. Here IBM service coordinators in Atlanta use a computer-based system to assign representatives to handle calls for service.

20. Selling computers to businesses and government agencies is a team effort that requires more than demonstrating hardware and software. Most organizations won't decide to purchase until they have received responses to a formal Request for Proposal (RFP), tested a working system, talked with prior customers, and negotiated a maintenance agreement. Here an IBM instructor trains U.S. Department of Agriculture employees as part of a contract that includes the installation of almost 2,900 computers.

21. Large retailers frequently offer seminars to help buyers become comfortable with their new personal computer systems. The focus of these seminars ranges from a basic introduction to advanced training in the use of specific applications.

22. Widespread use of personal computers has created many opportunities in retail sales. Success in computer sales requires a desire to work with people and the technical ability to find and demonstrate solutions to their problems.

tutoring, although slightly less expensive.[12] But other studies have found that the use of CAI over a year resulted in grade-level gains in student skills that averaged four and a half months per student, with a net cost nearly half as much as peer tutoring.[13] The hard fact, however, is that CAI has had little impact on present educational practice.[14] Drill-and-practice programs abound in the lower grades, and nearly every school system devotes part of the learning day to CAI. But the net effect has been neither revolutionary nor sweeping, as was predicted earlier.

Part of the reason for this lag lies in the poor design of many CAI programs. Some of them don't incorporate even basic educational principles in their programming. They give answers too quickly; they use intrusive and distracting sound effects and graphics; they don't permit immediate feedback from the user; and they fail to teach by *successive approximations*, in which a lesson is built incrementally on skills taught earlier.[15] Another possible reason why CAI programs haven't revolutionized education is teachers' resistance to being replaced by a machine.[16] This argument assumes that a computer is just as capable of imparting complex instruction as a teacher and that, consequently, a rivalry exists between human and machine. The truth is that CAI programs, no matter how sophisticated, can only complement teaching by a human, not replace it.

Computers In The Arts

Computers can assist humans in their capacity for creating and enjoying works of art. Here are some examples of how they are presently being used.

Motion Pictures

Computers have been used in the animation of motion pictures, but possibly their most controversial use in the motion picture industry is for the **colorization** of such classic films as *The Maltese Falcon, It's a Wonderful Life, Casablanca,* and *The Music Box.* The rationale behind colorization is plainly commercial: surveys indicate that movie watchers, especially those under 20, will buy color videos of the classics, but not black-and-white ones.[17] Colorization costs hundreds of thousands of dollars and consumes some four hours of computer time for every minute of film. But it is relatively inexpensive compared to remaking an old movie, which can cost millions.

To colorize a film, an art director transfers the 35mm footage to a 1-inch videotape, which is then cleaned up with image-enhancement techniques perfected by NASA for televising its Apollo pictures of the moon. Using a computer that can synthesize 16,700,000 colors, the art director patiently examines each frame of the film and decides — based on clues from the original script — what colors to use (see Figure 13.8). As the scene advances frame by frame, the computer compares the hue assigned to every pixel in the preceding frame and either "paints"

Figure 13.8
The colorization of a film. Workers in this colorization lab use a computer program that goes through a film frame by frame, "painting" in selected colors.

it anew or leaves it untouched. The ridge of a hat, for example, may have to be shaded from frame to frame as a character shifts position. At any time in the "painting" of a scene, the art director can intervene and make corrections.

Colorizing a film doesn't mean destroying the black-and-white original. For that matter, a television viewer can eliminate the effects of movie colorization by turning off the color on the set. What colorization offers viewers is a choice between the original film and the computer version. At least two companies plan to colorize many more of the classics in spite of protests from some critics and movie directors.

Art

What did the *Mona Lisa* look like when she was first created? She was painted by Leonardo da Vinci, around 1503. But in 1550, a restorer daubed at her hands and brows and added a coat of green-brown varnish as a preservative. Some 400 years later, she looks frumpy, thick-set, and gloomy. She poses against a background of muddy sky, and her face is fissured by *craquelure* — age crackling.

Working with a high-quality photograph obtained from the Louvre, image enhancers tried their hand at computer re-creation of da Vinci's masterpiece.

Figure 13.9
Mona Lisa undergoes computerized restoration. Pictured here is the digitized version of the painting, with certain areas of the painting highlighted.

Figure 13.9 shows *Mona Lisa* undergoing this process. The picture was digitized at NASA's Jet Propulsion Laboratory into 6 million pixels, and the overcoat varnish was subtracted from the image. The brown sky turned blue, the lady's skin changed from yellow to alabaster, and her gown acquired a greenish tint.[18] Similar experiments at image enhancement are being tried on other aging artistic masterpieces, if only to give us a fresher glimpse of how these canvases might have looked when first painted.

Literature

An intriguing branch of computer literature is the **interactive fiction** available today from several software houses. In interactive fiction, the reader participates in the story by feeding inputs into the plot. One of the earliest such programs was the Zork trilogy. Zork and other programs like it were made possible by the invention of sophisticated *parsers*, which enable the computer to understand plain English commands. For example, the story might say, "You are facing a cottage that is surrounded by a broken fence. Sitting on top of one of the posts is a key. The

Figure 13.10
Recording artist Stevie Wonder sits at the keyboard of a Kurzweil digital synthesizer, along with the instrument's inventor (left). Introduced in 1984, the Kurzweil 250 is known for its outstanding digital reproduction of the grand piano sound.

cottage door is closed, and there is no one around." If the reader then types, "Take key," the story branches off to one line of development.

Developed with the help of artificial intelligence techniques, parsers today contain vocabularies of hundreds of words, which allow computers to recognize such sophisticated commands as "Pick up the key and put it into the sack." More complicated novels and stories are consequently possible. For example, the novelist Ray Bradbury has collaborated with a software manufacturer to turn his *Fahrenheit 451* into an interactive work. Michael Crichton *(The Andromeda Strain, Terminal Man)* developed an interactive story entitled *Amazon*, which featured a sidekick parrot named Paco.

Music

Sound is a fluctuation of air pressure that can be measured as a waveform. Specific musical instruments produce sounds characterized by specific and measurable waveforms. By converting these waveforms into digital equivalents, storing them in memory and then playing them back, computers can be used to faithfully

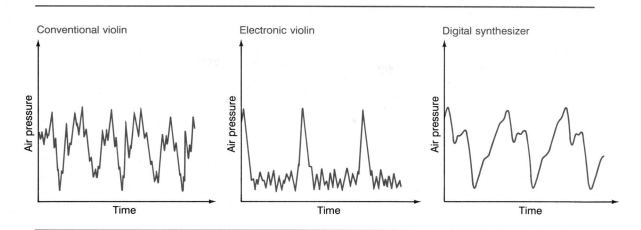

Figure 13.11

A graphic illustration of the waveforms of a conventional violin, electronic violin, and digital synthesizer.

reproduce the sound of any musical instrument. This is the basic principle behind digital recordings and computer-generated music, such as a digital synthesizer produces (Figure 13.10). Figure 13.11, for example, shows the waveform of a conventional violin, along with its equivalent reproduced by an electronic violin and a digital synthesizer.[19] Many orchestras and bands have added computer-generated music to their productions to obtain a richer sound than they otherwise would be able to get from their ensembles.

Lately composers and arrangers have also used computers to tinker with musical scores before recording. Before this new process, a composer who wished to experiment with an arrangement had to rent studio time and taping facilities — at considerable expense.[20] But with special software and a computer hooked up to a music synthesizer, an arrangement can now be played and stored on a floppy disk for editing. Bars may be moved from one part of the composition to another and the effect played back nearly instantly. A composer or arranger can quickly hear how a certain musical arrangement will sound. With the ability to run 16 musical synthesizers at once and to store the equivalent capacity of 99 tape recorders, the system gives composers a freedom to experiment that was unimaginable in an earlier era. Predictions have already been made that, within the near future, music studios will do most of their recording with computers.

Computers in Science

Computers are already part of the standard lab equipment of scientists in disciplines ranging from aerodynamics to sociology. Their effect on the progress of science is incalculable. One mathematician explained the usefulness of computers this way.

> Computers will affect science and technology at least as profoundly as did the invention of calculus. The reasons are the same. As with calculus, computers have increased and will increase enormously the range of solvable problems. The full development of these events will occupy decades and the rapid progress which we see currently is a strong sign that the impact of computing will be much greater in the future than it is today.[21]

It is easy enough for anyone familiar with computers to grasp that machines capable of swift and accurate numerical calculations should be indispensable to scientists who gather data. But computers do more than speed up practical and empirical research. They also make possible research that humans could never undertake without their help. In the discussion that follows, we will briefly mention some of the scientific experiments made possible by computers.

Simulation

No human researcher can ever get close enough to a black hole to empirically measure its gaseous flow. But it is possible to create a mathematical model of black holes that can simulate the flow of gases in them. Such a simulation can involve 25,600 variables in each step, consist of some 10,000 steps per experiment, and yield a solution amounting to 1.25 billion numbers.[22] Without the use of a supercomputer, such a simulation would be impossible.

Computers are also used in a variety of simulation exercises with consequences and results that are more immediate and practical. For example, the wind tunnel has been made obsolete by supercomputers, which are used to simulate the variables involved in airflow over the surface of a wing. Computers have enabled sociologists to apply mathematical modeling to understanding group behavior. They have been used to simulate the malleability of sheet metal and the characteristics of new chemicals and to predict the location of petroleum fields. Computers, in sum, not only help us to study scientific riddles that humans have studied for centuries, they also help us to formulate and explore entirely new problems.

Supercomputers

Supercomputers are the fastest computers made. Some supercomputers, such as the Cray 2, are capable of processing at speeds up to 1 billion operations of arithmetic per second. Most supercomputers use not the single-processor architecture of more typical computers, but **parallel processors** that work on several parts of a problem simultaneously. Supercomputers also contain vast storage capacities.

In the past, supercomputer facilities were maintained by separate government agencies, without coordination between them. NASA, for example, maintains its own supercomputer facilities, as does the Department of Atmospheric and Ocean Sciences. But in 1985 the federally funded National Science Foundation contributed $200 million in "seed" money, which will be used to establish national supercomputer centers at the University of Illinois, the University of California at San Diego,

Figure 13.12
The flight deck of the Space Shuttle Orbiter Columbia. The flight computer is between the pilots' seats. Above this three CRT screens display flight information to the crew.

Princeton, and Cornell. These facilities will be open to use by academic researchers, and industrial scientists.

The main use of supercomputers is to construct complex mathematical models and simulations. We've already mentioned the use of supercomputers to simulate the airflow over a wing or the flow of gases in black holes. Supercomputers have also been used to model the behavior of trillions of sand grains involved in rock slides or shifting sand dunes and thus contribute to an understanding of how three-dimensional particles behave.[23]

Space Exploration

Anyone who has ever seen a NASA launch canceled by a computer knows that space exploration depends heavily on computers. Computers are responsible for monitoring the engines and complex electronic systems of rockets. They perform the precise calculations necessary for achieving and maintaining orbit (see Figure 13.12). They regulate the life support systems of space vehicles.

But even more exotic uses of computers are contemplated for space stations. Computer-controlled robots will monitor electrical systems, maintain navigation and altitude control, communicate with tracking systems, maintain environmental controls for the crew, and be responsible for damage control and repair. The robots will, according to a report, be able to understand human speech, provide automated medical decisions on the health of the crew, detect leaks, and manage onboard manufacturing processes. Sounding suspiciously like HAL, the computer who went berserk in the movie *2001*, these machines are expected to be fully functional and working by the year 2010, according to a NASA report.[24]

Review

Key Terms

Computer-assisted instruction (CAI)
Courseware
Drill-and-practice program
Simulation
Tutorial

Colorization
Interactive fiction
Supercomputer
Parallel processors

Discussion Questions

1. What uses do governments make of computer systems?

2. What single principle seems to underlie all government use of computers?

3. What is especially troubling to some critics about the use of computers in the proposed *Star Wars* system?

4. What benefits does a geocoding database offer an enhanced 911 system?

5. What are the three main types of CAI? How do they differ?

6. Why has CAI not lived up to its promise?

7. What does computer colorization of a movie entail?

8. How does image enhancement help our appreciation of masterpieces?

9. What is interactive fiction? What software invention made interactive fiction possible?

10. How do computers reproduce the sounds of musical instruments?

11. What is a supercomputer? How are supercomputers used?

Projects

1. Contact your campus police or a local police department and find out if they use computer information systems. Ask if they use the NCIC network and why they do or don't use it. Find out what types of information on crimes, arrests, and convictions are available to the public.

2. Discuss the implications of making data from police investigations more publicly available or less so.

3. Define each of these computer-related systems and identify how it is used:

    EDGAR

    LEGIS

    COPAD

    FAPRS

    NORAD

    SDI

    AMRAAM

    NCIC

4. Compare and contrast instructional software for drill and practice, simulations, and tutorials. Use examples from your campus if possible.

5. Select a major application of computers in science (for example, system simulation, rocket control, or weather forecasting) and speculate on the difficulty of getting along without it.

Notes

1. Tom Logsdon, *Computers Today and Tomorrow* (Rockville, Md.: Computer Science Press, 1985).

2. F. Seghers, "Computerizing Uncle Sam's Data," *Business Week*, 15 December 1986, p. 102.

3. L. Wiener, "Computerizing Tax Returns," *U.S. News & World Report*, 8 December 1986, p. 66.

4. *United States Population Estimates and Components of Change: 1970 to 1986, 1987.*

5. DARPA report quoted in "The `Star Wars' Defense Won't Compute," *Atlantic Monthly*, June 1985.

6. Ibid.

7. Frank Barnaby, "How the Next War Will be Fought," *Technology Review*, October 1986.

8. "Taking a Byte Out of Crime," *Time*, 14 October 1985.

9. Ibid.

10. "Computer Tracking Plan for Suspects Gets Panels O.K.," *Atlanta Constitution*, 11 June 1987.

11. Julie S. Vargas, "Instructional Design Flaws in Computer-Assisted Instruction," *Phi Delta Kappan*, June 1986.

12. Henry M. Levin and Gail Meister, "Is CAI Cost-Effective?" *Phi Delta Kappan*, June 1986.

13. Richard P. Niemiec, Madeline C. Blackwell, and Herbert J. Walberg, "CAI Can Be Doubly Effective," *Phi Delta Kappan*, June 1986.

14. "Using Computers for Instruction," *Byte*, March 1987.

15. Vargas.

16. John F. Rockart and Michael S. Scott Morton, *Computers and the Learning Process in Higher Education* (New York: McGraw-Hill, 1975).

17. This discussion is based on Ken Sheldon, "A Film of a Different Color," *Byte*, March 1987.

18. John F. Asmus, "Digital Image Processing in Art Conservation," *Byte*, March 1987.

19. Max V. Mathews and John R. Pierce, "The Computer as a Musical Instrument," *Scientific American*, February 1987.

20. S. P. Sherman, "Musical Software," *Fortune*, 14 October 1985, p. 145.

21. James Glimm, quoted in Larry L. Smarr, "An Approach to Complexity: Numerical Computations," *Science*, April 1985.

22. Ibid.

23. Ivars Peterson, "Rolling Rocks and Tumbling Dice," *Science News*, 3 May 1986.

24. "NASA Report Urges Developing Robotics, Software for Station," *Aviation Week & Technology*, 22 April 1985.

14

Computers and Ethics

Preview   Increase the speed and efficiency with which information is collected and manipulated, and you get an information revolution. In turn the information revolution raises new concerns about the conflict between the individual's right to privacy and society's "need to know." What kind of personal information should be collected and stored in computers? Who should have access to it? The freedom to use computers in business and government must be balanced against freedom from unnecessary intrusions.

Computers also raise concerns about computer security. Computer crime is now responsible for losses in billions of dollars. The advent of microcomputers makes it possible for almost anyone to violate systems once thought reasonably secure. How can computer systems be made less vulnerable to such abuses? How do we resolve these issues? How do we treat the new ethical concerns that are just beginning to be discussed? The last part of this chapter explores information malpractice, intellectual property rights, the value of information and of human capital, and the need to ensure equal access to information services.

In this chapter, you'll learn:

- ■ Why the computer may be a threat to privacy
- ■ How to safeguard privacy
- ■ Types of computer-aided crime
- ■ How to make a computer system more secure
- ■ The ethics of using computers

Privacy

Privacy is the ability of individuals or organizations to control information about themselves. Privacy can best be understood by considering its absence. Imagine yourself growing up in a society in which anyone could find out anything about anyone else just by sitting down at a personal computer and searching files containing everyone's complete personal history. True, there would be benefits. You wouldn't have to fill out a job application, for instance, because your prospective employer could get a list of all your achievements and failures in past jobs. But in the absence of privacy, you wouldn't be able to date anyone new without your date's finding out everything you did on past dates. We tend to take privacy for granted, but our daily lives often depend on our ability to limit what others know about us.

The right to privacy is a cornerstone of a free society. While the U.S. Constitution doesn't explicitly mention it, privacy is recognized in common law and protected by several federal laws. Personal information is required by government agencies, such as the Internal Revenue Service, and by other organizations, such as schools and financial institutions. The central issue when discussing the right to privacy is the proper balance between organizations' need for information and individuals' right to withhold it (Figure 14.1). The advent of computers disturbs that balance in several ways.

The Computer as a Threat to Privacy

When the purpose for gathering information is known, its benefits clear, and its confidentiality assured, most people will cooperate with requests for personal data. They routinely fill out state and federal income tax returns, answer census questions, and sign information release forms for credit checks.

Public confidence in the proper use of information rests on past experience. In most precomputer information systems, the amount of information that could be collected and processed was severely limited, and little information was shared among systems. Computers allow the inclusion of more personal data on census forms, tax returns, school applications, marketing surveys, and credit applications. Computers also make it possible to collect detailed information about people's everyday activities, much of it without their knowledge. Each long-distance phone call, each credit card transaction, each check a person writes is recorded. New technology makes it possible to access, within seconds, any one of millions of records in a database.

Information can be gathered or shared without the knowledge or consent of those concerned. For example, AT&T uses information from surveys of customer billings for marketing purposes. Though the intent of the survey isn't malicious,

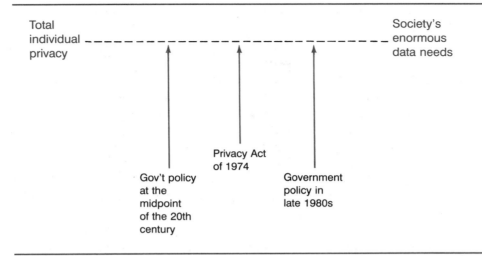

Figure 14.1
The balance: privacy policies fall along a continuum between support of total individual privacy and nearly unlimited need for data by organizations in society.

and no information about individual customers' calling habits is released, some people find the mere existence of the survey disquieting.

Electronic connections among computers make sharing massive amounts of information fast and simple. Computerized subscription and membership lists are regularly sold and traded. That's why we receive so much junk mail and so many computer-generated phone calls. What's more, some computers can search and combine information from several databases. Recently, the Department of Health and Human Services used its computer system to compare welfare recipients' social security numbers with those of employees in the Justice Department, the Department of Defense, and the Office of Personnel Management. The search identified federal employees who were receiving welfare benefits illegally.

Even if people have committed no crime, the information contained in computer files may embarrass or inconvenience them. Personal medical records are a good example. The existence of a national medical database could one day save someone's life; but it could also contain information about an abortion, psychiatric treatment, substance abuse, or AIDS. Given access to such information, a prospective employer might decline to hire someone. Similarly, a financial institution might not approve a loan application, or an insurance company might refuse to issue a policy. Just as in a manual system, computerized data may not be correct, complete, or current. Once inaccurate information is shared, it is very difficult to track down and correct all records containing the error. Computers can greatly increase the potential for misuse of information.

The problem of data integrity or quality has been most extensively studied in computerized criminal history (CCH) systems. The criminal justice system, from the FBI down to the local police officer, rely on these CCH records for daily decisions in their investigations of suspects. There are about 195 million criminal history records in the United States, and it is estimated that about one-third of the labor force has an arrest or court record in these files. A recent study of the quality of the data in these files concluded that at least 50 percent of the records contained inaccurate or out-of-date information.[1] Apparently, law enforcement agencies need more incentives to keep these files current. There is little question that CCH systems are a critical weapon in the fight against crime, but unless the data are maintained properly, the resulting benefits are open to question. From the point of view of an individual with an inaccurate arrest record, the system is unquestionably a threat to privacy.

If personal privacy were the only issue to consider, collecting and storing personal information in computer systems would have been outlawed years ago. But computerized information systems can be a powerful instrument for improving and maintaining service delivery. The most obvious examples are in package delivery services, such as Federal Express. Federal Express keeps your name and address on file, and a telephone call can dispatch a truck to anywhere in the United States to pick up a package for overnight delivery.

Automatic teller machines can now dispense cash, and point-of-sale terminals make it easier for retail business to obtain authorization for large credit purchases. Most people seem willing to accept the storage of data in return for the convenience of such services.

Safeguarding Privacy

How do you safeguard personal privacy without undermining society's informational needs? The following five proposed guidelines summarize the most commonly heard themes:

1. Give individuals the legal right to examine any information about them, and give them legal recourse should they not agree with what is recorded.
2. Make it a crime to obtain information fraudulently.
3. Make it a crime to keep the existence of a database secret.
4. Make it mandatory to discard information after a certain period of time.
5. Provide regulations and procedures for auditing databases to detect violations of law.[2]

For a variety of reasons, many of these recommendations have not been implemented. Cost and inertia tend to discourage their implementation. The most significant privacy legislation enacted in the United States is the *Privacy Act of 1974.* This landmark bill identified the right to privacy as a fundamental right and stated that "the increasing use of computers, while essential to the efficient operation of

TABLE 14.1
Chronology of Major U.S. Privacy Laws

Name	Description
Fair Credit Reporting Act of 1970	Gives citizens the right to examine their own credit records and provides procedures for correcting errors
Crime Control Act of 1973	Extends privacy provisions to criminal justice information systems developed with federal funds
Family Education Rights Act (1974)	Requires schools and colleges to give a student or a parent access to that student's records; limits disclosure of these records to others
Privacy Act of 1974	Restricts federal agencies from collecting, using, sharing, and disclosing personal data that directly or indirectly identify a specific individual
Tax Reform Act of 1976	Protects confidentiality of tax information by disallowing its nontax use with significant exceptions
Right to Financial Privacy (1978)	Spells out when banks can and cannot give out financial data for specific persons
Protection of Pupil Rights (1978)	Gives parents rights to inspect educational materials and restricts mandatory psychological testing
Privacy Protection Act of 1980	Prohibits unannounced searches of press offices
Electronic Funds Transfer Act (1980)	Requires banks offering EFT to notify customers if their account information is given out to third parties
Debt Collection Act of 1982	Establishes procedures for federal agencies to follow before releasing information about bad debts to credit bureaus
Reports Elimination Act of 1983	Eliminates some reporting requirements of the Privacy Act of 1974
Cable Communications Act of 1984	Requires a cable service to inform subscriber of all personally identifiable information collected; restricts use of such information

government, has greatly magnified the harm that occurs from any collection, maintenance, use, or dissemination of personal information." The Privacy Act of 1974 specifies rules for creating and managing federal data files and provides for individuals to review and challenge their personal data records. It stipulates that Congress must approve all exchanges or sharing of government-collected data. The act also establishes a commission to study the privacy protection issues of both public and private sectors.

Several other federal legislative actions relevant to privacy occurred about the same time as the Privacy Act of 1974. These are summarized in Table 14.1.

A law passed in Great Britain in 1984 may prove a sign of things to come. The act requires anyone who maintains a database containing personal data to register it with the government. There are a few limited exceptions; for example, payroll files don't need to be registered. The registration must include the name of the installation, the purpose for which the data are being held, the source of the data, the names of everyone to whom the data may be disclosed, the countries to which the data may be transferred, and the name of the person responsible for granting access to the data. No such legislative provisions have yet been passed in the United States.

Experts predict that the enforcement of privacy laws is more critical than their enactment. Kenneth Laudon, in *Dossier Society*, proposed the establishment of a new Privacy Protection Commission to monitor existing government information systems and evaluate proposals for new ones. With the aid of citizens, such an agency would answer the following questions about new or existing recordkeeping systems:

- *Need.*   Is there a compelling social need for the information?
- *Feasibility.*   How does or would the system work, and how well?
- *Alternatives.*   Are there other mechanisms for addressing the same need?
- *Accountability.*   Does or will the system include measures to ensure accountability for the responsible use of the data?

Once an information system with personal data has been created, the remaining safeguards are company policies, administrative procedures, and professional ethics. Most computer-related associations have written codes of ethics on privacy rights, which specify minimizing needless collection of data, developing access controls, ensuring data quality, and disposing of data as appropriate.

The debate on data privacy is far from settled. The conflict between organizational efficiency and personal privacy means that continued discussion and research will be required to ensure that legislation and administrative practice recognize the need for both.

Computer Crime

The *Computer Fraud and Abuse Act of 1986* now explicitly prohibits a wide range of computer-related crimes. With these laws in place, more cases are apt to go to trial and result in convictions and serious sentences.

Preventing computer crime depends on (1) limiting access by unauthorized users masquerading as legitimate users and (2) limiting rightful users to those parts of the system they are authorized to access.

Computer-abetted Crime

When the computer was first invented, *computer crime* referred to theft or sabotage of computers. Now the term **computer crime** includes the unauthorized use of computer systems, including software or data, for unlawful purposes. A new breed

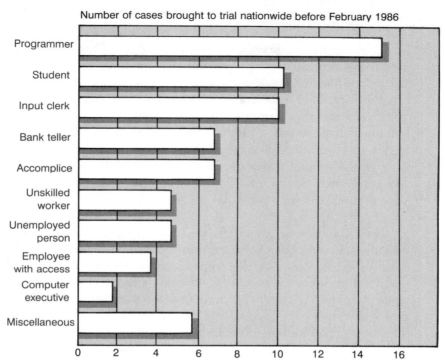

Number of cases brought to trial nationwide before February 1986

Information provided by the National Center for Computer Crime Data's Computer Crime Census. Figures based on a survey of 130 prosecutors in 38 states.

Figure 14.2
Who commits computer crime? Number of cases brought to trial nationwide by type of suspect.

of criminal has emerged who tackles the technical challenges while disregarding the moral or ethical implications of these criminal acts. Although most arrests for computer crime have involved young, highly skilled employees, Figure 14.2 shows that a wide range of other employees has also been involved.

Accurate data on computer crimes are lacking. The average loss appears from all reports to be large — perhaps as high as several hundred thousand dollars. Most of these crimes are committed by individuals who are authorized to use the system and have enough technical knowledge to exploit its weaknesses. Computer-abetted crimes are difficult to detect (many crimes are discovered by accident), and some aren't reported because doing so would undermine the confidence of the public or investors.

Electronic funds transfer systems (EFTS) are especially vulnerable to computer crime because of the high potential payoff. Embezzlers with detailed knowledge of a particular system can transfer money from one account — usually an inactive one

— to their personal account. Stanley Rifkin, for example, used his knowledge of a bank's procedures, a telephone, and an authorization code to transfer $10.8 million to a Swiss bank account. Eventually he was caught.

Some of the methods used in computer crime are novel, and a specialized jargon has evolved to describe them. Two of these unique methods are salami slicing and the Trojan horse method.

Auditors have a difficult time detecting smart embezzlers, because doctored computer-generated reports and listings seem to be correct. For example, in a **salami-slicing** scheme, a program is modified to round down all fractions of a penny in transactions like salary calculations and to add these amounts to the criminal's computer account or paycheck. Although these "slices" may not seem like very much, they can add up to a surprisingly large sum in a company with several thousand employees. Salami slicing is difficult to detect because the account totals balance.

In a **Trojan horse** scheme, named for the legendary Greek warriors who hid inside a hollow wooden horse, an unauthorized program is hidden within a legitimate program, such as a telecommunications control program. The hidden program might discover passwords by scanning the data passing through the legitimate program. The criminal then uses the stolen passwords to enter other accounts and pillage them.

The largest and most notorious computer fraud scheme involved Equity Funding Corporation, a large insurance firm based in Illinois and California.[3] To inflate the company's stock, top executives established within the company a second data processing department, ostensibly for research and development. This department actually programmed the company's computers to generate over 60,000 fictitious life insurance policies worth $2.1 billion. These fictitious policies were then sold to other insurance companies. Equity Funding received a commission on each fictitious policy sold, paid premiums on these policies to the reinsurers, and then generated fake medical records to show that some of the policy holders had died. Besides profiting from the sale of shares of Equity Funding stock, the executives also collected over $1 million as beneficiaries of the fake policies. They were caught when a disgruntled former employee revealed the fraud. More than 20 people were convicted of federal crimes, and several books were written on the scandal. When the company collapsed, shareholders lost an estimated $600 million, and life insurance policy holders lost an estimated $1 billion in the face values of their policies.

Hackers and Computer Trespassing

Not all security breaches have serious consequences, nor do they all involve the clear-cut commission of a crime. Many are the work of young computer hackers who merely want to access and "look around" computer systems. Once, *hacker* meant a person who was obsessed with writing and rewriting programs and exploring the capabilities of computer systems. Today **hacker** generally means someone who gains access to a computer system without authorization. This has upset "old-definition" hackers, who prefer that the term **cracker** (short for "security cracker") be used to describe computer trespassers.

This new breed of hackers is a product of the personal computer. Years ago, lists of authorized user names, passwords, trustworthy employees, and a secure computer room protected mainframe computers from trespassers. With the development of dial-up timesharing, however, anyone with a valid password, modem, and terminal could gain access by dialing the system's telephone number and supplying a valid user name/password combination. Today a personal computer modem can be programmed to penetrate computer security.

Is a hacker a criminal or a prankster? In one case, an ex-employee of a software company used his personal computer equipped with a modem to access his former employer's confidential records on products and customers. Even though his files had been removed from the computer system, he penetrated the security system by guessing other employees' passwords. He used the information he gained to develop similar products and to offer them to his former employer's customers at attractive discounts. Clearly this individual committed a crime.

Classifying the activities of hackers like the "Milwaukee 414" group (414 is the telephone area code in Milwaukee) isn't as straightforward. Twelve teenagers in Milwaukee used networks, such as GTE Telenet, to gain illegal access to over 60 government and business computer systems.[4] Getting into the GTE Telenet system required only a local telephone number and a two-digit access code. Once on the network, the teenagers were able to gain access to the computers at the Sloan-Kettering Cancer Institute; the nuclear weapons laboratory at Los Alamos, New Mexico; and a Los Angeles bank. They only looked around these computer systems, and they didn't damage any data. Nevertheless, their activities raised anger and anxiety. Was this an innocent prank, or was a crime committed?

Some people argue that the Milwaukee 414 and hackers like them help identify weak links in security and should be encouraged. Hackers claim that they should be able to access a computer system when it isn't being used (late at night or on weekends), because this is a good way to learn about programming and computers. Some hackers encourage this type of activity by exchanging telephone numbers and passwords through electronic bulletin boards.

Those who consider computer trespassing a crime point out that there is no difference between invading a computer system and breaking into an office to snoop in the file cabinets. That the intruder only browsed and didn't steal anything is immaterial. Information is a valuable resource, and the temptation to alter or misuse it is great. Unauthorized changes to medical, financial, or government records could be catastrophic, endangering life and greatly undermining confidence in public institutions. The records of private organizations, too, must be protected. Trade secrets, product information, and marketing data provide business with a crucial competitive edge.

Victims of computer crimes sometimes find themselves in a bind. Publicity might inspire others to attempt similar schemes and shatter public trust. A bank certainly wouldn't want to publicize a million-dollar embezzlement by personal computer, lest it suffer from additional crimes or lose customers. Although businesses are reluctant to prosecute hackers who just browse around their files, they have prosecuted computer trespassers who change or destroy information. News stories about the activities of hackers have heightened public apprehension about the vulnerability of computer systems and lax security.

Safeguarding Security

No computer system is perfectly secure. Administration controls and software safeguards are two critical elements that make a computer installation more secure.

Administrative controls are policies and procedures that discourage computer crime by making it more difficult for a crime to remain undetected. Typical administrative controls dictate that businesses

- Distribute sensitive duties among several employees. For example, organizations often assign the tasks of developing programs, operating the computer system, and generating data for the system to separate departments.
- Establish audit controls to monitor program changes, access to data files, and submission of data.
- Shred sensitive documents before discarding them.
- Limit employee access to only those computer facilities that are essential to their jobs (Figure 14.3).
- Thoroughly investigate the trustworthiness of individuals in sensitive positions.

Software safeguards are programs and procedures that prevent unauthorized access to computer files. Of all protective mechanisms, software safeguards are the most difficult to develop. In the wake of revelations about hackers, recommendations to computer networks and facilities have included the following steps:

- Change passwords frequently and avoid using common words (such as *test*, *system*, or people's names) as passwords. Passwords should include both digits and letters to make guessing more difficult.
- Remove invalid user names and passwords.
- Watch for unusual activity, such as a user who repeatedly gives an incorrect password when attempting to connect with the computer system.

These measures are only a first line of defense. Underground newspapers and some electronic bulletin boards undermine these safeguards by publishing phone numbers and passwords. Several technical schemes, including callback login, access monitoring, and data encryption, can thwart these attempts to gain unauthorized entry to computer systems.

Figure 14.3
Careful monitoring of computer access has become common practice at many computer centers. Honeywell employees must wave a passcard before a sensor to be admitted to computer facilities.

In a **callback login**, all calls are screened. Each user has an identification number and an authorized telephone number. A user dials in, enters the identification number with a push-button telephone, and hangs up. The callback system verifies the identification number, searches its directory for the authorized telephone number, dials the number, and waits for a one-digit connection code. If all the information is correct, the user is given access to the computer. Use of a callback normally adds about 30 seconds to the time needed to access the computer.

Access monitoring allows a user only a certain number of attempts (say, five) to give the correct password to access the computer system. Once that number is exceeded, the user's account is frozen until the manager of the computer system receives a valid explanation of the problem.

Encryption scrambles data in files and data transmitted over communication lines, so that they can't be read by someone who doesn't know the encryption

TABLE 14.2

An encrypted message. The ecryption code used here is a fairly simple one, which involves substituting one character for another

Actual Character	Coded Character	Actual Character	Coded Character
A	P	S	G
B	I	T	O
C	@	U	E
D	A	V	'
E	W	W	F
F	C	X	V
G	[blank]	Y	X
H	T	Z	/
I	B	!	D
J	Z	@	Y
K	!	#	.
L	#	$	%
M	U	%	K
N	L	[blank]	M
O	N	/	J
P	Q	.	$
Q	S	,	H
R	R		

Encripted Message: XNERMQRB'P@XMBGMTPRAMONMWLGERW$

Deciphered message: Your privacy is hard to ensure.

scheme (see Table 14.2). The disadvantages of encryption are the cost of the special equipment needed and the loss of transmission speed.

As technology improves, computers might be protected by devices that recognize voices and fingerprints. For now, these schemes are prohibitively expensive.

Emerging Issues in Information Ethics

When people start using technology in a new way, the ethical implications of such use are often unknown. When the ethical issues eventually crystallize, community consensus may develop to demand appropriate legislation. For instance, there were no laws against publishing obscene pictures until many decades after photographic technology made such pictures possible. Maximum-speed laws weren't enacted in this country until 1926; by then, over 15 million Model T Fords were stirring up dust on the roads. This phenomenon, called *cultural lag*, is likely for computer technology as well, because legal solutions to conflicts between old values and new technology take time to emerge.

The ethical problems of computerized information systems are only beginning to surface in the public consciousness. Inevitably, some issues will engender public

A WORD ABOUT
Software Piracy

Software piracy is the illegal or unauthorized copying of software. No one really knows the extent of software piracy; some people estimate that as many as half of all copies of software in use are pirated copies.

Software, like a book or an audio or video recording, is protected by copyright law. When you buy a software package you are actually buying the right to use it (a license); you are not buying the software itself. The license agreement restricts your right to copy the software and documentation. Because the publisher retains ownership, you are not free to treat the software as personal property.

For many years personal computer applications software was distributed on floppy diskettes that were copy-protected. The copy protection made it difficult to duplicate the diskette using a standard disk drive and the operating system copy command. This method worked well as long as the application was a game or other trivial program. However, it was difficult to copy applications to a hard disk or to make backup copies of the software. In some cases people would be unable to use the application for several days, if, for instance, the original diskette wore out or was damaged and a replacement had to be ordered.

For many consumers the inconvenience was simply too great and, whenever possible, they chose to purchase programs that were not copy-protected. Today copy-protected diskettes are extremely rare. Instead, publishers use publicity campaigns and an occasional lawsuit to inform and educate consumers about the ethical and legal issues involved in copying software. This has proven effective in large corporations, where piracy is easier to police. The adverse publicity and potential legal costs are far more important to the company than the money saved by stealing software.

There is one *practical* reason why you shouldn't illegally copy software: it isn't worth it. An application software package is much more than a few files on a diskette. The documentation can often run to several hundred pages or more, and if the software is sufficiently complex, you'll need to have all the documentation handy for reference. Photocopying is expensive, and the copy is rarely as easy to read or use as the original.

Another problem is that of software updates. Most complex software packages are continuously improved and adjusted to support new computers, printers, and features. When you purchase a software product you will usually receive a numbered registration card to mail back to the publisher. The publisher will then advise you of new releases of the software, and will often offer them to you at a discount. If you need technical support you can call the publisher on the telephone and receive prompt answers to your questions; however, the technical support department will generally *not* help you unless you are the official registered user.

When you consider the value of an ongoing relationship with the software publisher, along with the cost and bother of using copies, copying software just doesn't make sense. And the fact remains that software is legally protected by copyright law. Anyone who makes a copy of software to avoid paying for it is breaking the law.

debate, trigger new legislation, and permanently alter social mores. This chapter has already reviewed the major issues — privacy and crime — each of which deals with the ownership of information. The remainder of the chapter identifies five less obvious ethical issues, which are nevertheless at the cutting edge of computer information systems: malpractice in the use of information, intellectual property rights, the value of information, the value of human capital, and equal access to information.

Information Malpractice

Much as doctors worry about medical malpractice suits, information professionals fear information malpractice suits. Computer programmers who create information products have reason to be concerned about malpractice suits. In 1986 an error in the software controlling a radiation therapy machine turned on the wrong type of electron beam, killing one patient and injuring others. The determination of fault in this case hasn't yet been made, but programmers in prior cases of a similar nature have been found guilty of negligence. It is even possible for programmers whose programs fail to work as claimed to be found guilty of fraud. Organizations as well as information workers are susceptible to information malpractice and product liability. Any defect in a computerized information system is a potential liability for the designers, owners, and administrators of the system.

The most common deficiency of information systems is inaccurate data. Although data-entry errors and foul-ups in record updates seem inconsequential, they can have serious effects on individuals and corporations. Consider the trauma of Mr. and Mrs. Gorges. The Gorgeses both worked hard for years to save enough money to buy a house.[5] When they finally bought their dream home, they regularly took their monthly mortgage payment to the bank. One month they were notified that their last month's payment was past due. Mr. Gorges had evidence of having made the payment, but when he went to the bank, they couldn't find any trace of it in their computer system. The bank refused to acknowledge receipt of the payment and eventually sent out a notice of foreclosure. Upon reading the notice, Mrs. Gorges, who was already ill, collapsed with a near-fatal stroke. Finally, Mr. Gorges hired an attorney who obtained a sizeable settlement from the bank. The system software was apparently defective and didn't make reasonable checks for error conditions. It is likely that, in the future, computer operations will give greater attention to identifying and correcting such deficiencies. In addition, we can expect more and stricter standards for information practice and malpractice as our society grows more dependent on information.

Intellectual Property Rights

Concerned by widespread duplication of audio, video, and software recordings, the entertainment and software industries have pressured lawmakers for protection. The problems remain, and no quick and easy solutions are in sight. Copyright law today doesn't encompass important types of computer-related information. For instance, databases that are continuously updated can't be copyrighted, nor can ideas central to major software inventions, such as spreadsheets. And the law has yet to address the question of who owns the information produced by expert system software.

In 1986 the Office of Technology Assessment, a legislative department that helps Congress predict and prepare for new uses of technology, published *Intellectual Property Rights in an Age of Electronics and Information*, a 300-page report that concluded a long and extensive investigation. With input from hundreds of industry and academic specialists, the authors concluded that existing law for copyrights, patents, and trademarks needs to be replaced by a different legal framework. They proposed a major legal distinction between works of art, works of fact, and works of function. This proposal addresses the diversity of protection methods required by different types of intellectual properties.

The Value of Information

As we move rapidly toward an information economy, the value of information increases. Success in commerce depends more and more on information, so information itself gets treated like a proprietary commodity. In fact, information industries can't function unless information is designated as private property. Nonetheless, the public, as indicated by its large-scale violations of audio, video, and software copyrights, resists the notion of information ownership. The legal system has traditionally treated physical property and information as having different implications for liability. Consequently, we can expect ongoing debates on the meaning and ownership of different types of information.

The Value of Human Capital

The old issue of unemployment and automation is raised anew by computerization, as it begins to tackle work that demands a great deal of knowledge. When the knowledge of a human expert is implanted in an expert system, it raises challenging ethical questions of ownership as well as responsibility. What compensation is warranted for this exchange of intellectual property? Who should share in the credit for and profit from the performance of an expert system? We and future generations will have to resolve questions like these.

Equal Access to Information

Computer-accessed databases dramatically improve our ability to retrieve information, but people who want to access it need expensive computer equipment, and the whole process demands specialized training.

National studies have found that schools in poor communities are less likely than those in wealthy communities to teach computer skills to their students. The poor, then, are more likely to become "information dropouts," a situation that in the long run may be as serious as that of today's school dropouts. Setting up financial and educational obstacles to information access may promote a social system in which the poor get information-poor and the information-poor get poorer. Is this the direction in which our society is heading? Are people getting caught in a vicious cycle in which those who ignore information are likely to become poor, and once they become poor, they can no longer afford access to information?

Information access may be a problem for other social groups, in addition to the poor. This is especially likely if technological prowess is essential to information access. In part because of cultural attitudes and norms, certain groups, including women, racial minorities, and the elderly, have tended to shun computing skills. It is possible, but not inevitable, that this will put them at an information disadvantage. An Ohio project has given grants to school projects designed to reduce discrepancies in computer opportunities for females, minorities, and the disabled.

Review

Key Terms

Computer crime

Salami slicing

Trojan horse

Hacker

Cracker

Callback login

Access monitoring

Encryption

Discussion Questions

1. What rights should people have regarding information about themselves in computer databases? How might these rights interfere with the efficiency of a free market economy?

2. Do you support the establishment of a universal identifier card that would serve as a driver's license, credit card, and health record? What long-term benefits might this system have?

3. What information (if any) should owners of private databases be required to make publicly available?

4. Social security numbers are often used as a key in accessing personal information contained in several databases. Should some restrictions be placed on the use of a person's social security number?

5. Do you think the government's matching of computer files to find welfare cheaters was unethical or illegal? What portion of fraud and tax evasion do you think might be prevented if government agencies were allowed unlimited access to the records of financial institutions?

6. Authorities have raided several electronic bulletin boards used by "crackers" and seized their computing equipment and disks. They said that they hoped to "scare the kids." Should the person running the bulletin board be responsible for what callers write in the bulletin board?

7. Do you think a hacker should be able to access a computer system when it isn't busy? Is a computer system with inadequate security an attractive nuisance?

8. Is allowing computer software to be used on just one machine too restrictive? Can you suggest a more reasonable rule?

Projects

1. Find a reported case of computer crime. What type of security safeguards would have prevented the crime?

2. List some reasons why a bank might not prosecute a computer-abetted embezzler. List some reasons why they should prosecute.

3. Determine what laws (if any) your state has enacted concerning computer trespassing.

4. Interview the director of a computer center about security safeguards.

5. List some tasks a computer shouldn't perform. Justify your choices. Because a computer can't be convicted of a crime, who is responsible when a computer commits a criminal action? The programmer who wrote the program? The computer operator? The computer user? The computer's manufacturer?

Notes

1. Kenneth C. Laudon, *Dossier Society* (New York: Columbia University Press, 1986).

2. Deborah G. Johnson, *Computer Ethics* (Englewood Cliffs, N.J.: Prentice-Hall, 1985), p. 68.

3. Donn B. Parker, *Crime by Computer* (New York: Charles Scribner's & Sons, 1976).

4. "The 414 Gang Strikes Again," *Time*, 29 August 1983, p. 75.

5. Richard O. Mason, "Four Ethical Issues of the Information Age," *MIS Quarterly* 10, 1 (March 1986): 52-53.

15

Buying a Personal Computer

Preview   Throughout this book, you have been learning how to use a personal computer. You've also become familiar with several general-purpose applications. In this chapter, we'll give you some ideas for choosing a computer system of your own.

Buying a personal computer system involves decisions that don't lend themselves to clear-cut rules. You'll be inundated with other people's preferences and opinions. You'll have to use judgment and insight to sort through an immense number of conflicting messages.

Correctly projecting from your own application needs to the capabilities of a specific make and model of personal computer is the most important step for the first-time computer buyer.

In this chapter, you'll learn:

■ How to determine your needs
■ How to specify your applications
■ Where to find information
■ How to choose an MS-DOS-based computer
■ How to choose a Macintosh
■ How to choose a home computer
■ How to choose a portable computer
■ How to purchase your computer

Know Your Applications

Buying a personal computer system, like the problem-solving process we discussed in Chapter 3, starts with getting to know the problem. In thinking about buying a personal computer, the most important consideration is to know your applications and to buy for those applications. Don't rush off to the computer store before you do your homework.

Get to Know the Problem

First, examine your expectations about how you will use a personal computer. Some questions to consider include:

- Will you be interested in predominantly one application? Are you a writer (word processing), an accountant (spreadsheets or accounting software), a graphic designer (graphics), or a small-business owner (database or spreadsheet programs)? By eliminating the applications you don't need, you will simplify the decision-making process considerably.
- Will you use the computer in your profession? If your colleagues favor particular hardware and software, you might want to follow suit so that you will be able to easily exchange information with them.

Checklist for Getting to Know the Problem

- Get to know the problem: Think about how you will use a personal computer.
- Define the problem: Make a general list of the applications you need.
- Identify alternative solutions: Research and evaluate a variety of software packages and personal computer systems.
- Choose the best alternative: Narrow down the choices and decide which system works best for you.
- Implement the solution: Make your purchase.

- Are you computerizing a small business? A dentist might want a computer to keep track of patient records and billing. A lawyer might use a computer to help prepare legal contracts. The owner of a retail store might need a system for accounting and inventory. The widest variety of software for these specialized needs is available for MS-DOS-based computers.
- How often do you plan to use your computer? People who use their computers day in and day out want power, performance, and functionality.

They are willing to pay more, and they will often put up with complex, hard-to-learn systems to obtain these features. Casual users may prefer a simple, easy-to-learn system.

■ Are you planning to write programs or develop software? If so, you may not need any application software. Instead, you will want to find the computer system that best suits the applications you wish to develop, and the one that offers special tools, such as programming languages.

■ Do you travel? Will you want to take your computer with you? Find out whether a portable computer can run the software you need. A reporter, for instance, might want a computer that fits in a briefcase and offers word processing and communications functions. A manager might need a computer that he or she can take home to finish up the day's tasks.

■ Will the computer be primarily for your own use or for your children's education and entertainment? If business applications are not your primary consideration, a home computer will offer the best value and the widest variety of recreational and educational software.

Of course, you may have other ideas in mind. Generate your own questions in light of your needs. No one knows them better than you.

What Do You Want the Computer to Do?

Defining the problem means defining what you want the computer system to do. Start with a general list of applications geared to your needs. Some examples are writing (papers, articles, letters, novels), personal financial planning, inventory control, customer lists, mailing lists, tax preparation, budgeting, payroll, adventure games, simulations, tutorials, music, drawing, computer-aided design, scheduling, forecasting, stock market quotes, home banking, and conferencing.

Refine your general description into a specific description. Spell out your expectations in more detail. Define what it is you intend to do with your computer. Let's look at some examples:

■ A graphic designer wants a computer system to help create charts and graphs, layouts, and illustrations. She wants to draw the graphics, print them, and present them to clients.

■ A journalism student wants to develop a freelance writing and editing business while finishing graduate school. He needs to produce multiple-page proposals, articles, reports, and papers. The documents will include typographical elements like boldface, italics, and footnotes.

■ A musician wants a computer that connects to a keyboard synthesizer. The computer will be used to edit and arrange music, control the playback, and print sheet music using standard musical notation.

■ The owner of a retail shoe store wants computerized records of customers' names and addresses. She currently files customer records by name and zip code and types mailing labels for direct-mail campaigns. The number of customers has grown to 5,000, and the task is becoming unmanageable to do by hand.

- A contractor wants to prepare estimates and keep track of expenses, materials, and labor hours.
- A stockbroker wants to monitor stock prices, obtain and analyze financial data from on-line databases, and prepare summary reports featuring graphs.

Even before you've begun collecting information about specific hardware and software, jot down a list or description of all the ways you envision using the computer. These notes will help you to define the requirements of the system. By defining and refining your description of applications, you will clarify your alternatives and your priorities.

Information Sources

There are many ways to acquire the background information you need to evaluate your alternatives. Spend some time researching, reading, and talking to people before you make any purchases. This process will help you to narrow down your choices.

Computer Users

Talk to people who have similar application interests. Do you have any friends, professional contacts, or teachers who are already using a computer for the types of problems you are going to tackle? Ask people how they use their computers. Ask what problems they have encountered. Ask their opinions on various computer systems and software packages.

Computer Magazines

Computer magazines provide reviews of hardware and software, opinion columns, news, trends, and predictions. There are hundreds of personal computer magazines, targeted to various types of consumers. Magazines are targeted to educators, businesspeople, programmers, children, users of specific applications, and owners of specific computers.

For trends, news, and reviews, read magazines like the weekly *InfoWorld*, the monthly *Personal Computing*, or *Byte* and the quarterly *Whole Earth Review*. Magazines about specific computers and applications include *PC World*, *PC*, *Macworld*, *A+* (Apple), and *Amiga World*.

Public and school libraries often subscribe to specialized, expensive, or controlled-circulation magazines not available at newsstands or computer stores. These periodicals are a good source of information about particular applications. Names of some of these are *PC Week, The Seybold Report on Professional Computing, Data Sources,* and *Datapro's Microcomputer Software.*

Books

A relatively small investment in a pertinent, up-to-date book is a valuable way to familiarize yourself with computers and their uses before you buy. Look for user guides in the application areas in which you are interested, and books with hardware or program names in their titles. Before you buy a book, evaluate it as a learning tool and as a reference guide. Check the copyright date to see if the book is current. Read the preface or introduction to find out who the book is written for. Flip through the pages to see whether illustrations and graphics accompany the text. Then flip to the index and glossary at the back of the book, to see if the book is useful as a reference.

Your local or school library will probably have a small to medium-sized collection of computer books. (For an overview, check number 001.64 under the Dewey Decimal System; in Library of Congress systems, look under QA 76.) If you would rather buy, most bookstores and computer stores carry computer books and magazines.

Computer Shows

If you've ever been to an automobile or boat show, you already have an idea of what a computer show is all about. If you want to compare several computer systems and software packages, see demonstrations, or meet people with similar interests and needs, go to a computer show or conference. Check local newspapers for regional shows and magazines for national shows or conventions. Larger cities host many such shows and expositions yearly.

For maximum media and customer exposure, many companies wait for computer shows to announce their latest products. Shows are good places to look at new software and hardware systems, pick up company literature, and often buy products at a discount.

Many of the smaller local and regional shows are like flea markets, where bargains can be found in both used and new merchandise. Often, the "new" merchandise is actually slightly obsolete, but in the very fast-moving world of personal computers, last year's model can represent an outstanding value for the average user. After you've bought a computer, these shows are a good source for supplies like diskettes, printer paper, cables, and other accessories.

User Groups

User groups are loosely knit collections of people who meet periodically to listen to lectures, swap problems and solutions, publish newsletters, trade software, and meet other people with similar interests. They are usually organized around a

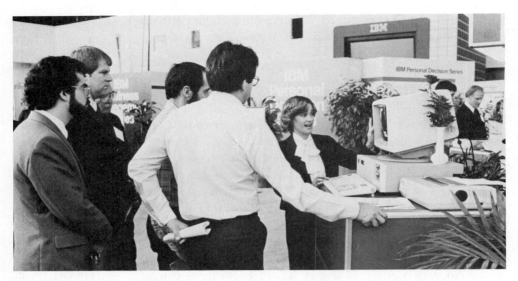

Computer shows and conferences are a good place to see new computer hardware and software and to compare systems.

particular brand of computer, such as an Apple Macintosh or an IBM Personal Computer. Some are organized around application software, such as a Lotus 1-2-3 user group, and others focus on particular professions (consultants, technical writers, small business systems, and the like). Joining a user group or attending meetings before you buy a computer is a good way to get advice and information.

Computer Stores

Computer stores are probably the best sources of information. There you can try out various systems, watch demonstrations, and ask questions. Check out several retail stores in your area. Ask about prices and the availability of various systems. Get a sense of the salespeople's attitude. Do they help customers solve problems? Do they appear knowledgeable about hardware and software? Do they ask you questions about your specific needs? Does the store cater to professionals or hobbyists, and which would you prefer? Ask about after-sale training and support.

Before you begin looking at systems in a store, have some concrete examples of your application in mind. Know specifically what the application must do. For example, "I need a database package that will store 10,000 names and addresses, produce a monthly summary report, and print mailing labels sorted by ZIP code. I also expect to add 5,000 new names to the file over the next year." Concrete examples help you to uncover hardware and software limitations and eliminate those systems from consideration.

At a computer store you can also obtain copies of the product literature supplied by software publishers and hardware manufacturers. Of course, descriptive infor-

Computer stores are often the best place to see demonstrations and compare different systems.

mation of this kind is written by the companies' marketing departments and should not be mistaken for objective evaluations. The product specification sheets do provide accurate technical information, however.

Documentation

The manuals that accompany hardware and software products are called **documentation.** You can get an excellent overview of most products by looking at their documentation. The quality and style of the documentation also reflect the ability of the manufacturer or publisher to market and support their products.

Evaluate the documentation as a teaching tool. Does it explain how to use the product? Does it proceed logically from the basics to more advanced functions? Are there plenty of examples? Does it include a tutorial disk? Does it contain illustrations and screen shots?

Then evaluate the documentation as a reference manual. Does it have an index? Does it explain error messages? Is there a quick reference guide? Is there a technical appendix?

Courses

Still in doubt about whether or not to buy? Look around for one-day or weekend seminars on such topics as "Using a Personal Computer" or "Purchasing Your

Personal Computer." Also look for application-oriented classes, such as "Word Processing for Personal Computers" or "Using Personal Computers in Small Business." Make sure the course offers hands-on experience.

How to Buy an MS-DOS-Based Computer

Recall from Chapter 1 that in personal computers that use disk drives, the operating system is usually called a disk operating system or, more casually, DOS. Most personal computers, such as IBM, Tandy, Compaq, and Hewlett-Packard, use MS-DOS (Microsoft Disk Operating System). MS-DOS is usually supplied by the manufacturer of a particular computer.

Because MS-DOS is the most widely used operating system for personal computers, it has become the de facto standard for personal computer operating systems.

IBM Personal System/2®

	Model 25	Model 30	Model 50	Model 50 Z	Model 60	Model 70 386	Model 80 386
Microprocessor	8086	8086	80286	80286	80286	80386	80386
Clock speed	8 MHz	8 MHz	10 MHz	10 MHz (0 Wait State)	10 MHz	16, 20 or 25 MHz	16 or 20 MHz
Potential system throughput[1]	More than 2 times Personal Computer	Up to 2½ times PC XT™	Up to 2 times Personal Computer AT*	Up to 3½ times Personal Computer AT	Up to 2 times Personal Computer AT	More than 8 times Personal Computer AT	More than 5 times Personal Computer AT
Standard memory	512, 640KB	640KB	1MB	1MB	1MB	Up to 2MB	Up to 2MB
Expandable to	640KB		16MB	16MB	16MB	16MB	16MB
Diskette size and capacity	3.5-inch 720KB	3.5-inch 720KB	3.5-inch 1.44MB	3.5-inch 1.44MB	3.5-inch 1.44MB	3.5-inch 1.44MB	3.5-inch 1.44MB
Fixed disk[2]		20MB	20MB	30,60MB	44, 70MB	60, 120, 120MB	44, 70, 115, 314MB
Additional options[5]	3.5-inch 720KB drive or 20MB fixed disk		60 MB fixed disk	60MB fixed disk for 031 version	44, 70, 115MB		44, 70, 115, 314MB
Maximum configuration[6]	20MB w/option	20MB	60MB	60MB	185MB	120MB	628MB
Expansion slots[3]	2[4]	3	3	3	7	3	7
Operating system(s)	DOS 3.3	DOS 3.3	DOS 3.3 and Operating System/2™	DOS 3.3 and Operating System/2	DOS 3.3 and Operating System/2	DOS 3.3, Operating System/2 and AIX PS/2	DOS 3.3, Operating System/2 and AIX™ PS/2

1. Based on testing of the most powerful configuration, as described in the IBM Personal System/2 Performance Guide. Your results may vary. 2. Model 30 also comes in a diskette-based configuration. 3. Model 25 and 30 accept most IBM PC and IBM PC XT option cards. Models 50, 60, 70 386 and 80 386 accept new IBM Micro Channel™ option cards. 4. One slot is 8 inches. 5. Model 25 version with an IBM Token-Ring Adapter Card also is available. 6. The IBM 3363 Optical Disk Drive can provide an additional 200MB to 1.6GB of on-line storage, depending on the model.

Figure 15.1
IBM Personal System/2 Model Comparison Chart.

IBM PS/2 Model 30.

IBM Products

IBM manufactures a family of personal computers called the Personal System/2 (PS/2). Figure 15.1 shows some characteristics of the major models in the family. You should note that there is room in the family for additional models (there is no Model 40, for example) and that by the time you read this book, new models will undoubtedly have been added.

The original IBM Personal Computer (PC), introduced in 1981, along with the IBM PC XT, a portable PC called the convertible, and the IBM PC AT, are no longer manufactured by IBM. Because of their popularity, however, you will still see many of these PCs in offices and schools.

The IBM PS/2 is an extremely popular personal computer. IBM is the world's largest computer manufacturer. This influences many buyers, who feel that the size and prestige of IBM, coupled with the service and backup it can offer, outweigh many other considerations.

Virtually every software company writes programs for IBM's personal computers. IBM has also spawned a large "third-party" industry of hardware

IBM PS/2 Model 50.

developers that manufacture accessory hardware compatible with IBM personal computers.

The PS/2 was designed as an open system. An **open system** is one in which components, both hardware and software, can be purchased from many different vendors and combined into a single system. This provides tremendous versatility and adaptability, but the tradeoff is that there are many decisions to make when buying a PS/2. You must decide which model, memory, disk drives, display, and so forth to buy. You also must decide whether to buy all components from IBM or whether to buy some parts, such as a display, from another company.

Model Considerations

The PS/2 family covers a very wide range of prices and performance. Models 25 and 30 are good starter systems suitable for home and office applications, but their expandability is somewhat limited. Models 50 and 70 are desktop computers suitable for most business and professional applications. Models 60 and 80 are floor standing units. They offer the most option slots but are more expensive than the other models. *Option slots* hold optional electronics packaged onto flat cards called circuit cards. You can add accessories to a computer, like a modem or additional memory, by plugging a circuit card into an option slot.

Additional memory for the PS/2 comes on circuit cards, which you can buy from IBM or from your choice of many other companies.

Disk Storage Considerations

You can configure your system to contain either one or two floppy disk drives, or one floppy and one hard disk. Two disk drives are preferable to one. The combination of floppy and hard disk gives you the most flexibility, versatility, and performance from your system. A hard disk increases the performance of virtually any software. Access time is much faster and storage capacity much greater; the tradeoff is a much higher price.

The standard floppy disk in the PS/2 is the 3½-inch size, although the older 5¼-inch floppies are available as an option. Both 5¼-inch and 3½-inch disk drives come in two flavors, one holding more data than the other. The older 5¼-inch technology stores either 360 kilobytes or 1.2 megabytes; the 3½-inch technology stores 720 kilobytes or 1.44 megabytes. Most new computers use either the 1.2 megabyte 5¼-inch drives, or the 1.44 megabyte 3½-inch drives.

Display Considerations

The two most important points to consider in comparing display devices are graphics and color. Buying an IBM PS/2 requires you to weigh the differences between display devices.

Display devices range from monochrome (the least expensive), to composite color monitors, to RGB color monitors (the most expensive). Which to choose depends largely on whether or not you will be using software that takes advantage of color and graphics displays. Word processing, for instance, is traditionally associated with monochrome display of text, but the newest word processors, such as Microsoft Word, display text graphically, and most word processors can utilize color displays to highlight various attributes.

The IBM PS/2 has a built-in graphics chip that supports several levels of resolution depending on the model you buy. In Models 25 and 30, the graphics chip supports only what is known as a MultiColor Graphics Array (MCGA) display. Models 50 and above support Video Graphics Array (VGA), which provides higher resolution and more colors.

For applications that require very high resolution, such as computer-aided drafting and design, IBM provides a graphics adapter, a card that plugs into one of the option slots and connects the PS/2 to the video display device.

Both the built-in graphics chip and the graphics adapter can be used with either a monochrome or a color display.

The Compaq Transportable 286 is compatible with the IBM PC AT.

Printer Considerations

The IBM's versatility means that virtually any type of printer can be connected to it. Figure out what your printing needs will be based on your application; then select the type of printer that suits your needs.

Printers fall into two categories — impact and non-impact. Of the non-impact printers, laser printers (the most expensive) offer the broadest range of desirable features: graphics, high speed, high quality, and quiet operation. Inkjet and thermal-transfer printers cost less, and are the best choice for high-resolution color printing.

Impact printers — dot-matrix and letter-quality — transfer an image by striking the paper. Letter-quality printers produce text that closely resembles the printing of an IBM Selectric typewriter, which is desirable for some business situations; the tradeoff is high noise and lack of graphics capability. Dot-matrix printers are the most common and least expensive printers for personal computer systems. They, too, are noisy, but can print graphics and high-quality text, and some can print in color.

Communication Considerations

There are two ways to add communication capability to a PS/2. The first is to use a modem card, which plugs into one of the option slots. The alternative is to connect an external modem to the computer using one of the external device connectors.

A Note on IBM Compatibility

The term **IBM PC–compatible computer,** sometimes called a *clone,* refers to a computer on which software designed for the IBM PC family can be run without alteration.

These computers usually feature a lower price and additional features. IBM PC–compatibles are made by a wide variety of companies from America, Europe, Japan, Korea, and Taiwan. Many of the companies that have made personal computers in the past have gone out of business. If you want to minimize the risk of buying a PC from a company that may be gone tomorrow, you can choose from IBM and several other giant companies like Japan's NEC, Italy's Olivetti, and Tandy, Compaq, and Zenith in the United States. If you are willing to accept some risk, you will usually find that the newest, fastest, and cheapest computer comes from one of the smaller companies that are less well known.

A Note on Operating Systems

Although MS-DOS is the de facto standard today, several other operating systems deserve consideration. The Apple Macintosh, for example, has a unique operating system. We will discuss the Macintosh in the next section.

IBM PS/2 Models 50 and above and many newer computers are designed to support IBM and Microsoft's new operating system called Operating System/2 (OS/2). OS/2 allows application software to use more memory, carry out more than one task at a time (a feature called *multitasking*), and display elaborate graphics that make complex software easier to use. OS/2 requires a more expensive computer than does MS-DOS, but for many applications the added features will be well worth the additional expense.

Yet another operating system called Unix is available for some personal computers. Unix is an operating system designed by AT&T for technical applications. It is not particularly suited for the average home- and business-related uses of personal computers.

How to Buy an Apple Macintosh

Apple borrowed graphics concepts and a mouse-driven interface from high-priced research and development computers and incorporated them into a personal computer. The difference between the Macintosh family and the IBM family is not what each can do, but how they do it. The Macintosh is very easy to use, and its built-in graphics and user interface set it apart from other personal computers.

The Macintosh family tree has two branches: the Macintosh SE and the Macintosh II. The Macintosh SE is similar to earlier models of the Macintosh family. It comes with one megabyte of memory expandable to four megabytes and one option slot. The standard model comes with two $3^1/2$-inch floppy disk drives, but an optional hard disk can be added. The Macintosh II differs physically from the Macintosh SE and in form more closely resembles the MS-DOS family of personal computers. It comes with one megabyte of memory, which can be expanded to eight megabytes, six option slots, one $3^1/2$-inch floppy drive, and a hard disk.

The Macintosh family of personal computers. On the left is the Macintosh II. On the right, the Macintosh SE.

Memory Considerations

The standard Macintosh comes with 1 megabyte of memory. Although most of the software developed for the Macintosh will run in that amount of memory, the operating system will take advantage of more memory to fit more than one application in memory at the same time.

Disk Storage Considerations

To expand on the built-in floppy, you can add an external floppy drive, or an external or internal hard disk drive. The external floppy drive is the least expensive alternative. An external hard disk drive offers greater storage, whereas the internal hard disk drive offers greater storage plus higher speed. The tradeoff is higher price.

Printer Considerations

The Macintosh supports two families of printers. The ImageWriters are low-cost dot-matrix printers that can accurately reproduce the graphic images produced on the Macintosh screen. The LaserWriters are a family of laser printers that can print near-typeset-quality text and high-resolution graphic images. However, the average LaserWriter is ten times as expensive as an ImageWriter.

How to Buy a Home Computer

Home computer is a generic term for personal computers designed primarily for entertainment and instructional programs. Home computers vary widely in function and price. At the low end, they are closed systems that do not support much in the way of peripherals, add-ons, or general-purpose application software. Word processors, spreadsheets, and database programs may be supplied with the system or are available at a low price, but they tend to be limited in scope and function.

If you mainly want access to recreational and educational software, or if you are uncertain how much you will use a computer, start with a low-cost system for exploratory purposes. A home computer like the Commodore is your best choice. High-end home computers, such as the Amiga, the Atari 520, or the Apple II, are close to desktop personal computers in functions and price.

The Apple II Family

The original Apple II was introduced in 1978. It was followed by the Apple II+, IIe, transportable IIc, and IIGS. An extremely wide variety of software exists for the Apple II family.

The IIGS is an open system, like the IBM or Macintosh. You can add more memory, a monochrome or color display, floppy or hard disks, and specialized input devices, such as a mouse. Apple manufactures most of these components,

The Apple IIGS personal computer.

but they can also be bought from other manufacturers. The IIc is a closed system. The system unit houses a keyboard, processor, and memory, a 5¼-inch floppy drive, and places to connect a monitor, printer, and other input/output devices.

If you want simplicity and a transportable computer that you can take out of the box, plug in, and begin using right away, choose the IIc. If you want expandability and the versatility that goes with it, and you don't mind adding components yourself, choose the IIGS.

How to Buy a Portable Computer

Portable computers range from hand-held to laptop and transportable models. **Hand-held personal computers** might be thought of as the next generation of programmable calculators. They fit in your pocket and are battery powered. They

Portable computers come in a wide variety of sizes and prices. Hand-held personal computers, such as the Sharp, are like programmable calculators. Laptop computers, such as the Hewlett-Packard portable, are notebook-sized computers. Transportable computers, such as the Apple IIc, offer functions similar to desktop personal computers.

offer a single-line liquid crystal display. Software consists of built-in BASIC and a simple text editor. Optional attachments include cassette recorders, for storing programs, and thermal printers. Radio Shack sells an inexpensive line of hand-held personal computers that resemble business pocket calculators, whereas Hewlett-Packard offers a far more expensive line of computers that resemble programmable scientific calculators.

Laptop computers, such as the TRS-80 Model 200, the Toshiba family, and the Grid family, are sometimes called "notebook-sized" computers. They often feature a built-in set of applications, such as a simple word processor, a spreadsheet, and BASIC programming. Most are MS-DOS computers. They are battery powered in their normal operation, contain a liquid crystal display screen, typically come with a built-in modem, and can be plugged into peripheral devices, such as printers, plotters, or disk drives. High-end laptop computers are as powerful as their desktop cousins but are higher priced.

Transportable computers, such as the Compaq family, the Apple IIc, and the Kaypro, are self-contained units that include a CRT display and disk drives and come with a case for fairly easy carrying. They require AC electrical power and generally weigh 20 to 40 pounds. They usually offer all of the functionality of a desktop computer, at a slightly higher price, and should be considered if transportability is a requirement.

Choose the Best Alternative

What is the best personal computer system to buy? Each has its own style, features, advantages, and disadvantages. You have to decide which system works best for you. Price usually dictates the overall performance level and functionality of a system.

To find a reasonably priced system that offers everything you want, implemented the way you would like it, you will probably have to make compromises, whether in price, functionality, or simplicity and clarity. Compare hardware prices from several sources using a chart like Figure 15.2. Choosing the best alternative will be easier if you follow these guidelines:

- *Keep your system simple.* It is easy to be intimidated by the technobabble of features, functions, performance, and power. Look for simplicity and clarity in a computer system. Computer design is changing. Keep in mind that simple no longer means less useful or less powerful.

- *Add functions only as you need them.* A simple, less-powerful system is often the best choice for the first-time buyer. Your computer system is like a toolbox. A few general-purpose tools can be far more useful than a toolbox crammed with special-purpose tools. With most computers, you can add more later.

Figure 15.2

Comparing hardware costs. When shopping for a computer system, make a list of everything you will need. Then compare prices from several sources.

Store name	_____	_____	_____	_____
Address	_____	_____	_____	_____
Phone	_____	_____	_____	_____
System unit:	_____	_____	_____	_____
Base price	_____	_____	_____	_____
Extra memory	_____	_____	_____	_____
Disk Storage:	_____	_____	_____	_____
Floppy (KB)	_____	_____	_____	_____
Hard (MB)	_____	_____	_____	_____
Display:	_____	_____	_____	_____
Monitor	_____	_____	_____	_____
Adapter	_____	_____	_____	_____
Printer	_____	_____	_____	_____
Printer cable	_____	_____	_____	_____
Other:	_____	_____	_____	_____
Modem	_____	_____	_____	_____
10 disks	_____	_____	_____	_____
Paper (1 box)	_____	_____	_____	_____
Accessories	_____	_____	_____	_____
Sales tax	_____	_____	_____	_____
Total	_____	_____	_____	_____

■ *Let the system evolve as your learning evolves.* Build your computer skills and expertise by accumulating a series of small successes. Only after you experience tangible benefits and results should you move on to more advanced functions.

How to Make Your Purchase

Many first-time buyers should buy from a computer store that offers service and support. Insist that the dealer show you how to set up the hardware, how to connect the cables, and how to install the software. Establish a clear understanding of what support and training the dealer will provide. Find out if support and training are separately priced. Ask what happens, and whom to call, if your computer breaks down. Find out the policies of the hardware manufacturer and

A WORD ABOUT
What To Do After You Buy a Computer

Buying the personal computer system of your choice is the first step toward a potentially rewarding experience. However, buying a computer isn't like buying a toaster or a television. You can't just take it out of the box and begin to use it. It takes a little time and patience to get a new computer set up and ready to go. Here are some tips to make the process flow smoothly:

1. Unpack the boxes and check to see if everything is there. Notify the seller immediately if anything is missing.

2. Plug the components into each other; then plug them into the wall socket and turn them on. This process is similar to setting up a stereo or VCR.

3. Install the operating system software. If your computer has a hard disk, you may need to format it first. If your computer has only floppy disks, you will need to make copies of the operating system disks for day-to-day use.

4. If you encounter a problem, don't fight it. Call the store where you bought the computer or call your friends. Sometimes things don't work instantly and instructions may be difficult to follow. Although hardware and software are thoroughly tested before being sold, they may still be faulty.

5. If you have purchased word processing application software, install it next. In the case of MS-DOS you will need to edit special files to properly configure your operating system. This is much easier if you have installed a word processor that you already know how to use.

6. Try using the printer. A cable should connect the printer to the correct socket at the back of the computer. The word processor needs to know what kind of printer is connected. If the correct words are printed, but they don't look right, the software needs to be adjusted. If the words are wrong, or the printer doesn't work at all, the hardware setup isn't right.

7. Play with your computer system. The best time to experiment is when the system is new. Press keys, explore, discover, and make mistakes. Mistakes made now will be less costly than those made further on down the line.

8. Send in the warranty cards. For hardware, this establishes the initial date of ownership; warranties are usually for either 90 days or 1 year. For software, sending in a warranty card will put you on the company's mailing list. They will probably keep you informed of software updates which fix bugs and add new features. You will often get a discounted price on these new versions of the software. For both hardware and software, jot down all the serial numbers and telephone numbers to call for service.

9. To learn more about your new computer you may want to join a *users group.* To find out what users groups are available in your area, ask at your local computer store.

10. Check out computer books and magazines. Now that you own a computer you may want to subscribe to a magazine; especially if you don't have time to join a users group. Most chain and college bookstores feature a huge selection of paperbacks on computers and software. If you were a smart shopper you probably looked at some of them *before* you bought your computer. Look again; they will seem a lot more interesting now that you, too, have your very own personal computer.

software publisher on damaged or faulty equipment, faulty disks, updates, copy protection, and telephone hotline services.

If you have a number of friends who already have personal computers or have other sources for advice and technical help, you may want to consider buying a computer from a discount store. Mail order retailers, such as *47th Street Photo* in New York City, sell computers at steep discounts to bargain hunters willing to shop by phone. If you live near a "high-tech" area, like California's Silicon Valley, you can often locate businesses that specialize in selling computers that are assembled from a variety of sources and come with dramatically lower price tags than those that carry a brand name. When dealing with mail order or otherwise questionable sources, purchase only with a credit card. If your computer arrives broken or fails in a few days, the credit card company will generally make the vendor take the merchandise back and give you a refund.

Is this kind of bargain hunting worth the risk? Yes and no. If you have the money, it is a lot easier to buy a brand name machine from a first-rate store. Also, if you must be able to run the newest application programs, it is best to have the newest brand name machine. Sometimes the most complex new software doesn't work perfectly on the less popular computers. On the other hand, if your requirements are simple and your budget is modest, by all means bargain hunt if that means the difference between having a computer and going without. Although bargain hunting may seem risky, computers are incredibly reliable. If you get one that works for a month without breaking, there is a good chance you will outgrow it before it ever fails.

Remember to leave some room in your budget for applications software. Other costs that will crop up in your initial purchase include blank disks, disk storage boxes, ribbons or cartridges, and paper for your printer.

Review

Key Terms

User group
Documentation
Open system
IBM PC-compatible computer

Home computer
Hand-held personal computer
Laptop computer
Transportable computer

Discussion Questions

1. What are some advantages and disadvantages of an open system?

2. What applications would benefit most from a portable computer? What applications would benefit least?

3. Consider where you live and your access to information about personal computers. What would your first steps be to find out more about buying your own computer?

Projects

1. Pick an application, such as word processing, spreadsheets, or database management. Search magazine reviews of packaged software for that application. Make a comparison list of prices and features.

2. Check your daily newspaper for computer sales. (The business and sports sections contain most computer ads.) Compare prices for various systems, noting what is included in the sale price.

3. Make an exploratory visit to a local computer store to inquire about hardware, software, and prices. Caution: be honest with the salespeople. Tell them that you are working on a class assignment.

4. Survey your school's library to familiarize yourself with books and periodicals that will help you find information quickly.

5. Develop a requirements list for a personal computer system. Shop and compare prices by phone.

Appendix A
Using MS-DOS
and Works

MS-DOS is an acronym for *Microsoft Disk Operating System,* the operating system originally developed for the IBM Personal Computer. Now it has become a standard operating system, available for IBM Personal System/2 computers and nearly all IBM workalike personal computers, such as Tandy, Compaq, Zenith, and PC's Limited.

An operating system controls the computer. It interfaces with you; with application software, such as Works; and with hardware, such as the keyboard, disk drives, memory, and display screen. You interact with MS-DOS by typing instructions on the keyboard. These instructions allow you to create, store, and retrieve files; run programs; and access printers and disk drives.

MS-DOS uses a single letter to designate each disk drive in your computer. It always assigns *A* and *B* to floppy disk drives. If your computer has a hard disk, it is assigned *C.*

The Keyboard and MS-DOS

The following keys and key combinations are often used to perform functions when using MS-DOS.

- The [Enter] key enters a command that has been typed.
- The [Backspace] key moves the cursor to the left, deleting one character per keystroke.
- The [F1] function key copies and displays the previously entered line.
- The right arrow key moves the cursor to the right and "uncovers" a character from the previously entered line.

With the following commands, it is necessary to press the indicated keys simultaneously. To indicate this, we use the plus (+) sign.

- Pressing the [Shift] + [PrtSc] (print screen) keys causes the printer to print everything displayed on the screen.
- Pressing the [Ctrl] + [Alt] + [Del] keys causes a system reset.

All About Files

All files in an MS-DOS directory must have unique names. The name of a file can consist of up to four parts: a drive designator, one or more directory names, a filename, and an extension. The file and directory names consist of a maximum of eight characters each; the optional extension consists of a period (.) and up to three characters. The following table shows examples of filenames:

Valid Filenames	Invalid Filenames
1QTR	FirstQuarter (too long)
File1	File 1 (no blank spaces)
11-89	11/89 (uses DOS character [/])

Drive designators are a single letter followed by a colon. The following name specifies file *report.wps* on floppy disk drive *A:*

```
a:report.wps
```

The extension *wps* is used to designate this file as a word processing file. The extension *wks* would designate a spreadsheet file; *wdb*, a database file; and *wcm*, a communications file.

Uppercase and lowercase letters are ignored. For example, the following name will choose the same file as that above:

```
A:REPORT.WPS
```

A directory name is indicated by the backslash character (\). The following name chooses a file in the Reports directory on drive *C:*

```
c:\reports\english.wps
```

There can also be more than one directory name, as follows:

```
c:\john\reports\math.wps
```

Some commands allow you to name many files at once, based on a pattern of characters in the name. For instance, "a:*.wks" will choose all files that have the "wks" extension. The "*" selects any sequence of characters; the "?" selects any single character. Many patterns are possible:

- All files on disk *A* that start with *x* and have the extension *wps:*

```
a:x*.wps
```

■ Files of any extension called *study:*

```
study.*
```

■ Files starting with *xyz* and ending in any two characters. The extension must start with *w*, but the other two characters can be anything:

```
xyz??.w??
```

MS-DOS Commands

The following are brief descriptions of selected MS-DOS commands and programs. Some of these commands have extra options that are not discussed, and there are many other commands available from MS-DOS. However, these are the most commonly used commands. The MS-DOS manual that comes with your computer describes all MS-DOS commands in greater detail.

Most of these commands are actually built into MS-DOS and are available at any time. Commands followed by (Ext) are external programs that come on one of the MS-DOS diskettes. To give these commands you must have a copy of the program on one of your disk drives before you can use the command.

DIR
Display a list of files in a directory.
To display the files on drive A:

```
dir a:
```

To display the files in directory *mary:*

```
dir \mary
```

To display the files in the current directory:

```
dir
```

COPY
Copy one or more files from one drive or directory to another.
To copy all of the wps files on drive C to drive A:

```
copy c:*.wps a:
```

DISKCOPY (Ext)
Copy an entire diskette from drive to drive.
To copy the diskette in drive A to the diskette in drive B:

```
diskcopy a: b:
```

DEL
ERASE
Delete files.

> To delete all the backup files in the current directory:

```
del *.bak
```

DATE
TIME
Set the date and time in the computer's internal clock.

> Files are marked with both the current date and the time each time they are changed. The time must be entered in 24-hour format.

```
date mm/dd/yy
time hh:mm:ss
```

CD
Change directory.

> MS-DOS "remembers" a current disk drive designator and directory. Any filename that does not explicitly specify a disk drive or directory will be interpreted relative to the current directory. For instance, the command

```
cd \john
```

makes "\john" the current directory. A filename like *math.wps* would then refer to the file *\john\math.wps*.

CHKDSK (Ext)
Check disk; verify the disk integrity for a drive.

> Check the integrity of the diskette in drive A:

```
chkdsk a:
```

FORMAT
Format a blank disk so that it can be used to store files.

> To format the disk in drive A:

```
format a:
```

> Be careful with this command, it will erase *all* the files on the disk being formatted.

CLS
Clears the screen of all text.

MD
Creates a subdirectory on the specified disk.

RENAME
REN

To change the name of a file from *abc* to *xyz*:

```
rename abc.wps xyz.wps
```

RD

Removes a subdirectory from the specified disk.

Be careful with this command, since removing a subdirectory necessitates erasing all the files in the subdirectory.

Appendix B
Special Mouse
Shortcuts

Keyboards are not the only way to communicate with a computer. Moving the cursor and executing commands can also be accomplished with a *pointing device* — a device for interacting with a display screen. Some pointing devices with which you may be familiar are the joystick and the trackball, which are often found in video games. Moving the handle of a joystick or spinning the ball on a trackball controls a corresponding movement on the display screen. For personal computers, the most common pointing device is called a *mouse* (See Figure B.A.).

A mouse is a small box connected to a computer by a cord (the "tail" of the mouse). As the mouse rolls across the work surface, signals are sent to the computer. The mouse has at least one button on its case; pressing the button also sends a signal to the computer.

The Works Mouse

When you run Works, it will automatically sense whether a mouse is present. Works will allow you to use the mouse to select, scroll, view menus, and press buttons on dialog boxes. Works alters the screen slightly when a mouse is being used. Figure B.C shows what a screen looks like when a mouse is installed. The major differences are the appearance of (1) scroll bars on the right and bottom edges of the screen and (2) a special cursor on the screen called the *mouse pointer*.

When you move the mouse, the mouse pointer makes a corresponding movement on the screen. By moving the mouse pointer, you can point at different parts of the screen. The mouse pointer is similar to the cursor, but it doesn't blink.

Though your mouse may have more than one button on it, Works uses only one button. If you have more than one button, use the leftmost button.

There are two mouse-button commands to which Works responds. A *click* is a button press followed immediately by a button release. A *drag* is performed by pressing the button, holding it down, and moving the mouse while it is held down.

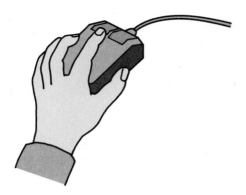

Figure B.A
A mouse pointing device.

The Mouse and Menus

When you point at a menu title and click, the menu is displayed. You then point at one of the commands on the menu and click again to activate the command. You can also point at the menu title and drag. As you drag, a highlight moves up and down the menu. When you release the mouse button, the highlighted command is performed.

The Mouse and Dialog Boxes

Dialog buttons are activated by pointing at them with the mouse pointer and clicking. Instead of using the [Tab] key to move the cursor from field to field in the dialog box, simply point at a field and click. The cursor will then move to that field. You can also select items in choice boxes, list boxes, and option boxes by pointing and clicking.

The Mouse and Scroll Bars

A *scroll bar* is a horizontal or vertical stripe with buttons on it, used, with the mouse, to scroll. Figure B.C shows both horizontal and a vertical scroll bars used by the word processor. Most Works screens have scroll bars when a mouse is present. Inside of dialogs, list boxes have vertical scroll bars.

Several kinds of scrolling can be accomplished with a scroll bar and the mouse. If you point at one of the scroll arrows and click, text will scroll one line per click. The position of the scroll box in the scroll bar indicates what part of the file the screen is showing. For instance, if the scroll box is in the middle of the scroll bar,

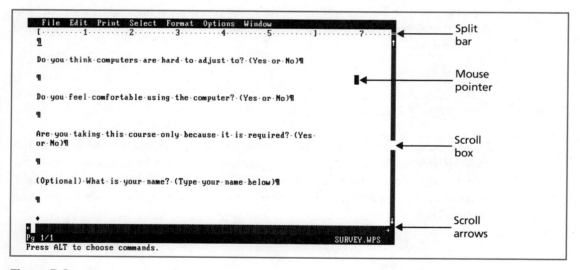

Figure B.B
A screen without scroll bars.

Figure B.C
The same screen with scroll bars.

then the screen represents the information at approximately the middle of the file. You can drag the scroll box with the mouse to quickly scroll to a location in the file. If you click on the scroll bar above the scroll box, you will scroll up about one screenful; if you click below the scroll box, you will scroll down about one screenful.

Some scroll bars display a *split bar* symbol. You can drag the symbol to split the window. When you release the mouse button, the scroll bar splits into two scroll bars, representing two independently scrollable views of the file. To close a split, drag the split bar to one end of the scroll bar.

The Mouse and Selecting

Without a mouse, the selection of text, spreadsheet cells, and other information is performed by holding down the [Shift] key and using the arrow keys. With the mouse, simply point at the beginning of the selection and drag. Information is selected as you drag the mouse pointer over the screen; when the ending point of the selection is reached, release the mouse button.

In the spreadsheet and database programs, you can select entire rows and columns by pointing and clicking on their column and row titles. This technique is much quicker than using the commands in the Select menu.

The Mouse and the Keyboard

Even if you have a mouse, you can still use the keyboard commands mentioned throughout this book. You can switch between mouse and keyboard at any time. For instance, you can display a menu with the mouse, but still use the arrow keys or the [Alt] key to activate a command on the menu.

Most people find that the mouse is easier to use for editing and browsing. However, if you are typing a great deal, then your hands will probably be over the keyboard; when this happens, it is often easier to use a keyboard command.

Another common style is to use the mouse for almost everything, but when a series of commands need to be repeated over and over, the keyboard method is used because it is quicker.

Most people like the mouse, once they get used to it. However, it does require a bit of eye-hand coordination. Try it and see if it suits you.

Appendix C
Spreadsheet and
Database Functions

A **function** is a built-in calculation, a procedure that takes some input, called *parameters*, and returns an answer. This appendix describes the Works functions and gives examples of their use in spreadsheet and database formulas.

A function consists of a short name followed by a pair of parentheses, which group zero or more parameters. For instance, the following example shows a function called *fun* that takes two parameters, *p1* and *p2*.

```
fun(p1,p2)
```

Each parameter can be a number or a reference to a cell (in the spreadsheet) or a field (in the database). Here, *fun* uses the value 2 for the first parameter and the value in cell A3 for the second parameter:

```
fun(2,A3)
```

In some functions, a parameter can be a range reference. A range reference is a pair of cell references separated by a colon. For instance the range reference A1:A20 refers to cells A1, A2, A3, and so on, through A20. Here, *fun* takes a range reference for the second parameter:

```
fun(2,A1:A20)
```

A parameter can also be an expression that calculates a value. Here the first parameter to *fun* is the value of cell B2 + 5.

```
fun(B2+5,A1:A20)
```

A parameter can also be an expression that contains another function. Here the first parameter to *fun* is calculated by another function called *zap* that takes the number 5 as a parameter.

```
fun(zap(5),A1:A20)
```

Some parameters will be numbers with fractions like 5.5 and 17.623, and some parameters will be whole numbers like 2 and 765. Some parameters are special numbers that represent the time or date.

Some functions will take a variable number of parameters. Here *fun* takes at least one parameter, but ellipses (...) indicate there can be more.

```
fun(p1,...)
```

For instance, both fun(5) and fun(5,6,7) would be valid uses.

ABS(n)
Calculate the absolute (positive) value of *n*. ABS(5) is 5 and ABS(-5) is 5, too.

ACOS(n)
Calculate the arc cosine (the angle whose cosine is *n*). The variable *n* must be in the range -1 through +1; the result will be in radians for an angle of 0 through 180 degrees.

ASIN(n)
Calculate the arc sine (the angle whose sine is *n*) of *n*. The variable *n* must be in the range -1 through +1; the result will be in radians for an angle of -90 through +90 degrees.

ATAN(n)
Calculate the arc tangent (the angle whose tangent is *n*). The variable *n* must be in the range -1 through +1; the result will be in radians for an angle of -90 through +90 degrees.

ATAN2(x,y)
Calculate the angle of a line from (0,0) to (*x*,*y*). The result will be in radians for an angle of -180 degrees to +180 degrees.

AVG(r,...)
Calculate the average of the values in *r*, which is usually a range reference but can be a single-cell reference. There can be more than one parameter; the average of all cells in all parameters is computed. In a range reference like A1:A20, blank cells are ignored (they don't affect the average). In references to a single cell, blank cells are counted as 0. In all cases, text cells are counted as 0.

CHOOSE(c,p0,p1,...)
Parameters *p0*, *p1*, and so on are the value of this function, depending on the value of *c*. If *c* is 0, then use *p0*, if *c* is 1 use *p1*, and so on.

COLS(r)
Compute the number of columns in range reference *r*. A range reference can refer to a rectangle of cells. For instance, A1:B2 describes the four cells A1, B1, A2, and B2. The value of COLS(A1:B2) is 2. (See ROWS to compute rows.)

COS(n)

Calculate the cosine of n, an angle measured in radians.

COUNT(r,...)

Count the number of nonblank cells in r, which is usually a range reference but can be a single-cell reference. There can be more than one parameter; the count for all cells in all parameters is computed. In a range reference like A1:A20, blank cells are ignored (they don't affect the count). In references to a single cell, blank cells add 1 to the count.

For purposes of the count function, a cell with any text or number value, ERR or NA is counted.

CTERM(r,v,i)

Calculate the term (number of compounding periods) needed for investment i to grow to the value v at interest rate r.

DATE(y,m,d)

Computes a Works date number for the date specified by year y, month m, and day d. Works dates are represented by numbers from 1 to 65534, which denote the days from January 1, 1900, to June 3, 2079. (See TIME.)

Use this function to enter a specific date into a cell. You can also use the NOW function to enter the current date into a cell. Be sure to format the cell as a date; otherwise, a time/date number will be displayed instead of a date. Use the functions DAY, MONTH, and YEAR to display date components meaningfully.

DAY(d)
MONTH(d)
YEAR(d)

The parameter is a Works date number. DAY computes a number from 1 to 31; MONTH computes a number from 1 to 12; YEAR computes a number from 0 to 179. (See DATE.)

DDB(c,s,l,p)

Calculate depreciation for period p using the double declining balance method. Parameter c is the cost of an asset, and s is the salvage value of the asset at the end of lifespan l. Parameter p is a period during lifespan l for which the calculation will be made. For tax purposes, l and p are usually years. (See SLN and SYD.)

ERR()

This function forces a cell to display ERR, indicating that an error has been made in a calculation. Any calculation that uses this value will result in ERR as well. Use this to catch erroneous calculations. Many of the functions described here compute ERR if their parameters are incorrect. (See NA and ISERR.)

EXP(n)

Calculates the base number of natural logarithms to the *nth* power. The base number of natural logarithms is 2.71828. (See LN for the inverse function.)

FALSE()

The logical value of FALSE is represented by the number 0 in Works. Use this function to compute FALSE and make logical calculations more readable. A 0 could be mistaken for an arithmetic calculation. (See TRUE.)

FV(d,r,t)

Calculate future value. A deposit of value *d* earns interest at rate *r*. Each term *t*, a deposit is made and interest is calculated. Use to compute the effect of compound interest. (See TERM.)

For instance, you deposit $10 into a savings account each month and earn interest at the rate of 0.5 percent per month. At the end of 5 years (60 months), the account would be worth FV(10,0.5%,60) dollars.

HLOOKUP(v,r,row)
VLOOKUP(v,r,col)

These functions use a table of cells indicated by range reference *r*. Value *v* is found in the table, and the value at either the row or the column position indicated by parameter 3 is used. HLOOKUP finds *v* in the first (top) row of the table; VLOOKUP finds *v* in the first (left) column. The values located by *v* should be in ascending order by row for HLOOKUP and by column for VLOOKUP.

Use this function to look up values in tables where the top row or the left column serves as an index to information in corresponding columns or rows. (See INDEX.)

HOUR(t)
MINUTE(t)
SECOND(t)

The parameter is a Works time number. HOUR computes a number from 0 to 23; MINUTE and SECOND compute numbers from 0 to 59. (See TIME.)

IF(l,t,f)

If the value *l* is TRUE, then the value *t* is used, otherwise the value *f* is used. Parameter *l* is usually an expression that computes a logical value. For example,

```
IF(A3 > 100,B10,B11)
```

tests whether the value in cell A3 is greater than 100. If so, the value in B10 is used; otherwise, the value in B11 is used.

INDEX(r,col,row)

Gives the value at the intersection of the column and row in the table represented by range reference *r*. (See HLOOKUP, VLOOKUP.)

INT(n)

Gives an integer (whole) number; only digits to the left of the decimal point are used. For instance, INT(45.83) is 45. (See ROUND.)

IRR(g,r)

Calculate the internal rate of return for a cash flow series in range *r*. The result is the interest rate that yields a net present value of 0. Parameter *g* is a guess at what the interest rate might be; the function returns ERR if the result cannot be computed after 20 attempts. When this happens, the value of *g* is too far off, and a better guess must be made. (See NPV.)

ISERR(n)

Is TRUE if *n* is the value ERR; otherwise it is FALSE. Use to test for ERR values in a spreadsheet. (See ERR.)

ISNA(n)

Is TRUE if *n* is the value NA; otherwise it is FALSE. Use to test for NA values in a spreadsheet. (See NA.)

LN(n)

Calculate the natural logarithm of *n*.

LOG(n)

Calculate the base 10 logarithm of *n*.

MAX(r,...)
MIN(r,...)

Find the largest (MAX) or smallest (MIN) number in *r*, which is usually a range reference. There can be more than one parameter, which can be ranges or single cells; the largest or smallest number in all cells in all parameters is found.

MINUTE(t)

See HOUR, MINUTE, SECOND.

MOD(n,d)

Calculate the remainder (modulus) for the division n/d. MOD(4,3) is 1. MOD(4,4) is 0.

MONTH(d)

See DAY, MONTH, YEAR.

NA()

This function forces a cell to value NA, indicating that a value is not available. (See ERR and ISNA.)

NOW()

Using the internal clock and calendar of the computer, compute the time and date as a Works time and date number. (See HOUR, MINUTE, SECOND; DAY, MONTH, YEAR.)

NPV(i,r)

Calculate the net present value for a cash flow series in range *r*. The cash flow is discounted at interest rate *i*.

PI()

Give the constant number 3.14159.

PMT(p,r,t)

Calculate the payment for a loan. The amount borrowed (the principal) is *p*, the interest rate is *r*, and the length of the loan (the term) is *t*. If *t* is in months then the interest rate *r* should be for one month; if *t* is in years, then *r* should be annual interest.

PV(p,r,t)

Calculate the present value of a series of payments in the amount of *p*, using an interest rate of *r*, for a term *t*.

RAND()

Calculate a random number between 0 and 1. Multiply or divide RAND by another number to get larger or smaller random numbers.

RATE(f,p,t)

Calculate the fixed interest rate needed to achieve a future value of *f*, from a present value of *p*, over term *t*.

ROUND(n,p)

Round *n* to *p* digits. If *p* is positive, digits to the right of the decimal point are rounded. If *p* is negative, digits to the left of the decimal point are rounded. If *p* is 0, *n* is rounded to the nearest integer (whole number). For instance, ROUND(45.83,0) is 46. (See INT.)

ROWS(r)

Compute the number of rows in range reference *r*. A range reference can refer to a rectangle of cells. For instance, A1:B2 describes the four cells, A1, B1, A2, and B2. The value of ROWS(A1:B2) is 2. (See COLS to compute columns.)

SECOND(t)

See HOUR, MINUTE, SECOND.

SIN(n)

Calculate the sine of *n* measured in radians.

SLN(c,s,l)

Calculate depreciation for one period using the straight-line method. Parameter c is the cost of an asset, and s is the salvage value of the asset at the end of lifespan l. For tax purposes, l is usually in years. (See DDB and SYD.)

SQRT(n)

Calculate the square root of n. If n is negative, the value is ERR.

STD(r,...)

Calculate the standard deviation for the population in r, which is usually a range reference but can be a single-cell reference. There can be more than one parameter; the deviation for all cells in all parameters is computed. In a range reference like A1:A20, blank cells are ignored (they don't affect the deviation). In references to a single cell, blank cells are counted as 0. In all cases, text cells are counted as 0.

SUM(r,...)

Sum all the nonblank cells in r, which is usually a range reference but can be a single-cell reference. There can be more than one parameter; the sum of all cells in all parameters is computed. Blank cells have a value of 0, so they never affect the sum.

SYD(c,s,l,p)

Calculate depreciation for period p using the sum-of-the-years method. Parameter c is the cost of an asset, and s is the salvage value of the asset at the end of lifespan l. Parameter p is a period during lifespan l for which the calculation will be made. For tax purposes, l and p are usually years. (See DDB and SLN.)

TAN(n)

Calculate the tangent of n, an angle measured in radians. (See ATAN and ATAN2.)

TERM(p,r,f)

Calculate the number of payments needed in the amount of p, earning interest rate r, to grow to the future value f. Use to compute the effect of compound interest. (See FV.)

For instance, each month you deposit $10 into a savings account earning interest at the rate of 0.5 percent per month. For the account to grow to $3,000, it will take TERM(10,0.5%,3000) months.

TIME(h,m,s)

Computes a Works time number for the time specified by hour h, minute m, and second s. Works times are represented by fractions from 0 to 0.999, which denote 24-hour time from 00:00:00 to 23:59:59. (See DATE.)

Use this function to enter a specific time into a cell. You can also use the NOW function to enter the current time into a cell. Be sure to format the cell as a time; otherwise, a time/date number will be displayed instead of a time. Use the functions HOUR, MINUTE, and SECOND to display time components meaningfully.

TRUE( )

The logical value of TRUE is represented by the number 1 in Works. Use this function to compute TRUE and make logical calculations more readable. A 1 could be mistaken for an arithmetic calculation. (See FALSE.)

VAR(r,...)

Calculate the variance for the population in *r*, which is usually a range reference but can be a single-cell reference. There can be more than one parameter; the variance for all cells in all parameters is computed. In a range reference like A1:A20, blank cells are ignored (they don't affect the variance). In references to a single cell, blank cells are counted as 0. In all cases, text cells are counted as 0.

VLOOKUP(v,r,col)

See HLOOKUP, VLOOKUP.

YEAR(d)

See DAY, MONTH, YEAR.

Appendix D
Menus and Commands

Works displays a menu bar across the top of the screen. The menu bar is a list of menu titles like "File Edit Print," each of which corresponds to an individual menu. Commands in the menu bar are invoked by pressing the [Alt] key. If you hold down the [Alt] key, one character in each menu title is highlighted. For instance, the "F" in the "File" menu is highlighted. If you press F, the File menu will be displayed. You can also just press and release the [Alt] key and then use the arrow keys to display menus and move the highlight up and down each menu.

Each menu item also contains a highlighted character. Each item represents one command. Once the menu is displayed, pressing this character will invoke that command. For instance, when the File menu is displayed, the "Save" command has a highlighted "S." Pressing [Alt], F, and S in sequence will activate the Save command in the File menu. If the highlight is missing, the command is not possible for some reason. For instance, in the word processor, if no text is selected, then the "Delete" command cannot delete anything. Thus, the "D" in "Delete" is not highlighted.

At times, some menus' items will have a bullet next to them. These commands are like switches that can be either on or off. The bullet indicates that the switch is on; activating the command will turn it on or off. For instance, in the word processor, the "Show All Characters" command in the Options menu can have a bullet. If the bullet is present, it means that special characters are showing; if the bullet is missing, it means that the special characters are hidden.

Not all menus with the same title are exactly the same. For instance, the Print menu in the charting program is slightly different from the Print menu in the word processor.

Commands followed by ellipses (...) cause a dialog box to appear. A dialog box is like a questionnaire that you must fill out to complete the command. The dialog box will contain the additional instructions, options, and text-entry fields needed to complete the command. After you have completed the dialog, press the [Enter] key to carry out the command.

Dialog boxes always allow you to cancel the command by pressing the [Esc] key. Some dialog boxes feature a <Cancel> button, which has the same effect.

Summary of Commands by Application and Menu

The following sections describe each Works menu bar in detail. Each command is described by both the menu title and the command on the menu. For instance, "File/Save" signifies the Save command in the File menu.

Main Menu Bar Commands

The Works main menu appears when you first start the Works program, before any application is running.

File/New...
Start your choice of the word processor, spreadsheet, database, or communications application with a new, blank file.

File/Open...
Open a file that already exists and start the corresponding application. Browse through the disks and directories to locate the file.

File/DOS...
Temporarily suspend Works and return to MS-DOS. Return to Works by typing "exit" as an MS-DOS command.

File/Exit
Exit Works entirely.

Window/Help Index
Window/Tutorial Index
These two commands are not implemented in the textbook edition of Works. In the full version, they display quick reference information and a tutorial on the screen.

Window/Settings...
Adapt the Works software. Set screen colors, the default measurement system, and keyboard/country for accented characters. The backup option determines whether files are duplicated before they are opened.

Word Processor Commands

File/New...
Start another application with a new, blank file. The display will change to the new application. The current word processing file will appear in the Window menu.

File/Open...
Start another application by opening a file that already exists. Browse through the disks and directories to locate the file. The current word processing file will appear in the Window menu.

File/Save
Save the current file using the current name.

File/Save As...
Save the current file using a different name, directory, or disk drive.

File/Save All
Save all the open files. These are the files that appear at the bottom of the Window menu.

File/Close
Close the current file. If it has been changed, a dialog will ask if it should be saved first.

File/DOS...
Temporarily suspend Works and return to MS-DOS. Return to Works by typing "exit" as an MS-DOS command.

File/Exit
Exit Works entirely. If any open files have been changed, one or more dialogs will appear, asking if they should be saved first.

Edit/Undo
Reverse the effect of the last command. If text was deleted, paste it back, and so on. Works only for the most recent command, and not all commands can be reversed.

Edit/Move
Move the selected text to a new location. The cursor is moved to the desired location; when [Enter] is pressed, the selected text is moved. The "File/New," "File/Open" and "Window/" commands can be used to move the text to a completely different file. The [Esc] key cancels the move.

Edit/Copy
The same as "Edit/Move," except that the text is duplicated at the new location.

Edit/Copy Special...
The same as "Edit/Copy," except that attributes of the text are copied, not the text itself.

Edit/Delete
Delete the selected text.

Edit/Insert Special...
Insert a special character into the file at the cursor position.

Edit/Insert Field...
Insert a database field into the file at the cursor position. Choose field from any open database file. When using the "Print/Print Merge" command, actual values from selected records are substituted. Used to print form letters from a database.

Edit/Insert Chart...
Similar to "Insert Field" command, except that a chart from an open spreadsheet is inserted. The chart will not appear on the screen but will appear on the printed document.

Print/Print...
Print the document.

Print/Layout...
Choose the page margins and other printing options.

Print/Merge...
Print one copy of the document for every record selected in a database. Field values are inserted into the document at points determined by the "Insert Field" command.

Print/Labels...
A special form of "Print/Merge" used when adhesive mailing labels are printed.

Print/Select Text Printer...
Adjust Works to the printer that will be used to print the document.

Select/Search...
Select/Replace...
Search for a word or phrase. Search for a word or phrase and replace it with a different word or phrase. Searching starts from the cursor position and stops at the end of the document.

Format/Plain Text
Format/Bold
Format/Underline
Format/Italic
Format/Character...

Change a character attribute of the currently selected text or use the CHARACTER dialog box to change several attributes at once.

Format/Normal Paragraph
Format/Left
Format/Center
Format/Justified
Format/Single Space
Format/Paragraph...

Change a paragraph attribute of the currently selected text or use the PARAGRAPH dialog box to change several attributes at once.

Format/Tabs...

Change the tab settings for selected paragraphs. Tabs are displayed on the ruler line.

Options/Split

Use arrow keys to move a horizontal split bar up and down. The split bar divides the screen into two sections that are independently scrollable views of the document. Use "Split" when you need to look at two paragraphs that are otherwise too far apart.

Options/Show Ruler

Turn display of the ruler line on and off.

Options/Show All Characters

Turn display of special characters, such as the paragraph symbol, on and off.

Options/Headers & Footers

Turn display of the special header and footer lines on and off. They appear at the top of the document with an "H" and "F" in the left margin.

Options/Check Spelling...

This command is not implemented in the textbook edition of Works. In the full version, it uses a dictionary to check the spelling of each word in the document.

Options/Manual Pagination

Turn manual pagination on and off. Pagination is the division of the document into pages. Page break symbols appear in the left margin and indicate the beginning of a new page. The pages change constantly as the document is edited. If you would prefer that the page break symbols correspond to the document pages as of the last printing, turn manual pagination on before you start editing. The document will not be paginated again until you print it again or use the "Paginate Now" command.

Options/Paginate Now
Divide the document into pages now.

Window/Help Index
Window/Tutorial Index
Window/Settings...
These three Window commands are identical to those in the Works Main Menu Bar. (See page 371.)

Window/1 FILENAME
Window/2 FILENAME
etc.
At the end of the Window menu, a numbered list of filenames appears. Each names a currently open file. Choosing one of these commands causes the display to switch to the corresponding file.

Spreadsheet Commands

File/...
The File menu in the spreadsheet is identical to that of the word processor. (See page 372.)

Edit/Move
Move the selected cells to a new location. The cursor is moved to the desired location; when [Enter] is pressed, the selected cells are moved. Works adjusts all references to the moved cells. The "File/New," "File/Open," and "Window/" commands can be used to move the cells to a completely different file. The [Esc] key cancels the move.

Edit/Copy
The same as "Edit/Move," except that the cells are duplicated at the new location. Works adjusts all references to the copied cells.

Edit/Copy Special...

Three options, to (1) copy the value and format of selected cells only, leaving the formula behind; (2) add the selected cell values to cell values in another part of the spreadsheet; or (3) subtract the selected cell values to cell values in another part of the spreadsheet.

Edit/Clear

Erase the contents of selected cells. Cell formats are unaffected.

Edit/Delete

Remove selected rows or columns from the spreadsheet. Note that you must use the "Select/Row" or "Select/Column" command first to select the entire row or column to delete it.

Edit/Insert

Insert blank rows or columns between existing rows or columns. Works inserts as many rows or columns as you have selected. Adjusts all references to the moved rows or columns.

Edit/Fill Right

Replicate the cells in the leftmost column of the selection into their adjacent selected cells to the right.

Edit/Fill Down

Replicate the cells in the topmost row of the selection into their adjacent selected cells below.

Edit/Name...

Create or delete a name for a cell or range of cells. For instance, the range A1:A12 could be named *sales*. The formula *sum(sales)* would then produce the same result as *sum(A1:A12)*. Using names instead of cell numbers can make a complex spreadsheet more understandable.

Print/Print...

Print the spreadsheet.

Print/Layout...

Choose the page margins and other printing options.

Print/Set Print Area

Print a selected portion of a spreadsheet in lieu of printing the entire spreadsheet.

Print/Insert Page Break

Insert a page break to the left of a selected column or above a selected row.

Print/Delete Page Break

Delete page breaks you placed in the spreadsheet with the "Insert Page Break" command.

Print/Font...

This command is not implemented in the textbook edition of Works. In the full version, it selects the font used when printing the spreadsheet.

Print/Print Chart...

Print the active chart from the spreadsheet.

Print/Select Text Printer...

Adjust Works to the printer that will be used to print the spreadsheet.

Select/Row
Select/Column

Extend the selection to include the entire row or column.

Select/Go To...

Select the cell, range, or name. For example, if you are in cell A1 and want to move the cursor to cell J32, type *J32* in the dialog box.

Select/Search...

Search cells for a series of specified characters. You can search for a specific item or search row by row or column by column.

Format/General
Format/Fixed...
Format/Dollar...
Format/Comma...
Format/Percent...
Format/Exponential

Change the attributes of selected numeric cells.

Format/Logical

Selected cells display TRUE or FALSE in lieu of numeric values. Cells whose values are zero display FALSE; all nonzero cells display TRUE.

Format/Time/Date...

Convert numeric values to a time or date. Options include how much of the time or date you want to display, 12- or 24-hour time, and whether to display months as text (for instance, *Jan*) or numbers.

Format/Style...

Align (general, left, right, center); format (bold, underline, italic); and lock or unlock cells. Locking a cell prevents its contents from accidentally being changed.

Format/Width...

Change the width of selected columns. Maximum width is 79 characters. Minimum width, 0, hides the column.

Options/Freeze Titles

The rows and/or columns above and to the left of the cursor will "stick" to the screen and no longer scroll. Used to keep caption text visible while repeated information scrolls.

Options/Unfreeze Titles

Reverse the "Freeze Titles" command.

Options/Split

Use arrow keys to move a horizontal split bar up and down or a vertical split bar left and right. The split bars divide the screen into two or four sections. Adjacent windows scroll together along the direction of the split. Use "Split" when you need to look at different sections of a spreadsheet that are otherwise too far apart.

Options/Show Formulas

Display the formulas rather than the values in cells of a spreadsheet. Repeating the command returns the spreadsheet to its original condition.

Options/Protect

Turn protection on and off. Cells that have been locked with the "Format/Style" command cannot be changed when protection is on.

Options/Manual Calculation
Options/Calculate Now

"Manual Calculation" turns automatic formula calculation on and off. When off, formulas are not updated until you choose the "Options/Calculate Now" command.

Chart/Define

Switch to the chart screen and the active chart from the spreadsheet screen.

Chart/New

Switch to the chart screen from the spreadsheet screen, and create a new chart using the current selection as *Y*-axis data.

Chart/View

View the active chart. To return to the spreadsheet screen, press any key.

Chart/Charts...
Chart/1 CHARTNAME
Chart/2 CHARTNAME
etc.
Use the CHARTS dialog box to copy, delete, and rename charts. If any charts have been defined, their names appear at the bottom of the menu. The active chart will have a bullet next to it. Select one of the chart names to make it active.

Window/...
The Window menu in the spreadsheet is identical to that of the word processor. (See page 375.)

Chart Screen Commands

Chart/Exit Chart
Switch to the spreadsheet screen from the chart screen; only the menu bar changes.

Chart/New
Create a new chart and make it active.

Chart/View
View the active chart. To return to the chart screen, press any key.

Chart/Charts...
Chart/1 CHARTNAME
Chart/2 CHARTNAME
etc.
Use the CHARTS dialog box to copy, delete, and rename charts. If any charts have been defined, their names appear at the bottom of the menu. The active chart will have a bullet next to it. Select one of the chart names to make it active.

Print/Print...
Print the active chart.

Print/Layout...
Choose the page margins and other printing options.

Print/Title Font...
Print/Other Font...
These commands are not used in the textbook edition of Works. In the full version, they select optional fonts used when printing the chart.

Print/Select Chart Printer...
Adjust Works to the printer that will be used to print the chart.

Data/1st Y-Series
Data/2nd Y-Series
Data/3rd Y-Series
Data/4th Y-Series
Data/5th Y-Series
Data/6th Y-Series
Data/X-Series
The current selection is made *Y* series 1 through 6 or the *X* series.

Data/Series...
Use this dialog box to set a series by typing in cell ranges. Also use to delete a series and see which series are defined.

Data/Titles...
Data/Legends...
Enter text for chart titles and legends. Text can be entered directly, or a cell reference can be used.

Data/Data Labels...
Enter text for series labels. Text can be entered directly or a cell reference can be used.

Format/Bar
Format/Stacked Bar
Format/100% Bar
Format/Line
Format/Area Line
Format/Hi-Lo-Close
Format/Pie
Format/X-Y
Choose a chart style.

Format/Data Format...
Choose the colors, line styles, and markers used to draw each series.

Options/X-Axis...
Options/Y-Axis...
Choose the range of values used to label each axis, whether grid lines are drawn for each axis value, and whether a logarithmic scale is used.

Options/Right Y-Axis...
Options/Two Y-Axes...

Create a right Y axis to accompany the normal left Y axis. Use to compare two different kinds of Y-axis data in the same chart. Assign different Y series to one axis or the other. Choose axis options for the right Y axis.

Options/Mixed Line & Bar...

Use a mixture of lines and bars in the same chart. Assign different Y series to be drawn with lines or bars.

Options/Format For B&W
Options/List Printer Formats

If you have a color display, turn "Format For B&W" on to see what your chart will look like when printed on a black–and–white printer. If you want the "Format/ Data Format" dialog box to list the effects that your printer can print, then turn on "List Printer Formats"; when turned off, the effects that your screen can display are listed.

Options/Show Printer Fonts

This command is not meaningful in the textbook edition of Works, since there is only one font for both the screen and the printer. In the full version, it displays text on the screen exactly as it will appear in the printed chart.

Options/Show Legends
Options/Show Border

Turn the display of chart legends or a border around the chart on and off.

Window/

The Window menu in charting is identical to that in the word processor. (See page 375.)

Database Commands

Design Screen Commands

The Design screen is used to create or change the record structure of a database. When you open a new database file, you are initially in the Design screen.

Edit/Exit Design

Switch to the Form screen.

Edit/Move

Move selected fields to a new location on the Design screen. Use to change a form's layout.

Edit/Copy

Copy selected fields to a new location.

Edit/Delete

Remove a selected field from the database. If the cursor is on a blank line, a line is removed from the form and information below moves up.

Edit/Insert

Insert a blank line into the form.

Format/General
Format/Fixed...
Format/Dollar...
Format/Comma...
Format/Percent...
Format/Exponential

Change the attributes of selected numeric fields.

Format/Logical

Selected fields display TRUE or FALSE in lieu of numeric values. Fields whose values are zero display FALSE; all nonzero fields display TRUE.

Format/Time/Date...

Convert numeric values to a time or date. Options include how much of the time or date you want to display, 12- or 24-hour time, and whether to display months as text (for instance, *Jan*) or numbers.

Format/Style...

Align (general, left, right, center); format (bold, underline, italic); and lock or unlock fields. Locking a field prevents its contents from accidentally being changed.

Format/Width...

Change the width of selected fields. Maximum width is 79 characters. Minimum width, 0, hides the field.

Format/Show Field Name

Hide or display the selected field's field name.

Window/...

The Window menu in the database is identical to that in the word processor. (See page 375.)

Form and List Screen Commands

The main screen of the database features two views: Form view and List view; the menu bar is the same for both. The default is Form view. Both Form view and List view are used to examine and change database records and view the results of queries on the database.

File/...

The File menu in the database is identical to that in the word processor. (See page 372.)

Edit/Move

Move records and fields to a new location within a database. In the List screen, you can rearrange the order of the fields (columns). In the Form screen, you can only move records to a new location. Normally the ordering of records should be the result of sorting the database rather than of manual rearrangement.

Edit/Copy

Copy selected records to a new location. You can copy information into word processing documents.

Edit/Clear

Erase the contents of selected fields. Has no affect on fields containing field formulas.

Edit/Delete

Remove selected records from the database.

Edit/Insert

Insert a blank record into the database in front of the selected record.

Print/Print...
Print the database.

Print/Layout...
Choose the page margins and other printing options.

Print/Font...
This command is not implemented in the textbook edition of Works. In the full version, it selects the font used when printing the database.

Print/Print Report...
Prints the active report.

Print/Select Text Printer...
Adjust Works to the printer that will be used to print the database.

Select/Record
Select/Field
Extend the selection to include the entire record (row) or field (column). This command is meaningful only with the List view.

Select/Go To...
Select by record number and field name. Used to move to a specific location in the database.

Select/Search...
Searches fields for a series of specified characters. You can search for a specific item or search record by record or field by field.

Format/General
Format/Fixed...
Format/Dollar...
Format/Comma...
Format/Percent...
Format/Exponential
Change the attributes of selected numeric fields.

Format/Logical
Selected fields display TRUE or FALSE in lieu of numeric values. Fields whose values are zero display FALSE; all nonzero fields display TRUE.

Format/Time/Date...
Convert numeric values to a time or date. Options include how much of the time or date you want to display, 12- or 24-hour time, and whether to display months as text (for instance, *Jan*) or numbers.

Format/Style...
Align (general, left, right, center); format (bold, underline, italic); and lock or unlock fields. Locking a field prevents its contents from being accidentally changed.

Format/Width...
Change the width of selected fields (columns). Maximum width is 79 characters. Minimum width, 0, hides the field. This command is meaningful only with the List view.

Options/Define Form
Switch to the Design screen.

Options/Protect

Turn protection on and off. Fields that have been locked with the "Format/Style" command cannot be changed when protection is on.

Options/View List

Switches to the List view.

Options/Split

Use arrow keys to move a horizontal split bar up and down or a vertical split bar left and right. The split bars divide the screen into two or four sections. Adjacent windows scroll together along the direction of the split. Use "Split" when you need to look at different sections of a database that are otherwise too far apart. This command is meaningful only with the List view.

Options/View Form

Switches to the Form view.

Query/Define

Switch to the Query screen to define a query.

Query/Apply Query

Apply the active query. Only records that match the query rules are displayed; other records are hidden.

Query/Hide Record

Hide selected records. Hidden records are not displayed, printed in reports, or deleted by the Delete command. Normally, a query is used to hide unwanted records that don't match the query rules.

Query/Show All Records

Display hidden records. Use after the "Query/Apply Query" command to redisplay the entire database.

Query/Switch Hidden Records

Swap the displayed and hidden records; the hidden records become visible, and the visible records are hidden.

Query/Sort...

Sort all database records in either ascending or descending order. Up to three fields can be specified for sorting purposes.

Report/Define

Switch to the Report screen.

Report/New
Create a new report.

Report/View
Display the active report.

Report/Save As...
Save the summary and totals information in a report for use in the database, spreadsheet, or word processor.

Report/Reports...
Report/1 REPORTNAME
Report/2 REPORTNAME
etc.
Use the REPORTS dialog box to copy, delete, and rename reports. If any reports have been defined, their names appear at the bottom of the menu. The active report will have a bullet next to it. Select one of the report names to make it active.

Query Screen Commands

The Query screen is used to define or change a query.

Edit/Exit Query
Switch to the Form and List screen.

Edit/Clear
Erase the query rules of selected fields.

Edit/Delete
Erase the current query so that you can enter new rules.

Window/...
The Window menu in the Query screen is identical to that in the word processor. (See page 375.)

Report Screen Commands
The Report screen is used to define or change a report.

Report/New
Create a new report.

Report/View
Display the active report.

Report/Save As...
Save the summary and totals information in a report for use in the database, spreadsheet, or word processor.

Report/Reports...
Report/1 REPORTNAME
Report/2 REPORTNAME
etc.
Use the REPORTS dialog box to copy, delete, and rename reports. If any reports have been defined, their names appear at the bottom of the menu. The active report will have a bullet next to it. Select one of the report names to make it active.

Edit/Move
Move records and fields to a new location within a report.

Edit/Copy
Copy the selected information to a new location.

Edit/Clear
Erase the contents of selected fields. Has no effect on fields containing field formulas.

Edit/Delete
Remove selected information from the report.

Edit/Insert
Insert a blank record into the report in front of the selected record.

Edit/Field Name...
Enter a database field name into the selected report field.

Edit/Field Value...
Create a formula to retrieve values from the database and put them into the report.

Edit/Field Summary...
Enter a statistical formula into the selected report field. Choose from Sum, Avg, Count, Max, Min, Std, Var.

Print/Print...
Print the report.

Print/Layout...
Choose the page margins and other printing options.

Print/Insert Page Break
Insert a page break above the selected row or to the left of the selected column.

Print/Delete Page Break
Delete the selected page break.

Print/Font...
Not implemented in the textbook edition of Works. In the full version, it selects the font used when printing the report.

Print/Select Text Printer...
Adjust Works to the printer that will be used to print the report.

Select/Row
Select/Column
Extend the selection to include the entire record (row) or field (column).

Format/General
Format/Fixed...
Format/Dollar...
Format/Comma...
Format/Percent...
Format/Exponential
Change the attributes of selected numeric fields.

Format/Logical
Selected fields display TRUE or FALSE in lieu of numeric values. Fields whose values are zero display FALSE; all nonzero fields display TRUE.

Format/Time/Date...
Convert numeric values to a time or date. Options include how much of the time or date you want to display, 12- or 24-hour time, and whether to display months as text (for instance, *Jan*) or numbers.

Format/Style...
Align (general, left, right, center); format (bold, underline, italic); and lock or unlock fields. Locking a field prevents its contents from being accidentally changed.

Format/Width...
Change the width of selected fields. Maximum width is 79 characters. Minimum width, 0, hides the field.

Query/Define
Switch to the Query screen.

Query/Sort...
Sort all report records in either ascending or descending order. Up to three fields can be specified for sorting purposes. Sort fields are also break fields unless you specify otherwise.

Window/...
The Window menu in the Report screen is identical to that in the word processor. (See page 375.)

Communications Commands

File/New...
The File menu in communications is identical to that in the word processor. (See page 372.)

Connect/Connect
Dial the phone number entered in the PHONE dialog box and establish a connection when the other computer responds.

Connect/Dial Again
Redial the phone number in the PHONE dialog box. Use this command when you get a busy signal.

Connect/Pause
Tell the other computer to stop sending information until it receives a continue signal. Use when the other computer is sending information so fast that you cannot read it.

Connect/Break
Try to get the other computer's attention and ask it to interrupt the program it is running.

Connect/Sign-On
Automatically "plays" a recorded sign-on sequence.

Connect/Record Sign-On
Record a sign-on sequence (the commands, such as identification name and password) for later playback.

Transfer/Capture Text...

Save the text that is displayed on the screen in a file. The file can then be viewed later with the word processor.

Transfer/End Capture Text

Stops the capture of text.

Transfer/Send Text...

Send an ASCII text file to another computer with no error correction protocol. The file is transmitted as if it were typed at the keyboard.

Transfer/Send Protocol...
Transfer/Receive Protocol...

Send and receive files to and from another computer using the XMODEM error detection and correction protocol.

Options/Terminal...

Adjust how your computer responds to the data sent to it by another computer during a communications session.

Options/Communication...

Adjust the settings that control the way your computer exchanges information with another computer.

Options/Phone...

Adjust the commands Works will send to your modem when you start a communications session.

Window/...

The Window menu in communications is identical to that in the word processor. (See page 375.)

Glossary

Absolute cell reference. A cell reference that does not change.

Access monitoring. A technique in which a user is allowed a specified number of attempts to give a correct password to access a computer system. When the preset number of attempts is exceeded, the user is denied further access.

Acronym. A word formed from the first letters or sounds in a phrase. For example, DOS is an acronym for *disk operating system*.

Active cell. The cell at which the cursor is pointing. (See Cell.)

Application. The use to which a computer system is put.

Application development. A problem-solving process that begins with the needs of the user and ends with a system that does what the user wants it to do.

Application program. A computer program that enables a user to perform a particular kind of task.

Artificial intelligence. The branch of computer science that attempts to understand human intelligence and to program computers to perform tasks that require qualities such as reasoning and perception.

Ascending order. Sequential arrangement from lowest to highest; for example, a telephone directory lists names in ascending order. (See Descending order.)

ASCII. An acronym for *American Standard Code for Information Interchange*. A code that specifies and standardizes the binary digits used internally by most computers to represent letters, digits, and special characters.

Automated teller machine (ATM). An interactive device that allows customers to access a bank's computer and complete transactions, such as cash withdrawal, without direct human intervention.

Backup file. A copy of a file made for safekeeping in case the original is lost or damaged.

Bar chart. A chart that represents numbers with rectangles of varying heights. (See Charting.)

BASIC. An acronym for *Beginners All-Purpose Symbolic Instruction Code*. A programming language commonly used on personal computers.

Bit. Short for **bi**nary digi**t**. The smallest unit of information in a computer system, represented by an electronic circuit that can be either on or off.

Bit map. A special segment of RAM where bits represent pixels on a display screen. (See Pixel.)

Blinking cursor. A visual aid in the word processor that indicates where the next character you type will appear on the display screen.

Block. In word processing, text that is consecutive and can therefore be manipulated as an entity, such as by moving, copying, or deleting it.

Boldface. Text that appears thicker or darker on the screen or printout for purposes of emphasis. For example, the terms listed in this glossary are in **boldface** type; the explanations are in ordinary type.

Booting. Starting up a computer, accomplished by a set of instructions called the *bootstrap program.*

Brainstorming. Unrestrained thought or discussion, without prejudging or rejecting any ideas.

Buffer. A temporary memory-storage area.

Bug. An error. A software bug is a programming error; a hardware bug is a malfunction or design error.

Builder-user. A person who designs and develops an application for his or her own use.

Button. In a dialog box, a field enclosed in < > used to carry out or cancel a command, or to answer a question.

Byte. A unit of storage that can hold one character of information. Equivalent to eight consecutive bits.

Callback. A technique in which incoming calls to a computer are screened for legitimacy.

Cell. In a spreadsheet, the space representing the intersection of a row and column.

Cell reference. (1) In a formula, the column letter and row number that are together used to refer to a particular cell. (2) A portion of the Works status line that indicates which cell is the active cell. (See Active cell.)

Centering. Aligning a paragraph of text to be an equal distance from the left and right margins.

Central processing unit (CPU). The part of a computer system that executes instructions, such as arithmetic, logical operations, and storage input and output. (See Microprocessor, Processor.)

Channel. A pathway for the transmission of data to and from a computer system.

Character. Any letter, number, punctuation mark, or other symbol that a computer can read, process, store, and write.

Charting. A technique for turning numbers into pictures.

Choice box. In a dialog, a box which displays a fixed set of choices. A choice is selected by moving the bullet character next to it. Only one item can be chosen. (See Dialog box.)

Command. An action which tells a program what operation to perform.

Command processor. An operating system program that interprets and responds to the commands typed in on the keyboard.

Communication. (1) The process of exchanging information using a commonly agreed-upon set of symbols. (2) From an engineering standpoint, the movement of electronic data from one point to another.

Communications satellite. A relay station in outer space that receives data beamed at it from a ground station and relays that data to other ground stations.

Communications software. Programs that enable computers to communicate with one another.

Computer-assisted instruction (CAI). The use of computers to teach.

Computer axial tomography (CAT). A medical imaging method that involves collecting cross-sections of x-rays, then assembling a three-dimensional composite image.

Computer communications. The movement of information from one computer to another.

Computer conference. A technology which allows groups of people to communicate about a mutual problem through electronic mail.

Computer crime. The use of computer systems for unlawful purposes.

Computer-integrated manufacturing (CIM). The linking of programmable automated systems through databases that plan, schedule, and control a manufacturing process.

Computer system. A system consisting of a computer, the programs that control it, the problem-solving procedures for accomplishing tasks, and the people who use it.

Control [Ctrl] key. A keyboard key that activates a particular function when pressed in combination with other keys.

Copy. To replicate information, leaving the original intact.

Copy protect. A technique used to make a disk difficult or impossible to copy.

Courseware. Programs whose main task is teaching.

Cracker. Short for *security cracker.* A term used to describe computer trespassers. (See Hacker.)

Cursor. A visual aid on the display screen, denoting the position that will be affected. For example, in word processing, a rectangular blinking box indicates where the next character you type will appear on the display screen.

Cursor-movement keys. Keys that move the cursor in a particular direction when pressed.

Data. (1) The raw facts that are used to create information. (2) A general term for all the information that can be produced or processed by a computer system. (See Information.)

Database. A collection of various categories of data, organized according to a logical structure.

Database management system. The hardware and software that organize and provide access to databases.

Database program. A computerized record-keeping program that stores, organizes, manipulates, retrieves, and summarizes data.

Data integrity. The accuracy and validity of the data in a database.

Data processing. Collectively, all the logical, arithmetic, and input and output operations that can be performed by a computer.

Data security. Techniques for protecting a database against unauthorized access.

Decision making. A problem-solving approach for situations in which only partial information is available about a problem.

Decision support system (DSS). Software that allows management to simulate business conditions and perform *what-if* analysis.

Dedicated system. A computer dedicated to a single task; for example, a computer dedicated to the task of word processing.

Default. An action or value that the computer automatically assumes unless a different action or value is specified.

Delete. To remove information from the screen or a disk.

Descending order. Arrangement of information in sequence from highest to lowest. (See Ascending order.)

Desktop publishing. The use of personal computers and page composition software to prepare and print typeset- or near-typeset-quality documents.

Dialog box. An on-screen box in which the user responds to the system's request for more information.

Directory. A listing of all the files on a disk.

Disk. A circular platter coated with a magnetic or optical material, which can store information.

Disk drive. The device that can read information from a disk, and write new information on it. A disk drive mounts the disk on a spindle, which spins it around like a record player while reading and/or writing.

Disk operating system (DOS). The operating system in personal computers that use disk drives.

Display screen. An output device for displaying information from a computer system. Commonly a cathode-ray tube (CRT), sometimes a liquid-crystal display (LCD), light-emitting diode (LED), electroluminescent display (ELD), or plasma screen.

Distributed processing. Information processing distributed among physically separate computer systems.

Document. Any text or collection of characters (letters, numbers, spaces, punctuation marks and other symbols).

Documentation. The books or manuals that accompany a software package, hardware component, or computer system.

DOS. An acronym for *disk operating system*. (See Operating system.)

Dot-matrix printer. An impact printer that prints characters and images composed of patterns of dots.

Drill and practice programs. Programs that reinforce lessons.

Dynamic values. In a spreadsheet, values that change automatically if the values that they depend on change. (See Static values.)

Editing. The process of composing text, revising (inserting, deleting, correcting, and formatting) it, and periodically saving the document onto disk.

Electronic funds transfer system (EFTS). A computerized system that processes information about financial transactions and facilitates the exchange of this information.

Electronic library. Files stored in a mainframe or minicomputer disk storage system, which can be accessed by terminals or personal computers.

Electronic mail. A technology for sending and receiving electronic messages.

Electronic mailboxes. Individual files used to hold individual electronic mail accounts stored on the computer system's disks.

Electronic spreadsheet. The part of a spreadsheet program displayed on the screen as rows and columns.

Encryption. A technique for scrambling data to keep it private.

End-user computing. In organizations, a configuration in which computers are controlled by users rather than by the MIS or data-processing department.

Enter key. A keyboard key used to enter commands, respond to prompts, and begin new paragraphs. (Also called the Return key.)

Ergonomics. The science of adapting the working environment to suit the worker.

Escape [Esc] key. A keyboard key used to cancel a command. For example, in Works the [Esc] key will cause a dialog box to disappear without performing a command.

Execute. To carry out a specified command.

Expert system. A computer program that solves specialized problems at or near the level of a human expert.

Field. The smallest unit of meaningful information in a record. (See Record.)

Field formula. An equation used in the database to calculate a field's value. Field formulas are similar to formulas in the spreadsheet.

File. A collection of logically related information.

Fixed information. Information that does not change, such as the captions in a report.

Floppy disk. A flexible platter, coated with magnetic oxide and encased in a protective jacket, capable of storing information. (See Disk.)

Footer. A line of text that appears at the bottom of each printed page. Footers are entered only

once; they are inserted on each page during printing. (See Header.)

Form. (1) In a database program, a list of fields illustrating the structure of a record and the correspondence between field names and sizes. (2) In word processing, a standard document for sending to a number of recipients.

Format. The way information is physically organized on a display screen, printed page, or disk.

Freezing titles. A spreadsheet technique in which column or row titles can be kept in view while scrolling.

Formula bar. A line directly underneath the menu bar. In the word processor, it is called a *ruler* and shows the locations of the margins and tab settings. In the spreadsheet and database, it is used to display the contents of the active cell or field.

Front-end processor. A processor that collects information from local sources, performs a limited amount of processing on it, and forwards it to another computer system.

Function. A predefined routine or formula.

Function keys. Keyboard keys used to initiate commands or operations that would otherwise require several keystrokes.

Functional specification. A problem definition that specifies the functions a system must perform.

General-purpose application software. Software designed to handle a wide variety of tasks that employ the same general capabilities; for example, word processing, spreadsheet, database management, graphics, and communications.

Gigabyte (GB). A unit of measure equal to 2^{30} or 1,073,741,824 bytes.

Global search. In word processing, an instruction to search through an entire document to find a particular word or phrase.

Graphics. The methods and techniques used to draw pictures or images.

Hacker. A person who gains access to a computer system without authorization. (See Cracker.)

Hard disk. A disk made with a rigid base such as aluminum, then coated with a magnetic or reflective recording surface, capable of storing information.

Hardware. (1) The electronic and mechanical components of a computer or other system. (2) The tangible part of a system. (See Software.)

Header. A line of text that appears at the top of each printed page. Headers are entered only once; they are inserted on each page during printing. (See Footer.)

Highlighting. Emphasizing information on a display screen, often in reverse video, for the purpose of selecting or manipulating it.

Hi-low chart. A chart that represents number pairs with lines. The top of the line represents the high number and the bottom of the line represents the low number. (See Charting.)

Hi-low-close chart. A chart that represents number triples with lines. The top of the line represents the high number and the bottom of the line represents the low number; the middle number is represented by a mark on the line. (See Hi-low chart.)

Horizontal scrolling. Shifting the contents of the screen to the left or the right in order to view information that is wider than the screen display.

Icon. A picture on a display screen that symbolizes an object such as a file, a wastebasket, an in-basket, or a memo representing a particular function.

IF function. A function that tests a value and then generates one of two possible results based on the test.

Imaging. Reading, then graphically displaying and analyzing, data.

Index. A list of the contents of a file or document, with references for locating each item.

Information. Data used in decision making. (See Data.)

Information processing. Performing systematic operations on information, such as typing, adding, sorting, and thinking.

Information system. A set of interconnected parts whose purpose is to gather, manipulate, store, transmit, and communicate information.

Information utility. A service which provides subscribers with access to data or transactions via computer networks.

Input. (1) The process of transferring data into a computer system. (2) Devices that convert data into a form that a computer's processor and memory can use.

Instruction. A basic unit of a program, which specifies what action is to be performed on what data.

Integrated software. Software that combines two or more functions with the ability to share data among the functions. For example, Works integrates word processing, spreadsheets, databases, and communications.

Interactive fiction. Computerized literature in which the reader participates in the story by feeding inputs into the plot.

Interface. (See User interface.)

Justify. In word processing, to align text at both the left and right margins.

Key. In a database program, a field in a record used for sorting or retrieval.

Keyboard. A panel of buttons that convert finger pressure into electronic codes a computer can recognize.

Kilobyte (K). A unit of measure equal to 2^{10} or 1024 bytes.

Laser printer. A printer that uses a laser to transfer an image to a drum, and then records the impression on paper.

Layout commands. Commands that enable the user to change the appearance of a document, spreadsheet, or database.

Letter-quality printer. An impact printer that closely simulates the printing of an IBM Selectric typewriter.

Linking spreadsheets. A technique for consolidating information from two or more spreadsheets. When data change in one spreadsheet, the other spreadsheet is automatically updated.

List. A particular view of a database in which many records are shown.

List box. In a dialog, a box which displays choices in a list of varying length. (See Dialog box.)

Local-area network (LAN). A geographically-limited communication channel linking personal computers for the purpose of (1) communicating with one another and (2) sharing such resources as a mass storage device or a printer.

Logical operators. A set of operators used in database queries consisting of (1) an equality operator (=) and (2) the comparison operators (<, <=, >, >=).

Macro. A single command that invokes a sequence of commands.

Macro language. A programming-like facility found in spreadsheets and database programs, used to create macros.

Mainframe. Room-sized high-performance computers, capable of running complex programs that would be impractical or impossible on smaller computers.

Management information system (MIS). The use of computers and other systems to generate the information necessary for management to perform its major functions: planning, organizing, directing, and controlling.

Manual page break. A user-inserted page break. (See Page break.)

Manual recalculation. In a spreadsheet program, an option in which formulas are evaluated only when the user issues a command to do so.

Margin. The left or right boundary of a document.

Mass storage. Devices that store a lot of information, such as disks and tapes.

Megabyte (MB). A unit of measure equal to 2^{20} or 1,048,576 bytes.

Memory. The component of a computer system that stores information used by the processor.

Menu. A list of commands available for a computer user to choose from.

Menu bar. A horizontal list of menus at the top of the screen.

Message line. The last line on the screen. It is used to display descriptions of what commands and dialog boxes do, and occasionally to display instructions on how to finish a command in progress.

Microcomputer. A computer system whose central processing unit is a microprocessor. Also called a personal computer.

Microprocessor. (1) The part of a computer that controls its operation. (2) A silicon chip that contains a central processing unit. (See Central processing unit.)

Microsecond. A unit of time equal to one-millionth of a second.

Minicomputer. A medium-sized medium-capacity computer system whose performance rivals that of a small mainframe. (See Mainframe.)

MIPS. An acronym for *million instructions per second*. A unit of measure for comparing the processing speeds of different computers.

Model. A simulation of a real-world event or phenomenon. (See Simulation.)

Modem. A hardware device that enables computers to exchange data over standard telephone lines.

Monitor. (See Display screen.)

Mouse. A device used to move the cursor on the display screen and to select commands or functions.

Move. To remove text, cells, or records from their original location to a different location.

Multiprocessing. Two or more processors sharing the same memory and input-output devices.

Multiuser system. A computer system that allows multiple users to share the processor, memory, disk storage, and software simultaneously.

Nanosecond. A unit of time equal to one billionth of a second.

Natural-language interface. A user interface that accepts commands or requests typed in ordinary English, and then translates them into equivalent commands or actions.

Network. A group of interrelated computers capable of exchanging information.

Numeric model. A simulation of a number-based problem.

Office automation. The application of computer and communication technologies to enhance office functions and procedures.

100% bar chart. A bar chart where all bars are of equal height. Each y series is drawn using a different color or pattern; like a pie chart, it is possible to see how much each value contributes to a 100% total. (See Bar chart.)

On-line system. A system in which input is transmitted immediately from the point of origin to a central location for processing.

Operating system. A set of programs that controls the operation and manages the resources of a computer system; for example, MS-DOS, OS/2, UNIX, Macintosh Operating System.

Option box. In a dialog, a box which displays a fixed set of options. An option is selected by placing a check next to it. (See Dialog box.)

Organizational constraints. In developing applications, the non-technical considerations that constrain a system, like budgets, deadlines, and people's capabilities.

Orphan. In word processing, the first line of a paragraph when it appears at the bottom of a page, separating it from the rest of the paragraph on the next page.

Output. (1) The results of information processing. (2) Devices that convert the results of processing into information that people can use; for example, display terminals, printers, and plotters.

Page break. The point in a document where one page ends and another begins.

Paragraph symbol. The character (¶) that the word processor uses to designate the end of a paragraph.

Parallel processors. Multiple processors that work on several parts of a computing problem simultaneously.

Password. A secret code the user needs to prove he or she has the right to access a computer system.

Peripheral. A device that operates in conjunction with a computer, but is not part of the computer; for example, a printer or disk drive.

Personal computer. A computer small enough to fit on a desktop, affordable enough to be owned by a single person, yet powerful enough to perform many different tasks. Also called a microcomputer.

Pie chart. A chart where numbers are drawn as the wedges of a circular pie. It is easy to see how much each number contributes to a 100% total. (See Charting.)

Pixel. Short for *picture element*. A light or dark point on the surface of a display screen.

Point-of-sale (POS) system. A series of computer terminals located where goods and services are paid for.

Printer. A device that produces printed output by transferring characters and images onto paper.

Printout. A document or listing, printed on paper.

Problem. Any question or matter characterized by doubt, uncertainty, or difficulty.

Procedure. A sequence of steps that specifies one or more actions and the order in which they must be taken.

Process. A systematic series of actions aimed at a specific goal.

Processor. The part of a computer system that performs the actual information processing and supervises and controls the operation of the entire system. (See Central processing unit.)

Program. A sequence of instructions that make the computer carry out a given set of tasks.

Programmable automation. The use of robots and other automated technology in manufacturing.

Programmer. A person who creates computer programs.

Programming language. A set of precise rules for formulating statements so that a computer can understand them; for example, BASIC, Pascal, C, Ada, COBOL, RPG.

Prompt. A request from the system for input from the user.

Protocol. A formal set of rules for specifying the format and relationships of information transmitted between two or more communicating devices.

Pull-down menu. A normally hidden menu that drops down from the menu bar when it is needed. (See Menu bar.)

Query. A question or request for information.

Query language. A language for questioning or requesting information from a database.

RAM. An acronym for *random-access memory*. A processor's temporary working area, which stores data and programs while the computer is on. (See Memory.)

Range search. In database programs, a search for records that fall between two criteria; for example, a search for all names between *L* and *N*.

Record. A collection of information consisting of one or more related items or fields. (See Field.)

Relational database. A database that organizes files into tabular rows and columns, and enables the user to relate two or more files through a field they share.

Relative reference. In spreadsheets, the ability to adjust a formula's cell reference in accordance with its new location.

Replace. The substitution of one piece of information for another, in combination with *Search*.

Report generator. The part of a database program that allows a user to define and produce printed output.

Reverse video. Highlighting of selected data on a display screen by reversing the normal light-dark contrast between the characters and the background area.

Robot. Automated machinery under the control of a computer program.

ROM. An acronym for *read-only memory*. A permanent memory, containing data and instructions loaded into it at the time of manufacture.

Salami slicing. A technique for rounding down all fractions of a penny in transactions like salary calculations, and illegally adding these amounts to one's own account. (See Computer crime.)

Save. To store information in a file.

Scanner. An input device that scans a drawing or photo and translates it into information that desktop publishing or other software can use.

Scatter chart. A chart that represents number pairs with marks on the chart grid. The pattern of the marks will reveal patterns in the number pairs. (See Charting.)

Scroll. To move the contents of a display screen up, down, left, or right to bring hidden parts of the document, spreadsheet, or database into view.

Search-and-Replace. The capability of a word processor to search a document for a particular word or phrase, and to replace it wherever it occurs with another word or phrase.

Sector. The smallest unit of data that can be written to or read from a disk. (See Track.)

Selection. The choosing (highlighting) of data for the purpose of manipulating it. In word processing, for example, a block of text can be selected for deletion.

Sequential. A method of organizing information in a series based on one or more key fields.

Shared-logic system. A computer system that connects several terminals to a single microcomputer or minicomputer's processor.

Simulation. A computerized representation of a process or a set of activities or events. (See Model.)

Software. The programs that control the operation of a computer.

Software package. One or more floppy disks on which a program resides. The package should also include documentation.

Solution. An answer or explanation to a problem.

Sort. To arrange a set of items in a predetermined sequence. For example, the telephone book is sorted alphabetically by customer name.

Special-purpose application software. Software designed for the special needs of particular kinds of businesses, education, or professions; for example, medical billing, patient tracking, or contract writing.

Speech recognition. (See Voice interface.)

Spelling checker. A program that checks documents for spelling errors.

Spreadsheet program. A program that helps solve problems that can be expressed in numbers and formulas. It organizes information into rows and columns, stores numbers, formulas and text, performs automatic calculations, and saves the results for future reference.

Stacked bar chart. A bar chart where each y series is drawn using a different color or pattern and the patterns are stacked on top of each other to form a bar. The height of each bar is the sum of its *y* series values. (See Bar chart.)

Static values. In spreadsheets, values that do not change unless a new number or text is entered manually. (See Dynamic values.)

Status line. The next-to-last line on the screen. It displays information about what you are viewing in the work area, as well as the name of the file you are editing.

Style checker. An electronic proofreader that hyphenates words, checks for punctuation errors, and flags awkward or redundant usage and wordiness.

Supercomputers. The fastest computers made.

System. A set of parts, each with a specific purpose, which work together to accomplish a desired goal.

System restart. A procedure used to restore the operation of a computer system to its original start-up mode without turning the computer off.

Systems analyst. A person who interprets needs, analyzes requirements, and develops functional specifications for a system.

Tab. A stopping-point along the horizontal dimension of a document.

Tab key. A keyboard key used to move the cursor to a prespecified location to the left or right, or above or below, its current location.

Technical constraints. In applications development, the limitations imposed by the hardware and the software.

Template. A partially completed worksheet, containing text and formulas but not data.

Terminal. An input/output device used to enter and receive information.

Terminal emulation. Software in a personal computer that simulates a terminal.

Text box. In a dialog, a box in which a line of text can be edited. (See Dialog box.)

Toggle. To alternate between functions by means of successive presses of a particular key.

Top-down design. A problem-solving method in which the solution is first specified in general terms, and then broken down into finer and finer detail.

Touch screen. A plastic membrane or set of infrared sensors are placed over a display screen to sense the presence of a finger. The user can select commands and actions by touching the screen.

Track. One of many concentric circles on which data is stored on a disk.

Transaction. A distinct input which causes processing to be activated in a system.

Transaction-oriented system. A system in which transactions activate processing; for example, an airline reservation system or a credit-approval system.

Trojan horse. A technique in which an unauthorized program is hidden within a legitimate program.

Tutorial. An interactive teaching tool, often a program, designed to help you learn to use a software package.

Typing cursor. An underline or reverse-video box that indicates the location on the screen of the next character you type. (See Cursor.)

Undo. A feature that enables a user to recover data deleted by the preceding command.

Universal product code (UPC). A bar code often used on packaged goods in supermarkets.

Update. To modify information by replacing it with more timely information.

User interface. Software that acts as an intermediary between an application program and the person using it.

Utilities. Programs that perform functions required by many of the application programs using the system; for example, utilities can copy, rename, and delete files.

Variable information. Information that changes on each occurance of a record in a report.

VDT. Short for *video display terminal.* Any computer terminal consisting of a CRT (cathode ray tube) screen and a keyboard.

Voice interface. (1) An input technology that enables the computer to recognize spoken words or phrases. (2) An output technology that simulates the human voice.

Volatile. In memory, the characteristic of losing contents when electrical power is shut off.

What-if **analysis.** Use of a spreadsheet to compare alternatives.

Wide-area network. A network that spans a very large geographic distance.

Widow. In word processing, the last line of a paragraph when it appears at the top of a page, separating it from the rest of the paragraph on the preceding page.

Wildcard search. A search that uses a shorthand notation to fill in an incomplete search criterion.

Winchester disk. A hard disk sealed in a container to prevent contaminants from touching the disk's surface (from the code name of the IBM project team that developed it).

Windows. A technique for dividing the display screen in order to view different sets of information simultaneously.

Word processing. Software that aids in the composition, revision, storage, and printing of text.

Word wrap. In word processing, the automatic carryover of text to the next line, along with the cursor.

Workgroup system. The use of computer and communication technologies to help a group of people work together better and more efficiently.

WYSIWYG. An acronym for *what-you-see-is-what-you-get*. A computer display that at all times accurately reflects what the computer is doing. In word processing, the display of information in a form that resembles very closely what will eventually be printed.

X **axis.** In a chart, the horizontal axis.

X **series.** In a chart, a series of numbers or words used to categorize each value from a *Y* series.

XY **chart.** Another term for scatter chart. (See Scatter chart.)

Y **axis.** In a chart, the vertical axis.

Y **series.** In a chart, a series of numbers that are represented visually.

List of Art Credits

Figure 1A Courtesy of International Business Machines Corporation

Figure 1B Courtesy of International Business Machines Corporation

Figure 1C Courtesy of Chrysler Corporation

Figure 1.2 Excelerator™ from Index Technology Corporation, Cambridge, MA

Figure 1D Courtesy of International Business Machines Corporation

Figure 1.7 Courtesy of ©Lotus Development Corporation. Screen provided by Apple Computer, Inc.

Figure 1.12 Courtesy of International Business Machines Corporation

Box Art 1B Courtesy of Microsoft Corporation/ Bruce Surber ©1987

Figure 2.2 Courtesy of Digital Research, Inc., Monterey, CA

Figure 2.3 Courtesy of International Business Machines Corporation

Box Art 2A Courtesy of MIT Media Laboratory

Box Art 2B Courtesy of Princeton Graphics System ©1986

Figure 3A Courtesy of International Business Machines Corporation

Figure 5B Courtesy of International Business Machines Corporation

Figure 5.13 Courtesy of Aldus Corporation

Figure 6A Courtesy of International Business Machines Corporation

Figure 10A Courtesy of Princeton Graphics Systems ©1986

Box Art 10A Courtesy of Eastman Kodak Co.

Figure 11A Courtesy of Hewlett-Packard Company

Figure 11B Courtesy of Satellite Broadcast Network

Figure 11D Courtesy of Mead Data Central, Inc.

Figure 11E Courtesy of Microsoft Corporation

Figure 11F a) Courtesy of Prentice Corporation
b) Courtesy of Hayes Microcomputer Products, Inc.

Figure 12.1 Courtesy of Apple Computer, Inc.

Figure 12.2 Courtesy of AT&T Corporation

Figure 12.7 Courtesy of General Motors Corporation

Figure 12.8 Courtesy of NYT Pictures

Figure 12.9 Courtesy of Ford Motor Company

Figure 12.10 Courtesy of First Interstate Bank

Figure 12.12 Spencer Grant III/Stock, Boston

Figure 12.13 Courtesy of National Medical Enterprises

Figure 12.14 Courtesy of Hewlett-Packard Company

Figure 13.2 Courtesy of NORAD

Figure 13.3 Courtesy of Bell Laboratories Record

Figure 13.4 Courtesy of NEC

Figure 13.5 Bohdan Hrynewich/Stock, Boston

Figure 13.6 Courtesy of Microsoft Flight Simulator

Figure 13.8 & 9 John Asmus

Figure 13.10 Courtesy of Kurzwell Music Systems

Figure 13.12 Courtesy of NASA/Michael Flynn

Figure 14.3 Courtesy of Honeywell, Inc.

Figure 15.1 Courtesy of International Business Machines Corporation

Figure 15C Courtesy of International Business Machines Corporation

Figure 15D Courtesy of International Business Machines Corporation

Figure 15E Courtesy of COMPAQ® Computer Corporation

Figure 15F Courtesy of Apple Computer, Inc.

Figure 15G Courtesy of Apple Computer, Inc.

Figure 15H Courtesy of Sharp Corporation, Hewlett-Packard Company, Apple Computer, Inc.

COLOR INSERTS

Window 1

Figure 1 Courtesy NCR Corporation
Figure 2 Courtesy Bank of Hawaii
Figure 3 Courtesy First Interstate Bancorp
Figure 4-6 Courtesy Intel Corporation
Figure 7 Courtesy of International Business Machines Corporation
Figure 8 Courtesy of Motorola, Inc.
Figure 9 Courtesy of Commodore Electronics Ltd.
Figure 10-11 Courtesy of International Business Machines Corporation
Figure 12 Courtesy Xerox Corporation
Figure 13 Courtesy of ROLM, an IBM Corporation
Figure 14 Courtesy Compaq Computer Corporation
Figure 15 Courtesy Xerox Corporation
Figure 16-17 Courtesy of International Business Machines Corporation
Figure 18 Courtesy of Apple Computer, Inc.
Figure 19 Courtesy of International Business Machines Corporation
Figure 20 Courtesy of Hewlett-Packard Company
Figure 21-22 Courtesy of Northern Telecom, Inc.
Figure 23 Courtesy of Unisys Corporation
Figure 24 Courtesy of International Business Machines Corporation
Figure 25 Courtesy of Hewlett-Packard Company
Figure 26 Courtesy Compaq Computer Corporation
Figure 27 Courtesy of Texas Instruments

Window 2

Figure 1 Courtesy of American Electric Power
Figure 2 Courtesy of TRW, Inc.
Figure 3-4 John Blaustein Photography
Figure 5 Courtesy of International Business Machines Corporation
Figure 6 Courtesy of AT&T
Figure 7 Courtesy of Caere Corporation
Figure 8 Courtesy of Data Entry Systems
Figure 9-10 Courtesy of International Business Machines Corporation
Figure 11 Courtesy of Radio Shack, a division of Tandy Corporation
Figure 12 Courtesy of Texas Instruments
Figure 13 Courtesy of Paradyne Corporation, Largo, Florida
Figure 14 Courtesy of TRW, Inc.
Figure 15 Courtesy of Gerber Scientific, Inc.
Figure 16 Courtesy of International Business Machines Corporation

Figure 17 Courtesy of Intergraph Corporation, Huntsville, Alabama
Figure 18 Living Videotext, Inc.
Figure 19 Courtesy of Toshiba America, Inc., Information Systems Division
Figure 20 Courtesy of TRW, Inc.
Figure 21 Courtesy of Commodore Electronics Ltd.
Figure 22 Sweet-P Plotters by Enter Computer, Inc., 6867 Nancy Ridge Drive, San Diego, California 92121, 619-450-0601
Figure 23 Courtesy of Gerber Scientific, Inc.
Figure 24-25 Courtesy of Hewlett-Packard Company
Figure 26 Courtesy of Monarch Marking Systems, a subsidiary of Pitney Bowes
Figure 27 Courtesy of Hewlett-Packard Company

Window 3

Figure 1-2 Courtesy of Hewlett-Packard Company
Figure 3 Courtesy of International Business Machines Corporation
Figure 4 Courtesy of ROLM, an IBM Corporation
Figure 5 Courtesy of International Business Machines Corporation
Figure 6 Courtesy The Gillette Company
Figure 7 Courtesy of Gerber Garment Technology, Inc.
Figure 8 Bill Varie/Fleetwood Enterprises, Inc.
Figure 9 Courtesy of Gerber Scientific, Inc.
Figure 10 Westinghouse Electric Corporation
Figure 11-12 Courtesy of Hewlett-Packard Company
Figure 13 Courtesy Compaq Computer Corporation
Figure 14 Courtesy of Westinghouse Automation Division/Unimation Incorporated
Figure 15 Courtesy of Gerber Scientific, Inc.
Figure 16-17 Courtesy of Hewlett-Packard Company
Figure 18 Courtesy of AT&T
Figure 19 Courtesy of International Business Machines Corporation
Figure 20 Courtesy Compaq Computer Corporation
Figure 21 Courtesy of International Business Machines Corporation
Figure 22 Courtesy Compaq Computer Corporation
Figure 23 Courtesy of International Business Machines Corporation
Figure 24 Westinghouse Electric Corporation
Figure 25 Courtesy of Compugraphic Corporation, Wilmington, Massachusetts
Figure 26 Courtesy of Atex, Inc., a Kodak Company, Bedford, Massachusetts
Figure 27 Courtesy of Hewlett-Packard Company
Figure 28 Courtesy of Aldus Corporation

Window 4

Figure 1 Courtesy of TRW, Inc.
Figure 2-4 Courtesy of Monsanto
Figure 5 Courtesy of International Business Machines Corporation
Figure 6 Courtesy of National Semiconductor Corporation
Figure 7 Courtesy of Commodore Electronics Ltd.
Figure 8 Courtesy of Memorex Corporation
Figure 9 Courtesy of Commodore Electronics Ltd.
Figure 10-11 Courtesy of National Semiconductor Corporation
Figure 12 Courtesy Intel Corporation
Figure 13 Loral Corporation/Ovak Arslanian
Figure 14 Courtesy of Commodore Electronics Ltd.
Figure 15-16 Courtesy of Gerber Scientific, Inc.
Figure 17-18 Courtesy of Cray Research, Inc.
Figure 19 Courtesy of Memorex Corporation
Figure 20 Courtesy of Storage Technology Corporation © 1984
Figure 21 Courtesy of Northern Telecom
Figure 22 Courtesy of International Business Machines Corporation
Figure 23 Courtesy of Hewlett-Packard Company
Figure 24 Courtesy of Storage Technology Corporation © 1984
Figure 25 Courtesy of TRW, Inc.

Figure 26-27 Courtesy of Hewlett-Packard Company
Figure 28 Zenith

Window 5

Figure 1 Courtesy of TRW, Inc.
Figure 2-3 Courtesy of Cray Research, Inc.
Figure 4 Courtesy of TRW, Inc.
Figure 5 Courtesy of Hewlett-Packard Company
Figure 6 Courtesy of International Business Machines Corporation
Figure 7 Courtesy of Telex Computer Products, Inc., Tulsa, Oklahoma
Figure 8 Courtesy of International Business Machines Corporation
Figure 9-10 Courtesy COMSAT
Figure 11 Courtesy of Electronic Data Systems, Dallas, Texas
Figure 12 Courtesy of TRW, Inc.
Figure 13 Courtesy of RCA
Figure 14 Courtesy Xerox Corporation
Figure 15 Courtesy of ROLM, an IBM Company
Figure 16 Courtesy of Commodore Electronics Ltd.
Figure 17 Courtesy of TRW, Inc.
Figure 18-20 Courtesy of International Business Machines Corporation
Figure 21 Courtesy of Apple Computer, Inc.
Figure 22 Courtesy of C. Itoh Electronics, Inc.

Index

Absolute references, 168
Access monitoring, 325
Accounting functions, computerization of, 269
Accounts Payable (AP) software, 271
Accounts Receivable (AR) software, 271
Accuracy, of computers, 72
Acoustic-coupled modems, 253
Active cell, 145
  updating, 148-149
Administrative controls, security and, 324
Agenda, 216
"Agrimation" robots, 279
AGV, *see* Automatic guided vehicles
AI, *see* Artificial intelligence
Alert boxes, 57
Alternate (Alt) key, 54
Amazon, 306
Amiga, 347
AMRAAM (advanced medium-range air-to-air missile), 296
Animation, 303
AP, *see* Accounts Payable software
Apple II family, 347-348
Apple Macintosh, 53, 345
  how to buy, 345-346
  mouse and, 47-48
Application(s), 30
  buying personal computer and, 334-336

Application development, 200-206
  evaluating results and, 204-206
  getting to know application and, 200
  identifying constraints and, 202-203
  implementing database program and, 203-204
  specifying requirements and, 200-202
Application programs, 31
AR, *see* Accounts Receivable software
Argo, 279
Arithmetic operations, hierarchy of, 150-151
Art(s), computers in, 303-307
Artificial intelligence (AI), 81
  personal computers as agents and, 257
AT&T, information sharing and, 316-317
Atari 520, 347
Automated fingerprint identification systems, 298
Automated teller machines (ATMs), 280-281
Automatic guided vehicles (AGV), 277

Backspace key, 34, 353
Backup file, 215

Banking, computers in, 280-281
Bank President, 301
Bar chart, 88, 224
Bedside information systems, 284
Bell companies, 257
Bifocals, 268
Bit, 13
Blinking cursor, 61, 100
Boldface, 132
Books, as source of information, 337
Booting, 12-13, 34, 56
Bootstrap program, 12-13
Brainstorming, 77
Break, grouping records and, 208
Business, 26-30
  management information systems and, 28-30
  transaction-oriented systems in, 26-27
  workgroup systems in, 27-28
Business transactions, computerization of, 269-271
Bytes, 13, 20

CADUCEUS, 284
CAI, *see* Computer-assisted instruction
Callback login, 325
Caps Lock key, 34
Cashless society, 280
CAT, *see* Computer axial

tomography

Catch-a-Cake, 300

CATLAB, 301

CCH, *see* Computerized criminal history systems

Cell(s)
active, 145, 148-149
distinguishing name from value of, 150

Cell references, 88, 145
absolute, 168
relative, 153-154

Charts, 44, 219-239
building, 226-233
charting from database and, 234-237
components of, 221-222
presentation graphics and, 238-239
printing, 237
types of, 223-226
visualizing numbers and, 220

Chart screen, commands for, 379-381

CIM, *see* Computer-integrated manufacturing

CIRRUS, 281

Click, 358

Clones, 344-345

Colorization, 303-304

Color monitors, 343

Columns
hidden, 161
width of, in spreadsheet, 149, 160-161

Commands, 370-390
chart screen, 379-381
communications, 389-390
database, 381-382
form and list screen, 383-386
main menu bar, 371
MS-DOS, 355-357
query screen, 386-389
for spreadsheet, 375-379
for word processor, 372-375

Commodore, 347

Communication(s), 22-26, 244-258, 264-265
buying a computer and, 344
commands for, 389-390
communications industry issues and, 256-258
computer networks and, 245-250
distributed processing systems and, 26
hardware for, 250-253
making connection and, 255-256
multiuser system and, 24-26
sample Works file and, 253-256
single-user system and, 23-24
small-scale systems for, 22
software for, 253

Communications industry, 256-258

Communications satellite, 246

Communications software, 22, 45-46

Comparison operators, 192

Computer(s). *See also* Personal computers; Portable computers
characteristics of, 72-73
in the arts, 303-307
in education, 299-303
in finance, banking, and retailing, 280-283
in industry, 275-283
in offices, 262-269
as problem-solving tools, 71-74
in professions, 283-288
in science, 307-310

Computer-assisted instruction (CAI), 300-302
drawbacks to, 302-303

Computer axial tomography (CAT), 284-285

Computer conferencing, 265-266

Computer crime, 320-326

Computer Fraud and Abuse Act of 1986, 320

Computer-integrated manufacturing (CIM), 277

Computerized criminal history (CCH) systems, 318

Computer networks, 22, 245-250
electronic mail and, 23, 247-248, 265
information utilities and, 248-250
local area networks and, 25, 250

Computer shows, as source of information, 337

Computer skills, acquiring, 8

Computer stores, as source of information, 338-339

Computer systems, 8-9
distributed processing, 26
multiuser, 24-26
single-user, 22-23
small-scale, 22
types of, 20-22

using, 30-34

Computer trespassing, 322-324

Computer users, as source of information, 336

Constraints
organizational, 202
technical, 202-203

Contents, 134

Control (Ctrl) key, 54

Controlling, management information systems and, 272

Copy command, with word processor, 104-105

Copy protection, software piracy and, 327

Copyright law
intellectual property and, 328-329
software piracy and, 327

Courses, as source of information, 339-340

Courseware, 300

"Cowbots," 279

Cracker, 323

Cray 2, 308

Credit cards, 26-27

Crime
computer, 320-326
computer-abetted, 320-322

Cultural lag, information ethics and, 326-327

Cursor, 36
blinking, 61, 100
mouse and, 47, 358

Cursor movement, 54
cursor-movement keys and, 54
scrolling and, 108
Tab key and, 54

Data, 11. *See also* Information

Database(s), 29, 45, 181-196, 199-216
application development process and, 200-206
charting from, 234-237
commands for, 381-382
complex searches and, 194
data integrity and, 214-215
data security and, 214
designing, 184-189
editing, 191
entering data into, 189-191
fields and, 45
form design screen and, 186-188
functions and, 362-369

large, 216
libraries and, 184
printing data from, 196
problem solving and, 182-183
query facility and, 45
querying, 192-194
records and, 45
registration form generation
with, 206-207
relational, 212-213
removing data from, 191
report generation with,
207-212
sample application of, 183-184
size of, 213-214
sorting records and, 195-196
starting program and, 186
wildcard searches and, 214
Database management, 263
Data entry
into database, 189-191
into spreadsheet, 147, 153-154
Data integrity, 214-215
Data manipulation, in database,
191-196
Data processing, distinguished
from word processing, 97
Data security, 214
Decision making, 79-80
Decision support systems (DSS),
275
Dedicated systems, 97
Default, for printing layout, 114
Defense, computers in, 294-296
Delete (Del) key, 54-55
Deleting
of block of text, 107
in database, 191
Department of Health and
Human Services, informa-
tion sharing and, 317
Design process, 81-85
Desktop publishing, 136-139
Dialog, 48
Dialog boxes, 57, 370
mouse and, 359-360
Directing, management informa-
tion systems and, 272
Directory name, 354
Disk(s), 15-16
floppy, 16, 343
formatting, 36-37
handling, 34-35
hard, 16, 343
optical, 17-18
tracks and sectors of, 30
write-protecting, 38
Disk drives, 15-16
buying a computer and, 343,

346
Diskettes, 16
Disk operating system (DOS), 20,
31-32, 345
functions of, 30-31
loading, 35-36
system files of, 39
using, 31-32
Display enhancements, 135-136
Display screen, 16, 18, 48-49
buying a computer and, 343
effects on health, 267
Display technology, 53-54
Distributed processing systems,
26
Document(s), 44
appearance on screen, 100
creating, 100
defined, 98-100
printing, 114
saving, 113-114
switching between, 131-132
types of, 98-100
Documentation, 19
as source of information, 339
spreadsheets and, 176
DOS, *see* Disk operating system
Dot-matrix printers, 344, 346
Dotted line, entering into
spreadsheet, 153
Double spacing, 124
Dow Jones & Company, 257
Drag, 358
Drive designators, 354
Drug conflict programs, 286
DSS, *see* Decision support
systems
Dynamic values, 147

EDGAR, (*See* Electronic Data
Gathering Analysis and
Retrieval system)
Edit checks, 214-215
Edit formula, 148
Editing, 100
in database, 191
shortcuts in, 106-107
of spreadsheet, 147-149
with word processor, 61-62,
106-107, 112
Education, computers in, 299-303
Electronic Data Gathering
Analysis and Retrieval
system (EDGAR), 294
Electronic funds transfer systems
(EFTS), 280
crime and, 321-322
Electronic mail, 23-24, 247-248,

265
Electronic proofreaders, 133-134
Embezzlers, 321-322
Encryption, 325-326
End key, cursor movement
with, 108
Enter key, 34, 353
Equality operator, 192, 194
Equity Funding Corporation,
322
Ergonomics, 266-269
Errors, correcting, with word
processor, 112
Escape (Esc) key, 52
Ethics, 315-330
computer crime and, 320-326
emerging issues in, 326-330
privacy and, 316-320
Excel, 159
Expert systems, 81
Extension, 354
Eye-tracking system, 50-51
Eyestrain, 268

F1 function key, 353
Facsimile transmission (fax), 266
Fahrenheit 451, 306
FAPRS (Federal Assistance
Program Resource System),
294
Federal Communications
Commission (FCC), 258
Federal Data Agency, 299
Federal Express, 318
Federal government, computers
in, 292-296
Feeling, people and, 73
Fields, 45, 184-185
File(s), 354-355
system, 39
FILE ERROR, 65
Filenames, 354
Fixed information, 202
Flexibility, people and, 73
Flight Simulator, 301
Floppy disks, 16, 343
Footers, 129-130
Footnotes, 134
Form, 185
Format menu, 124-125
FORMAT program, 36-37
Formatting, 124-133
of disks, 36-37
of spreadsheet, changing,
154-156
of text, 108
Form design screen, 186-188
commands for, 383-386

Formula(s), 150
  editing, 148
  entering into spreadsheet, 147, 153-154
Formula bar, 87, 144-145
Formula/ruler bar, 60
Freezing titles, 169
Front-end processors, 29
Function, 89, 152, 362-369
Functional specification, 76-77
Function keys, 51, 353

General ledger, computerization of, 269
General-purpose application software, 19
Glasses, 268
Go To command, spreadsheet and, 145
Government, computers in, 292-299
Graphic adapter, 343
Graphics, 264
  presentation, 238-239
Graphics chip, 343
Graphics display file, copying, 39-40
Grid Compass, 253

Hackers, 322-324
Hand-held personal computers, 348-349
Handicapped persons, user interfaces for, 48
Hard disks, 16, 343
Hardware, 9-18
Headers, 129-130
Health professions, computers in, 284-286
Hi-low chart, 225
Hi-low-close chart, 225
Hidden column, 161
Home computer, *see* Personal computers
Home key, cursor movement with, 108
Human capital, value of, 329
Hypercard, 216
Hypermedia, 109
Hypertext, 109
Hyphenation, 108-109

IBM compatibility, 344-345
IBM Personal Computer (PC), 159, 341, 342
IBM Personal System/2 (PS/2),

53, 341, 342, 342-343
  mouse and, 47-48
IF function, 175
ImageWriters, 346
Impact printers, 344
Indexes, 134
Industry, computers in, 275-283
Information
  access to, information utilities and, 248-249
  equal access to, 329-330
  fixed and variable, 202
  inaccurate, information malpractice and, 328
  sources of, buying a computer and, 336-340
  value of, 329
Information ethics, *see* Ethics
Information malpractice, 328
Information processing, 8-9
Information systems, 269-275
  bedside, 284
Information utilities, 248-250
  access to data and, 248-249
  access to transactions and, 249-250
Inkjet printers, 344
Input devices, 9, 11
Insert (Ins) key, 54
Integrated program, 44
Integration, spreadsheets and, 171-177
Intellectual property rights, 328-329
Intensive care units, computers in, 284
Interactive fiction, 305-306
Internal modems, 252
Internal Revenue Service (IRS), computers in, 292-293
Intuition, people and, 73
Inventory, as database application, 183-184
IRS, *see* Internal Revenue Service
Italics, 132

Jazz, 159
Journalism, computers in, 287-288
Joystick, 358
Judgment, people and, 73

Key(s)
  function, 51
  special, 52, 54-55
Keyboard, 11, 33, 49, 51-52, 54-55

mouse and, 360-361
MS-DOS and, 353-354
using, 32-34
Kilobyte, 20
Knight-Ridder Newspapers, 257
Knowledge representation, people and, 73-74

Languages
  macro, 178
  programming, 19-20
LANs, *see* Local area networks
Laptop computers, 287-288, 349
Laser printers, 135, 344, 346
LaserWriters, 346
Law, computers in, 286-287
Law enforcement, computers in, 297-299
Layout, of spreadsheet, 150-152
LAYOUT dialog box, 114-116
Legislation, privacy and, 318-319
Legislative branch, computers in, 294
LEGIS system, 294
Letter, to write, 111-118
Letter-quality printers, 344
LEXIS, 286-287
Libraries, databases and, 184
Lighting, 267-268
Line charts, 222-223
Linking, of spreadsheets, 178
List, 185
List box, 59
List screen, commands for, 383-386
Literature, computers in, 305-306
Local area networks (LANs), 25-26, 250
Local government, computers in, 296-297
Logic, of computers, 73
Logical operators, 192
Lotus 1-2-3, 159

Macro language, 178
Macros, spreadsheets and, 178
Magazines, as source of information, 336-337
Magnetic ink character recognition (MICR) systems, 280
Mail order retailers, buying computers from, 352
Mainframes, processing power of, 21
Management, levels of, 272-274
Management information sys-

tems (MIS), 28-30, 271-275
basis of, 274-275
levels of management and, 272-274
Manual recalculation, 178
Manufacturing, robotics and, 275-280
Mass storage, 9, 14-16
MasterType, 300
MCGA display, *see* MultiColor Graphic Array display
Medical education and consulting, computers in, 285-286
Medical imaging, 284-285
Medical records, information sharing and, 317
Membership lists, computerized, 317
Memo, writing with spreadsheet, 171-172
Memory, 9, 12-14
buying a computer and, 346
random-access, 12
read-only, 12
read/write, 12
size of, 13, 14, 20
volatile, 12
Menu(s), 47
mouse and, 359-360
Menu bar, 60, 370
commands and, 371
Message line, 60
MICR, *see* Magnetic ink character recognition systems
Microcomputers, *see* Personal computers
Microprocessor, 12
Microsoft, 32
Microsoft Works, *see* Works
Millionaire, 301
"Milwaukee 414" group, 323
Minicomputers
as front-end processors, 29
processing power of, 22
MIPS, 20-22
MIS, *see* Management information systems
Model(s)
building with spreadsheet, 52, 164-170
numeric, 142-143
Modeling, 71
Modem, 22, 46, 250, 252, 288
hackers and, 323
Monitor, 16, 18
Monochrome monitor, 343
Motion pictures, computers in, 303-304

Mouse, 11, 47
desktop publishing and, 137
dialog boxes and, 359
keyboard and, 360-361
menus and, 359
scroll bars and, 359-360
selecting and, 360
shortcuts for, 358-361
Mouse pointer, 358
Move command, with word processor, 105-106
MS-DOS, 353-357. *See also* Disk operating system
commands and, 355-357
files and, 354-355
keyboard and, 353-354
MS-DOS-based computer, how to buy, 340-345
MultiColor Graphic Array (MCGA) display, 343
Multiprocessor systems, 25
Multitasking, 345
Multiuser system, 24-26
local area networks as, 25-26
multiprocessor, 25
shared-logic, 24
Music, computers in, 306-307
MYCIN, 284

NASA, 308, 309-310
National Crime Information Center (NCIC), 297
NCIC, *see* National Crime Information Center
Neatness, of computers, 73
Networks, *see* Computer networks
NEW dialog box, 57
NEXIS, 288
911 emergency system, 296-297
North American Defense Command (NORAD), computers in, 294
Nuclear magnetic resonance (NMR), 285
Numbers
entering into spreadsheet, 147, 154
visualizing with charts, 220
Numeric keypad, 54
Numeric model, 142-143
Num Lock key, 54

OCR, *see* Optical character recognition systems
Office automation (OA), 262-269

Office of Technology Assessment, 329
100 percent bar chart, 226
On-line systems, 26
OPEN dialog box, 59
Open system, 342
Operating system, *see* Disk operating system
Operating System/2 (OS/2), 159, 345
Operational level, management information systems and, 273
Optical character recognition (OCR) systems, 280
Optical disk, 17-18
Option box, 58
Organizational constraints, 202
Organizing, management information systems and, 272
Organ matching, 286
Orphans, 125
Output devices, 9, 16, 18

PA, *see* Programmable automation
Page breaks, 125-127
in spreadsheet, 158, 160
PageMaker, 137, 138
Paragraphs, 110
Paragraph sign, 60-61, 110
Parameters, 89, 362
Passwords, 214, 253, 255, 324
access monitoring and, 325
stolen, 322
People, problem solving and, 73-74
Personal computers, 5
as agents, 257
buying, 333-352
display screen and, 48-49
hackers and, 323
hand-held, 348-349
interacting with, 46-55
keyboard and, 49, 51-52, 54-55
processing power of, 20
revolution and, 6, 159
user interface and, 47-48
uses of, 6-8
what to do after buying, 351
in wide-area networks, 29
Personal information management, 216
PgUp and PgDn keys, cursor movement with, 108
Pie chart, 89, 224
Pixel, 53

Planning, management information systems and, 271
PLATO system, 285-286, 302
Pointing device, 358
Point-of-sale (POS) systems, 281-283
Portable computers
    hand-held, 348-349
    how to buy, 348-349
    laptop, 287-288, 349
    transportable, 349
POS, *see* Point-of-sale systems
Presentation graphics, 238-239
Prewriting, 82
PRINT dialog box, 63
Printer(s), 18
    buying, 344, 346
    types of, 135
PRINT ERROR, 65
Printing, 63-65
    from database, 196, 212
    of graphs, 237
    of spreadsheet, 91, 158, 160
    with word processor, 114
Printing enhancements, 134-135
Privacy, 316-320
    computer as threat to, 316-318
    safeguarding, 318-320
Privacy Act of 1974, 318-319
Privacy laws, 318-319
Problem, 70
    defining, 76-77
    getting to know, 75-76
Problem solving, 70-91
    computers as tools for, 71-74
    database programs and, 182-183
    process of, 74-79
    spreadsheets and, 85-91, 142-143
    variations on, 79-85
Procedure, 74
Process, 70
Processing power, 20-22
Processor(s), 9, 11-12
    front-end, 29
Professions, computers in, 283-288
Program(s), *see* Software
Programmable automation (PA), 277
Programming languages, 19-20
Prompt, 36
PUFF, 284

QL Systems, 286
Query facility, 45

Querying, in database, 192-194
Query screen, commands for, 386-389
Quick reference card, 19

Random-access memory (RAM), 12, 14
Read-only memory (ROM), 12
Read/write memory, *see* Random-access memory
Recalculation, 156-157
    manual, 178
Records, 45, 185
    grouping, 208-209
    sorting, 195, 208-209
Registration form, creating, 206-207
Relational databases, 212-213
Relative references, 153-154
Remote Mobile Investigator, 278-279
Report
    defining, 209
    viewing and printing, 212
Report generation, database and, 207-212
Response time, 26
Résumé writing, as problem-solving process, 82-85
Retailing
    computers in, 281-283
    management information systems in, 29-30
Reverse video, 49
Revising, 82
    with word processor, 112-113, 121
Right arrow, double, 61
Right arrow key, 353
Robotics
    applications of, 279
    manufacturing and, 275-280
ROM, *see* Read-only memory
Row type, 209
Run for the Money, 301

Salami-slicing scheme, 322
Sales analysis model, building with spreadsheet, 164-168
Sales forecast model, building with spreadsheet, 171-175
Saving, 62-63
    of spreadsheet, 157-158
    with word processor, 113-114
Scale, 222
Scanner, desktop publishing

and, 137
Scatter charts, 224-225
Science, computers in, 307-310
Scroll bars, mouse and, 359-360
Scrolling, 49, 107
    freezing titles and, 169
    in spreadsheet, 145
    with word processor, 107-108
SDI, *see* Strategic Defense Initiative
Search(es)
    in database, 194
    wildcard, 214
Search and replace, 121-123
Sectors, 30
Securities and Exchange Commission (SEC), computers in, 294
Security, safeguarding, 324-326
Selection
    mouse and, 360
    with word processor, 102-104, 107
Shared-logic systems, 24
Shift key, 32
Signing off, 255
Signing on, 255, 256
Simulations, 71, 308
    in education, 301
Single-user system, 22-23
Small-scale systems, 22
Social Security Administration, computers in, 293
Software, 5, 18-20
    application, general-purpose, 19
    application, special-purpose, 19
    communications, 22, 253
    operating-system, 20
Software package, 19
Software piracy, 327
Software safeguards, security and, 324
Solution(s), 70-71
    choosing, 77-78
    evaluating results of, 78-79
    identifying, 77
    implementing, 78
SOPAD (Summary of Proceedings and Debates), 294
Sort(s), nested, 196
Sorting, database and, 195, 208-209
Space, between words, 61, 110
Space exploration, 309-310
Spacing, 124
Special-purpose application

software, 19-20
Speech recognizer, 50
Speed, of computers, 72
Spelling checkers, 133
Split bar, 360
Spreadsheets, 44-45, 85-91, 141-
    161, 160, 163-178, 263
  adding to, 156
  appearance of, 144-145
  building models and, 152, 164-
    168, 171-175
  changing formats and, 154-156
  column width in, 149, 160-161
  commands for, 375-379
  designing layout and, 150-152
  documentation and, 176
  editing, 147-149
  electronic, 144-149
  entering formulas into,
    153-154
  entering numbers into, 146-
    147, 154
  entering text into, 152-153
  example using, 85-86
  formatting, 160-161
  functions and, 362-369
  limitations of, 176-177
  macros and, 178
  moving around in, 145-146
  multiple, linking, 178
  printing, 91, 158
  problem solving and, 142-143
  recalculating, 156-157
  sample problem for, 149-161
  saving, 157-158
  templates and, 177
  very large, 177-178
  what-if analysis and, 87-91,
    169, 175-176
  writing memos and, 171-172
Stacked bar chart, 225
Staffing, management informa-
    tion systems and, 272
Standalone modems, 252
Star Wars, 294-296
Static values, 147
Status line, 60
Work area, 60
Strategic Defense Initiative
    (SDI), 294-296
Strategic level, management
    information systems
    and, 274
Structure, of records, 185
Style checkers, 133-134
Subscription lists, computerized,
    317
Supercomputers, 308-309
Switching, between documents,

131-132
System, 8. *See also* Computer
    systems
System files, 39
Systems analyst, 200

Tab key, 54
Table of contents, 134
Tabs, 127-129
TABS dialog box, 128
Tactical level, management
    information systems and,
    273-274
Tandy 100, 253, 287-288
Tandy 200, 253
Technical constraints, 202-203
Technical reference manual, 19
Technostress, 268
Telephone system, 245-246
Templates, spreadsheets and,
    177
Terminal(s), 22
  communications and, 250
Terminal emulation, 46
Text, entering into spreadsheet,
    152-153
Text box, 59
Thermal-transfer printers, 344
Times Mirror Company, 257
Top-down design, 80
Touch-sensitive screen, 50
TOW (Tube-launched, optically
    tracked, wired guided)
    missile, 296
Track(s), 30
Trackball, 358
Transaction(s), 26
  access to, information utilities
    and, 249-250
Transaction-oriented systems,
    26-27
Transportable computers, 349
Trespassing, 322-324
Trojan horse scheme, 322
Tutorials, 19, 301-302

Undo command, 104
  word processor and, 107
U.S. Census Bureau, computers
    in, 293
Universal product code (UPC),
    282-283
Unix, 345
Updating, *see* Editing
User groups, as source of infor-
    mation, 337-338

User ID, 253, 255
User interface, 47-48, 50-51
  for handicapped, 48
User's guide, 19

Variable information, 202
Video Graphic Array (VGA),
    343
Viewing, of database report, 212
VisiCalc, 159
Volatility, of memory, 12

Westlaw, 286
What-if analysis, 87-91
  with spreadsheet, 169, 175-176
What-you-see-is-what-you-get
    (WYSIWYG), 135
Wide-area networks, 29
Widows, 125
Wildcard searches, 214
Windows, 47, 136, 178
Word processing, 44, 96-116, 263
  advanced, 133-136
  commands and, 372-375
  copying with, 104-105
  display in, 100, 108-109
  distinguished from data proc-
    essing, 97
  document creation and, 100
  documents and, 98-100
  editing shortcuts with,
    106-107
  editing with, 61-62, 100,
    106-109, 112
  exercise in, 58-61
  experimenting with, 101-110
  formatting and, 124-132
  future of, 109
  LAYOUT dialog with, 114-116
  moving with, 105-106
  paragraphs in, 110
  printing with, 63-65, 114
  problem solving and, 97-98
  revising with, 112-113, 121
  saving with, 62-63, 113-114
  scrolling with, 107-108
  search and replace with and,
    121-123
  selection with, 102-104
  writing and, 111-139
Word wrap, 108-109
Work area, 60
Workgroup computing, 265
Workgroup systems, 27-28
Works, 43-65
  communications program of,

45-46
copying, 37-39
database of, 45
ending session with, 40
getting started with, 55-65
installing, 34-40
NEW dialog box of, 57
printing with, 63-65
saving and, 62-63
spreadsheet of, 44-45
word processor of, 44, 58-62
Workstations, physical layout of,
268
Write-protecting, 38
Writing, 119-139
of additional drafts, 124-132
advanced word processing
features and, 133-136
desktop publishing and,
136-139
of first draft, 120-123
formatting and, 132-133
as problem-solving process, 82
Writing enhancements, 133-134
WYSIWYG (what-you-see-is-
what-you-get), 135

X axis, 221
XY chart, 224

Y axis, 221

Zork trilogy, 305